COUNTERCULTURES AND POPULAR MUSIC

A translated and edited edition of a special issue of *Volume! The French Journal of Popular Music Studies* (Éditions Mélanie Seteun).

Additional articles published in both 'countercultures' issues of *Volume!* can be found at: http://www.cairn.info/revue-volume.htm and http://volume.revues.org.

Volume! is the only French peer-reviewed popular music studies journal. Created in 2002 by Marie-Pierre Bonniol, Samuel Étienne and Gérôme Guibert, it is published independently by the Éditions Mélanie Seteun, a publishing association specialising since 1998 in the cultural sociology of popular music. Biannual special issues deal with various topics in popular music studies, in a multidisciplinary perspective. It is also included on the online international academic portals Cairn.info and Revues.org. *Volume!* is classified by the French AERES and abstracted/indexed on the International Index to Music Periodicals, the Répertoire International de Littérature Musicale and the Music Index.

Countercultures and Popular Music

Edited by

SHEILA WHITELEY
University of Salford, UK

JEDEDIAH SKLOWER
Université Sorbonne Nouvelle, Paris 3, France

LONDON AND NEW YORK

First published 2014 by Ashgate Publishing

Published 2016 by Routledge
2 Park Square, Milton Park, Abingdon, Oxfordshire OX14 4RN
711 Third Avenue, New York, NY 10017, USA

First issued in paperback 2016

Routledge is an imprint of the Taylor & Francis Group, an informa business

Copyright © 2014 Sheila Whiteley and Jedediah Sklower and the contributors

Sheila Whiteley and Jedediah Sklower have asserted their rights under the Copyright, Designs and Patents Act, 1988, to be identified as the editors of this work.

All rights reserved. No part of this book may be reprinted or reproduced or utilised in any form or by any electronic, mechanical, or other means, now known or hereafter invented, including photocopying and recording, or in any information storage or retrieval system, without permission in writing from the publishers.

Notices:
Product or corporate names may be trademarks or registered trademarks, and are used only for identification and explanation without intent to infringe.

British Library Cataloguing in Publication Data
A catalogue record for this book is available from the British Library.

The Library of Congress has cataloged the printed edition as follows:
Countercultures and popular music / edited by Sheila Whiteley and Jedediah Sklower.
    pages cm. – (Ashgate Popular and folk music series)
    Includes bibliographical references and index.
    ISBN 978-1-4724-2106-7 (hardcover : alk. paper)

    1. Popular music – Social aspects. 2. Counterculture. I. Whiteley, Sheila, 1941– II. Sklower, Jedediah.

    ML3918.P67C73 2014
    306.4'8424–dc23

2013047641

ISBN 13: 978-1-138-24994-3 (pbk)
ISBN 13: 978-1-4724-2106-7 (hbk)

Contents

List of Figures	*vii*
General Editors' Preface	*ix*
Notes on Contributors	*xi*
Preface: Dissent within Dissent *Jedediah Sklower*	*xv*

INTRODUCTION

Countercultures and Popular Music   3
Sheila Whiteley

Reappraising 'Counterculture'   17
Andy Bennett

PART I   THEORISING COUNTERCULTURES

1. Break on Through: The Counterculture and the Climax of American Modernism   29
Ryan Moore

2. The Banality of Degradation: Andy Warhol, the Velvet Underground and the Trash Aesthetic   45
Simon Warner

3. Were British Subcultures the Beginning of Multitude?   65
Charles Mueller

PART II   UTOPIAS, DYSTOPIAS AND THE APOCALYPTIC

4. The Rock Counterculture from Modernist Utopianism to the Development of an Alternative Music Scene   81
Christophe Den Tandt

5. 'Helter Skelter' and Sixties Revisionism   95
Gerald Carlin and Mark Jones

6. Apocalyptic Music: Reflections on Countercultural Christian Influence   109
Shawn David Young

| 7 | Nobody's Army: Contradictory Cultural Rhetoric in *Woodstock* and *Gimme Shelter*
Gina Arnold | 123 |

PART III SONIC ANARCHY AND FREAKS

8	The Long Freak Out: Unfinished Music and Countercultural Madness in Avant-Garde Rock of the 1960s and 1970s Jay Keister	141
9	The Grateful Dead and Friedrich Nietzsche: Transformation in Music and Consciousness Stanley J. Spector	157
10	Scream from the Heart: Yoko Ono's Rock and Roll Revolution Shelina Brown	171
11	From Countercultures to Suburban Cultures: Frank Zappa after 1968 Benjamin Halligan	187

PART IV COUNTERCULTURAL SCENES – MUSIC AND PLACE

12	Countercultural Space Does Not Persist: Christiania and the Role of Music Thorbjörg Daphne Hall	205
13	A Border-Crossing Soundscape of Pop: The Auditory Traces of Subcultural Practices in 1960s Berlin Heiner Stahl	223
14	Music and Countercultures in Italy: The Neapolitan Scene Giovanni Vacca	237

Bibliography   *251*
Discography   *275*
Filmography   *281*
Index   *283*

List of Figures

12.1 The entrance into Christiania. Photo: Thorbjörg Daphne Hall — 210

12.2 The stage by Nemoland. Photo: Thorbjörg Daphne Hall — 211

12.3 Outside Loppen. Photo: Thorbjörg Daphne Hall — 214

12.4 The tourist information hut where guided tours are offered. Photo: Thorbjörg Daphne Hall — 215

General Editors' Preface

Popular musicology embraces the field of musicological study that engages with popular forms of music, especially music associated with commerce, entertainment and leisure activities. The Ashgate Popular and Folk Music series aims to present the best research in this field. Authors are concerned with criticism and analysis of the music itself, as well as locating musical practices, values and meanings in cultural context. The focus of the series is on popular music of the twentieth and twenty-first centuries, with a remit to encompass the entirety of the world's popular music.

Critical and analytical tools employed in the study of popular music are being continually developed and refined in the twenty-first century. Perspectives on the transcultural and intercultural uses of popular music have enriched understanding of social context, reception and subject position. Popular genres as distinct as reggae, township, bhangra, and flamenco are features of a shrinking, transnational world. The series recognises and addresses the emergence of mixed genres and new global fusions, and utilises a wide range of theoretical models drawn from anthropology, sociology, psychoanalysis, media studies, semiotics, postcolonial studies, feminism, gender studies and queer studies.

Stan Hawkins, Professor of Popular Musicology, University of Oslo &
Derek B. Scott, Professor of Critical Musicology, University of Leeds

Notes on Contributors

Gina Arnold received her PhD in Stanford's programme of Modern Thought and Literature in June 2011. She is the author of two books, *Route 666: On the Road To Nirvana* (1993) and *Kiss This: Punk in the Present Tense* (1997). Her contribution to the 33 1/3rd series *Exile in Guyville* is forthcoming.

Andy Bennett is Professor of Cultural Sociology and Director of the Griffith Centre for Cultural Research at Griffith University in Queensland, Australia. He has authored and edited numerous books including *Music, Style and Aging*, *Popular Music and Youth Culture*, *Cultures of Popular Music*, *Remembering Woodstock* and *Music Scenes* (with Richard A. Peterson). Bennett was lead chief investigator on a three-year, five-country project funded by the Australian Research Council entitled 'Popular Music and Cultural Memory' (DP1092910). He is a faculty fellow of the Center for Cultural Sociology, Yale University, and an associate member of PopuLUs, the Centre for the Study of the World's Popular Musics, Leeds University.

Shelina Brown was born in Vancouver, Canada, and raised in Kyoto, Japan. She is bilingual in Japanese and English and has a keen interest in Japanese literature and music. Since 2008, she has been pursuing doctoral studies at the University of California, Los Angeles. Her research centres on feminist cultural resistance in punk music from the late 1970s to the present. For her dissertation project, she plans to focus on Yoko Ono – the grandmother of punk and new wave. In her spare time, Shelina plays guitar and drums in several DIY post-punk bands in Echo Park, Los Angeles.

Gerald Carlin is Senior Lecturer in English at the University of Wolverhampton. He has published on modernism, critical theory and aspects of 1960s popular culture.

Christophe Den Tandt teaches Anglo-American literature and cultural theory at the Université Libre de Bruxelles (ULB). He is the author of studies on the representation of the urban scene in American fiction as well as of articles on popular culture – fiction, film and music.

Thorbjörg Daphne Hall is an adjunct and a program director of musicology at the Iceland Academy of the Arts. She holds an MA in Musicology from the University of Nottingham and an MA in Cultural Studies from the University of Iceland and Bifrost University. Her research interests focus on classical and popular music of the twentieth and twenty-first century in connection to images, identity, place, space and nationalism.

Benjamin Halligan is the Director of Postgraduate Research Studies for the College of Arts and Social Sciences at the University of Salford, and lectures in the areas of critical theory, media studies and performance. Publications include *Michael Reeves* (2003) and, as co-editor, *Mark E. Smith and The Fall* (2010), *Reverberations: The Philosophy, Aesthetics and Politics of Noise* (2012) and *Resonances: Noise and Music* (2013) and *The Music Documentary* (2013) in addition to numerous articles and chapters on audiovisual practices.

Mark Jones is Senior Lecturer in English and Award Leader for MA Popular Culture at the University of Wolverhampton. He has published on horror, science fiction, pornography and aspects of 1960s popular culture.

Jay Keister is currently Associate Professor at the University of Colorado, Boulder. His book *Shaped by Japanese Music: Kikuoka Hiroaki and Nagauta Shamisen in Tokyo* (2004) focuses on traditional music in modern Japan. He has published articles on Japanese music in the journals *Ethnomusicology*, *Asian Music* and *The World of Music* and on Japanese dance in *Asian Theatre Journal*. He also co-authored an article on progressive rock in the journal *Popular Music*.

Ryan Moore is Associate Professor of Sociology at Florida Atlantic University and the author of *Sells Like Teen Spirit: Music, Youth Culture, and Social Crisis* (2009). His broad research and teaching interests are in the areas of cultural sociology, critical theory, social movements and urban studies. He is currently working on a new project that draws on the critical theory of Henri Lefebvre to examine rhythm, noise and music in American cities.

Charles Mueller is a professional guitarist and studio musician in Portland, Oregon. He earned a Master's degree in Music Education from Portland State University and a PhD in historical musicology from Florida State University where he wrote a dissertation on the goth subculture. His scholarship continues to focus on music and subcultures, and the effect of the Cold War on popular music.

Jedediah Sklower specialises in the political and cultural history of popular music in the twentieth century. He teaches communication studies at Sciences Po Paris and popular music history and aesthetics at the Catholic University of Lille. He has been an active co-editor of the French peer-reviewed popular music studies journal *Volume!* since 2008. He published *Free jazz, la catastrophe féconde* (2006), edited a special issue of *Volume!* dedicated to listening (2013), and co-organised (with ASPM and IASPM-bfe) the 'Changing the Tune: Popular Music and Politics in the XXIst Century' Strasbourg international conference (June 2013), whose selected proceedings will be published in 2014.

Stanley J. Spector, who received his PhD in Philosophy from the University of Colorado, specialises in modern European thought, including phenomenology, transcendental philosophy, existential philosophy, and hermeneutics. He has published a number of articles on the interface between the Grateful Dead phenomenon and the philosophies of Nietzsche, Heidegger and Merleau-Ponty. Both a professor of philosophy at Modesto Junior College and a certified advanced Rolfer, Spector integrates the central methodologies of Continental philosophy and Rolfing to frame investigations of bodily existence. He co-edited *The Grateful Dead in Concert: Essays in Live Improvisation* (2010), and he is currently writing *The Grateful Dead and Nietzsche: Transformation in Life and Music*, a theory of art phrased in terms of the body and its application to the Grateful Dead experience.

Heiner Stahl is a post-doctoral researcher in the Department of Communication Studies at the University of Erfurt, Germany. He wrote his PhD on the broadcasting history in West and East Berlin in the 1960s, supervised by Prof. Dr Thomas Lindenberger and Prof. Dr Konrad H. Jarausch. He has published *Youth Radio Programmes in Cold War Berlin: Berlin as a Soundscape of Pop (1962–1973)* (2010). His lectures include the history of media and communication, media theory and comparative literary studies, including mediascapes, the theory of pop culture in literature, sound, silence and noise, and the history of media in the GDR. He is currently investigating the relational space concerning sound, noise and environment in public, political and academic discourse in the twentieth century.

Giovanni Vacca has a degree in Foreign Languages, a doctorate in Ethnomusicology, and has been a freelance journalist since 1992. He has worked extensively on traditional music and folk culture in Southern Italy, particularly in the area of Naples, and has published two books (*Il Vesuvio nel motore*, 1999, and *Nel corpo della tradizione*, 2004) on this subject. He is also a songwriter and has occasionally written lyrics for Neapolitan world music groups such as Spaccanapoli and Pietrarsa. He is currently working on a book about Neapolitan song, and co-editing (with Allan F. Moore) new research on the English folksinger Ewan MacColl, which includes the transcription of a long interview he himself recorded in 1987 and 1988, and critical essays by Dave Laing and Franco Fabbri (forthcoming).

Simon Warner is a lecturer and writer on popular music issues who teaches in Leeds University's School of Music. He takes a particular interest in the ways in which social, political and cultural history have connected with the evolution of pop and rock styles in the post-war period. A former live reviewer with *The Guardian*, his publications include the edited collections *Howl for Now* (2005), a study of Allen Ginsberg's ground-breaking poem, and *Summer of Love: The Beatles, Art and Culture in the Sixties* (2008). His latest volume, *Text and Drugs and Rock'n'Roll*, which considers the links between the US Beat poets and subsequent rock culture, appeared in 2013.

Sheila Whiteley is Professor Emeritus at the University of Salford, and Research Fellow at the Bader International Study Centre, Queen's University (Canada), Herstmonceux. As a feminist musicologist with strong research interests in issues of identity and subjectivity, she is known for her work on gender and sexuality as well as for longstanding interests in popular culture. She is author of *The Space Between the Notes: Rock and the Counter Culture* (1992), *Women and Popular Music: Popular Music and Gender* (2000), *Too Much Too Young: Popular Music, Age and Identity* (2005), and editor of *Sexing the Groove: Popular Music and Gender* (1996) and *Christmas, Ideology and Popular Culture* (2008). She is currently editing the OUP Handbook of Music and Queerness with Fred Maus, and the OUP Handbook of Music and Virtuality with Shara Rambarran.

Shawn David Young received his PhD from Michigan State University, and is Director of Music Management Studies and Assistant Professor of Music at Clayton State University in Morrow, Georgia. He has earned degrees in Music Industry Studies and American Studies, and has performed jazz, classical, Celtic and rock music for over 20 years on the electric bass guitar and trumpet. He has published research on the rock music history, the counterculture of the 1960s, communal living, music festivals, the politics of popular music, Christian rock and the changing landscape of popular religious music. He specialises in American popular music and religion, concert promotions, artist development and critical theory.

Preface: Dissent within Dissent

Jedediah Sklower

When *Volume!*'s editorial team began considering what directions a critical collection of new texts on the relationships between popular music and the concept of counterculture should take, we imagined papers that would explore the movement's margins and ambiguities, and question elements concerning its social, gender and racial relations.[1] We also expected texts that would explore the movement's aftermath, or how elements of the minimal, essential definition of the concept as it was theorised back then by Roszak – its anti-technocratic nature – and Reich – the research for new levels of consciousness[2] – would later be appropriated by other musical subcultures whose values could eventually diverge from the original movement's left-wing ideology, while using similar strategies and discourses. Interestingly, papers submitted by French scholars that were published in the original edition of this special issue (Whiteley 2012a and 2012b) did explore the movements' aftermath, with analyses of the skinhead movement (Lescop), Do It Yourself ethics (Hein) and Taqwacore Muslim punks (Macke), while those submitted by Anglo-Saxon scholars focused on the founding period.

The Counterculture as a Set of Antagonistic Fields

While theorists and *in situ* enthusiasts could see what – for a short period of time – bound the movement together in its opposition to mainstream society and the technocracy, what appears a novel theme in the contributions is how the 1960s counterculture fostered not only united resistance, but also multiple forms of inner dissent – a variety of contradictory facets of counterculture with different historical roots and various legacies beyond the 1960s. This, I believe, can at least partially account for what Andy Bennett identifies as a 'received, mediated memory' (Introduction: 25), and maybe even a polemical one. As such, it would appear that the antagonistic dimension of this legacy was more than simply the sum of the usual retrospective evaluations made by former participants and later generations – the result of an epic duel between nostalgic memory[3] and vengeful

---

[1] Something Sheila Whiteley explores in her recent article on Jimi Hendrix (2012c).
[2] See Sheila Whiteley's and Andy Bennett's introductory chapters, as well as Stanley Spector's analysis of the Grateful Dead's music (Chapter 9).
[3] See Hall (Chapter 12) on the Christiania community and Arnold (Chapter 7) on Woodstock and Altamont.

representations.[4] There was also a cultural, ideological struggle going on within the movement from the start.

Explicitly or not, many of the chapters presented here analyse the counterculture in the wake of twentieth-century artistic modernism.[5] Yet although the definition and delimitations of the concept diverge somewhat from one chapter to the next, three recurring elements seem to define it:

1. aesthetic vanguardism as an individualistic attack on formal tradition;
2. the belief in the capacity of art to change society and individual consciousness;
3. a specific relationship to modern life, whereby art either 1) flees from modern life to find aesthetic absolute in the absurd, madness, the unconscious, abstraction, other civilisations, or 2) on the contrary, in the postmodern phase beginning in the 1950s, 'harnesses its creative energies in order to transcend its limits' (Moore, Chapter 1: 32), greeting it 'as a field of artistic experimentation' (Den Tandt, Chapter 4: 85).

The current collection of chapters reveals how these trends were recycled by 1960s musicians and aesthetics. Be it via their artistic practices or their political goals – and the means they used to achieve these, such as psychedelic drugs, new interactions between musicians, amplification, or the recording studio, to name but a few – the minds behind the musics of the 1960s indeed followed the steps laid down by this tradition. These, then, constituted the key medium through which seemingly diverse tools and goals were synchronised, so suggesting a certain homology between cultural and musical characteristics. This countercultural coalition depended greatly upon the power of rock to federate the youth. Yet, pursuing artistic autonomy via unrelenting experimentation and sonic anarchy, 'even at the cost of alienating listeners with unlistenable noise' (Keister, Chapter 8: 142), meant that at some point, the avant-gardist trends within 1960s rock would contradict the fundamental rock ethos – serious popular music, yes, but appreciated by the masses and legitimised by the charts (Keightley 2001).

Modernism, however, as useful as it might be to scholars as a retroactive concept, was not an underlying substance that would generate solidarity or homogeneity between the various artistic factions of the counterculture. The concrete, strategic applications of the modernist agenda – whether conscious or not – were extremely varied. The fact that the concept is used to characterise such politically opposed movements and figures as Dadaism and Futurism, Ezra Pound and André Breton already hints at this heterogeneity. Merged with other historical roots, situations,

---

[4] See Halligan (Chapter 11) on Zappa's consistent disdain for pop, throughout the 1970s and 80s, as well as Carlin and Jones's '"Helter Skelter" and Sixties Revisionism' (Chapter 5).

[5] Particularly Warner (Chapter 2), Den Tandt (Chapter 4), Moore (Chapter 1), Keister (Chapter 8), Spector (Chapter 9) and Brown (Chapter 10).

lifestyles, and ideological and aesthetic projects, the practices and discourses of the counterculture sent the movement's subcultures and leaders (beat-hip bohemians, hippies, freaks, Jesus freaks, avant-garde performers, radicals and New Left social critics...) in diverging directions that were then reflected within the music world.

Consider two signature series of events: Ken Kesey's Acid Tests and Andy Warhol's *Exploding Plastic Inevitable*. Both protagonists staged synaesthetic drug-infused psychedelic performances meant to 'derange the senses'. Yet Simon Warner's and Jay Keister's chapters reveal two opposing aesthetic and moral projects. The former 'was meant to be a kind of rite of passage in which the individual, provided with free LSD, would become immersed in an alternative environment of free expression, interaction and experience without boundaries, and could eventually return to everyday life a newly enlightened person' (Keister, Chapter 8: 146). Contrary to this, Warhol's stagings, using, significantly, speed and heroin rather than LSD, abandoned 'moral purpose, social conscience or political ethos' (Warner, Chapter 2: 46), and were meant to violently shock the senses, not to awaken the mind. As for the Velvet Underground, who 'immersed themselves in a dystopian downtown, evoking a scene through their words and music that was neurotic and hyperactive, numbed and anaesthetised', their music explored 'psychic disturbances', rejecting 'the simmering, summery optimism of psychedelia' (ibid.: 62) conveyed by the music of the Grateful Dead. Identical means can conceal opposite creeds, and vice versa.

Musicians even had to struggle with their own contradictions: Bob Dylan's more introspective texts clashed with folk music's allegiance to social realism; acid rock's use of typically modern, industrial and technological tools with the communal, anti-capitalist mythology it had recycled from folk; avant-garde experimentation in rock with the pop ideology it inherited from the rock and roll era; freak out's self-conscious amateurism with the cult of guitar-hero virtuosity; politically-committed jazzmen's free-form improvisations with their populist ambitions (Sklower 2006); the Velvet Underground's fascination with surface, camp, androgyny, deviant sex and depression with rock's happy, sentimental and macho posturing; and so on.

Of course, the point is not to demonstrate that the counterculture was breeding cultural civil war without knowing it. Things worked out harmoniously for a few years, in quite good spirit, it seems; besides which, individual contradictions or inconsistencies do not necessarily lead to torment. Nonetheless, the counterculture was not only a collaborative art world (Becker 1982), but also a cultural *field* (Bourdieu 1992), a space of tensions that was probably 'doomed' to crack under the centrifugal pressures of its contradictions. Gerald Carlin and Mark Jones's chapter clearly demonstrates this via the Beatles' and the Rolling Stones' duelling visions of popular violence and political change ('Revolution' vs. 'Street Fighting Man'), or the diverging representations of Charles Manson by hippies and radicals, as a demon or a 'victim', which 'catalysed the splintering of the decade's countercultural coalition' (Chapter 5: 99). As such the counterculture's experimental, freely creative, centrifugal drive, its libertarian, democratic impulse, may account for its early fragmentation just as much as the political and economic factors traditionally summoned to explain the 'death of the 1960s'.

Apocalypse, Utopia and Beyond

As mentioned, the counterculture's representation of music's capacity to change the world was one of many symptoms of a modernist influence. Another of these undercurrents reveals itself in several of the chapters of this volume: apocalypticism. The cultural history of rock in the 1960s is not simply a continuation of/variation on a single trend in twentieth-century popular music history, but that of a multiplicity of strange, entangled roots. Modernism itself, as an 'annihilation of tradition and formal standards' (Moore, Chapter 1: 30), contains the proposal or provokes the perceived threat of aesthetic apocalypse.[6] Contemporary reactions by fans or foes to Bob Dylan going electric (ibid.: 31), rock music or free jazz (Sklower 2008) further demonstrate this point. As Christophe Den Tandt writes, apocalypse considered as a time of revelation 'requires the annihilation of the present' (Chapter 4: 84), a creed held in common by many hippies, freaks and avant-garde musicians. The times were ripe for utopian or dystopian fantasies.

Apocalypticism animated as much the optimistic revolutionary programme of rock as it did the Jesus Movement, the modernist ethos and the condemnation of society's moral decadence, utopian Acid Tests and the dystopian *Exploding Plastic Inevitable*. Utopia accomplished under a hippy rainbow is paradise lost for conservatives, and, obviously, the same is true in reverse. In the aftermath of music-related events such as the Manson Family murders, the violence at Altamont, the Beatles' break-up, the death of many prominent rock icons, but also violence at the Democratic National Convention in Chicago, the murder of Martin Luther King and Bobby Kennedy in 1968 or the Kent State shootings in 1970, countercultural enthusiasts started tasting their own brand of disenchantment. A significant number of members of the counterculture ended up rejecting the movement and its shortcomings, some abandoning the project altogether to reintegrate into mainstream society, others looking for political or spiritual alternatives. George Harrison, for example, quit LSD after a disappointing trip to Haight-Ashbury, and decided to dig deeper into Hinduism to further the pursuit of his ideals by other means (Scorsese 2011). In Chapter 6, Shawn David Young shows how Christian millennialist themes started influencing former members of the counterculture and how many hippie freaks turned to evangelical Christianity. The radicalisation of left-wing students who resorted to terrorism (the Weathermen Underground) can just as well be interpreted as an apocalyptic reaction to the failure of the

---

[6] It is quite telling that the chapters that deal with modernism analyse apocalyptic influences within 1960s popular music: see Moore (Chapter 1), Warner (Chapter 2), Den Tandt (Chapter 4), Carlin and Jones (Chapter 5), Young (Chapter 6) and Keister (Chapter 8).

counterculture to overthrow capitalism and the technocracy. Lost utopia leaves one with so many options.

Analyses of how capitalism redefined itself by integrating the counterculture's principles into its ideology,[7] organisation and management techniques are numerous (see, for example, Boltanski and Chiapello 1999). Once again, however, there is also a lesson for cultural history, beyond the more classic political or economic historical narratives. The darker side of rock music, 'more obsessed with destruction than with the hopeful outcome of transfiguration' (ibid.), is something that Gerald Carlin and Mark Jones's research on the numerous cover versions of 'Helter Skelter' demonstrates best. They revealing the way many metal, post-punk, industrial and goth bands later interpreted the song to criticise the countercultural project by stressing Charles Manson's aura and thus shed light on the movement's sombre legacy. As they write, 'the "dark" 1960s – gore films, bad trips and Satanism – were never entirely dispelled by the enlightenment ideals of the counterculture, and they would flourish in the 1970s mélange of paranoia and camp' (Chapter 5: 104), a mixture foreshadowed by freak explorations of madness, Yoko Ono's 'abject vocalisations' (Brown, Chapter 10)and the Velvet's and Nico's play with gender identity (Warner, Chapter 2).[8]

The progressives among my generation have had to mourn two major political setbacks in the twentieth century: the failure both of classic Marxist avant-garde politics and the regimes they gave birth to and of pacific transformation of society by 'the masses'. Despite what I mentioned above, the chapters in this volume do not leave us in utter despair. The 1960s counterculture represents an outstanding period of authentic democratic creativity – its music being one of its more fruitful legacies. As Christophe Den Tandt writes, 'utopian impulses only enjoy partial fulfilment in the field of practice. They must therefore be evaluated as a function of the residual accomplishments they leave in their wake – the practices, works and social changes their empowering momentum makes possible' (Chapter 4: 86). The music of the 1960s offered much in this regard for future generations to appropriate in new circumstances. A recent conference I co-organised in Strasbourg[9] on the relationships between popular music and politics in the twenty-first century showed how music, as a tool of political empowerment and democratic agency, remains a key component of political change. Recent events in the Middle East, Chile and Canada, and the examples of the '*indignados*' and #Occupy movements across the Western world, all attest to popular music's

---

[7] See Gina Arnold's chapter in this volume (Chapter 7) on the paradoxical rhetorics of two iconic documentary films of the period, *Woodstock* (Wadleigh 1994 [1970]) and *Gimme Shelter* (Maysles and Maysles 1970).

[8] See Keister (Chapter 8), Brown (Chapter 10) and Warner (Chapter 2).

[9] The international conference 'Changing the Tune: Popular Music and Politics in the XXIst Century' was co-organised by the ASPM, the French-speaking branch of the IASPM and *Volume!* and took place on 7–8 June 2013 at the University of Strasbourg. The programme and abstracts are available at: http://volume.revues.org/3444. The selected proceedings of the conference will be published in France in 2014, in the Enlish-speaking world in 2015.

everlasting strength and necessity in popular struggles around the globe.[10] This of course also means music can be hijacked by repressive states or advertising, and its efficiency can be as helpful to skinheads or Tea Partiers as it is to left-wing radicals. The counterculture may have been betrayed by some of its icons,[11] its history may have become a polemical legacy, and the chapters herein may demonstrate the frailty of the coalition it constituted, it nonetheless remains a significant creative and democratic moment in twentieth-century cultural and social history, a provocative promotion of aesthetic marginality and radicality, a set of 'emancipatory gestures that redraw the social and cultural field' (ibid..: 88) – the concrete inheritance of its utopian promises. New subcultures and political movements still feed on this to find new capacities, new agencies for political and cultural change. The counterculture: an apocalypse maybe, but a prolific one!

Working with Sheila Whiteley on the preparation of both issues of *Volume!* as well as this translated and edited version was a wonderful intellectual experience – I thank her deeply for her part in such a challenging and yet smooth collaboration and the rewarding opportunity she gave us. I am grateful also to Heidi Bishop, Derek Scott and all the people at Ashgate for supporting this project – having the occasion to disseminate our work beyond the frontiers of the French-speaking world is a wonderful gift. Thanks also to Chelsea Keenan for her father's wonderful photograph, used on the cover, and to Simon Warner for leading us to Larry Keenan's fantastic work. Of course, I also salute my *Volume!* comrades, Catherine Guesde, Gérôme Guibert, Emmanuel Parent, Béatrice Ratréma, Dario Rudy and Matthieu Saladin, on such splendid – as usual! – independent, DIY, collectiv[ist] teamwork.

---

[10] Charles Mueller (Chapter 3) offers new perspectives on this link between musical subcultures and political emancipation, via Hardt and Negri's work on the concept of Multitude.

[11] An ambivalent example of this could be Frank Zappa. Benjamin Halligan analyses Zappa's disdain for disco music, gay sexuality and suburban cultures as 'inevitably open[ing] up common ground between Zappa and reactionary, moralistic elements then ascendant in the public and political spheres' (Chapter 11: 192), all of this while remaining faithful to his satire of Christian morals, probably thus opposing many former Jesus Freaks converted to conservative politics (Young, Chapter 6). Giovanni Vacca's analysis (Chapter 14) of the Neapolitan countercultural scene and its legacy also provides insight on such reversals.

INTRODUCTION

Countercultures and Popular Music

Sheila Whiteley

As Andy Bennett writes in 'Reappraising "Counterculture"', while 'issues such as the essentially diverse, heterogeneous nature of both individuals and socio-political and cultural ideologies' have been thoroughly explored in relation to 'subculture', there has been far less engagement with the counterculture and, as such, it remains a problematic concept (p. 22). What is emerging, from the chapters submitted to *Countercultures and Popular Music* is counterculture's non-specificity: 'it was an entity with a significant degree of fluidity such that it could incorporate diverse groupings and, thus, manifest itself differently at specific times and within specific places depending on local socio-economic, cultural and demographic circumstances' (ibid.) While the previous lack of attention given to the 1960s counterculture accounts for our timely intervention, it is also apparent that there have always been certain issues that have, as yet, to be fully explored, not least demographic diversity and identity politics within 'the underlying unity of the countercultural variety' (Roszak 1970: 66). As I wrote in *The Space between the Notes*,

> Initially there appears to be an underlying tension between the political activism of the student New Left and the 'Fuck the System' bohemianism of the hippies and the yippies. At a deeper level, however, both extremes were united in their attack on the traditional institutions that reproduce dominant cultural-ideological relations – the family, education, media, marriage and the sexual division of labour. There was a shared emphasis on the freedom to question and experiment, a commitment to personal action, and an intensive examination of the self (Whiteley 1992: 83),

whether pathologically invasive or creatively expressive.
As Roszak observed,

> Beat-hip bohemianism may be too withdrawn from social action to suit New Left Radicalism; but the withdrawal is a direction the activist can readily understand ... We see the underlying unity of the countercultural variety, then, if we see beat-hip bohemianism as an effort to work out the personality and total life style that follow from New Left social criticism. At their best, these young bohemians are the would-be utopian pioneers of the world that lies beyond an intellectual rejection of the Great Society. They seek to invent a cultural base for New Left politics, to discover new types of community, new family patterns,

new sexual mores, new kinds of livelihood, new aesthetic forms, new personal identities on the far side of power politics, the bourgeois home, and the consumer society. (1970: 66)

On re-visiting my earlier research into rock and the counterculture, it occurred that chaos and uncertainty, allied to the impact of noise (inharmonious sound, distortion, dissonance and the connotations surrounding discord itself) could be interpreted as underpinning a revolutionary agenda suggestive of a state of creative anarchy,[1] which is arguably distinct from the more soft-focus connotations of 'All You Need Is Love' and the pacifist agenda implicit in such slogans as 'Make Love Not War'.[2] If, however, Roszak was correct in identifying 'beat-hip bohemianism as an effort to work out the personality and total life style that follow from New Left social criticism', then the forming of countercultural communities, such as the commune that emerged in, for example, Christiania (see Hall in this volume), could appear a logical development in 'providing a particular location for self-identity' (Whiteley 2000: 23). Discord and the darker extremes of 'noise' associated with performers such as the Grateful Dead, Captain Beefheart, Jimi Hendrix and MC5 would thus come into focus as the first stage in the countercultural agenda of establishing a relevant and alternative life-style.[3] As Jeff Nuttall observed, two of the aims of the Underground were to 'release forces into the prevailing culture that would dislocate society, untie its stabilising knots of morality, punctuality, servility and property; and [to] expand the range of human consciousness outside the continuing and ultimately soul-destroying boundaries of the political utilitarian frame of reference' (1970: 249), a philosophy that resonated with the *International Times* identification of rock as a political weapon.[4]

But was this the whole story and is the concept of counterculture still meaningful? It would appear from the chapters that follow that 'despite the theoretical arguments that can be raised against the sociological value of

---

[1] To an extent, this can be traced back to the romantic anarchism of the Beats, with its interest in Eastern mysticism, poetry, jazz and drugs and writers Jack Kerouac and Allen Ginsberg.

[2] Although it is recognised that the fight against middle-class prurience led increasingly towards an explicit identification of sexual freedom with total freedom which, at its extreme, embraced pornography (including the so-termed 'velvet underground' advertisements for blue movies and classified ads, and *Play Power*'s 'Female Fuckability Test' (Neville 1971: 14). As such, while love was fundamental to the philosophy of the counterculture, there was nevertheless a marked difference between the transcendental spirituality promised to followers of the Maharishi Mahesh Yogi and the revolutionary liberation of the Yippie Party's Jerry Rubin and his symbolic call for patricide.

[3] As Jacques Attali observed, noise contains prophetic powers. 'It makes audible the new world that will gradually become visible' (1985: 11).

[4] 'The mood is right for us to fight politics with music, because rock is now a media. Sure it's basically recreation but because we've now applied new rules to the way it's run, it's also a weapon' (*IT*, 56 [1969]).

counterculture as a meaningful term for categorising social action, like subculture, the term lives on as a concept in social and cultural theory ... [to] become part of a received, mediated memory' (Bennett: 25) What emerges from the chapters that appear in *Countercultures and Popular Music* is that this involved not simply the utopian but also the dystopian and that while festivals such as those held at Monterey and Woodstock might appear to embrace the former, the deaths of such iconic figures as Brian Jones, Jimi Hendrix, Jim Morrison and Janis Joplin, the nihilistic mayhem at Altamont, and the shadowy figure of Charles Manson cast a darker light on its underlying agenda, one that reminds us that 'pathological issues [are] still very much at large in today's world' (ibid.).

An Overview of the Chapters

We are privileged to have an introductory chapter by Andy Bennett, whose extensive research and publications on subcultures, cultures and cultural memory have established his reputation as a leading international academic on cultural theory. 'Reappraising "Counterculture"' re-visits and re-evaluates earlier and on-going instances of counter anti-hegemonic ideology, practice and belief, and how the emergence of the term in the late 1960s has been redeployed in more recent decades in relation to other forms of cultural and socio-political phenomena. As he explains, recent developments in sociological theory complicate and problematise theories developed in the 1960s, with digital technology, for example, providing an impetus for new understandings of counterculture. What is intriguing is the way in which current movements and groups have been referred to as countercultural, so raising the question of how we position the latter.

Part I: Theorising Countercultures

In many ways, the first part of *Countercultures and Popular Music* extends and develops many of the issues raised by Bennett, so providing a reflective space in which to consider different ways of explaining and exploring both the relevance and the diversity inherent in the concept. Ryan Moore's chapter, 'Break on Through: The Counterculture and the Climax of American Modernism', investigates the mediating link between music and 1960s modernism, focusing attention on the shared spirit of innovation and progress, with the celebration of 'youth' providing an iconic symbol of hope and transformation. With its origins in the free jazz and folk music scenes in New York at the beginning of the 1960s, Moore's discussion of Ornette Coleman and Bob Dylan then moves west to consider the different variations of rock music that emerged from San Francisco and Los Angeles, 'the homeland of the counterculture and the terminal point of American modernisation in the 1960s' (Chapter 1: 33), identifying LSD and acid rock as symbolic of 'the spirit of modernity and its ironies' (ibid.: 35). Simon Warner also draws attention to the significance of New York in 'The Banality of Degradation: Andy Warhol, the Velvet Underground and the Trash Aesthetic'. As he successfully argues, Warhol was at the heart of one of the key countercultural gestures of the era.

> By stressing surface and the superficial over depth and substance and by rejecting traditional motivations – issues of moral purpose, social conscience or political ethos, for instance – the artist and his disciples created an enclosed aesthetic universe that was profoundly alternative to both the mid-1960s mainstream and also those who would challenge it in more conventional ways. (Chapter 2: 45–6)

Not least, the introspective, amphetamine-induced music of Warhol's resident band, the Velvet Underground, was in stark contrast to both 'the psychedelic jams of San Francisco and the acid-drenched and dandy stylings of London' (ibid.: 60), 'marrying instead elements of the high and the low, the cultural leftfield and the arts underground, harsh rhythms, repetitive drones and minimalist arrangements with stories of low-life transgression, conjured, at least in part, by the toxic charge of speed and heroin' (ibid.: 61). The trash aesthetic associated with Warhol and the Velvet Underground was to influence artists as diverse as musician Genesis P-Orridge and photographer Cindy Sherman and even more mainstream examples – from Boy George to RuPaul and k.d. lang and, indeed, earlier performances by David Bowie, Iggy Pop and Lou Reed where camp, drag, sexual diversity, gender controversies and violence were an integral and conscious part of their artistic strategy.

The impasse faced in the last decade concerning subcultures and post-subcultural critique discussed earlier in Bennett's introductory chapter, is addressed in Charles Mueller's chapter, 'Were British Subcultures the Beginning of Multitude?'. Drawing on the theories of Michael Hardt and Antonio Negri, which present a social, economic and philosophical description and critique of globalisation and the multinational capitalism that has formed the foundation of Western societies since the early 1970s, Mueller explores the idea that subcultures may be a part of the early stages of Multitude. Defined as a set of singularities (not unlike the loose organisation of subcultures), and drawing both on Spinoza's theory of immanence and Foucault's concept of biopolitics (the process of harnessing human potential as a group), attention is focussed on the 'outsiders' who 'begin to form new alternative networks of affection and social organization' (Hardt and Negri 2004: 193). Mueller's discussion of 1970s and 1980s subcultures who conform to Negri's definition of subversion as 'the radical nature of truth' (Negri 2005: 59) provides a thought-provoking insight into the newer political counter and subcultures that are emerging in contemporary society, and hence why the concept of Multitude offers a plausible explanation for their social construction, style and existence. In addition it raises the question of 'what can we do to help popular music and popular culture bring about a more developed social conscience' (Chapter 3: 78), and the extent to which the sign-value of subcultural style continues to be both a subversive and life-affirming symbol when capital continuously makes new demands on the workforce and the struggle for justice, time and quality of life assumes an international dimension. A question yet to be resolved.

Part II: Utopias, Dystopias and the Apocalyptic

Christophe Den Tandt's ground-breaking chapter 'The Rock Counterculture from Modernist Utopianism to the Development of an Alternative Music Scene' poses an important question: how do the centrifugal gestures of rock leave 'residual traces' in the cultural field, in the form of musical practices, but also specific practices, places and institutions (Chapter 4: 83)? Den Tandt begins by examining the paradoxes inherent in rock. As he notes, there is no consensus on its aesthetic vocation or on the social function of its supposed rebellion, albeit its frequent interpretation as 'resisting through rituals' and the Adornian-like criticisms if it fails. His identification of 'the utopian' (as theorised by Jameson and Hassan) opens out the possibility that 'in rock, the refusal the refusal of co-optation (social, academic or even artistic) expresses the aspiration to exceed a condition lived as alienated, thus opening up a utopian perspective' (ibid.: 83) that can be interpreted as 'apocalyptic' (revelation requiring the annihilation of the present). For academics, this dimension enables a historicisation of rock within broader twentieth-century trends. Hassan, for example, interprets the desire to free oneself of a social universe perceived to be non-authentic as one of the fundamental features of early twentieth-century modern art. By the late 1950s, the aesthetic disqualification of the social world loses its virulence and with the emergence of the Beat movement, John Cage, Pop Art and psychedelics, everyday life is no longer rejected and becomes, instead, the source of artistic experimentation. Rock's violence is thus expressive of the desire both to master the industrial environment and its own violence. Yet as Den Tandt observes, 'it is the essence of rock never to fulfil its desires – its project can only be evaluated as a function of the residual accomplishments they leave in their wake – the practices, works, social changes their empowering momentum makes possible' (ibid.: 86). As such, 'the legacy of artistic utopiansm aren't the works themselves, but the emancipatory gestures that redraw the social and cultural field' (ibid.). Den Tandt then questions how a utopian model can be applied to profit-based mass culture, providing examples drawn from rock and roll and the ways in which emancipation was synonymous both with rhythm and blues sensuality and the praise of consumerist pleasures, and the hippie movement's satire of ostentatiousness (Chuck Berry's 'Cadillac Coupe' v. Janis Joplin's 'Mercedes Benz'). Musical excellence is also cited as both a mark of autonomy (the Beatles, 'Eleanor Rigby') and punk rejection. Rock's structures of production and distribution are then subjected to scrutiny, so offering a further point of discussion on issues of authenticity and the market, with some small independent labels trying to make a profit, while the majors enable Bob Dylan to emerge, thanks to commercial experimentations.[5] Den Tandt concludes by exploring rock as a culture of professionalism, aimed at a social integration characterised by non-alienated work – so continuing mass culture's meta-industrial dimension. Its comparison with literature (thrillers) and film (westerns) suggests that its heroes preserve their existential and economic autonomy by fighting against structures of authority while proposing conservative models of masculine aggressiveness, homophobia, racism and misogyny.

Den Tandt's discussion provides a compelling backdrop for the issues raised in this part. Mark Jones and Gerald Carlin explore the heritage of the Beatles' 1968 track, 'Helter Skelter' and its association with the psychotic killer, Charles Manson. As they reveal, in '"Helter Skelter" and Sixties Revisionism', 'the "dark" 1960s – gore films, bad trips and Satanism – were never entirely dispelled by the enlightenment ideals of the counterculture, and they would flourish in the 1970s mélange of paranoia and camp' (Chapter 5: 103–4). As a continuing figure in this resurgence of the sinister sixties, Manson becomes the 'tabloid bogeyman, the subject of numerous pulp treatments in various media, as well as in heavy metal where he is used to invoke the devil or to herald the apocalypse' (ibid.: 104). Initially difficult to classify, 'Helter Skelter' assumed a growing notoriety due to its subsequent associations with the Manson Family. As the authors reveal, while 'Helter Skelter' was largely overlooked for several years, the existing early covers are, stylistically, hard rock. Later, the song was covered in more diverse and/or deviant idioms, so reinflecting the original as a critique of the sixties and its legacies. While Paul McCartney's 2009 live album *Good Evening New York City* has exorcised many of its demons, 'Helter Skelter' nevertheless remains one of the few cultural objects that can still summon forth its revolutionary spectre. Yet as Jones and Carlin tellingly observe, 'after over 40 years in which "Helter Skelter" has variously signalled the failure of the sixties, a hard rock heritage, metallic origins, schlock horror and apocalyptic race war, it now communicates an institutionally respectable radical chic' (ibid.: 107).

The Book of Revelations is also central to Shawn David Young's discussion of 'Apocalyptic Music: Reflections on Countercultural Christian Influence'. As his research suggests, the development of the so-termed Jesus Movement became 'a critical part of the decade rather than an aberration' (Luhr 2009: 74), allowing the counterculture to be 'reintegrated into the continuing American consensus' (ibid.: 68). The conversion to Christianity of such iconic musicians as Bob Dylan, Eric Clapton, Barry McGuire, Johnny Cash and Fleetwood Mac's Jeremy Spencer – the last to 'the rigid and controversial commune the Children of God, a notable doomsday group' (Chapter 6: 115) – as well as such songs as the Byrds' 'Jesus Is Just Alright' (1969), Ocean's 'Put Your Hand in the Hand' (1970), Creedence Clearwater Revival's 'Bad Moon Rising' (1969) and Norman Greenbaum's 'Spirit in the Sky' (1969), suggested that the counterculture

---

[5] A topic that Fabien Hein explores in the French version of this book, about the DIY ethic in punk (2012).

was beginning to change its focus, but as tales of Judgement Day were woven into lyrics the doomsday feel intensified. Catastrophic global events were interpreted as predictors of Armageddon, with heavy metal drawing on the rhetoric of chaos rooted in Judeo-Christianity. Meanwhile, musicals such as *Jesus Christ Superstar* and *Godspell* added to the already spiritually drenched atmosphere of countercultural Christendom, 'bringing what was, to some extent, a vestige of Christian thinking into every sphere of pop culture ...[:] a cosmology that was both triumphalist/postmillenialist (God's kingdom can be realised on earth as Christianity gains global influence) and premillennialist (Jesus would return in the Rapture to escort believers to Heaven)' (ibid.: 116).

While Woodstock and Altamont have often been interpreted as indicative of the utopian and dystopian polarities of countercultural mythology, Gina Arnold's chapter, 'Nobody's Army: Contradictory Cultural Rhetoric in *Woodstock* and *Gimme Shelter*' provides an insight into the significance of the films in shaping the ideology of the rock festival *qua* festival. As she explains, while Woodstock and other historic festivals have 'worked ideologically to legitimate the highly contradictory beliefs and actions of rock fans at present day festivals' (Chapter 7: 124), Altamont 'followed more in the tradition of the free Rolling Stones concert in Hyde Park in July of 1969 that served as a memorial for guitarist Brian Jones' (ibid.: 125). 'What is significant is the way in which certain cultural rhetorics about festivals were circulated via two specific films', and the ways in which the mediated attributes of entertainment, escapism and worldliness had less to do with the festivals themselves, and more to do with the artistic license taken by their filmmakers. In effect, both films work as cultural propaganda, conveying an intangible aura, a feeling, an experience, a sense of participation. Arnold's close analysis of *Woodstock: Three Days of Peace and Music* reveals its use of film gimmickry (e.g. split-screen effects to enhance its representational power) and news documentary techniques to reinforce its narrative: the redemptive vision of the festival, the peaceful and passive crowd, and the popularisation of rock bands which has inspired almost half a century of rock festivals. In contrast, *Gimme Shelter* attempted to 'live' the film: 'at the concert's height the filmmakers deployed 35 camera people in the field ... to capture crowd moments' (ibid.: 125). Both, however, use similar rhetorical strategies to valorise the significance of being part of a rock community and hence, taking part in a historical moment. Not least, the horrifying climax to Altamont is put into a contrived perspective as the first half of the film shows the Stones' concert at Madison Square Gardens where a rapt and peaceful crowd shower Mick Jagger with rose petals. It is, perhaps, no coincidence that both films have been compared with the work of Leni Riefenstahl, 'generally considered to be the finest producer of twentieth-century political propaganda' (ibid.: 136). As Arnold concludes, *Woodstock* and *Gimme Shelter* disseminate a vision that continues to exert a powerful ideological presence on contemporary rock festivals where concert goers/the crowd define themselves as rebellious, countercultural and liberal when, in fact, they are largely docile, passive and conservative. Moreover, both imply that attending rock concerts is 'a crucial way of participating in the history of an era' (ibid.: 135), a possible reason for their continuing popularity.

Part III: Sonic Anarchy and Freaks

It is no coincidence that the four chapters that follow provide both an in-depth analysis of key bands associated with what Jay Keister terms 'freak culture', while referring outwards both to other chapters in this section and to those mentioned earlier in 'Theorising Countercultures'. Young's earlier observations on the Jesus Movement and its relationship to the American consensus of respectability has a curious resonance with Benjamin Halligan's chapter, 'From Countercultures to Suburban Cultures: Frank Zappa after 1968', while Stanley J. Spector and Shelina Brown confirm the relationship between anarchy, chaos and noise discussed earlier in my Introduction.

Jay Keister's chapter, 'The Long Freak Out: Unfinished Music and Countercultural Madness in Avant-Garde Rock of the 1960s and 1970s' provides a thoughtful context for album tracks where sonic anarchy creates an underlying connotation of madness, and where amateur techniques suggest conceptual absurdity, so highlighting their significance within the discourse of rock rebellion. However, as Keister subsequently points out, while the blend of anarchy and the absurd are distinguishing characteristics of freak, 'amateurism is clearly by design' (Chapter 8: 142). Andy Warhol's *Exploding Plastic Inevitable* and the Velvet Underground's 'feedback-drenched track "European Son"' (1967), the Grateful Dead's album *Anthem of the Sun* (1968), Yoko Ono and John Lennon's *Two Virgins* (1968) and *Freak Out!* (1966) by the Mothers of Invention led by Frank Zappa all providing examples of avant-garde techniques. Post-punk, industrial and post-industrial groups that celebrated the destruction of song form, both in amateurish values of musicianship and conceptual absurdity, were also indicative of the enduring attraction of freak out, while hallucinatory insanity, as boosting creativity, was exemplified in the improvisational approach of the Grateful Dead who, as Stanley J. Spector observes, was the quintessential '"psychedelic" or "acid rock"' band (Chapter 9: 158). Spector's identification of associative improvisation during musical explorations, and transformational improvisation during the climax of that exploration provides new insights into the Grateful Dead's improvisational techniques, which culminated in what David Malvini terms a 'transformational' quality, which he traces to 'the space and tension' between the hierarchical and associative forms of improvisation (2007: 5). 'The Grateful Dead and Friedrich Nietzsche: Transformation in Music and Consciousness' is a thought-provoking introduction to the Dead's psychedelic rock, stressing 'scarifying, chaotic feedback' (Lesh 2005: 191), an abandonment of structure and form, and the exploratory space that was to characterise their acid-drenched improvisations during 1968–69.

While Keister includes Yoko Ono within his discussion of freak, Shelina Brown identifies her experimental musical works within a framework of revolutionary feminist politics and Julia Kristeva's writings on abjection. As 'Scream from the Heart: Yoko Ono's Rock and Roll Revolution' tellingly observes,

> Ono's screams emerge from the depths of her body, unleashing a subversive vocality that threatens to destabilise not only the boundary between music and noise, but also the gendered and racialised sonic codes that delineate acceptable modes of vocal musical expression. In their politicised interpretation, Ono's unruly vocalisations thus point back to the deepest reaches of her own unique, albeit gendered and racialised body. (Chapter 10: 173)

Brown's analysis of Ono's extreme vocalisations situates the scream as sonic abjection, 'focusing awareness of Yoko's very real existence' (Levitz 2005: 223), 'a sense of a fragmented bodily interiority' (Brown op.cit.: 176) as exemplified in, for example, her lament for her lost daughter, 'Don't Worry Kyoko (Mommy's Only Looking for Her Hand in the Snow)'. It was, however, her collaborative work with John Lennon (*Unfinished Music No. 1: Two Virgins*, 1968), an avant-garde tape composition, spliced together over the course of a night-long acid trip, that most attracted attention both to her role as an avant-garde artist and as a formative influence on the counterculture. As Brown observes, 'it is fitting that Yoko Ono, a Japanese woman, would surface as a powerful public figure in the US at this historical moment' (ibid.: 180).

There is little doubt that the late 1960s/1970s caused many to reflect on what appeared to be the failure of the counterculture; the realisation that the party was over and that the freedoms promised by the cultural revolution were little more than a stoned dream. Then, as the 1970s turned into the 1980s and 'the long 1960s' were finally routed by the dawn of the Reagan era, Frank Zappa, 'the ringmaster of freaks, a mother to the North American counterculture, and champion of outsiders, would find himself outnumbered and outmanoeuvred by the rising tide of "plastic people"' (Chapter 11: 188). Benjamin Halligan's 'From Countercultures to Suburban Cultures: Frank Zappa after 1968' offers a perceptive discussion of the Reagan years 'when revolutionary impulses and radical subjectivities had been near-fully buffered by and absorbed into a new suburbia', when 'what was once a target, had now become a destination ... for those baby boomers ... [who] took the reins of power, and the keys to the institutions, from their parents' (ibid.: 189). Not least, sex itself had been edged into commercial domains and for Zappa the results were a matter for ridicule. 'Sex has been feminised, to become the preoccupation or pastime of the sexually aggressive female, "*pace*" feminism, and of the "femininity" of the character of the passive male homosexual, receiver rather than giver' (ibid.: 192). As Halligan explains,

> rounding on sexuality in this way, with sex as the optic through which suburban cultures are presented, examined and decried, inevitably opened up common ground between Zappa and reactionary, moralistic elements then ascendant in the public and political spheres. Zappa's concern is not so much diagnosing mass sexual dysfunctionality (in the manner of Wilhelm Reich's writing of the 1930s) as spinning a Chaucerian picaresque, drawing on specific case studies of sexual bad practice. (ibid. 192–3)

His premise is supported by a close analysis of key albums: *Sheik Yerbouti*, 'with its valley girls and soulless computer muzak' (ibid.: 199), and 'the contemporary sheen' of *You Are What You Is* (ibid.: 201), which 'remains one of the most ambitious public stands against Reaganism in the 1980s' (Watson 1993: 395). In documenting the trajectory from 'the Summer of Love, and "freak" cultures, to the onset of neoliberalism and "Valley Girl" cultures', Halligan's chapter provides a much-needed reappraisal of Zappa's work. As his chapter reveals, Zappa's engagement with suburbia is indicative of the end of ideological radicalism and liberation while marking the terminus of his satirical project.

Part IV: Countercultural Scenes – Music and Place

Music played a significant part in the way that the counterculture authored space in relation to articulations of community by providing a shared sense of collective identity. Not least, the heady mixture of genres provided a socio-cultural-political backdrop for distinctive musical practices and innovations which, in relation to counterculture ideology, offered a rich experiential setting whereby different groups defined their relationship both to the local and international dimensions of the movement. As such, there was a growing sense of locality, community and collective identity. As Richard Neville wrote at the time: 'From Berlin to Berkeley, from Zurich to Notting Hill, Movement members exchange a gut solidarity, sharing common aspirations, inspirations, strategy, style, mood and vocabulary. Long hair is their declaration of independence, pop music their Esperanto and they puff pot in their peace pipe' (1971: 14). Neville's identification of what he calls the counterculture's 'intense, spontaneous internationalism' is explored initially in Thorbjörg Daphne Hall's chapter 'Countercultural Space Does Not Persist: Christiania and the Role of Music'. Founded by the '*Slumstormere*' [Slum Stormers][6] in 1971 as an alternative city within the city of Copenhagen, and officially recognised by the Danish parliament as a 'social experiment' in 1973, Christiania developed as an area populated both by student activists and by drop-outs, junkies and criminals who saw it as 'a refuge, an opportunity to escape from the problems which they had experienced in the metropolis'

---

[6] '*Slumstormere*' were a mixture of homeless people from Christianshavn and political activists that protested against the renovation that was taking place in the area and the lack of housing.

(Baldvig 1982: 11). Hall's research into Christiania's musical venues and genres provides a detailed reading of contrasting and contesting scenes, including the traditional Danish practice of communal singing, and '*slagsange*' [protest songs], which reflect the constant battle for independence. Both contrast with the newer practice of supporting records by non-political inhabitants, which have gradually shifted towards a more localised and atmospheric depiction of Christiania as idyllic, and the cover band culture of the drop-outs. As Hall observes, music 'creates an ambiguous construction of locality and the idea of independence versus commercialism' (Chapter 12: 220) and, it would seem, Christiania no longer constitutes a countercultural space, but rather relies for its existence on tourism which, in turn, fosters and nurtures nostalgia for its past. In effect, it has been transformed into an 'outdoor museum for the culture of the 1960s and 1970s, which, because of a fence, has survived in a world that would otherwise have destroyed it years ago' (Kvorning 2004: 85).

The recognition that musical processes take place within a particular space and place, and are shaped both by specific musical practices and by the pressures and dynamics of political and economic circumstances, provides a telling context for the ways in which a countercultural ideology informed both East and West Berlin during the period of the Cold War. As Heiner Stahl explains, to be heard in public is to generate attention: to be seen by others, and to perform in front of others is a social practice that draws lines of aesthetic demarcation (Chapter 13: 224). While this observation is relevant to all the chapters in Part IV, the focus of Stahl's research is on 'A Border-Crossing Soundscape of Pop: The Auditory Traces of Subcultural Practices in 1960s Berlin' where 'experiencing entertainment' and competing images from the past and present of popular music combined to take on new and additional meaning at a local level (ibid.: 223). Stahl's investigation into the acoustic dimension of everyday life in Berlin unveils hidden layers of social, cultural and political power relations. Not least, 'controlling auditory space is recognised as a powerful tool in both creating and consolidating communities'. This was evidenced in East Berlin's proliferation of youth clubs and rock bands during the 1960s and the influence of Berlin Radio and its youth programme Jugendstudio DT 64, which was heavily criticised by Erich Honecker (secretary of the Central Committee's office) for spreading the 'capitalist evil' of pop and dance music and undermining socialist morality and decency. The Rolling Stones concert at the West Berlin outdoor venue, Waldbühne, on 15 September 1965, was identified as fostering hysteria, feeding what can be described as moral panic on both sides of the Berlin Wall. The significance of youth-oriented radio is also identified in West Berlin's Wir-um zwanzig (launched in October 1965) and S-f-beat (March 1967) under the auspices of the Broadcasting Station of Free Berlin. In addition to contemporary pop, the stations also fostered a new generation of journalists whose investigative approach to issues of authority and power (such as West Berlin's repressive policing) challenged the image of liberal West Berlin that the Station of Free Berlin was so keen to stage. As Stahl concludes, 'By actively grabbing "foreign" acoustic and aesthetic influences [they contested] the liberal rhetorics of Cold War democracy [by challenging] their claims of cultural openness' (ibid.: 234). Meanwhile, in East Berlin, 'The auditory presence of "Jugendstudio DT 64" constantly conflicted with an idealised approach to socialist cultural politics' (ibid.). Both reflected the mediated power of subcultural pop and its practices to mirror and oppose the cultural codes of mainstream society.

Giovanni Vacca also focuses attention on the 1960s, a time when the first seeds of rock and roll and the ideology surrounding the counterculture were penetrating Italian culture. As he reveals in his chapter 'Music and Countercultures in Italy: The Neapolitan Scene', it was a period when British and American rock stars began to include Italy in their world tours and Italian rock bands found a more defined political identity as progressive rock superseded beat. Then, during the accelerating conflicts of the 1970s a new radical political culture developed. Born outside the Communist Party, criticism was addressed to 'the system' in all its articulations: family, education, politics, work and entertainment. Within this highly-charged context the folk music revival and the political song assumed a new significance as popular genres and the classic Neapolitan song were reclaimed and reshaped. As Vacca explains, the song, in Neapolitan tradition, developed both 'as an important part of the identity of the local emerging middle class' while being 'taken up and continuously revisited by the lower classes' (Chapter 14: 239). The strength of these traditions was such that 'the Neapolitan song had to be violated, debunked, stripped bare of its stock conventions and bent to unheard expressive possibilities' (ibid.: 240) if it was to embrace and reflect the changes inherent in the countercultural agenda. Vacca's detailed discussion of Neapolitan bands that revitalised traditional songs through influences as diverse as jazz, rhythm and blues (the Showmen), progressive and psychedelic rock (Osanna and Il Balletto di Bronzo) also focused on lyrics that encapsulated the two major poles of Italian countercultures: India, which for many Italian hippies 'represented the myth of an alternative civilisation, custodian of an ancestral wisdom lost in the industrial world', and the factory, which was 'at the centre of theoretical Marxist speculations of the radical left wing born outside the Communist Party' (ibid.: 241). Sorrenti's apocryphal ballad 'Vorrei incontrati' (1972) thus 'foreshadows the late eighties when the fragmentation of large factories and the re-allocation of industrial production to countries with a less expensive labour force lead to growing unemployment and the transformation of what once were working-class areas into a waste land' (ibid.: 246). The subsequent takeover of its derelict buildings as 'occupied self-managed social centres' led to a new Italian music, which incorporated rap, ragamuffin and reggae and which also brought with it a rediscovery of folk music and the Neapolitan song. As Vacca concludes, 'it took three decades for Neapolitan musicians to find their own way into modern song and popular music and, at the same time, to recover a glorious tradition' (ibid.: 249), and today the Neapolitan song has become a favourite genre by a new generation of performers.

Coda

I would like to acknowledge and thank my co-editor Jedediah Sklower for his support and enthusiasm throughout our planning and design of *Countercultures and Popular Music*. What could have been a laborious task was instead a joyful exploration of the counterculture's history, as well as its diverse manifestations.

I would also like to thank Simon Warner for introducing us to Chelsea Keenan, and to Chelsea for allowing us to use her father's photo 'Daughter of the New American Revolution, Spring Mobilization' as our cover illustration for *Countercultures and Popular Music*.

Reappraising 'Counterculture'

Andy Bennett

Since its emergence as a key socio-political term during the late 1960s, the concept of counterculture has reappeared periodically in literature, media and vernacular discourse as a means of articulating aspects of counter-hegemonic ideology, practice and belief. Generally speaking, 'counterculture' is used to denote a point of disjuncture between what are represented as *dominant* or *mainstream* values and alternative value systems that, although the purview of a minority, are articulated through various forms of media – music, writing, art, protest and so on; these serve to amplify the collective voice of a counterculture in such a way that a minority becomes a 'significant' minority. In terms of academic theorisation, counterculture has been dramatically overshadowed by the term 'subculture', the latter having become a key conceptual framework for the examination of counter- and anti-hegemonic practice, particularly among youth. Indeed, subculture has also become a subject of ongoing critical debate between theorists as to the validity – or not – of the concept, given its fixation around issues of class and social structure. At one level, such a perspective, it is argued, carries increasingly less significance in a social world characterised by reflexivity, fragmentation and cultural pluralism (see Bennett 2011). By and large, the concept of counterculture has remained beyond the ambit of such debates. Yet, as a conceptual framework, counterculture presents an equally potent series of questions, not least because of the way in which it has been applied to ongoing trends in socio-political action and thought – particularly in relation to new social movements and alternative lifestyles, but also on occasion in the context of other aspects of social life, such as organised religion (Elliott 1990) and racism (van Donselaar 1993).

The purpose of this introductory chapter is to critically revisit and re-evaluate the term 'counterculture' as a means of examining and explicating previous and ongoing instances of counter- and anti-hegemonic ideology, practice and beliefs. The chapter begins by looking at the emergence of the term 'counterculture' in the late 1960s, and its associations with the hippie movement. This is followed by a consideration of how more recent developments in sociological theory complicate and problematise the 1960s definition of counterculture, and also the way in which this definition has been redeployed in more recent decades in relation to other forms of cultural and socio-political phenomena. This is followed by an investigation of how new social trends and associated developments – notably in digital technology – provide an impetus for new understandings of counterculture. Finally, the chapter will examine some current examples of movements and groups that have been referred as countercultures and consider new ways of positioning this concept.

The Origins of Counterculture

While the precise origins of counterculture are unclear, the term acquired popular currency during the late 1960s when it became associated with the hippie movement. Taking some of their inspiration from the Beat era, the hippies created an alternative cultural milieu in which music, drugs, literature and lifestyle combined to create a series of perceived alternatives to the dominant capitalist society inhabited by their parents and other members of the 'parent culture' (Hall 1968). Music was undoubtedly an important driver for the separation that the hippies sought from the parent culture (Whiteley 1992). Building on generations of protest song, artists such as Bob Dylan, the Beatles and the Rolling Stones infused rock music with a level of social and cultural critique that was quickly acknowledged, emulated and developed by other emergent artists of the late 1960s (Bennett 2001). As Frith (1981, 1983) observes, such was the power of rock music in this respect that it came to bespeak notions of an alternative community that the hippies believed could be experienced and realised through the music itself. As Frith observes, such claims about the power of music to create a physical, alternative community were ill-founded and spurious. Nevertheless, signature events of the countercultural era, such as the Woodstock Music and Arts Fair (see Bennett 2004) and the emergence of rural communes (see Webster 1976), gave rise to a collective sense – albeit a short-lived one – among the hippies that a fully-fledged alternative lifestyle was possible. It was this mythical and romanticised notion of an alternative lifestyle, and its intimations of an alternative community, that provided the impetus for the countercultural ideology of the hippie movement.

Equally important in this respect was the global character of the counterculture. While most of the youth cultures and gangs of the 1950s and early 1960s – for example, the Teddy Boys – had been locally specific manifestations (Hall and Jefferson 1976), the hippie movement quickly established a presence throughout the Western world and also in some parts of South America, Asia and the former Soviet Bloc (see Easton 1989). Again, music was highly important in this respect. Utilising the possibilities of the then rapidly increasing global communications technologies, popular music artists of the day were able to communicate their music – and their message – across a wide geographic area in a single performance. A significant example of this was the Beatles' song 'All You Need Is Love', which was first aired as a semi-live performance by the Beatles as part of the *Our World* programme, the world's first live global television link-up. The programme was broadcast via satellite on 25 June 1967 and was viewed by an estimated 400 million people in 26 countries throughout the world.

Popular representations of the counterculture also interpreted it as a socio-cultural phenomenon with the potential to create a new cultural sphere, beyond and ideologically separated from the parent culture. Wolfe's (1968) *The Electric Kool-Aid Acid Test* was a highly influential piece of writing in this sense. Documenting the road-trip of Ken Kesey and his 'Merry Pranksters' around the United States during the mid-1960s, Wolfe vividly portrays the use of LSD in multimedia events designed to create new levels of perception and awareness among participants (see Moore and Keister in this volume). Similarly, Thompson's (1971) *Fear and Loathing in Las Vegas*, although published in the early 1970s, pays due homage to the countercultural legacy and its vision of a new world deflected from the mainstream society's economic greed and obsession with technological growth.

Such matters also piqued the interest of a number of academic theorists during the late 1960s and early 1970s. Of particular significance and interest for many academic writers was the fact that the counterculture, unlike earlier examples of youth culture, appeared to focus on middle-class youth. Thus, as Clarke et al. (1976) observe in their introductory essay to the now seminal text on youth culture, *Resistance through Rituals*, the counterculture

> spear headed a dissent from their own, dominant, 'parent' culture. Their disaffiliation was principally ideological and cultural. They directed their attack mainly against those institutions which reproduce the dominant cultural ideological relations – the family, education, the media, marriage, the sexual division of labour. (1976: 62)

In the United States, too, there was a sense amongst academic theorists that the counterculture was challenging the hegemonic hold of the middle class from within.

In his book, *The Making of a Counter-Culture*, Roszak (1969) takes the argument a step further, arguing that the counterculture was not simply opposed to the hegemonic power of their parent culture but also to the technocracy the parent culture had created. By technocracy, Roszak refers to the increasing reliance upon technology and rational-scientific reasoning. During the late 1960s, the atrocities of Nazi Germany and the horrific realisation of the destructive power of the atomic bomb were disturbing facets of a recent past, while the Cold War and the escalating conflict in Vietnam served as current reminders of the highly pathological aspects of the technocratic society (see Bennett 2005). Roszak describes the counterculture as 'technocracy's children' – disaffected middle-class youth who wished to break away from the bourgeois and technocratic world of their parents. Thus, observes Roszak,

> By way of a dialectic Marx could never have imagined, technocratic America produces a potentially revolutionary element among its own youth. The bourgeoisie, instead of discovering the class enemy in its factories, finds it across the breakfast table in the person of its own pampered children. (1969: 34)

In *The Greening of America*, Reich (1971) advances the notion of a countercultural, middle-class youth breaking away from the social and cultural bonds of the parent culture and simultaneously challenging its authority through his concept of Consciousness III. For Reich, this describes a new level of consciousness and being that encapsulates the potential for social change through achieving a new level of experience and understanding in which individuals work collectively for the good of the community and the well-being of future generations. This involves a rejection of the values of capitalism, which fosters an individualistic and short-term set of goals through its emphasis on the accumulation of wealth tied to individual comfort and security. According to Reich, the counterculture provided a platform for youth to subvert such dominant, received ideology and supplant it with a new series of values relating to sustainability – social, economic and environmental.

Problematising Counterculture

It was observed earlier in this chapter that some of the basic tenets of the countercultural ideology – notably its emphasis upon alternative notions of community based around common investment in musical taste – amounted to a relatively idealist and romanticised notion of social change. Arguably, a significant element of such romanticism also taints much of the writing about counterculture published during the late 1960s and early 1970s. In this writing, counterculture is held up as a model for social change, a perspective informed by a wider body of work grounded in critical theory and cultural Marxism. By naming middle-class youth as the key drivers of a countercultural revolution, a new means is found of explicating the transformation of class consciousness as a way of subverting the oppressive class relations seen to underpin capitalism. In this sense, there are some parallels between 'counterculture' and 'subculture' in that both concepts have been taken up and used in academic writing as a means of addressing the inequalities underpinning class relations and the potential for social change.

The application of both counterculture and subculture presupposes a class-based ownership of a specific mode of style-based youth identity in which music, fashion, drugs and associated resources are deployed homologically in the pursuit of a singly defined expression of counter-hegemonic action against the institutions of the ruling hegemony. This approach is typified in Willis's (1978) study, *Profane Culture*. Thus Willis's 'working-class' bikers and 'middle-class' hippies – although they occupy different social strata – are both engaged in a symbolic show of resistance against a common enemy: the dominant, middle-class society.

In certain respects, the problems inherent in the concept of counterculture are similar to those that have been identified with subculture. A number of writers have previously criticised subcultural theory for its neat equation of subculture with working-class youth, the contention being that this produces a self-serving argument linked to a cultural Marxist critique of late capitalism (e.g. see Redhead 1990; Muggleton 2000). This is supported by a further level of critical debate, which argues that little empirical evidence exists to suggest that the early examples of youth subcultures were exclusively working class, while in the case of later subcultures, such as punk and goth, it is clear that memberships have been cross-class (Bennett 1999). A similar case can be made in relation to the term 'counterculture', in that sweeping assumptions are made about its class composition and consequent ideological intent.

There are two main problems with the way in which the late 1960s counterculture has been conceptualised in previous writing. First, there was a clear disjuncture between the forms of social change that the counterculture envisaged and those that social theorists at the time envisaged. Certainly, there were highly political elements within the counterculture, but the movement was not uniformly politicised in a way that dictated that the only way forward was to overthrow the capitalist system by whatever means. Indeed, there was, in many ways, an inherent contradiction in this understanding of the counterculture, in that the very foundations of countercultural ideology were based on products and resources made possible through mass media and mass consumption – the latter both representing significant arms of late capitalism. Furthermore, within the hippie rhetoric itself, there were clear and inevitable inconsistencies in the way in which the countercultural aesthetic was understood and expressed. For example, at two of the 'great' countercultural music events, the Woodstock Music and Arts Fair in 1969 and the Isle of Wight Festival of 1970, while there was much discussion of music being part of the counterculture and of youth having a right to freely access music, this only became a reality after failed attempts to ticket both of these events.

The other problem inherent in academic renderings of the counterculture is the assumption that it wholly or mainly comprised white, middle-class youth. Such an interpretation depends very much on the particular argument rehearsed with reference to the counterculture. Indeed, according to Clecak (1983), the equation of counterculture with a white, middle-class, hippie movement is an inherently narrow interpretation. According to Clecak, not only were there people from a variety of social and cultural groups involved in the counterculture, but 'counterculture' itself was an umbrella term for an amorphous range of activities and ideologies that, for a brief period at the end of the 1960s, found a common voice. Indeed, observes Clecak, the counterculture enabled a wide range of different groups and individuals 'to find symbolic shapes for their social and spiritual discontents and hopes' (ibid.: 18). These groups included:

> (1) The civil-rights movement, beginning with blacks but quickly encompassing such other racial minorities as American Indians, Hispanic Americans, and Asian-Americans; (2) the young, especially college students and disaffected intellectuals; (3) the peace and anti-war movements; (4) the poor; (5) women; (6) the human-potential movement; (7) prisoners and other 'outcasts'; (8) gays and lesbians; (9) consumers; (10) environmentalists; (11) the old; and (12) the physically different (the disabled, the very fat, the very tall, the very short). (ibid.: 18)

A similar point is made in a more recent study by Eyerman and Jamison (1998) who, in their own analytical evaluation of the counterculture made some 15 years after Clecak, suggest that:

> During the 1960s youth not only gained self-consciousness, it became the model and set standards for the rest of society in many spheres of culture, from the most superficial like clothing and hair-styles, to the most deeply rooted like the basic social interactions of men and women and blacks and whites. (1998: 113)

The respective observations of Clecak and Eyerman and Jamison, are significant for several reasons. First, they each point to the essentially diverse, heterogeneous nature of both the individuals and socio-political and cultural ideologies that either merged or coexisted within the countercultural movement of the late 1960s. Second, and in association, these accounts each portray the counterculture not as a specific socio-cultural entity, but rather an entity with a significant degree of fluidity such that it could incorporate diverse groupings, and thus manifest itself differently at specific times and within specific places, depending on local socio-economic, cultural and demographic circumstances. While these issues have been explored thoroughly in relation to 'subculture', largely through the critical work of post-subcultural theorists such as Bennett (1999), Miles (2000) and Muggleton (2000), there has been far less engagement with the limitations of counterculture when used as a rigid concept for denoting relatively narrow forms of style-based social action at the expense of a detailed consideration of the impact of local circumstances on the nature of countercultural practices and processes.

Re-theorising Counterculture

As the above observations suggest, although counterculture has evaded many of the criticisms levelled at subculture over the last 20 years, in many respects it is no less problematic a concept. Indeed, it can be argued that counterculture suffers from many of the problems associated with subculture. Most significant in this respect is the fact that counterculture, like subculture, emerges from a specific set of theoretical concerns embedded in sociology and cultural studies, which seek to render social conflict and struggle visible through mapping them on to contemporary cultural practices grounded in particular forms of leisure, consumption and lifestyle. As noted earlier, the form of homological interpretation that results from this produces characteristically rigid forms of explanation that do not necessarily sit well with the actual ways in which such cultural practices play out in everyday life. The 'cultural turn' in social and cultural theory during the early 1990s brought with it a new range of perspectives for understanding how socio-cultural identities – both individual and collective – are made and remade in ways that may reference but do not directly reflect the social structure. Giddens' (1991) notion of reflexive modernity is particularly important in this respect, as it offers new ways of understanding how identities are reflexively constructed by individuals with reference to the cultural commodities and resources with which they engage and that they appropriate in the course of their daily lives. According to Giddens, such is the impact of reflexive modernity on the individual that identity can no longer be considered a given. Rather, it is contingent upon a range of individual life experiences and the interface between the individual and the plethora of objects, images and texts made available through the cultural industries.

Chaney (1996, 2002) makes a similar range of arguments concerning the way in which individuals and groups are empowered through their engagement with cultural resources. For Chaney, there are two salient points emerging from such engagement. First, individual appropriations of specific cultural resources give rise to what he terms lifestyle sites and strategies. The latter bespeak the physical appropriation and symbolic inscription of cultural resources within the context of everyday life in such a way that the latter come to represent specific meanings in specific local contexts. Second, such is the plurality of lifestyles in late modern society that it becomes inherently difficult, and therefore largely impractical, to insist on sub-/dominant binaries when talking about the cultural forms and practices that characterise contemporary everyday life. Considering this in relation to the concept of subculture, Chaney offers the following observation:

> [I]f values, relationships and identities are being constructed in the manipulation of vocabularies of style, then material culture becomes the terrain – albeit an unstable, relative terrain – though which social order is constituted. This, it seems to me, is one of the most important aspects of the rise of lifestyles as 'sites and strategies' for new forms of affiliation and identification ... that is, culture becomes more clearly a resource than an inheritance. Thus, what were once described as subcultures could now be regarded as collective lifestyle statements, which reflexively negotiate rather than directly mirror the experience of social class. (2004: 41–2)

Chaney's notion of the cultural terrain of contemporary everyday life comprising a diverse series of lifestyle sites and strategies, in which aspects of class, race, gender and sexuality may converge just as much as they may be held separate from each other, signifies an important shift in our understanding and interpretation of the term 'counterculture'. Indeed, just as Clecak (1983) suggested that the late 1960s counterculture was in fact an umbrella term for a range of different and highly diverse social groupings, so the physical manifestations of many 'so-called' countercultures in a contemporary context are no less diverse in terms of their socio-economic and demographic composition.

Countercultures as Lifestyle Sites and Strategies

Following the theoretical arguments of Giddens and Chaney regarding the increasingly complex array of reflexive lifestyles that characterise late modern society, there is a case for arguing that the term 'counterculture' – despite its seductive resonance as an aesthetic and ideological term of opposition – actually denotes a contemporary social process through which the cultural fabric of everyday life is diversifying in ever more rapid cycles of change. The terrain of everyday life in late modernity is such that a variety of different lifestyle sites and strategies emerge and coalesce into collective forms of social life, each embodying specific sets of aesthetic and political sensibilities through which groups and individuals articulate their sense of 'difference' from others who occupy the same urban and regional spaces and places. Such articulations embed a range of ideological positions in which aspects of, for example, personal taste, political, religious, sexual and ethnic identity are imbricated in myriad ways, fashioning collective identities that resonate sharply with specific local, trans-local and, increasingly, global circumstances.

In relation to this latter point, the time–space compression created through digital communication technologies and the more ready global flow of information plays a significant part. Through the latter, groups and individuals from different places around the globe are able to form critical alliances and coordinate trans-local or global forms of collective practice and/or action aimed towards specific outcomes. Likewise, such trans-local and global connections may also facilitate entirely passive forms of interaction – mundane, unspectacular, yet equally significant in their underscoring of the diverse pathways and objectives that mark the ways in which groups and individuals in contemporary societies negotiate everyday life and create physical and symbolic nodes of meaning. Equally important here is the global flow of people, goods and resources; this adds a further layer of possibilities for socio-cultural connections to be made between groups and individuals with similar lifestyle orientations and sensibilities.

The concept of lifestyle has been criticised in the past for allegedly bespeaking a largely celebratory position in relation to cultural consumption and the creation of social identity (e.g. see McGuigan 1992). Admittedly, in previous applications of the term – and through its use in market research and advertising – lifestyle has assumed a resonance with leisure-orientated consumerism and the hedonistic sensibilities that often pre-figure this (e.g. see Featherstone 1991). However, the notion of lifestyle sites and strategies denotes a more socially and culturally complex way of positioning lifestyle as a conceptual framework for understanding aspects of opposition and change. Thus lifestyle sites and strategies pertain not only to the objects, images and texts that individuals consume, but also how they inscribe them with specific meanings, which in turn are embedded in the everyday realities with which groups and individuals are confronted.

Moreover, lifestyle sites and strategies provide scope for different lifestyle projects, with points of commonality but also points of difference, to find pathways to convergence – thus building towards broader socio-cultural ends. Such a description arguably befits the counterculture of the late 1960s. Thus, although superficially the counterculture appeared to coalesce around a common series of resources that, as noted above, included music, drugs and literature, in truth it marked a far more complex and diverse array of lifestyle sites and strategies that were able to coalesce – albeit for a limited period – under a single descriptive banner. Indeed, while some of the more radically political elements of the counterculture harnessed music, style and the hippie argot and rhetoric to make powerful statements against government (as with the anti-Vietnam War movement), other elements were more invested in an essentially passive, greenist, back-to-the-land ideology (as in the commune movement), while others were attracted to happenings and other 'total experience' events informed by drugs and literature such as Huxley's *Doors of Perception* (1954). Still others, while aware of such elements coexisting and overlapping in the counterculture, were less invested in such articulations of hippie lifestyle, but largely took an interest in the music, style and in being part of a particular urban scene (as seen in the example of the so-called hippie Mecca, San Francisco's Haight-Ashbury district).

Counterculture in a Contemporary Context

Despite the theoretical arguments that can be raised against the sociological value of 'counterculture' as a meaningful term for categorising social action, like the term 'subculture', it lives on as a concept in social and cultural theory. Arguably, however, the continuing resonance of counterculture in academic scholarship has much to do with the way the term is now deployed and assimilated at a broader everyday level. As with subculture, counterculture has now become an embedded aspect of the discourses employed by the cultural industries and thus in everyday vernacular discourse. This partly relates to the past associations and legacy of the term 'counterculture' and the way in which this has been represented and redeployed by the popular and 'quality' media. Through its omnipresence in the global 'mediascape' (Appadurai 1990), counterculture retains its aura as a potent discursive symbol for forms of social action and/or alternative lifestyles and belief that all appear – or can be made to appear – to link with the aesthetic, political and cultural trends associated with the late 1960s manifestation of counterculture.

This goes further than merely a nostalgic yearning on the part of the baby boomer generation. Through its rich historical legacy and continued representation as a mode for expressions of 'otherness' from a 'mainstream' ideology, the term 'counterculture' now occupies a special place in the popular imagination. From the point of view of post-1960s generations, counterculture has become part of a received, mediated memory (van Dijck 2007; Bennett 2010) that bespeaks a reaction to a series of pathological issues still very much at large in today's world. Whereas subculture is held to represent small-scale, perhaps underground or quasi-devious solutions to social problems, counterculture connotes something larger in scale – a movement or series of movements directed towards and orientated to address large, globally dispersed socio-economic problems and issues. For this central reason, it retains significant currency in the minds of many who participate in, report or reflect on, various forms of counter-hegemonic activity in contemporary social settings. Global movements centred on current issues such as environment, human and animal rights and the financial crisis all in some way absorb and rehearse oppositional discourses that took on their initial shape during the late 1960s. Indeed, McKay (1996) identifies what he regards as a palpable connection between the styles of activism that acquired global momentum in the late 1960s and those that have emerged during subsequent decades.

As a form of popular narrative, counterculture asserts its relevance in our perceptions and understandings of the hegemonic struggles that continue to inform everyday life in myriad societies and cultures across the globe. Beyond these semantic features of counterculture, however, are more complex forms of social interaction and trans-local communication and bonding that only begin to make critical sense, in sociological terms, when one applies the theoretical lenses produced through the cultural turn. When viewed from this perspective, the term 'counterculture' is seen to encompass a highly complex and diffuse range of lifestyles, sensibilities and beliefs that, although clearly connecting at some level, are rooted in varying biographical pathways and trajectories, each with their own connections to other specific cultural milieu and lifeworlds. As such, at a theoretical level, counterculture – like subculture – cannot effectively work as a form of cultural categorisation that defines social groups as distinct from each other in a counter-/dominant binary fashion. Rather, the term 'counterculture' acts as a mechanism for describing particular points of convergence through which individuals are able to connect temporarily in the pursuit of specific goals. Countercultures are, in effect, fluid and mutable expressions of sociality that manifest themselves as individuals temporarily bond to express their support of and/or participation in a common cause, but whose everyday lives are in fact simultaneously played out across a range of other cultural terrains.

PART I
Theorising Countercultures

Chapter 1
Break on Through: The Counterculture and the Climax of American Modernism

Ryan Moore

At the dawn of the 1960s, two musical movements developing only a few blocks from each other in New York City were poised to irreversibly shift the trajectory of American music. In the final weeks of 1959, the Five Spot café in the Bowery hosted a series of performances by the Ornette Coleman Quartet that sparked enormous controversy among New York's jazz enthusiasts, who were immediately polarised over Coleman's improvisational style that would change the course of jazz while also influencing psychedelic rock later in the decade. Whereas it was once condemned as 'the devil's music', by the end of the 1950s jazz had reached a pinnacle of cultural legitimacy: it was promoted internationally as 'America's art form', taught in thousands of American colleges and high schools, and appraised by a new generation of intellectuals who developed the field of jazz criticism. Having released an album with the audacious title *The Shape of Jazz to Come* earlier in the year, the Ornette Coleman Quartet came to the Five Spot in November 1959 and invented a form of collective improvisation that violated all the musical conventions that were understood as fundamental to jazz (Anderson 2007). The cultural elite of New York's jazz scene were passionately divided over the Coleman Quartet's performances, with *Time* (1960) magazine's story on the controversy quoting the legendary trumpeter Dizzy Gillespie: 'I don't know what he's playing, but it's not jazz.'

Both the enthusiasm for and opposition to Coleman's music were a testament to its ground-breaking nature, as he desecrated the solidifying orthodoxy of jazz in the name of improvisational freedom. Those who took offence at his free jazz typically disparaged it as nothing but noise: undisciplined, disorderly and technically deficient. Yet free jazz would indeed be the shape of jazz to come in the 1960s, a decade we now know for a succession of cultural and political revolts against conventions and authorities throughout the social system. Within jazz music but also far beyond it, an improvisational style would pose a challenge to orthodoxies of all sorts that had congealed during the middle of the twentieth century. Coleman was one among an assortment of artists and activists who sought to liberate individual parts from overbearing wholes and rescue transitory moments of time from scheduled orders of progress and repetition. This cohort would wage war on the official forms of modernism that were instituted during the post-war years, yet the counterculture they created in the 1960s also expressed the modernist ideal that development and transcendence could be achieved through the annihilation of tradition and formal standards. Their revolt against order and tradition in the quest for freedom and innovation also included the dangers of atomisation, anarchy and self-annihilation that felled the counterculture as the 1960s came to an end with a succession of drug overdoses, violent episodes and generally bad vibes. The Ornette Coleman Quartet personified a potentially higher synthesis of this conflict between the individual and society in their practice of *collective* improvisation, but this was not the direction the 1960s took as the counterculture became increasingly libertarian in a strictly individualistic sense, eventually devolving into a self-absorbed culture of personal growth in the 1970s.

Just a few blocks north and west of where controversy was raging at the Five Spot, a revival of folk music had been ongoing in Greenwich Village and developed into a full-fledged subculture by the end of the 1950s. Hundreds of young people wielding a wide assortment of stringed instruments were gathering in Washington Square Park on the weekends to sing folk songs, while nearby MacDougal Street had become home to Izzy Young's Folklore Center and a number of coffeehouses where people in the folk scene congregated (Hajdu 2001). The folk music subculture embodied a dual character that would ultimately prove unsustainable in the 1960s: while one part expressed folk culture's romantic attachment to pre-industrial America, thereby exalting sincerity and an aesthetic of social realism, a second, divergent path was shaped by the urban bohemianism of Greenwich Village, where experiments with representation and form were opposed to social realism, and the search for the authenticity was undertaken as a process of becoming rather than being. Folk music is rooted in tradition and inherently suspicious of modernity: Raymond Williams (1983: 136–7) has traced the usage of 'folk' from 'a general meaning of "people"' in the seventeenth century to the nostalgic connotations it developed in the nineteenth century, as 'a complex set of responses to the new industrial and urban society' in which folk songs 'came to be influentially specialised to the pre-industrial, pre-urban, pre-literate world'. Folk music maintained a presence in American society in large part through the labour movement and the political Left, where folk was celebrated not only for its lyrics about popular struggle but also for the participatory form of its common ownership and accessibility to anyone with relatively simple instruments. The neighbourhood of Greenwich Village that became a central point for the folk revival had previously been the setting for collaborations between bohemia and the American Left in the period roughly between 1890 and 1920, when the anarchist Emma Goldman was regularly rabble-rousing in the streets, John Reed wrote *Ten Days that Shook the World* after witnessing the Bolshevik Revolution, and intellectuals, artists and labour activists intermingled at the salon of heiress Mabel Dodge (Stansell 2000). At the end of the 1950s, a reprise of this tenuous alliance between folkie populism, Left politics and bohemian modernism was developing again in Greenwich Village's folk scene.

Folk had become the most popular genre of music among more intellectual and politically engaged young people, particularly on the expanding college campuses, when in January 1961 Robert Zimmerman arrived in Greenwich Village from Minnesota, adopted many of the affectations of Woody Guthrie, and began performing regularly in the coffeehouses using the name Bob Dylan. Alongside Joan Baez, Dylan took folk to the apex of both its commercial popularity and social significance, but he also pushed the contradiction between folk realism and bohemian modernism to its breaking point, from which a new synthesis developed in the second half of the 1960s. In his early years, Dylan crafted his image and style to meet the expectations of his audience, which grew from the folk scene in Greenwich Village to the college campus circuit across the US during the peak years of the Civil Rights Movement. Dylan's stardom immediately created contradictions within the culture of folk music, for the image of sincerity in Dylan's pose as a proletarian troubadour was largely contrived, enabling him to achieve fame as something like a folkie pin-up in a scene that defined itself in opposition to commercialism. The sincerity and social realism demanded by the folk scene was also an immediate fetter on the creativity of Dylan's music and lyrics, as even before changing to a rock sound he had been criticised by the folk community for writing songs that were more personally introspective than politically topical. When he dropped the folkie image in favour of dark sunglasses, motorcycle gear and an electric rock band, Dylan was greeted with a polarity of responses akin to those that faced Ornette Coleman: as many believed they were witnessing an artistic breakthrough to the new shape of things to come, those attached to the standards and traditions of folk music correctly perceived a threat to their culture and the community it supported. Dylan abandoned the cultural field of folk, but in doing so he created a new field of possibilities for rock, mainly by linking the music and his new image to the lineages of Romanticism and the defiant poets and painters of modernity. In the second half of the 1960s, musicians began to approach rock as a means of experimentation and self-exploration, and music became an intellectual, emotional and physical medium of social change surpassing what folk had once been.

Modernisation and Modernism in the 1960s

My argument situates the music and counterculture of the 1960s within the forms of modernism and the processes of modernisation that spanned from the end of the Second World War until the economic and geopolitical crises of the early 1970s. This particular stage of modernisation was fuelled by monopoly capitalism with a greater degree of state management and planning, one which has been supplanted by a more chaotic, global yet decentralised form of neo-liberal capitalism since the 1970s (Harvey 2007). In the post-war years, capital conceded to pay higher wages because they stimulated lifestyles of mass consumption among the working populace while securing their loyalty to the corporation, thus resolving the crisis of under consumption and class warfare that threatened capital during the interwar years. As the 1960s began, American capitalism had reached new peaks of prosperity after more than a decade as the dominant power in the world economy, and this prosperity translated into roughly equal increases in the standard of living of people throughout the class structure. The US state played a crucial role in shaping the direction of post-war modernisation by launching 'urban renewal' projects to demolish older city neighbourhoods while subsidising the construction of new suburban housing and highways, thus remaking the American landscape into a more de-centred, atomised sprawl that facilitated conformity and mass consumption. The state's role in post-war modernisation also included major investments in the public system of higher education, whose expansion was crucial for scientific and technological research in the Cold War. In the second half of the 1960s, these colleges and universities would be flooded by massive numbers of young people conceived during the giddy years of post-war triumph, the 'baby boomers' raised with the confidence that they would be the most educated and prosperous generation in American history (Gitlin 1987).

My understanding of the dialectical relationship between modernisation and modernism has primarily been shaped by Marshall Berman (1982: 16), who defines modernism as 'an amazing variety of visions and ideas that aim to make men and women the subjects as well as the objects of modernisation, to give them the power to change the world that is changing them, to make their way through the maelstrom and make it their own'. For Berman, this maelstrom is energised by the collision of numerous social processes, but its centrifugal force is capitalism's profit motive, which fuels investment and innovation, demands rationalisation and calculability, incites mass migration and the growth of cities, and compresses spatial distance through mass communications. The common effect of all these social processes is to create a modern world characterised by an uncertainty of values and an accelerating pace of change, a volatile and frenzied world where 'all that is solid melts into air, all that is holy is profaned', as Marx and Engels (1998: 38) put it.

The experience of modernity is constituted by this dialectical relationship between modernisation and modernism. Considering the modernism of the 1960s, Berman identifies three tendencies of cultural response to the conditions of modern life: affirmation, negation and withdrawal. The affirmative voices of the 1960s welcomed the continuing evolution of the electronic media and the erosion of the boundaries separating art from commercial culture, whereas those who advocated withdrawal sought to maintain their ideals for the autonomy of art via self-referential formalism. Most of all, the modernism of the 1960s expressed a spirit of negation, an adversarial culture dedicated to destroying conventions and desecrating traditions. Berman remains dissatisfied with each of these affirmative, negative and withdrawn responses, but his survey of 1960s modernism primarily examines high culture, urban architecture and the intelligentsia while saying little about popular music. I believe that a closer look at the music of the 1960s, along with the counterculture surrounding it, will reveal a dialectical ambivalence that Berman finds in an earlier generation of modernists – from Goethe and Marx to Baudelaire and Dostoyevsky – who did not simply affirm or reject modern life but instead tried to harness its creative energies in order to transcend its limits. Berman contends that this form of modernism 'is ironic and contradictory, polyphonic and dialectical, denouncing modern life in the name of values that modernity itself has created, hoping – often against hope – that the modernities of tomorrow and the day after tomorrow will heal the wounds that wreck the modern men and women of today' (1982: 23).

In the analytic narrative that follows, my method is to fleetingly traverse the times and spaces of the 1960s in a modernist style, initially focusing on youth and its relation to modernity, and then moving west to California – the homeland of the counterculture and the terminal point of American modernisation in the 1960s – to examine the rivalling scenes that developed in San Francisco and Los Angeles. In the preceding section, we began to identify some of the different symbolic responses to modernisation that were already emerging in New York's free jazz and folk scenes at the beginning of the 1960s. Against the processes of modernisation that praise novelty for its own sake, the folk revivalists sought to anchor themselves in the past, preserve the means of expression established by previous generations, and rediscover forms of community that had been shattered in the name of progress. This anti-modernisation style of modernism could also be seen in early 1960s New York, where Jane Jacobs (1961) outlined an alternative conception of urban life in opposition to the sprawling, automobile-centred projects of Robert Moses, whose plan to build an expressway through lower Manhattan was thwarted by neighbourhood opposition led by Jacobs. On the other hand, the free jazz of the same time embraced the spirit of modernisation with its frenetic pace, disdain for convention and tradition, and celebration of individual freedom from the collective. This type of modernism that aligned itself with the velocity and volatility of modernisation was also a recurring cultural tendency of the 1960s, especially within the counterculture that was energised by an experimental approach to raising its collective consciousness while utilising the newest electronic media and chemical concoctions in the pursuit of self-expression. However, in both free jazz and the folk revival we also see glimpses of an alternative, more ambivalent response, one that transcends the dichotomy of affirmative or negative responses to modernisation. Although free jazz was an improvisational form that broke with the usual constraints of pitch, tempo, bar and chord, it did not amount to musical anarchy but instead established a new collective form in which one player's freedom opened opportunities for the others to contribute to the performance in new ways. Meanwhile, if the folk revival sought refuge from modernisation in clinging to tradition and community, a new crop of electrified rock bands were poised to demolish the cultural boundaries of folk in the process of opening new avenues for music.

Youth, Modernity and the Counterculture

To fully understand the significance of the counterculture and its music during the 1960s, we must consider the experience of youth which forms an intermediary relation between music and society. As Theodore Roszak (1969) was the first to argue, the 'counterculture' was composed of college students and young people in both the hippie/acid rock culture and the movements of the New Left, who Roszak believed should be grouped together, despite all their differences, because both were created by the young in opposition to the American 'technocracy' (also see Keniston 1968). The technocracy that developed from post-war forms of modernisation provided this counterculture with its various targets for revolt: the heartless American war machine; the conformity of the organisation man; intractable government bureaucracies; an atomised landscape of suburbs and highways; soulless consumer materialism and the standardisation of mass culture; the rationalisation of an educational system enmeshed with industry and the military. However, young people of the counterculture did not rebel simply in opposition to modernisation, but also to realise the promises of social and personal development that are the hallmarks of modernity. These were not simply movements of resistance but also experiments in renewal, growth and possibility. The search for sources of personal and social transformation – and the confidence that they would eventually find those sources – characterised both the hippies and the New Left, even if they differed on what needed changing and how to realise those changes. The rebellions of the 1960s took shape in opposition to technocracy, but they were conceived in a maelstrom of flux and growth and nourished by the utopian vision of a post-scarcity society.

In the 1960s, the experience of youth mediated between the conditions of modernity and the formation of a counterculture. Henri Lefebvre (1995: 195) noted this ambivalent relationship between youth and modernity in 1961, seven years before millions of students and workers took to the streets of Paris to 'demand the impossible':

> Everywhere we see [young people] showing signs of dissatisfaction and rebellion. Why? It is because they themselves are new and thirsty for innovation – that is, modernity – and are therefore experiencing all of modernity's unresolved problems for themselves. Their finest qualities are the ones which cause them the most pain. Their vitality exposes them and makes them vulnerable. Attracted by it, yet repeatedly disappointed by it, they live out the 'new' and all its empty moments. It is they who are worst hit by the disjunction between representation and living, between ideology and practice, between the possible and the impossible. It is they who continue the uninterrupted dialogue between ideal and experiment.

Millions of young people rebelled against the social system in the 1960s, yet their rebellion was enabled and shaped by the system itself, especially because their sense of generational self-importance was fuelled by the apparently limitless abundance of the capitalist economy. The counterculture mocked the stability and predictability of modernisation while taking its productivity for granted, thus creating a utopian vision where the values of leisure, spontaneity and self-expression would triumph over work, discipline and instrumental rationality.

Young people occupy a privileged position relative to modernity's spirit of novelty and innovation, especially because they embrace the latest things and the possibilities of the future while casting tradition and security aside. The extension of higher education, postponement of work, advancement of birth control technologies, and other social changes have created youth as a distinct phase of the life cycle, a 'psychosocial moratorium' (Erikson 1968) which allows the young to try out different identities while maintaining distance from adult social roles. The baby boom generation was uniquely privileged in the sense that they inherited the confidence of the post-war years and symbolised the apparently bright future of American society. Baby boomers would be doted on in countless parenting manuals, courted as a multibillion-dollar teen market and pack university campuses infused with military spending. Politicians, educators and self-proclaimed childrearing experts declared that this was a special generation that would benefit from all the difficult sacrifices of the past and the infinite opportunities of the future. As the 1960s progressed, it was evident that much of this generation took these messages about their collective importance to heart, but not in the way that authorities had intended.

Better Living through Chemistry: LSD and Acid Rock in San Francisco

Few things symbolise the 1960s spirit of modernity and its ironies better than LSD. After being discovered by the Swiss chemist Albert Hoffman during the Second World War, the US Central Intelligence Agency (CIA) conducted experiments with LSD as part of their search for mind control drugs in the 1950s, administering doses to everyone from military personnel and college students to prostitutes and the mentally ill in studies of its psychoactive effects (Lee and Shlain 1985). Among other places, LSD then found its way into Harvard's psychology department, where it was studied in the experiments of the Harvard Psilocybin Project and transformed two of the lead researchers – Dr Timothy Leary and Dr Richard Alpert – into advocates of a psychedelic and spiritual change of consciousness. At roughly the same time on the opposite coast, Ken Kesey was also participating in the CIA's research on LSD at Stanford University. In the ensuing years, Kesey wrote his acclaimed novel *One Flew Over the Cuckoo's Nest* (1962) and gathered his group of 'Merry Pranksters' to host 'acid tests' where LSD was distributed, accompanied by the music of a band that would later be known as the Grateful Dead. LSD and its infiltration of American society were thus the products of post-war American modernisation, of military research in the context of the Cold War and scientific research at the nation's top universities. And yet as LSD became the chemical inspiration behind the counterculture that developed in the 1960s, it activated modes of consciousness that not only opposed the American government and its war machine but also contradicted the calculating, mechanical thinking that fuels modernisation in its totality.

LSD had a decisive influence on the music of the 1960s, particularly in the San Francisco psychedelic rock scene that began forming in the Haight-Ashbury neighbourhood in 1965. The San Francisco scene began as a continuation of the folk revival and the Beat literary movement that was centred in the city's North Beach neighbourhood. By 1965, musicians, writers and various eccentrics had begun moving into the Haight-Ashbury's dilapidated, low-rent Victorian houses (Perry 1984). The new crop of San Francisco bands were a mix of the communitarian ethos of folk and the improvisational spirit of jazz and the Beats, but they ruptured the boundaries and surpassed the limits of both cultural traditions by adding an explosive concoction of LSD and electrified rock and roll. Concurrent with the prime years of LSD's exploration, the Beatles and the other bands of the British Invasion, along with a newly electrified Bob Dylan, had begun to open new possibilities for the creation of rock music as a meaningful form of cultural expression. In the second half of the 1960s, LSD and rock music blended to create a collective expression of modernity's quest for elevation and expansion, one that promised to cultivate higher states of consciousness and being among individuals nurtured within a loving community. Along with LSD, rock music presented a challenge to American institutions and social norms, but it too was nurtured by scientific and technological modernisation, by multicoloured light shows, massive amplification and new innovations in the recording studio. So-called acid rock was imagined to be a liberator of minds and bodies, uniting musicians and audiences in a community of the young, taking them higher and further with experimental recordings and improvisational performances. By the end of the 1960s, however, this vision would lie defeated and exhausted: unable to change reality in accordance with its collective imagination, the counterculture imploded, went into retreat and gradually dissolved.

The Grateful Dead combined all of these musical and cultural elements, under the influence of LSD and other psychedelics, to help create the countercultural daydream for an emerging community that was expanding from its nucleus in northern California. The members of the Grateful Dead initially met during the early 1960s in Palo Alto near Stanford University (approximately 30 miles south of San Francisco), where the mix of folk music and Beat literature had generated a flourishing bohemian community. Jerry Garcia was initially inspired to learn guitar as an adolescent after hearing Bo Diddley and Chuck Berry, but in Palo Alto he was one of many folkies who played guitar and banjo in bluegrass and jug bands. On the other hand, Phil Lesh was a classically trained musician who played the trumpet in high school and had a keen interest in jazz improvisation and avant-garde classical music, which led him to explore new methods for playing the electric bass as more like a second lead than a time-keeping instrument of rhythm. Ron 'Pigpen' McKernan represented a third musical trajectory, at least until his death from cirrhosis in 1973: he grew up listening to the blues and rhythm and blues (his father was a local disc jockey), and in the Grateful Dead he played the harmonica and blues organ, looked like a Hells Angels biker, and sang in a rugged voice coated with alcohol. Finally, the rhythm section that was an essential part of the improvisational process included not one but two percussionists, thus doubling the complex web of musical interactions during a jam session (McNally 2002 and Spector in this volume).

Musically and culturally, the Grateful Dead were an amalgamation of all the countercultural components that had accumulated up to the mid-1960s, amplifying the traditionalism of the folk revival into an improvisational practice that was expanding from a community of folkie bohemians into a more colourful movement of hippie freaks. They personified the duelling musical responses to modernisation – folk and experimentalism – but also the promise that a youthful counterculture was poised to transcend this duality in an alternative vision (or hallucination, if you prefer) of modernity. The Dead's roots were in the folk scene, but their ascent into a rock band was fully connected with the spread of LSD and Kesey's Merry Pranksters. By 1966, the emerging hippie scene concentrated in the Haight-Ashbury had become a veritable 'psychedelic city-state' with its own neighbourhood head shop (the Psychedelic Shop) and underground newspaper (the *San Francisco Oracle*) (Lee and Shlain 1985: 141–9). A rapidly growing community of musicians with backgrounds in folk, jazz and the blues was also forming in the neighbourhood. Marty Balin had opened a venue in San Francisco called the Matrix after witnessing the emergence of folk rock, and he formed Jefferson Airplane by adding a trio of guitar and bass players who played folk, country and the blues. Similarly, the founding members of Big Brother and the Holding Company had begun their musical careers in San Francisco's folk circuit, while their drummer came from a jazz background. Months later, the local hippie concert promoter Chet Helms introduced Big Brother to their newest member: a blues singer who had just arrived from Texas named Janis Joplin (Echols 1999).

Social solidarity was a core ideal of the folk scene, and it continued to be prominent even as music ventured in experimental directions during the second half of the 1960s. One prospect of the counterculture was that it might overcome the opposition between individualism and collectivism by forming a collaborative community of creative people who could inspire and influence one another in the development of a unique self. This collective vision formed in opposition to postwar modernisation and the suburbanised life of the American middle class, whose atomised existence in cars and cul-de-sacs made people anxious to conform and unwilling to deviate, thus creating neither community nor individuality but instead a 'lonely crowd' in the words of sociologist David Riesman (1950). As with free jazz, the psychedelic rock bands could be seen as microcosms of this countercultural model of social relations, especially as the collective process of music-making involves individual musicians working within an interdependent collective, one where each member makes a unique contribution to the sonic whole by utilising their particular skills in a continuous interplay with the others. The collective improvisation of the acid rock bands was surely enhanced by the fact that their members often lived together – at different times, the Grateful Dead cohabitated at 710 Ashbury St, Jefferson Airplane at 2400 Fulton St., and Big Brother and the Holding Company had a house in neighbouring Marin County – and therefore allowed creative bonds and improvisational familiarity to develop among some extremely unique individuals. On a larger scale, live performances and festivals became the most significant medium for creating a sense of community within the counterculture. As the rock audience grew into the multitude of Woodstock Nation, rock music concerts created an environment similar to religious rituals or festivals – Emile Durkheim (1915: 245–55) called it 'collective effervescence' – where the intensity of social interaction produces a state of euphoria among people who feel elevated beyond their ordinary, everyday selves.

Just as folk music was being absorbed and surpassed by psychedelic rock, the communitarian politics of folk culture took on more colourful and theatrical forms that expressed not just resistance but also collective joy. The Diggers, for instance, evolved from the San Francisco Mime Troupe, a group of actors who had been staging improvisational forms of radical theatre in the city's streets and parks. After holding a parade on Haight Street to celebrate 'The Death of Money and the Birth of the Free' in 1966, the Diggers began giving away food and clothing on a regular basis at the panhandle in front of Golden Gate Park and established a free store, a free bakery and even a free medical clinic (a precursor of the revered Haight-Ashbury Free Clinic). They took their name from a seventeenth-century agrarian movement that arose in England to resist the Enclosure Acts and rising food prices. These seventeenth-century Diggers claimed squatters' rights for common lands and engaged in digging the soil (hence the name) and planting vegetable gardens to feed the needy. The San Francisco Diggers, by contrast, were products of modernity and urbanisation, forming a movement based on the appropriation of an enormous surplus produced by a prosperous economy, a surplus they imagined could be redistributed to allow people to avoid wage labour and live freely. A strong distrust of money and commercialism was shared by the folk and the bohemian cultural traditions, and in the 1960s this was expressed in concerns about the commercialisation of music and conflicts between rock bands and their record labels. Within the San Francisco scene, these conflicts over commerce and music created a rivalry between Bill Graham and Chet Helms and the Family Dog commune: while Graham was an unabashed businessman who was on the way to becoming the leading rock concert promoter of his time, Helms and the Family Dog promoted concerts as vehicles of liberation that minimised the role of money (Perry 1984).

Rock Music and Consumer Capitalism in Los Angeles

The San Francisco music scene formed largely in opposition to the mainstream pop music of the recording industry, and those commercial forces were concentrated in the city's hated rival to the south, Los Angeles. Over the course of the 1960s, the centre of the American music industry shifted away from New York City, where the biggest labels were headquartered and the country's most successful songwriters and publishers worked in Tin Pan Alley and the Brill Building. In 1960, the movie industry still greatly overshadowed the music industry in Los Angeles: several of the major labels were subservient divisions of the movie studios (e.g. MGM, Warner Brothers) in search of teen idols that could cross over to film and television. This left Capitol Records as the most significant player – its local supremacy signified by a skyscraper designed like a stack of records, erected in 1954 – along with a cluster of independent labels like Dot, Liberty, and Specialty Records, all of which were housed on Sunset Boulevard in Hollywood. However, Los Angeles had become synonymous with the commercial side of pop music by the time of the Monterey Pop Festival in June 1967, and so as the festival was being organised by Lou Adler (a record producer who had recently become a millionaire following the sale of Dunhill Records) and John Phillips (leader of the commercially successful LA-based folk act the Mamas and the Papas), the conflict between the two scenes was palpable. As Adler recalled, 'The San Francisco groups had a very bad taste in their mouths about LA commercialism ... And it's true that we were a business-minded industry. It wasn't a hobby. They called it slick, and I'd have to agree with them' (cited in Hoskyns 1996: 145).

Los Angeles emerged as a centre for innovations in popular music during the early 1960s, when Phil Spector was developing his 'wall of sound' approach to recording at Gold Coast Studios, while at the same time surf music expressed the carefree leisure of young people raised on American abundance. Spector made advancements on the Brill Building sound after apprenticing with the songwriting duo of Leiber and Stoller in New York, bringing greater volume and depth to studio recordings by utilising an orchestra of instruments playing simultaneously to create a dense, lush composition surrounding the vocal harmonies of the groups he was producing. Spector's wall of sound was engineered to carry through to jukeboxes and AM radio, leading to a string of hit singles by the Crystals, the Ronettes, and the Righteous Brothers from 1962 to 1965, prompting Tom Wolfe to christen him 'The Tycoon of Teen'. But the music that resonated most with great numbers of young people in the early 1960s was surf music, particularly the music linked to a wider cultural celebration of surfing, the beach and spring break vacation depicted in a succession of teen movies. Although southern California's surfing subculture originated among rebellious individuals in refuge from wage labour and social convention, its evocations of leisure, youthfulness and sex were perfectly suited to serve as advertisements for consumer hedonism among affluent white teens. The reverberating sound of surf music was originally developed by guitarists and instrumental groups like the Ventures and Dick Dale, and the formula for writing songs about surfing, cars and fleeting summertime romances was established in a succession of hit singles from 1961 though 1965 by Jan and Dean and the Beach Boys (Hoskyns 1996).

The prosperity and leisure of southern California's 'endless summer' of the early 1960s contained an underside of racial exclusion that confined Blacks and Latinos within an environment of poverty, unemployment and police brutality. In August 1965, at the same time that the Beach Boys' 'California Girls' was climbing the singles chart, the ghetto of Watts exploded in an uprising that lasted for five days and required the dispatch of 15,000 troops from the National Guard before it was finally suppressed (McCone Report 1995). The significance of the Watts rebellion as a watershed moment in the struggle for racial equality, and as an opening signal of the militant turn of the late 1960s, can hardly be overstated. Beginning only days after passage of the Voting Rights Act had abolished the last vestiges of legal segregation, Watts exposed the limits of liberal democratic remedies for racial injustice and activated a more radical turn toward issues of political economy and state repression in the Black social movements of the late 1960s. Watts was a stark reminder that there was something rotten in the land of sunshine, for the local African-American community was continually subjected to racist police violence while being denied access to the affluence surrounding them in the white suburbs and the electronic media beaming out of greater Los Angeles. Guy Debord (2007: 197) of the Situationist International saw the rebellion and destruction in Watts as nothing less than a negation of the 'spectacle-commodity economy' erupting on the perimeter of Hollywood's dream factory:

> The looting of the Watts district was the most direct realisation of the distorted principle: 'To each according to their *false* needs' – needs determined and produced by the economic system which the very act of looting rejects. But once the vaunted abundance is taken at face value and directly *seized*, instead of being eternally pursued in the rat-race of alienated labor and increasing unmet social needs, real desires begin to be expressed in festive celebration, in playful self-assertion, in the *potlatch* of destruction. People who destroy commodities show their human superiority over commodities.

Only a few months after the Watts riots, Brian Wilson of the Beach Boys began working at his home in Beverly Hills to record an album that would rise to the challenge recently set forth by the Beatles' *Rubber Soul* (Granata 2003: 68). Wilson continued to utilise and further develop the dense musical landscapes and expansive harmonies employed in previous Beach Boys songs, but *Pet Sounds* also featured a deep undercurrent of loneliness and estrangement, one that threatened to negate the fun-in-the-sun sound and image that had become the group's trademark. During this time, critics of 'mass society' maintained that behind the glossy façade of the consumer culture and suburban lifestyles afforded by post-war modernisation was an atomised society of isolated individuals – as Phillip Slater (1970: 7) argued in his treatise *The Pursuit of Loneliness*, 'Americans attempt to minimise, circumvent, or deny the interdependence upon which all human societies are based ... We seek more and more privacy, and feel more and more alienated and lonely when we get it.' While he and the other Beach Boys had been writing and singing about surfing, cruising and summertime, in reality Brian Wilson was far too reclusive and awkward to have enjoyed much of this life of youthful leisure, and so it had been a dreamworld for him in the same way it was for most of his audience. Now, in 1966, having recently discovered LSD, and with the symptoms of an emerging mental illness beginning to surface,

Wilson's growing sense of estrangement formed an antithesis within *Pet Sounds* to offset the upbeat harmonising and carefree hedonism of the Beach Boys' sound. The signs of alienation appear immediately on *Pet Sounds*, when a cheery song about teenage lovers is unsettled with the question 'Wouldn't it be nice to live together in the kind of world where we belong?' and the observation that 'You know it seems the more we talk about it/It only makes it worse to live without it.' On the surface, the gorgeously sad falsettos of *Pet Sounds* appear to stem from personal heartbreak, but a closer listen also reveals a young man suffering from a more social or even political kind of disconnection, a feeling that he 'just wasn't made for these times'.

In short, if the Watts riots were a destructive assault waged by those excluded from the 'spectacle-commodity economy', *Pet Sounds* was an early sign of the dissatisfaction and estrangement developing from inside the spectacle among those born into a position of privilege within this economy. Though Wilson and the Beach Boys approached them from a different direction, along with the San Francisco bands they too pushed against the limits of post-war modernisation and modernity, exposing the need to overcome its contradictions to progress further. *Pet Sounds* did indeed become known as one of the greatest rock albums of all time, but not in 1966: the album was initially a commercial failure and mostly ignored by the burgeoning rock community, and only subsequently has it accumulated the massive symbolic capital it now possesses. By 1966 the torch had already been passed to a new cohort of folk rock bands, some of whom (the Byrds, Love, Buffalo Springfield) had built a following within the counterculture through their performances at nightclubs on the Sunset Strip. Sunset Boulevard hosted a small riot of its own in 1966, when plans to demolish a folk rock hotspot called Pandora's Box sparked a confrontation between police and young people that began in November 1966 and continued sporadically for the next two years (Davis 2007). As the hippie subculture was emerging and a moral panic about youth, music and drugs began to spread, the LAPD tried to vigorously enforce a 10 p.m. curfew while routinely harassing and beating long-haired youth outside the clubs; in appropriately Hollywood style, the melees were immortalised in both film (*Riot on the Sunset Strip*) and song (Buffalo Springfield's 'For What It's Worth'). Like the Watts riots, these confrontations with the police developed into festivals of joyous destruction that united the young in a collective identity forged in opposition to state power. A self-described Hollywood rock 'groupie', Pamela Des Barres (1987: 44) recalled the formative influence of these events for her:

> I felt like I belonged, united with a thousand other kids, protesting what THEY were doing to US ... I watched as Gorgeous Hollywood Boys overturned a bus, and I cheered on the offenders from my warm spot on the Sunset Boulevard blacktop. I gazed at Sonny and Cher, arms wrapped around each other, wearing matching polka-dot bell-bottoms and fake-fur vests, and realised that we were all one perfect hip force with one huge beating heart.

Coda: I Cannot Go Back to Yer Frownland

The story of how this loving community with its dreams of social progress and individual growth imploded internally while being repressed externally, and all the consequences that followed, is much too complicated to be explained here. It is, in brief, the story of modernity's exhaustion and the emergence of a postmodern sensibility that spread across a wide spectrum of cultural forms in the decades that followed. Musically, the sound of things falling apart can be clearly heard on an album released in the summer of 1969 that still continues to disturb the unsuspecting set of ears like few others can, Captain Beefheart's *Trout Mask Replica*. The 28 songs on *Trout Mask Replica* sound as if what Pamela Des Barres called the 'one huge beating heart' of the counterculture has been ripped into a thousand shreds, only to be stitched back together in ways that seem random and haphazard at first but eventually reveal a new system of chaos. The beat of this music, as Beefheart (Don Van Vliet) has explained, no longer approximates the soothing regularity of a heartbeat, but instead has been crushed into a mishmash of erratic rhythms that never carry on long enough for the listener to settle into a groove or state of tranquillity. Beefheart's music was a concoction of the disorderly noise and frenetic pace of free jazz, simulations of unpolished sounds from the earliest blues recordings and the disorienting clamour of psychedelic rock, all of which are accented by Vliet's gruff shouting of lyrical puns and nonsensical word associations. Langdon Winner (2007: 59) explained why *Trout Mask Replica*, venerated by some as a masterpiece but denigrated by many others as un-listenable noise, would be his choice as the one album he could bring to a deserted island: 'a desert island is possibly the only place where I could play the record without being asked by friends and neighbours to take the damned thing off' (on 'freak out' recordings and sonic anarchy, see Keister in this volume).

As the 1960s wore on, the collective hopes for development, transcendence and authenticity embedded in the counterculture's modernism began to fizzle out even faster than they appeared to arise. The tumultuous year of 1968 was the most significant turning point, the year when young people all over the world took to the streets and undertook radical projects of personal and political transformation because, as Lefebvre put it, they were 'experiencing all of modernity's unresolved problems for themselves'. Yet in their attempts to break through these contradictions of modernity, young people were met with massive exercises of state violence in both capitalist and communist societies. Meanwhile, in the late 1960s both the New Left and the counterculture were also imploding from within, the former as a result of the toxic mixture of sectarianism and state repression, the latter coinciding with an individualistic withdrawal from the vision of collective change. The modernism of the 1960s that was created by a youthful counterculture imagined new possibilities in the simultaneous pursuit of social change and personal growth, but by 1969 these possibilities had been extinguished and reduced to empty symbolic gestures circulating through the consumer culture. Young people exposed the limits and hypocrisies of post-war modernisation while representing an image of the new world that could take its place, but their attempts to make this collective dream into reality were resisted by the dual powers of state repression and commercial co-optation. A fragmented, postmodern culture – characterised by an absolute rejection of modernist notions of progress and development, authenticity and originality, and totality and universality – took root in this social context of despair.

Jacques Attali (1985: 11) has theorised that noise contains prophetic powers: 'It makes audible the new world that will gradually become visible.' Two months after the release of *Trout Mask Replica* – and not more than 20 miles from the Woodland Hills house where Vliet shacked up his entire band while insisting on complete authoritarian control over their rehearsal and recording – the Manson family committed a string of gruesome murders, including one at the Benedict Canyon home that Manson believed was still occupied by former Beach Boys producer Terry Melcher (see Carlin and Jones, in this volume). At the end of the 1960s, images of crazed hippies seized the media spotlight in the weeks following the celebration of peace and love at Woodstock, and this turn of events was reinforced in December 1969 by the violence at the Altamont festival in northern California. In explaining why news of the Manson murders came as less than a surprise to her and those she knew in Los Angeles at the time, Joan Didion (1979: 41) wrote, 'This mystical flirtation with the idea of "sin" – this sense that it was possible to go "too far", and that many people were doing it – was very much with us in Los Angeles in 1968 and 1969.' *Trout Mask Replica* stands as the most dramatic document of this time and space of social disintegration, analogous to the word salad and anti-art concocted by Dada in response to the senseless horrors of the First World War. The record begins with a flurry of sounds that seem to be coming from every direction as Vliet protests in his raspy voice, 'My smile is stuck/I cannot go back to yer frownland', as if he is being dragged back to a humdrum reality after momentarily basking in the sunshine of utopia. The record ends with a ferocious jam session to conclude the anti-war song, 'Veteran's Day Poppy'. Noise is always ahead of its time, according to Attali's definition, and so although *Trout Mask Replica* was a commercial flop in 1969, it accumulated influence over the course of the 1970s with a new cohort of punk musicians like Mark Mothersbaugh of Devo and Joe Strummer of the Clash, the latter of whom told Greil Marcus (1993: 31), 'When I was sixteen ... that was the only record I listened to – for a year.' 'What is noise to the old order', as Attali (1985: 11) put it, 'is harmony to the new.'

Chapter 2

The Banality of Degradation: Andy Warhol, the Velvet Underground and the Trash Aesthetic

Simon Warner

Introduction

> American culture is trash culture. (Hamelman 2004: 3)

Because he invested his energies in that promiscuous cultural intersection where Pop Art met both underground film and the methods of mass production, the artist Andy Warhol might be regarded as the king, or indeed queen, of the trash aesthetic. The fact that he also engineered a space in which an alternative language of rock and roll could be devised and dispersed through the medium of a band known as the Velvet Underground further places him in the vanguard of this potent counter-narrative to the history of art-making and art appreciation. This chapter will attempt an overview of the influences that shaped the rise of a trash aesthetic; the meanings that are attached to, and generated by, such an anti-philosophy; and the ways in which we might identify evidence of its style and expression within the world of Warhol and his Manhattan working environment the Factory, his house band the Velvet Underground and his 1966 live, multi-media presentation *Exploding Plastic Inevitable*.

Through image, sound and movement, Warhol's quixotic coven of artists, poets, film-makers, photographers, actors, dancers and musicians developed a stream of creativity that tested the tenets of several millennia of received wisdom about the nature of, the making of and the function of art. The Warholian 1960s, in fact, proved to be a kinetic crucible in which the boundaries were pushed and many rules re-written. At the heart of this process was the establishment of an aesthetic credo which disrespected, disrupted and dismissed, dismantled even, earlier conceptions of what art should comprise, communicate or represent, what Cagle has referred to as 'haute kitsch' (1995: 5). The philosophers who, over so many epochs, had debated art's founding and enduring principles – the towering pillars of truth and beauty, justice and morality – were challenged, perhaps fatally, by this fervent dissident wave. Warhol's part in this project, this aesthetic re-ordering and re-evaluation, places him, I would argue, at the heart of one of the key countercultural gestures of the era. By stressing surface and the superficial over depth and substance and by rejecting traditional motivations – issues of moral purpose, social conscience or political ethos, for instance – the artist and his disciples created an enclosed aesthetic universe that was profoundly alternative to both the mid-1960s mainstream and also those who would challenge it in more conventional ways.

Not that Warhol was the only figure in this aesthetic revolution – he was merely a link in a chain that had seen a number of twentieth-century artists, ideologues and cultural mavericks attack the citadel of orthodoxy and conceive fresh perceptions of the creative milieu itself: what it might do, what it might say, how it might say it. In short, this small, but influential, breed cultivated a system of thought built, at least substantially, on aspects of shock value. That Warhol was present in an era when both mass communication and social democratisation cross-fertilised so strikingly and effectively was serendipitous. It meant that his radical ideology became familiar not just to a narrow intellectual elite but to the global billions.

The result was that this flaring, this flowering, of productivity in the heart of, arguably, the most dynamic decade of the epoch, would not be confined in its impact to merely a few short years. Instead, the final quarter of the century would be infused and infected, influenced and affected, by the practices and preachings of this paradoxical figure – strange isolate and socialite scenester – whose most remembered quotation is that 'in the future everybody will be world famous for 15 minutes' (Fineberg 2000: 256) (even if it tends to be misquoted as 'in the future everyone will be famous for 15 minutes'). Within this argument rests a significant contradiction. Warhol's identification of ephemerality as a key feature of what we might describe as the postmodern condition was insightful. But his legacy has, ironically, seen transience become a sustained and repeating state. The flashing, flickering, fleeting focus of the lens, as the second millennium merges into the third, has become the norm, not the exception.

So how might we identify a trash aesthetic? First, we may perhaps think of the rise of a transient and high impact culture in the post-Second World War period, broadly an era of relative material plenty in the West which saw us enter times in which the art interests of the elite and the folk practices of ordinary people were essentially marginalised, if not superseded in many instances, by the powerful presence of a democratised experience, one constructed on the premise of mass production and mass consumption aided by the power of mass promotion. Not all mass or popular culture, as it became broadly known from the mid-twentieth century, could be designated trash but much of it was based on extravagant display and featured a strong note of the temporary. Richard Keller Simon, who is most interested in the relationship between popular and high culture in the realm of literature, claims that in his chosen field of enquiry '[m]any of the differences between trash culture and high culture show only that storytelling adapts to changing economic, social, and political conditions' (1999: 2). As he compares great literary texts and contemporary accounts in film and TV, magazines and newspapers, he argues: 'The connections between high and low are extensive and systematic ... trash culture replicates *all* of the major genres of literature' (ibid.: 3). For Hamelman, American trash culture embraces:

> Natural rights, baseball, apple pie, huge gas-guzzling cars, guns, blockbuster movies, strip malls, Disney/Pixar cinema, talk shows, billboards, theme parks, fast food, superheroes, superstars, little pink houses, Andy Warhol's prints of Marilyn Monroe, Elvis Presley and Campbell soup cans. Rock and roll music. The music of the Velvet Underground too. And garbage ... heinous beyond description, heavy beyond statistical calculation, beautiful beyond belief. American culture, American garbage, American art. (2004: 82)

And, within his sweeping overview, he cannot ignore the central paradox of the ugly, the throwaway, the transitory, as appealing, valuable even, despite its negative associations. Even more helpfully, he includes both Warhol and his protégé musical act of the mid-1960s in his long list of indicators. More pertinently, too, I would suggest that while Hamelman can place in line a sequence of representations which he feels stand for the culture of trash – and his book plays both freely and astutely with the literal meanings of throwaway materials and the term's metaphorical connotations linked to products of low artistic value – the only elements in the list which may be usefully associated with a trash aesthetic are the artworks by Warhol and the musical output of the Velvets.

For, even if we may claim that versions of trash culture have subsequently become almost ubiquitous in the capitalist world and beyond – in, for example, junk food and junk mail, reality television and celebrity obsession, scandal sheets and news-stand pornography, slot machines and stretch limousines – it does not follow that a trash aesthetic, as such, also exists. Rather, for such an aesthetic to establish its presence requires an artist or a movement to knowingly and self-consciously take the materials of a cultural moment and re-conceptualise those materials in such a way that they represent or comment upon that moment. Then, we may argue still further, that authoritative critical voices are then needed both to identify and to contextualise what the artist or movement have done, a process not dissimilar to the chain needed in the creation of myth that Barthes describes (2000: 113). The symbols have to stand for something else and there has to be recognition of what they stand for by the viewer before this form of signification effectively occurs. As Hunter and Kaye have proposed:

> Recent cultural criticism has explored more deeply than ever before the undergrowth of literature and popular film, shifting attention away from what ideal audiences should be reading and viewing to what real people actually enjoy. As well as discovering unexpected complexity in 'trash culture', the result has been a heightened awareness of the differences between audiences, and of the importance of specialised constituencies such as fans and cultists. (1997: 1)

The decoding skills and mediation of informed commentators and insightful interpreters – figures like Robert Hughes and Lawrence Alloway – to guide reception of this work were therefore particularly relevant as Warhol and his allies tended to present their work blankly and without explanation. While they frequently drew on and depicted the more excessive and controversial components of trash culture – confronting the taboos of sex, money and celebrity, drugs, violence and death – they did so non-judgementally. Furthermore, we need audiences capable of digesting this chain of information.

Subsequent disciples of the model have demonstrated a similar lack of sanctimony, a sustained moral ambivalence, to the sensitive topics they address and the materials they manipulate to make their statements. As an artistic practice or creative ethos, the trash aesthetic has taken a wide range of forms and shapes but so many of its features owe a debt to the work of Warhol and his cohorts, including the Velvet Underground. It has been linked to the cracking of sexual bounds through ambivalent gender display on screen and on stage; it can be perceived at once as feminised and effete and also macho and aggressive; it may be recognised in its pared down primitivism and its over-blown glamour; it may be linked to material and narcotic excess; it may be recognised in adornment – from piercings to tattoos – or other body modification; or we might perceive it in its adherence to low production values, which reject ideas of polish and professionalism and pursue, instead, the rough, the raw and the unrefined. In short, such transgressive cultural expressions, symbols which have become associated with notions of poor taste, the cheap and the lewd, the crude and the gross, have become cornerstones of this alternative aesthetic, infringing those boundaries familiar to mainstream social codes and traditional conceptions of artistic value. In this piece, I want to consider how the seeds of trash were sown in the first half of the last century and later blossomed; locate the ways in which Warhol and his brigade of creative mercenaries adopted, encouraged and adapted those new visions in the work they produced at the height of their powers; and touch briefly upon the legacy of those subversive adventures.

Dada and Duchamp's Urinal

> It is essential to grasp that Dada was never an art style, as Cubism was; nor did it begin with a pugnacious socio-political programme, like Futurism. It stood for a wholly eclectic freedom to experiment; it enshrined play as the highest human activity and its main tool was chance. (Hughes 1980: 61)

As the mud of Flanders and the wastes of the Eastern Front were churned and reddened by the guts of several million young soldiers, the members of Cabaret Voltaire,[1] an arts cell lodged in Zürich and residing in a neutral state but inflamed by the destruction choreographed by the feuding super-powers of that early-century, dreamt up their creative responses to the sanctioned madness of the trenches:

---

[1] Artists Hugo Ball and Jean Arp and poet Tristan Tzara and were among the group's members. Dada was 'a verbal alibi for inanity' and Tzara insisted that 'DADA DOES NOT MEAN ANYTHING' (Note: author's capitals) (Conrad 1998: 112).

they fired arrows of protest through disorientating performances, chaotic poetry randomly construed and unorthodox art statements. The sires of Dada, the Cabaret Voltaire would also later be the catalyst to the European Surrealists. While the latter were fascinated by the unconscious and Sigmund Freud's faith in the power of dreams and the painting of pictures which tapped into the tangled psychological briar patch of the brain, figures like Marcel Duchamp, semi-detached from both these streams of activity in New York, went still further.

With his 1917 sculpture, *Fountain* – a commercially-produced, porcelain urinal signed enigmatically by the artist as 'R. Mutt' – he produced and exhibited his first readymade in New York, arguing that the artist simply by displaying such a piece – domestic, quotidian, banal – imbued it with the aura of art.[2] Robert Hughes, long-time art critic of *Time*, said: 'Such things were manifestos. They proclaimed that the world was already so full of "interesting" objects that the artist need not add to them. Instead, he could just pick one, and this ironic act of choice was equivalent to creation – a choice of mind rather than of hand' (Hughes 1980: 66). The fact that he selected an object associated with pissing and the evacuations of bodily function might legitimately lead us to identify this, retrospectively, as the premiere act in the history of the trash aesthetic.

There were others, too, who would break moulds by recycling or re-manipulating what appeared to be mere detritus – Kurt Schwitters and his *Merz* collages, John Heartfield and his disruptive, cut-up photo-montages – to make social commentaries or political critiques. Yet, while these groups and individuals with quite unconventional visions did not entirely turn the art world on its head, all these threads would feed into the avant-garde impulse of the 1920s and 1930s. All brought taboo components to the table: sex, desire, madness, psychosis, junk reclaimed and re-positioned as art. These expressions, these gestures, would rattle the cage of artistic normality as the Second World War loomed without breaking its bars.

That said, the principal thrust of modern art, as the interwar years drew to their end, remained locked in a determined cycle of abstraction – a significant counter, in itself, to earlier aesthetic notions of art as a form of imitation – rather than representation. Abstraction even became an ideological weapon, too, an intriguing emblem of the free world, a perfect antidote to Hitler's pre-war assaults on degenerate[3] – that is, essentially, modern – art. As the global centre of art innovation moved from Paris to New York in the 1940s, the avant-garde

---

[2] British gallery curator Julian Spalding has claimed that Duchamp never actually put forward the item for display. He says that 'recent research has shown that the urinal was actually submitted by Baroness Elsa von Freytag-Loringhoven. Her gesture was an early feminist attack on a male society. She didn't claim the urinal was a work of art. She was taking the piss' (cf. Spalding 2012).

[3] A Nazi-sponsored exhibition showcasing – and attacking – modernist trends and abstraction in art, *Entartete Kunst* ('degenerate art'), opened in Munich in 1937 and then toured Germany and Austria.

was embraced as a sign that capitalism could freely nurture pioneering artist-visionaries while fascism would crush them under its heel. But the mood of the US art scene was ripe for transformation in the decade that followed the second great conflict. Pop Art's arrival from the mid-1950s would resist that prevailing, non-figurative form of extemporisation – typified by the abstract expressionist Action painters like Jackson Pollock – and celebrate instead the imagery and artefacts of the high street and the mass media.

Pop Art, Postmodernism and New Aesthetic Bearings

> Here was a realism that thrust itself knowingly in the face of a society that liked its garishness larger than life; a society ineluctably drawn to cartoon romance and tabloid scandal, to that particular species of glamour – in parts lurid, sexual and tragic – that was embodied by Elvis and Marilyn and Jackie. (Madoff 1997: xiv)

Pop Art, a movement that enjoyed separate and then eventually inter-mingling lives in the US, UK and Europe, did not, however, draw upon the usual devices of representational mimicry which may have returned the artistic project to a pre-avant-garde understanding of the aesthetics of art. Instead, this post-war form, originally dubbed New Realism (Livingstone 1991b: 12), utilised familiar signs and symbols of the mass marketplace in a literal manner, incorporating them into collages and constructions. These assemblages appeared simultaneously to celebrate *and* to question a new age of rampant consumerism: the absence of a clear line between endorsement and critique was a disorientating, even unsettling, experience for many. We might also propose that this adoption and adaptation of such recognisable features from the popular cultural landscape sabotaged the assumed certainties of abstraction, by then the accepted core of avant-garde thinking.

The US had enjoyed a consumer boom in the decade or so after the conclusion of the Second World War. It would take longer for Britain and other Western European nations to cast off the shadowy pallor of war and assume a role of free-spending bridesmaid to the glamorous American bride. But artists on both sides of the Atlantic, in independent gatherings, had begun to reflect on the impact and power of commercialism and the expanding media, both of which found common platforms in, for example, TV, radio, newspaper and magazine advertising. Cars, soap powders, soft drinks, cigarettes and the increasing range of convenience goods for the home were just part of this explosion of mass production and mass purchasing. While most Americans were quickly seduced by this pattern – to be followed by others in the West – sections of the arts community found the formula tasteless, crass and ultimately empty.

The Beat writers and black jazz musicians found themselves at the margins of this glossy American dream and wrote novels, poems and music which resisted the white hegemony of spend, consume, dispose and spend again. Jack Kerouac and Allen Ginsberg, Charles Mingus and Miles Davis set themselves against the presiding *Zeitgeist*: material indulgence, anti-communist paranoia, a terror of imminent nuclear annihilation and belief in continuing racial division. As the 1950s declined, other notable creative innovators, with New York City their prime crucible, would also confront the gleaming sheen of US prosperity, adopting a variety of media to spread their original and often oblique visions. Photographer Robert Frank, an immigrant heir perhaps to the Ashcan School,[4] those American painters who had created early-century, and considerate, portraits of the city's underbelly, brought a gritty Beat aesthetic of his own to a series of monochrome images and, in *The Americans*,[5] displayed pictures that eschewed glamour and prosperity and pursued the ordinary and often beaten-down characters he randomly located in the national landscape. Painter Allan Kaprow's 1959 work *18 Happenings in 6 Parts* would christen a radical new art form – the happening – a multi-media format in which performance and art-making were merged into one environment and even the lines between production and audience were blurred. Artists Jim Dine and Claes Oldenburg, both connected to the Pop surge of the time, would also be associated with this development. This ground-breaking form of presentation would be adopted, too, by the art group Fluxus, further re-defining notions of visual art in live settings. Says Banes:

> Both Happenings and Fluxus developed out of ideas from John Cage's class in 'Composition of Experimental Music', which he taught at the New School for Social Research from 1956 to 1960. Various members of the class, in which students made performances and discussed them, attributed the beginnings of Happenings to their experiences there. Influenced by the Italian Futurists, Dadaists, Zen Buddhism, and the theatre theories of Antonin Artaud, Cage's notion of music had expanded to become a nondramatic ... form of theatre ... Cage himself had organised a precursor to Happenings at Black Mountain College in 1952, but, for the most part, his performances remained classified as music. (1993: 52)

Additionally, the New American Cinema Group, led by Jonas Mekas[6] and including Stan Brakhage among its members, also developed challenging film-making

---

[4] This name of this school, forged in 1908, referred to 'the group's gritty urban subjects, general preference for a dark palette, and roughly sketched painting style. Ashcan realists rebelled against feminine prettiness and academic correctness to express a masculine, virile energy, primarily symbolised by the teeming humanity of an increasingly urbanised America' (Bjelajac 2000: 293).

[5] Robert Frank's 1959 photography collection included a preface from Jack Kerouac. Frank would make films, too, including *Pull My Daisy* with Kerouac in 1959 and the unreleased *Cocksucker Blues*, a highly charged account of the Rolling Stones' 1972 tour of the US.

[6] Mekas would engage with the Warhol community. He filmed the audience, alongside Barbara Rubin, when Warhol presented a controversial presentation, including the Velvet Underground, to the New York Society for Clinical Psychiatry at the Hotel Delmonico in New York City in January 1966 (Cagle 1995: 1).

formats presenting visions which ran counter to the establishment projections of mid-century US life. True to the edginess of the street and engaged with the activities of subterranean outsiders, these movies were also fervently committed to testing the limits of the law in respect of censorship. Speaking of an early 1960s wave of new cinematic works by his members, Mekas said that

> these movies are illuminating and opening up sensibilities and experiences never before recorded in the American arts; a content which Baudelaire, the Marquis de Sade, and Rimbaud gave to world literature a century ago and which Burroughs gave to American literature three years ago.[7] It is a world of flowers of evil, of illuminations, of torn and tortured flesh; a poetry which is at once beautiful and terrible, good and evil, delicate and dirty .... (quoted in Banes 1993: 165)

All of these novel approaches had a bearing on Warhol's rapidly emerging milieu. Furthermore, the fact that large numbers of these creative players stood outside the apparently omnipotent WASP (White Anglo-Saxon Protestant) hegemony – by nationality and politics, ethnic background and religion – makes their disruption of the smooth narrative of an immaculately back-lit American Dream all the more compelling. Many of these writers and artists employed radical tools of engagement, the fractured tropes of modernity – dissonance, distortion, derangement – to provide elliptical yet revealing statements. Sometimes the work possessed an underlying social commentary and a strain of the redemptive to it; much exhibited a critical consciousness that was also, on occasions, tied to serious political intent.[8]

The Pop artists were more ambiguous: for a start, they shared no filial unity, no clear manifesto;[9] and second, many of the painters and sculptors actually found inspiration in the brash electric steeples of the ever-rising city, the neon capitalism of the high street, the possibilities proffered by the multi-lane highway and the proliferation of goods on the supermarket shelves. Pop's mission was obsessed less with issues of beauty than matters of irony and paradox: the commercial directness and garishness of the ubiquitous trademark or the movie still, the cartoon frame or the urban billboard, appeared to be both flattered and questioned by their appropriation into works by Anglo-American artists of the 1950s and 1960s. As Sarat Maharaj asks: 'Do Pop Art signs replay the scene of consumerist desire,

---

[7] We must assume that Mekas was referring to Burroughs' experimental novel *Naked Lunch*, first issued in France in 1959, and subsequently the target of an obscenity case in the US.

[8] The Beats' 'New Vision', a manifesto of artistic intent, dated back to the mid-1940s (Watson 1995: 38–40) while the anti-censorship commitments of the new film-makers was central to their creative campaign (Banes 1993: 171–3).

[9] In the UK, proto-Pop painters like Richard Hamilton and Eduardo Paolozzi as members of the Independent Group did present statements offering explanations of their work from the mid-1950s (Alloway 1974: 27–66).

or do they prise open a critical gap in it?' (1991: 22). There was frequently, for sure, a cold disengagement from the materials at hand, which provided a perplexing counterpoint to what critics and audiences had previously expected of the artist – expressions of feeling, emotion and connection with the subject matter.

Andy Warhol, once of Pittsburgh but by now based in New York City, emerged as one of the prime practitioners of Pop Art, leaving behind the purely commercial world of shoe illustration – where his adept draughtsmanship had made him a valuable cog in the post-war, promotional rollercoaster and a lucrative earner[10] – to create a new art of his own. His paintings and silkscreen prints from around 1962 paid attention instead to the products of the food store – Coca Cola, Campbell's soup and Brillo pads – and the iconic emblems of the mass entertainment business – Mickey Mouse, Marilyn Monroe and Elvis Presley. As we have stated, fellow artists, loosely corralled under the heading Pop, also utilised the output of the mass media. But no one quite took on the trappings of mass culture so readily nor adopted its methods – reproduction on a huge scale, commercialism on industrial principles – like Warhol.

Writes Robert Hughes: 'What he extracted from mass culture was repetition. "I want to be a machine", he announced, in memorable contrast to Jackson Pollock, who fifteen years before had declared that he wanted to be nature: a mediumistic force, unpredictable, various, and full of energy' (1980: 348). He says that 'Warhol loved the peculiarly inert sameness of the mass product: an infinite series of identical objects – soup cans, Coke bottles, dollar bills, Mona Lisas, or the same head of Marilyn Monroe silkscreened over and over again' (ibid.: 348). By drawing on the most recognisable of conveyor-belt commodities and then replicating them in a near-parody of the principle of art as one-off, unrepeatable talisman, Warhol enraged the traditionalists of the inner art circle and outraged conservative gallery goers who knew what art should stand for and what it ought to look like.

However, by initially alienating the intellectual bastions of art past and the middle-class wardens of art present, Andy Warhol – alongside other Pop artists like Robert Rauschenberg, Jasper Johns, Roy Lichtenstein and Claes Oldenburg, and their British equivalents David Hockney, Peter Blake and Richard Hamilton – appeared to carve out a new domain for art and the artist. What Warhol initially lost in credibility found compensation in instant fame; then credibility also followed. A young generation alienated by antiquity and the classics, dissatisfied by abstraction, disenfranchised by the musty silence of museums, found, within this novel movement, a super-charged portrait of their times: paintings and sculpture which commented on television and movies, rock and roll and teen fashion. Warhol's images had the flash of the clothes they wore, the energy of the records they played, the Technicolor vibrancy of the cinema they watched, the streamlined swish of the futuristic automobiles they drove. It is little wonder that Pop Art and popular music, which despite their common adjective enjoyed a somewhat

---

[10] By 1959, Warhol was earning around $65,000 a year (Fineberg 2000: 251).

contrasting genealogy, should eventually share a bed in the shape of numerous high-profile album sleeves for the Beatles, the Rolling Stones and Cream.[11]

The fact that these various objects of desire, in which the new viewers revelled, had a built-in obsolescence, linked them intrinsically to the throwaway age and drew them to Warhol's operating methods and selected media. His work had an immediacy and transparency that appealed to the times. It also inevitably became associated with concepts of ephemerality and disposability. Some also regarded his oeuvre as empty and vacuous and the artist did little to deflect those attacks, content to ignore – even enjoy – such ambiguities rather than address them.

Out of such connections the concept of an 'anti-aesthetic', made concrete some little way down the line by thinkers such as Hal Foster (1993a: xiii), began to take shape. Thus art, previously considered absolute and ever-lasting, became rather, in this feckless re-configuration, instantaneous and passing. And out of this would emerge, in time, the more general notion of a trash aesthetic, a virulent sub-branch of the larger arts tree, an oxymoronic concept which was oppositional and subversive, not as a consequence of any radical programme or revolutionary dynamism, but rather through its determinedly shallow posturing and limp, world-weary listlessness.

Yet, in the fertile testing ground of the 60s, Warhol's approach – and that of his sidemen and women, his lieutenants and his foot-soldiers – was about more than just depicting everyday iconography. He was keen also to explore art subjects and art practices that moved beyond facile – if skilfully crafted – portraits of soda, soup and soap or Hollywood royalty. He was interested, too, in the darker realms of the psyche – death through execution or car crash, for instance – which he included in his print series but also cultural taboos – drugs and sex, generally, homosexuality and sexual perversity, more specifically – which he considered through a series of films created under his own name and also via the recordings that the Velvet Underground laid down and which, in each case, Warhol nominally supervised.[12]

By presenting those taboo-breaking devices within the context of the artwork – either moving picture, stage event or sound recording – Warhol further helped to engineer the break from conventional ideas of what art should contemplate or stand for, by inference a split from the Greco-Roman, Jewish and Christian codes on which aesthetics – truth, beauty, morality and, by very strong implication, *good*, as in worthwhile, valuable or improving – had been ultimately, and until this moment, generally founded. But we should also draw attention to wider philosophical shifts of the 1960s of which Pop Art and Warhol could be regarded as both trigger and mirror: the general move towards an aesthetic framework,

---

[11] Blake and Hamilton designed, respectively, the Beatles covers *Sgt. Pepper's Lonely Hearts Club Band* (1967) and *The Beatles* (1968); Jim Dine did *Best of Cream* (1969); and Warhol created *Sticky Fingers* for the Rolling Stones (1971).

[12] Paul Morrissey, Warhol's manager, was both adviser to the artist and a key figure in physically realising various of his movie and music ventures (Watson 2003: 221–3).

based on relative value rather than rigid and incontrovertible certainty, and the dismantling of the barriers that separated high art from low, elite art from the popular, art itself from the ancient straitjacket that fixed ideologies had wrapped around it.

The reception of Pop Art may be regarded as an excellent example of this changing basis of artistic analysis and assessment. Considered radical at first, the movement was not long in the cold. It speedily became a feature of the accepted circle of fine art exchange – absorbed into that establishment network built on galleries and dealers, buyers and critics – while simultaneously drawing its materials from the activities of mass culture, the antithesis on which that long-founded institutional nexus had been built. Scant surprise then, that John Storey should dub Pop Art 'postmodernism's first cultural flowering' (1998: 148) and Fredric Jameson include it in a long list of artistic, architectural and literary movements of the 1960s that were 'specific reactions against the established forms of high modernism, against this or that dominant high modernism which conquered the university, the museum, the art gallery network, and the foundations' (Jameson 1993: 111). Sylvia Harrison offered a more focused view of Pop's postmodern specificities. She explained that this style possessed features that 'resisted accommodation within existing formalist or realist critical canons'. Among these characteristics were 'anonymity' and 'a lack of "authorial presence"' evident in its 'depersonalised technique' and 'obscure or uninterpretable "message"' (Harrison 2001: 11).

This dispassionate distance from the artwork – apparent in various media he selected – which Warhol embraced, an almost Brechtian alienation from the subject matter, might also be regarded as a sign of the trash aesthetic: if the blandly mundane is transposed or the darkly dangerous is depicted, it is barely engaged with, nor commented upon, a kind of degradation through banality. If there is ambivalence in the piece on show, there is also an equivocal morality behind its construction.

Underground Movies and the Music of the Velvets: The Trash Aesthetic and the Factory Shift

> Even those who would hesitate to classify the arts as holy often feel that they form a sanctified enclave from which certain contaminating influences should be excluded – notably money and sex. (Carey 2005: ix)

> Warhol's autistic stare was the same for heroes and heroines as for death and disaster. (Hughes 1980: 351)

> [The Velvet Underground] became the model for an avant-garde within rock and roll, the source of a self-conscious, intellectual trash aesthetic. (Frith and Horne 1987: 112)

In what ways can we illustrate the trash aesthetic, this creative impulse that would benefit from its early tending by Warhol and his followers to recur in various artistic disciplines – music, fashion, film, theatre, dance, art and more – in the subsequent decades? We might start by reiterating Warhol's desire to be machine-like. It is surely no coincidence that, given his interest in the man as mechanised android, he should have christened his art studio in Manhattan, the Factory.

Today, our ability to see art as both cultural artefact and product with commercial potential – a sliding signifier, if you like – renders the chosen name of the artist's workspace, in retrospect, quite comprehensible. In the heart of the 1960s, when manufactories and art-making would have been most definitely viewed as mutually incompatible, Warhol confused his audiences with this tactic. The naming of the Factory reduced his art, by implication, to the equivalent of a component on a Detroit assembly line, subverting the language in aid of his strategy of aesthetic disinformation. In fact, we might even speculate that Warhol was striking at the very soul of the Romantic notion – the compact artists had previously made with the forces and fruits of nature was symbolically rejected within the cold, dark recesses of an abandoned industrial complex. Simultaneously he jettisoned the comfortable intellectual environment of the art establishment, which inhabited the rarefied and protective environment of the salon and the academy.

It is not without irony either that since then, in these post-industrial times, artists have flocked to disused mills and redundant factories to create their loft spaces, their studios and their galleries. Following Warhol's prescient example, the reclaimed factory has, in the present era, become a birthing-pool for art that is the offspring of the urban postmodern environment. But the artist's move to the building located in East 47th Street at the end of 1963 was only part of his re-making of the art experience. Jonathan Fineberg summarises the ethos – both unfamiliar and ground-breaking – that would infuse the place and his gathering circle. He comments: 'Andy Warhol's devotion to the aesthetic of television, society columns and fun magazines was opposed to the European model of the struggling avant-garde artist which the abstract expressionists had emulated' (2000: 250).

The Factory, Fineberg explains, 'evolved into an environment lined in silver foil and filled with drag queens, listless "beautiful people", chic fashion personalities, and the rock music underground, many of them wasted on drugs or engaged in bizarre behaviour' (ibid.: 256). But, amid these strange conjunctions, these decadent social experiments, the heartbeat of trash was evident in a wide array of Warhol's art and artefacts. If the power of the previous prevailing aesthetic code had been sited in joy, humanity and emotional involvement, the ambience of the Factory was premised on something else: detachment, distance and emotional disengagement.

On the canvases and in the movie reels that were produced there was a deliberate attempt to reduce the human component, drain the life-force, the pleasure, the humane pulse, the signs of the soul, that had formerly been the expected keynotes of an artwork. The value of felt life to legitimate art, explored and commemorated by such modernist literary philosophers as F.R. Leavis, was absent here. In the silkscreens and the film scenes, feelings and the felt were essentially excised.

What we can assert is that within this curious scene – a crossroads where upscale high life convened with degraded low life – the core of the trash aesthetic was hardened: a postmodern meeting of wealth and the gutter, of the famous and of freaks, of stars both genuine and *ersatz*, of flash and flesh, of the bright lights and the twilight, of the glamorous and the grotesque, of adulation and addiction, of uptown and downtown, a mingling of aspiring and even expiring, of the treasured and the trashy of the isle of Manhattan.

Although initially Warhol continued to make paintings and prints, conventional products depicting unconventional subject matter, and build his career as 'the decade's leading art star' (Fineberg 2000: 256), he eventually announced his retirement from painting and, from 1966, dedicated his principal output to film, performance and the celebrity scene which engrossed him. His films tended to embody the low-production values that would come to characterise our sense of trash, too: grainy, black and white footage concerned less with narrative than with visual texture, unscripted tributes to the lives of those at the edge who managed to escape the alienation and ostracism of society and the grime of the street to find a receptive cocoon within the Factory walls. Watson outlines the artist's film aesthetic saying that he

> found his signature cinematic style very quickly: an emotionally uninflected camera that neither panned nor zoomed, the use of real time instead of edited time, and a frame dominated by tightly cropped parts of the anatomy, usually a face. It is customary to think the movies sprang full-blown from the mind of Andy Warhol and that they were all the same. Saying something was a like a 'Warhol movie' became shorthand for saying it was boring, blank and long. (Watson 1995: 132)

Early cinematic ventures, including 1963's *Sleep*, a six-hour depiction of a sleeping poet called John Giorno, and the following year's *Empire*, an eight-hour, single view study of the Empire State Building in which only one piece of action, the switch-on of the skyscraper's lights, enlivened the plot, reflected Warhol's concern with the minor, inane details of life. Many dozens of similar pictures would follow. *The Chelsea Girls*[13] released in 1966, which starred Nico and was filmed at the celebrated bohemian haunt the Chelsea Hotel under the direction of Paul Morrissey who would oversee many of the Factory films, was characteristic. In Calvin Tomkins' summary, it was 'a three-hour, twin-screen examination of assorted freaks, drugs and transvestites' (Tomkins quoted in Fineberg 2000: 257). But he pointed out that the superficial sensationalism of these pieces was quite misleading. Warhol, claimed Tomkins, subtracted 'movement, incident and

---

[13] The film is also referred to as simply *Chelsea Girls*.

narrative interest from his movies, grinding out epically boring, technically awful films that failed signally to live up to their sex-and-perversion-billings' (ibid.).

These were hardly films for mainstream movie theatre viewing, but conceptual escapades, installations in celluloid – auguries of the manner in which film would become as integral a feature of art's lexicon as oil paint as the century came to a conclusion – funded by the most acclaimed and successful artist of his day and, fiscally, quite capable of indulging his every creative whim. Later film-works like *Flesh* (1968) and the significantly titled *Trash* (1970) were a bizarre weaving of hedonism and nihilism, superficially sexual extravaganzas but so coldly and dispassionately delivered that they were frankly drained of their erotic charge, a contrapuntal quality that would have probably pleased the curiously asexual Warhol.

His aim, we might say, was to socially engineer a playground in which division – by class or cash, by sexual deviation or narcotic reliance – was dispelled. However, the ringmaster of this exotic mélange was not a liberal meritocrat or a fevered reformer: he was a mischief-maker extraordinaire who revelled in the contradictions and juxtapositions he was able to manufacture in the varied dramatic scenarios he dreamt up, on screen or in life. Period interviews, like an example from 1964, in which his monosyllabic 'yes'/'no' retorts to a reporter's questions, suggest a powerful inclination to undermine the conventional critical discourse: is he robot or clown as he deflects his interrogator's queries, his automaton persona only just capable of masking the adolescent smirk? (Warhol 1964b). Yet Warhol's sponsorship of one of the more interesting art experiments of the period is worth more attention – the rock act the Velvet Underground, their recordings and their involvement in the greatest multi-media show of the era, *Exploding Plastic Inevitable* (*EPI*).

So what can we say of the band? Ellen Willis believes that 'the Velvets were the first important rock and roll artists who had no real chance of attracting a mass audience' (Willis 1996: 74). They made music that was 'too overtly intellectual, stylised and distanced to be commercial'. Their output, the status of which she linked to Pop Art, was 'anti-art art made by anti-elite elitists' (ibid.). Matthew Bannister reflects on the group's relation to the anti-philosophy that so intrigued their powerful sponsor. 'The trash aesthetic', he says, 'functions not so much as a democratisation of culture as a testament to the superior taste of a discerning elite who can find sublimity in abjection' (2006: 44). Hamelman states: 'To separate the Velvet Underground and trash would be to separate the nervous system and the skeleton. It can't be done' (2004: 80). To take the two key artefacts that would engage the Velvets' time and energy in 1966, let us reflect on the pair in roughly chronological order – the unveiling of *EPI* and the making of their debut album. The two projects would overlap and interweave with composed material common to each context, though the record itself would not see the light of day until well into the following year.

The musical ensemble that had taken shape in 1964 and 1965, operating under several guises and with various personnel, had finally taken the name the Velvet

Underground in tribute to a 1963 paperback of the same title by Michael Leigh, a volume which had charted the recent sexual activities of post-Kinsey subterraneana. Drawn to Warhol's attention by his aide and adviser Morrissey and brought into the Factory fold, the band would comprise original members Lou Reed, John Cale, Sterling Morrison and Maureen Tucker but now joined, at Warhol's insistence, by the German model, screen actor and would-be singer Nico.[14] Although the introduction of a leggy Teutonic chanteuse was not universally welcomed by the group, they could see the value of compromise. As Richard Williams states of their new bond with a high-profile Pop artist: '[T]he most significant part of the relationship was this: if the Velvet Underground were going to pursue a career based on demolishing the unwritten rules and conventions of rock and roll, then Andy Warhol would be the last person in the world to discourage them' (2009: 189).

The band, according to Wayne Koestenbaum, actually made their live debut under Warhol's aegis with the name Erupting Plastic Inevitable (2001: 100) in a show called *Up-Tight* for the New York Clinical Psychiatry Society banquet in January 1966, before *Exploding Plastic Inevitable*, now re-titled, began its run at the Dom in St Mark's Place in April. *EPI* was a piece that drew on all of the managed anarchy of Warhol's universe: his movies – *Couch* (1964) and *Vinyl* (1965) in this case – became the backdrop to the installation; his house band became the musical performers and soundtrack providers; his aides and superstars its *dramatis personae*. At the Dom, says Williams, 'Around four hundred people made it upstairs on opening night to be confronted by the Velvet Underground and Nico, plus lights, films ..., the onstage dancing of "superstars" Gerard Malanga and Mary Woronov, and – between sets – a sound system that occasionally played three records at once' (2009: 190). Koestenbaum comments:

> The theatrics enveloping Nico and the Velvets were jubilantly sadomasochistic. The decibel level of the Velvets tortured the audience's eardrums. Gerard's whip was a token punishment. Nico's lack of relation to the band ... was another kind of torture: she was a bane to the band, the band a bane to her .... (Koestenbaum 2001: 101)

The show itself had much of the trash quotient with which Warhol had become almost eponymous – sex, violence, noise, mystery and menace – and Ronald Nameth's film, a record of a later Chicago production in June of that year, captures the essence of these ingredients, framing the chaotic disorder of the live performance. Neither Reed, absent through illness, nor Nico appear in this version. Although Nameth's documentary is shot in colour rather than monochrome, it distils the show's shambolic spirit: the jumble of swirling light – the gel projections akin to blazing flames – and the frenetically gyrating bodies, indistinctly identified and almost hermaphrodite, are the main points of visual concern (Nameth 1966).

---

[14] Nico's real name was Christa Päffgen (Koestenbaum 2001: 100).

In fact, the movie portrays a scene that evokes, somewhat ironically, something closer to the abstractions of a Pollock drip painting come to life than the bare, spare, flat representations of the Warhol printing press. It is interesting though that this mélange of disorientating light and shadow, dancers enacting sinister sexual games, and the sensory disturbances of music played at high volume were in keeping with the anti-aesthetic values that the Factory clan had so energetically pursued. *EPI*'s 'swirl of sound and sensation epitomised a nascent genre', says Koestenbaum (2001: 101) and the songs that formed the musical component within the multi-media enactment would, in due course, enjoy a second life on a debut record that would become one of the most pervasive collections of all time. Eventually released in March 1967, *The Velvet Underground and Nico*, proved initially to be a slow-burner but one that would, over the next decade, have an infernal impact.

The material it presented was a considerable way from the musical fare which would characterise the period as the Summer of Love approached, a sunny optimism that stretched from the southern California sands to the psychedelic jams of San Francisco and the acid-drenched and dandy stylings of London – represented by artists like the Beach Boys, the Mamas and the Papas and Jefferson Airplane, Pink Floyd, Jimi Hendrix and the Beatles. The hippy haven of Haight-Ashbury was in bloom, the Monterey Festival was soon to be enacted and the arrival of the classic album of that year, *Sgt. Pepper's Lonely Hearts Club Band*, was imminent.

But the Velvets' debut had little of the airy brightness, the upbeat sense of personal liberation, that those other artists would share with the rock public over these hyperactive weeks and months. Instead there were darker trends at large – the hard drugs of 'Heroin'[15] and 'Waiting for the Man' – and discomforting themes in play – the sado-masochist hints of 'Venus in Furs' – and the reflections on the mysteries of the Factory terrain – 'Femme Fatale', a tribute to doomed Warhol superstar Edie Sedgwick, and 'All Tomorrow's Parties', sometimes thought to be about the painter's controversial Manhattan commune but actually pre-dating Lou Reed's attachment to that scene.

There was no specific or unifying musical style that connected the 11 tracks but there was a monochromatic grain to the record that eschewed the multi-tracking ambition, the multi-layered vocal pyrotechnics of Brian Wilson, John Phillips, Syd Barrett or John Lennon and Paul McCartney. If those composers were bringing a kaleidoscopic, possibly chemically-induced, glee to the technological playground, the Velvets were more introspective, amphetamine expressionists exploring the psychic disturbances within rather than the phantasmagoria without. New York City, a frenetic, hard-wired East Coast metropolis, seemed out of step with the

---

[15] Lou Reed commented of the song and the wider LP: 'I'm not advocating anything ... It's just we had "Heroin", "I'm Waiting for the Man" and "Venus in Furs" all on the first album, and that just about set the tone. It's like we had "Sunday Morning" which was so pretty and "I'll Be Your Mirror", but everyone psyched into the other stuff' (Bockris and Malanga 2003: 117).

West Coast's mellow flavours and the nostalgic eclecticism of Carnaby Street. Cagle believes that the prevailing trends 'fostered sentiments against the alienated, nihilistic visions of the Velvet Underground. Perhaps their songs seemed too jaded and barbaric for a generation that was rallying against nihilism and despair' (1995: 92).

Although rock and roll had been regarded as a rough and ready amalgam of black and white musical forms since the mid-1950s, a symbolic miscegenation that threatened to further inflame the intense racial tensions of the time, by 1967, the rock vanguard had entered a new and mature phase. McCartney had acknowledged an interest in avant-garde Italian composer Luciano Berio and, as Gendron reports (2002), the US critical community, just like its hundreds of thousands of hysterical adolescents, had been seduced by the ever-burgeoning inventiveness of the Fab Four. The artistic *modus operandi* of the group and other leading players was becoming apparent: the adoption of an art method coupled to the dynamic possibilities promised by advanced studio facilities. At odds with this general inclination, the Velvets' album had been recorded around a year before, concurrent with the various *EPI* premieres, with Warhol nominally cited as producer but it seems his essential role was merely in funding and green-lighting of the project. It was the only LP release to see the light of day while the artist and the band shared a professional association.

If the Velvet Underground did not reject an art method *per se*, the one they pursued unquestionably ran counter to the creative ambience of the time. Centrally, the band avoided a policy of re-recording, re-mixing and re-touching the tracks to manicure and polish their sonic canvases. The principle of 'first thought, best thought', an existential belief borrowed from Buddhist sources that had informed the writings of the Beats, appears to be a key driver here. And it was really in this frayed unrefinement – the first engineer who worked with the Velvet Underground advised that single takes were the best way to capture the spirit of the pieces, though a more experienced producer in Tom Wilson also shaped some of the cuts – that set it apart from the competition of the day and set it up as such an influential example, in the years that followed, to a plethora of subsequent acts.

Distorted? Dissonant? Dishevelled? Amateurish? Unfinished? Ugly? There is scant doubt that the material that made up *The Velvet Underground and Nico* met standards that were quite out of step with the dominating ethos of the moment, one that was moving in the direction of refined sophistication and cerebral stimulation and away from notions of the three-minute pop song and the ephemeral teen anthem. Reed, Cale and co. rejected both the new art rock and the old trite pop, marrying instead elements of the high and the low, the cultural leftfield and the arts underground, harsh rhythms, repetitive drones and minimalist arrangements with stories of low-life transgression: drug use and abuse, sexual deviance and perversion, the thrills and spills of a dangerous palace of delights. Beauty thrown overboard; the sublime displaced by the degraded; traditional morality skewed by a libertarian abuse of the brain and body and undermined by a dismissal of accepted sexual mores. An anti-aesthetic, the trash aesthetic indeed, was surely embodied in this parade of distortion, discordance and contortion: radio friendly this was not. The Velvet Underground rejected the simmering, summery optimism of psychedelia and immersed themselves in a dystopian downtown, evoking a scene through their words and music that was neurotic and hyperactive, numbed and anaesthetised[16] by turn, conjured, at least in part, by the toxic charge of speed and heroin.

But what of truth, that other critical pillar in the temple of the older aesthetic? Well, yes, there was a truth intrinsic to and reflective of the Velvets' own experiences, even if they were only dramatising individuals, scenes and events they knew, but it was a truth that spoke not of enlightenment and salvation and goodness. On the contrary, here was a world-view something akin to hell fire on God's Earth, an authentic depiction of a Boschian place perhaps, a land recognisable to Sade and Baudelaire maybe, but one that was utterly antipathetical to those notions of truth as the philosophers had historically understood and described the concept. Ugly was not the new beautiful but it may have been considered, from the perspective of the subversive art-makers, the new true. The Velvets and their wider family played out their baser instincts on a strange cusp between life and art, leisure and creativity, whether at the Factory or Max's Kansas City or the various cities where *Exploding Plastic Inevitable* went on tour, the West Coast and Mid-West included. Where dubious pleasures ended and artistic work commenced was never entirely clear.

The record drew on a number of important influences: Beat poetry's stream of consciousness; Cale's affinity with US avant-garde composers such as La Monte Young; the fraught dissonance of Ornette Coleman's free jazz; Bob Dylan's spoken vocal mannerism; the swing-free pulse of Tucker's drumming; and Reed's rejection of the conveyor belt pop of New York City's Brill Building,[17] a world that the singer-lyricist had briefly – and unsatisfyingly – engaged with before forming a Velvets prototype called the Primitives in 1964. Williams sees the band as 'a natural fit' with the artist who had mentored them. He explains:

> The Velvet Underground were the only possible group for Warhol. First came songs reflecting their interest in the sort of transgressive activities that characterised the activities at the Factory. Second came the use of repetition and the acceptance of what the straight world would see as boredom, ennui or *la noia*: an existential angst apparently stripped of meaning. The incessant hammered piano figures and unvarying rhythm beds, not so distantly related to the pulse of *In C*,[18] could be seen as analogues of the multiple versions of the

---

[16] Anaesthesia – 'insensibility', 'loss of feeling' (*Chambers English Dictionary* 1988) and, by extension, without an aesthetic.

[17] The crucible of much teen-aimed pop of the late 1950s and 1960s, the Brill Building was located at 1619 Broadway and provided a composing base for Carole King, Neil Sedaka and many others (Clarke 1990: 157).

[18] Terry Riley's composition, conceived in 1964, was a ground-breaking piece, 'a series of fifty-three short musical figures to be performed in sequence by a group of players –

same image (Elvis, Marilyn, car crashes, electric chairs, etc.) churned out by the silkscreen printers working at the Factory. (Williams 2009: 189)

Ultimately though, for all its rule-breaking posturing, and maybe even because of that, the group's debut LP, wrapped eye-catchingly if perversely, in its Warhol-designed Pop Art banana sleeve,[19] had scant commercial impact and faded from the very lower reaches of the *Billboard* album chart speedily. Yet it was heard by an important coterie of musicians, critics and scenesters on both sides of the Atlantic. The fact that its genesis was so closely entwined with the machinations of a world-renowned visual artist hardly hindered the attention it garnered from those in the know. However, the seeds sown in the humid haze of that Summer of Love would lie dormant only to prosper, Triffid-like, as a rampant, mutant crop some years on, throttling the more delicate flowers of the abandoned hippy garden.

The Velvet Underground had not just been set against traditional cultural values; they would also reject the protocols of the counterculture itself, that broad-based movement which sought to test society's bounds through energetic engagement, employing political activism and preaching a utopian ideology in a campaign of confrontation and resistance, street demonstration and soapbox rhetoric. In that sense, therefore, we might see Warhol's band as doubly transgressive – disrespecting both the conventional mainstream and the radical reaction to it as well. In doing so, they shaped another countercultural position, subterranean in spirit and outsider in character, one that would help sustain an enduring assault on social and artistic norms long after the hippies and their anti-Vietnam protests had been largely laid to rest. In fact, the band's subversive behaviour and aesthetic stance would have a much more profound and lasting effect on subsequent popular music practices, certainly those linked to notions of an alternative or independent ethos, than the peace and love inspired psychedelic sounds of the time.[20] The Velvets' style became the seedbed of wave after wave of rock that leant towards minimalism over decoration, raw noise over manicured manipulation,

---

any number of them, using any kind of instruments – who could choose their moment of entry and the number of times they repeated each motif before moving on' (Williams 2009: 171).

[19] The cover's stuck-on banana image could be peeled back in early editions, revealing beneath a flesh-coloured fruit with the obvious phallic connotations. Paul Morrissey: 'The cover was one of the many obscene suggestions put forward ... No one remembers who suggested it, but everyone agrees that it was dirty enough' (quoted in Thorgerson and Powell 1999: 149).

[20] The acid rock bands of San Francisco – the Grateful Dead and Jefferson Airplane, Quicksilver Messenger Service and Moby Grape – and the psychedelic acts launched in London – Syd Barrett's Pink Floyd, the Crazy World of Arthur Brown and even Jimi Hendrix – all distilled the spirit of the time but their legacy was limited after the 1960s drew to a close. Hoskyns claims that, by 1973, San Francisco was 'all but dead as a music town' (1997: 217). In England, Barrett's mental decline and departure from the group in 1967, the dissolution of Brown's band in 1969 and Hendrix's death in 1970 all symbolised the fleeting nature of the moment.

economy and brevity over ornate and laboured indulgence. In contrast, the more baroque manners of the LSD surge became the subject of only occasional and quaint re-visitations and revivals in the decades that followed.

By the time the Velvets moved on to their second studio set, *White Light/White Heat*, at the end of 1967 with Tom Wilson now fully installed in the producer's seat, the band had severed their links with Warhol not to say their imposing – and imposed – female vocalist Nico, who would go on to a solo career. The group's project to make jarring music that was at odds with the contemporary canon – both in style and content, texturally and textually – was not de-railed but the group's post-Factory output had little more mainstream acclaim than the original release itself enjoyed. It would take the band's final and disorderly dissolution in the early 1970s – by which time Reed and Cale had already departed – before the Velvet Underground's fractured sound and vision became the blueprint for a thousand Anglo-American acts who would trigger a string of crucial rock manifestations in the 1970s and 1980s: glam and glitter, punk and new wave, industrial, goth and grunge.

Chapter 3
Were British Subcultures the Beginning of Multitude?

Charles Mueller

Few aspects of popular culture have been more scrutinised by academics than the development of youth subcultures in the United Kingdom from the late 1960s through the 1980s, a fascination that can be attributed to a number of different factors. Scholars have been intrigued by the creative manipulation of signifiers employed by subcultures in crafting their styles, the way in which they inspire and release passion, and their ability to create relationships and provide camaraderie in the face of twentieth-century alienation. But perhaps most significantly, published research into subcultures by members of the Birmingham Centre for Contemporary Cultural Studies [BCCCS], Dick Hebdige, Angela McRobbie and others were a product of the backlash against criticisms of mass-culture by the Frankfurt School. As Paul Passavant explains, the intellectual environment after the 1960s tended to give consumers credit for being wiser, and recognised that people exercised a degree of autonomy in how they used and created meanings for the products that they purchased. As a result, the idea of the 'duped masses' being manipulated by industry began to wane in academic circles (Passavant 2004a: 1). Subculture theory was undoubtedly part of this trend.

The gamut of twentieth-century intellectual traditions was used to analyse subcultures: Marxism, semiotics, postmodernism, sociology, gender studies and the theories of Weber, Bourdieu, Gramsci and Barthes among others. This research led to many disparate interpretations. Some saw subcultures as the heirs to the revolutionary counterculture of the 1960s fighting a rearguard action in a lost battle for substantial socio-economic change and maintaining the spark of some of its ideas. Subcultures were also interpreted as a demoralised bohemianism, a noteworthy but pitiable expression of resistance during a time of conservativism when global capital penetrated all of society, and domination completely replaced value in work relations. Still others detected no counterculture component and came to view subcultures as recreational fan-cultures who represent only consumerism and excess. The importance of these studies to understand subcultures is undeniable, however, we should also be open to the possibility that subcultures can best be explained as part of the beginnings of a new social formation that transcends class, race, nationality and gender.

In two provocative books, *Empire* and *Multitude*, Michael Hardt and Antonio Negri present a social, economic and philosophical description and critique of globalisation and multinational capitalism that has formed the foundation of Western societies since the early 1970s. The texts substantiate their belief that this new world order is destructive and dehumanising and will gradually dissolve into a global socialism that recognises the value of every human life, and the interconnectedness of those lives on both the social and metaphysical level – what Benedictus de Spinoza referred to as immanence. These works, based in part on Negri's earlier volume *The Politics of Subversion*, describe counterculture activity that is much different from that of the past, a counterculture that is, at once, more subtle and gradual, but also more effective and far-reaching. The writings also represent an ambitious attempt to update the philosophies of Marx, which both Hardt and Negri feel are inadequate to critique a society that is no longer based on the Fordist factory labour model.

How Empire will give way to Multitude is a detail that Hardt and Negri leave open to conjecture, and they give us few signs to look for. But the idea that subcultures might be a part of the early stages of Multitude, and whether this best accounts for their social construction, modes of resistance and communication strategies (all of which involved music) is a question worthy of consideration. Negri himself opens the door for such an explanation when he remarks that earlier and inadequate attempts to reform Western societies politically were carried out to the rhythm of the Beatles (Negri 2005: 67), and that the tattoos, piercings and anti-establishment music of punk was a noteworthy gesture of resistance but did not go far enough (Laclau 2004: 28). What is most significant in this regard, however, is Negri's view that social outsiders, a group to which most members of subcultures certainly belonged, 'help others to recognise that we are all monsters – high school outcasts, sexual deviants, freaks, survivors of pathological families, and so forth. And more important these monsters begin to form new alternative networks of affection and social organisation' (Hardt and Negri 2004: 193).

This chapter begins by briefly summarising Hardt and Negri's arguments, and how previous research in subcultures and their music can be reconciled with a theory of Multitude. It then explores how British subcultures from the 1960s, 1970s and 1980s anticipated many of Hardt and Negri's ideas, and explains why reading subcultures in this way offers perhaps the most satisfactory explanation for their social construction, style and existence. The concluding paragraphs examine how subcultures provide insight into how popular culture, and music in particular, in the present and future could function as part of a new counterculture that undermines Empire and facilitates a state of Multitude.

Empire and Multitude: A Brief Overview

One must read *Empire* in its entirety to fully understand how Hardt and Negri perceive the current state of national and international politics. The book does, however, rearticulate common fears concerning globalisation already present in the public consciousness. They describe a system of abject, deregulated capitalism that has transformed the world into one gigantic factory, and brought about an all-consuming subsumption that pervades every aspect of human existence. The global imperative is the unfettered circulation of goods and services and the accumulation of profits. All other objectives and values must be marginalised or systematically eliminated. In discussing the actual size and scope of Empire, Paul Passavant states, 'in contrast to colonial empires of the past, this one has no boundaries', Empire's homogenising, disciplinary power is not just omnipresent, *it is life itself* – from the absorption of labour into the mechanisms of production, to messages in the mass media, Nike T-shirts, credit checks, surveillance videos, there is no 'outside' space to oppose it (Passavant 2004b: 100).

According to Hardt and Negri, production in Empire can be divided into the physical and affective spheres. Physical production is decentred, dispersed across the globe and often preoccupied with producing goods that are useless in terms of actual utility. Production and accumulation now frequently exist for their own sake rather than to fulfil needs. Affective labour is concerned with inciting desire, cultivating hospitality and creating culture, social relations, languages and information. In Empire affective labour has supplanted factory labour as the dominant and most influential type. Hardt and Negri are quick to point out that 'the hegemony of immaterial labour does not make all work rewarding, nor does it lessen the hierarchy and command in the workplace and the polarisation of the labour market' (2004: 111).

Although Hardt and Negri stress that Marxist criticism is still valid and traditional class struggles are still possible, they feel that new strategies are required to confront and dissolve Empire in ways that reflect new economic and social realities that are difficult to reconcile with Marx's ideas. Negri expands the definition of the proletariat to include all those who labour under the rule of capital and are subject to exploitation. He argues that even though the concept of real wages has lost its meaning in the postmodern era many people still live in abject poverty. For those who do have their biological needs met, the struggle is now about justice, security, time and quality of life (Negri 2005: 178). However, writing with Hardt, Negri believes that humankind's path to a richer, more rewarding life is through the emergence and development of Multitude, a new global socialist formation that guarantees its citizens a sustainable income, a basic education, freedom of information and unfettered communication. Multitude is not a mindless, unthinking mob but a global network of coordinated labour that leads to a state of absolute democracy and that transcends race and national boundaries to form an 'irreducible multiplicity' (Hardt and Negri 2004: 105). Hardt and Negri emphasise that perhaps the best way to understand their ideas is not to ask 'what is Multitude?' but 'what can Multitude become?' (ibid.: 105). They insist that Multitude is not a political call to action such as 'workers of the world unite' but a name given to describe what has been happening, and what will continue to happen in the social and political spheres (ibid.: 220).

The formation of Multitude is distinct from other forms of countercultural activity in that the transformation will occur gradually rather than through mass protest, although physical conflict can play a role in its development. Multitude is essentially a realisation of Gramsci's ideal of the working classes articulating a plurality of struggles (Haslett 2000: 273). Hardt and Negri recognise that since the 1960s the instability of the individual subject has made collective action difficult, and that planned socialism is perhaps not realistically possible in an advanced capitalist system. Hardt and Negri feel that alienation and anomie exists in such a chronic state that only the cumulative weight of communication and media technologies and the fruits of affective labour in their totality will help to rectify the radical deficit of empathy and connectedness that exists.

Multitude and Immanence

Hardt and Negri's theory of Multitude has a metaphysical basis in Spinoza's idea of immanence, the life force inherent in all beings that is both singular and part of a universal whole. They believe that a democracy based on immanence would be much stronger than any constitution offered by the state, and would ideally function in a manner similar to Spinoza's concept of the human body; a 'multitude of multitudes' comprising individual natures that act in concert without any hierarchy (2004: 190). Multitude is therefore not a representable totality but a set of singularities. Individuals and groups create Multitude through a 'plurality of actions that do not need to be articulated between themselves' (Laclau 2004: 26). Hardt and Negri's reading of Spinoza is selective, but it is not difficult to comprehend how Spinoza's writings could be used as a counterpoint to Empire. For example, based on Spinoza's belief that the best governance comes about when there is a balance of political forces, and that citizens have more rights when they act together than when they act alone, Hardt and Negri conclude that global capitalism has given people a misguided confidence in individualism that leaves them vulnerable. In Hardt/Negri's view global capital undermines the freedoms that Spinoza believed the state should guarantee, by circumventing the laws and will of the populace, and by destroying their intellect (the place where Spinoza believed immanence resided) through propaganda and the control of information.

In addition to Hardt/Negri's faith in the unifying power of immanence, Multitude's theoretical foundation has an additional component: Foucault's concept of biopolitics, the process of harnessing human potential as a group. The biopolitics of Multitude is a 'power of the flesh', a force of boundless potential. They describe an elemental power that continuously expands social being, producing in excess of every traditional political and economic measure of value (Hardt and Negri 2004: 192). This biopower is made possible through the types of social relations produced by global capitalism, the predominance of immaterial affective labour, and by the seamless interconnectedness of labour and life. Not only do these relationships create biopower in and of themselves, affective labour also creates a distinct kind of antagonism that adds fuel to the fire:

The wealth it [immaterial labour] creates is taken away and this is a source of its antagonism. Yet it retains its capacity to produce wealth and this is its power. In this combination of antagonism and power lies the making of revolutionary subjectivity. (ibid.: 153)

Multitude and the Study of Subcultures

Hardt and Negri explain the importance of the media and affective labour in creating new relationships that will facilitate the formation of Multitude. They do not explain what effect the culture created by these groups might have, or ways that these groups might effectively spread messages that undermine Empire. This presents an obstacle to understanding previous scholarship on subcultures in the context of Hardt and Negri's theories as many of these earlier studies are largely debates over whether subcultures (and the music and style associated with them) represent rebellion or consumerism. Presumably some critical discourse would be needed within these new networks; their mere formation would not be enough to promote change. They would need to acknowledge and bear witness to Empire's dehumanising effects. They would need to be driven by subversiveness, which Negri defines as 'the radical nature of truth' (Negri 2005: 59). Truths such as equality, freedom and the promotion of life would need to be kept within the public consciousness in order to counter Empire's deceptive messages.

If one accepts Negri's definition of subversion as 'the radical nature of truth' then the Marx-influenced theorists who viewed subcultures as a type of counterculture must necessarily be considered the forerunners to a reading of subcultures based on *Multitude*. For example, Hebdige's analysis recognised, for example, that mods and punks were not operating outside of Empire's system of alienation but were a part of it. The point is echoed by Hardt and Negri who write: 'When the flesh of Multitude is imprisoned and transformed into the body of global capital it finds itself both within and against the powers of capitalist globalisation' (2004: 101), a state of being that can be seen in both the music and style of subcultures. Marx-influenced readings of the art created by subcultures are not unlike Terry Eagleton's interpretations of the popular fiction produced by writers like Charles Dickens whose stories simultaneously express admiration and revulsion, amusement and fear of bourgeoisie capitalism, a conflict that gave his writing a tension that should be considered a strength rather than a weakness (Eagleton 1976: 35). The creativity of subcultures, and much of their music in particular, disrupted capital's ability to gain a monopoly over the affections and mode of thinking (affective labour) of individuals, an important step toward Multitude, for as Hardt and Negri point out, the commodities of affective labour largely constitute social life itself.

Hebdige understood the continuing importance of class in social relations. He indirectly foreshadowed Negri's position that outcasts and the poor are no longer politically inert, and that young people are now in a position to show workers the way forward by forming alternative networks and evacuating sites of power (Negri 2005: 48). Like Hardt and Negri, Hebdige was aware that alternative media such as indie music labels, pirate radio and fanzines were not only important in forming new relationships that challenged class stereotypes propagated by conventional media, but also represented an attempt at transforming the means of production with the limited resources that were available. Hebdige understood that even if subculture's revolt through style and music did perhaps reflect Hardt/Negri's point that 'the wretched of the earth want to go to Disneyland and not the barricades' (Bull 2004: 225) (echoing Baudrillard's sentiments that people favour signs more than revolution), resistance through sign-systems is still a gesture worth making, for if society is governed by sign values as much as economic production, then any attempts to express refusal or transform the public consciousness must take place, to a large degree, on the semiotic level.

Many subsequent theorists have found fault with Marxist readings, but their arguments do not necessarily undermine the idea of subcultures as an early sign of Multitude. For example, Dave Laing (1985), and Sarah Thornton (1996), call into question the idea of British subcultures as an authentic form of class-protest because they believe that participants were not truly operating from a Marxist mindset advocating the total overthrow of capitalism, and that the whole idea of an adversarial binary distinction between subcultures and 'mainstream' society is fictitious, and was projected onto, for example, punk and goth by the Marx-inspired theorists themselves. In *Empire*, however, Hardt/Negri do postulate that a 'mainstream' ideology and culture did exist, and continues to exist. It is a value system based on a misguided faith in individualism, and a celebration of globalised laissez-faire. The resulting effects of this ideology of Empire create conditions that can generate opposition, an opposition that was reflected in the fashion, literature and music created by subcultures to varying degrees. Art, however, does more than just reflect the concerns and ideologies of its time, it also provides a glimpse into what it feels like to live in those conditions, something that the music of subcultures arguably accomplished to a greater degree than most varieties of popular music. Music played a part in the postmodern and radical bohemian strategy of total refusal, total negativity (which Žižek reminds us is really all that the poor have with which to protest save violence) and the cultivation of extreme otherness that can be seen in most British subcultures (Žižek 2004: 260). The affective content of the style and music of subcultures pointed to needs that the larger code of capitalism did not allow for, and this holds significance for the development of Multitude. In a passage reminiscent of Hardt and Negri's thinking, Jean Baudrillard writes:

> Nonetheless this emergence of needs, however formal and subdued, is never without danger for the social order – as is the liberation of any productive forces. Apart from being the dimension of exploitation, it is also the origin of the most violent social contradictions, of class struggle. Who can say what historical contradictions the emergence and exploitation of this new productive force – that of needs – holds in store for us? (Baudrillard 1981: 84)

Multitude is Hardt and Negri's answer to Baudrillard's rhetorical question. The fact that not every subculture participant was a disciple of Marx did not render their concerns invalid or prove that the style and music of subcultures contained no countercultural element as Hardt and Negri emphasise that it is the collective weight of mass-dissatisfaction with Empire's conditions that will result in Multitude's evolution, not a Marxist ideology agreed upon by the populace.

Another reason why scholars such as Laing and Thornton are dismissive of aims to assign proletarian significance to the music and fashion of punk is because it was, in part, created by a few artists, promoters and producers, and spread through media exposure. In Hardt and Negri's theory, however, the influence of the media on subcultures does not negate their authenticity. If any social movement helps promote an awareness of immanence, it is of value regardless of how it is spread or created. Further, the affective content of commodities was shaped by subcultures and signified more than a celebration of capitalism. Music was particularly life-affirming in that the lyrics, timbres and rhythms inspired emotional connections that cannot be quantified in terms of value and utility. In this way music in subcultures represented an attempt to bring back a measure of the symbolic in a society made indifferent by Empire's domineering ideology of utility, value and accumulation. The ability of the affective content of music to overshadow its status as a commodity makes it invaluable to the development of Multitude. As British subcultures demonstrated, music was a primary means of achieving their alternative networks of affective and social organisation. British subcultures can be interpreted as an attempt at breaking the cycle of alienation and false individualism that helps to sustain Empire. The music associated with subcultures bore witness to Empire's dehumanising effects, and helped to radicalise the nature of truth. It served as an affective and important counterpoint to the propaganda of Empire.

The belief of Ian Chambers (1985) and Bo Reimer (1995) that subcultures represented an attempt to escape socio-economic class rather than represent or redefine it is likewise not antithetical to a Marxist interpretation as people typically do not try to escape, transcend or cover up that which is positive and pleasing. In this way their reading further illustrates the negative effects of Empire.

Much of the scholarship on subcultures produced after Hebdige has abandoned a Marxist or post-Marxist approach in favour of sociology, gender studies and examining subcultures in an international context, all of which are vital to understanding the subculture phenomenon. However, this tendency to downplay or reject the influence of economic factors on the development of subcultures, drawing attention away from Empire's devastating effects, could be seen as an example of what Hardt and Negri are referring to when they observe that 'such lack of focus, and such intense discussion and debate over this fragmentation is also symptomatic of the current weakness and impotence of the left since the 1970s' (2004: 219).[1]

---

[1] Although Negri has been unsympathetic to much postmodern theory, I have seen no evidence that neither he nor Michael Hardt question the value of non-Marxist criticism.

Subcultures and the Beginnings of Multitude

The distinct type of socialism outlined in *Multitude* was anticipated by British subcultures in a number of ways. First, Hardt/Negri make it clear that Multitude is a class concept and that classes are defined through their lines of collective struggle (2004: 104). Subcultures were one of a multitude of different struggles against the most destructive and alienating acts of capital. Hardt/Negri assert that 'the common currency that runs through so many struggles today – at local, regional, and global levels – is the desire for democracy' (ibid.: xvi). Much of the anger, fear and fetishisation of power that comes through in the music of subcultures sprang from people feeling that they had no control over their lives. Second, one must consider the relationships produced through the affective labour (and music in particular) of subcultures. The music and style produced by British subcultures provides strong support for Hardt and Negri's position that 'Despite the myriad mechanisms of hierarchy and subordination, the poor constantly express an enormous power of life and production'. 'The closer we look at the lives and activity of the poor we see how enormously creative and powerful they are, and indeed, we will argue, how much they are part of the circuits of social and biopolitical production' (ibid.: 129).

Subcultures were formed in an environment that included a massive shift in the focus of Britain's economy from industrial to affective labour, the relocation of jobs to markets overseas, the huge influx of immigrants from developing countries to England, and unprecedented job insecurity for native workers – all hallmarks of Empire. England had adopted numerous, modest socialist reforms by the time that subcultures were developing. But the pessimism, nihilism, preoccupation with the macabre, and the angst portrayed and/or expressed, both literally and metaphorically, in the fashion, art and especially the music associated with the majority of subcultures illustrates Negri's point that under Empire socialism is deliberately ineffectual as it is designed to serve the needs of global capitalism and not to help the needy or strengthen social bonds as it should.

Subcultural style also supports Hardt/Negri's belief that, in Empire and Multitude, all forms of labour power are involved in the process of social production. They write: 'to the extent that social production is increasingly defined by immaterial labour such as cooperation and the construction of social relationships and networks of communication, the activity of all in society, including the poor become more and more directly productive' (ibid.: 131). Subcultures gave the poor, unemployed and underemployed a particularly bold and dramatic voice and a means in which to take part in social production. As an example one need only consider the relationships born out of the remarkable creativity and imagination of the music associated with subcultures: the virtuosity and social commentary displayed in so much British heavy metal; the energy

---

They do suggest, however, that the importance of immanence and the problems of Empire often get lost in the vertigo of competing academic theories.

perception, wit and humour of punk; and the imaginative way that goth artists attacked Empire through feminism, camp, parody and the celebration of macabre culture. A particularly valuable type of social production created by the colourful, flamboyant and sometimes grotesque styles associated with subcultures was the way in which they kept the concerns of the lower classes within the public eye. A point raised repeatedly by Baudrillard is that in postmodernity the poor simply vanish because they are not part of the media culture (2002: 128–9). One can assert that even the most reactionary or anti-social of subcultures played a part in preventing the disappearance of the poor.

Another major criticism of Marxist interpretations of subcultures is based on the premise that subcultures were only concerned with consumerism, play and providing recreational space. It is suggested that the accusations of commodity fetishism against subcultures and countercultures have always been overblown (poor youths had little disposable income) and the recreational aspects of subculture participation is best understood in terms of Multitude. In Negri's analysis, for example, extensive destitution is a tool used by capital to keep individuals isolated since 'poverty leads to economic blackmail, the destruction of the imagination, the reawakening of atavistic fears, and encourages monstrous piety' (Negri 2005: 96). Subcultures, their style, music and values, can be seen as a way to combat economic blackmail, ward off atavistic fears and as an affirmation of the power of the imagination. Instead of seeing subcultures as hedonistic, one should recognise the limited ways in which people from the lowest classes could spend their free time, and the limitations of their life experiences. Striking a blow against the celebration of piety is also a blow against the life-draining ideology behind Empire. Negri believes that the relationship between capital and labour is not dialectical but antagonistic, no longer exclusively a battle for real wages. The struggle is now for justice, time and quality of life, as capital continuously makes new demands on the workforce (ibid.: 178). In these terms, free-time and the sign-value of subcultural style are both subversive and life-affirming symbols.[2]

The loose unity of subcultures, and the sense of individuality as well as camaraderie that they inspired among their members is similar to the ideal of unity in Multitude; 'singularities that act in common' but are not swallowed up by the whole (Hardt and Negri 2004: 105). Hardt/Negri agree with postmodern theorists that identities are subject to fracture and multiplicity but they do not feel that this stands in the way of creating social bonds.[3] In fact, hybrid identities, though not

---

[2] As an example see Hebdige's explanation of the lifestyle and subversiveness of the mod subculture (1979: 63). Also see Hardt and Negri's discussion of the importance of abandoning sites of power throughout *Empire* and *Multitude*.

[3] Scholars concerned with race and gender have expressed scepticism about hybrid identities believing that hybrid will inevitably mean 'white male'. Hardt and Negri do not dwell on how women and minorities might experience Multitude differently just as they do subcultures. Hardt/Negri state that they are focusing on class and labour in their writings as these areas have been neglected in recent years. They applaud racial and feminist activism

revolutionary in and of themselves, are a precondition for it (Bull 2004: 229). Even before they brought Spinoza's concept of immanence to bear on the idea of unity in the postmodern, Negri stated earlier that 'production, consumption, knowledge, the desire for transformation and equality do not produce equivalent and interchangeable individuals' (Negri 2005: 207), and in this way subcultures represent in microcosm an early manifestation of biopower. The more fragmented and mobile the postmodern subjects are, the more abstract their productive capabilities and the greater their potential for cooperation rather than functioning as interchangeable cogs in the machine of capital.

The theory of a Multitude made up of groups of singularities acting in common was anticipated not just by single subcultures but by all the British subcultures combined. Hardt/Negri explain:

> The multitude is composed of innumerable internal differences that can never be reduced to a single identity – different cultures, races, ethnicities, genders, and sexual orientations; different forms of labour; different ways of living; different views of the world; and different desires. The multitude is a multiplicity of all these differences. (2004: xiv)

They repeatedly stress that in Multitude social differences will remain different, but there will be a common that is shared, a common that is 'not so much discovered as it is produced'. Subcultures voiced opposition to powers and circumstances that can consistently be traced back to Empire, or were a symptom of a social problem that was rooted in the negative consequences of Empire.[4] This was their common. For example, skinheads attacked the subsumption of British traditions and daily life by global capital (Hebdige 1979: 55–8). Goth criticised Empire's origins in the masculine logic of production (Mueller 2008: 90–120), and punks rebelled against symbols of privilege, pillars of society and phony optimism through their abrasive rhetoric, fashion and music (Hebdige 1979, Laing 1985). Many of the same themes appear again and again in the music and symbolic language of punk, goth, mod and heavy metal rockers, their diverse styles reflecting many of the same social concerns.[5] One of the most common targets of subcultures

---

and make it clear that their vision of Multitude contains no racial or gender hierarchies. See Hardt and Negri (2004: 273–4, and especially 224).

[4] Although some may see nihilistic, or far-right subcultures as antithetical to Multitude it can be argued that these groups all stem from what Terry Eagleton refers to as 'a lack of nourishment'; the current social environment of 'sterile ideologies' that are 'unable to make significant connections or offer adequate discourses' (1976: 58). According to Hardt/Negri, Empire is the crux of the problem so these subcultures are not as divorced from the idea of Multitude as it may seem.

[5] Once again, it is not being suggested that all subcultures were driven by identical concerns, only that there was a considerable overlapping of the same concerns among different subcultures.

was nuclear proliferation, which Negri identifies as one of Empire's most potent symbols declaring that 'nuclear terror appears as fixed accumulation, as fixed social capital'. He writes:

> If the brutality of social relationships is at a maximum, terror must be extreme. In material terms, capital's drive toward terror is orchestrated by the practice and ideology of nuclear power. It is important, even if banal, at this stage, to emphasise that the drive toward terror is not a result of some demonical quality of capital. Rather the origin and mechanism of such a tendency find their origin in the dialectic of capital's expropriation of productive cooperation from which they derive their degree of intensity. (Negri 2005: 123)

In other words, capital expropriates labour and alienates the worker but imposes a social unity by forcing them to be a part of state violence of which the bomb is the ultimate symbol. The music of heavy metal rockers disavowed nuclear weapons and their enforced social relations most forcefully in songs such as 'Electric Funeral' by Black Sabbath, and 'Revelation (Mother Earth)' by Ozzy Osbourne.[6] Anti-nuclear songs, however, can be found in the punk musical cannon with tracks like the Ramones' 'Planet Earth 1988' and 'Stop the World' by the Clash, as well as in the music from the goth movement with songs such as 'Black Planet' by the Sisters of Mercy and 'Blow the House Down' by Siouxsie and the Banshees.

Although the participants of England's youth cultures probably did not see themselves as global citizens to the degree that Hardt/Negri envision for a future Multitude, they did resist attempts by global capital to define and appropriate nationalism and patriotism. Under Empire the loyalty of the poor and working classes to the nation-state gradually fades as social programmes are cut, workplace safety and environmental standards are weakened, and the government places the desires of global capital ahead of the needs of the population. The loss of industrial labour as the primary site for friendships and social bonding also exacerbates this decline in feelings of national identity (Sassen 2004: 183).

Subcultures flourished at a time when British nationalism was enjoying a resurgence with the Falklands War, the celebration of the royal wedding, and the rise of Thatcher's conservativism. Subcultures helped to reclaim attempts by the political right to homogenise and define British national identity. Their strategies included turning signifiers of Britishness against their original meanings[7] or by making use of culture with subversive connotations in British society. For example, goth appropriated elements of English gothic literature and signifiers from classic horror films, which have traditionally carried degenerate connotations in British society (Mueller 2008: 69–90). Subcultures not only seemed to confound

---

[6] Although it should be self-evident the music being discussed here is British heavy metal and not the American style of glam metal which was quite distinct from its European counterpart.

[7] See Hebdige's remarks on punk and the Teddy Boys throughout *Subculture*.

expectations about people's position in the social structure, they also undermined definitions of patriotism that benefited Empire over the people of Britain.

The subcultures of the 1970s and 1980s, along with the fashion, music, art and writing that gave them a sense of identity, serve as an early example of Hardt/Negri's vision of the potential of affective labour, and their observation that the production of capital *is* the production of social life in the postmodern era. When they speak of commodities such as music inciting passion, excitement and a thirst for life, Hardt/Negri do not see commodity fetishism in the way that a traditional Marxist critic would, or see people being dominated and ruled by objects the way Baudrillard did. Instead they equate this passion with liberation for two reasons: first, this passion creates relationships that invite unity that in turn creates the biopower necessary for Multitude; second, this passion and these relationships have important semiotic value symbolising social wealth and the inability of capital to subsume, capture and control all aspects of the human experience (Hardt and Negri 2004: 147). Under Empire it is a subversive act to suggest that there is a life beyond the legal, national or financial (Passavant 2004a: 9).

Of course Hardt and Negri are speaking of the present in their writings and of the typical citizen's relationship with the products of affective labour, however, during the time when subcultures flourished in Britain their commodities inspired passion due to their subversive sign-value, so at the time some commodities had more liberating potential than others. The passion felt by, for example, mods, goths, punks and so on for their style and music was also inspired by their working-class background, and because, as Hebdige points out, it helped them say the right things at the right time and signify a sensibility (Hebdige 1979: 122).

Affects, Hardt and Negri remind us, refer equally to the body and mind. Affects such as joy and sadness reveal the present state of life in the entire organism, expressing a certain state of the body along with a certain mode of thinking (2004: 108). Because of this affective ability the music, fashion and artwork produced by subcultures was more than just an outward show of refusal through the manipulation of signifiers; the sentiment of refusal permeated the individual's entire being. This explains why the art and style of each distinct subculture was dominated by one overriding affect.

Subcultures further illustrate the potential power of affective labour to create social unity by the way these movements energised and influenced one another. Hebdige documents how most of Britain's subcultures were linked in some way to the culture of the black population, which was itself an amalgamation of carefully selected elements from their Jamaican heritage (1979: 48–9). The hardships endured by one ethnic group inspired a style that was given a fresh context and new layers of meaning by another group.[8] What is most significant for the concept of Multitude, however, is that subcultures produced a relationship with

---

[8] Hardt and Negri believe that the ascendancy of Empire is the root cause of most racial problems since the 1960s because Empire has everything to gain by dividing the populace through racism. They feel that race is determined politically more by collective

one another. Hardt/Negri observe that the creation of new languages (of which subcultural styles and music are an example) is one of the primary products of immaterial labour that produces Multitude (2004: 108). At this point subcultures were united by sharing signs of refusal, but in Hardt/Negri's theory the element of refusal would not necessarily have to be present; the interaction of languages and groups is what is most important. The manifestation of biopower that subcultures represent demands that their political significance be reconsidered.

Subcultures and the Future of Multitude

The individuals who participated in subcultures were only showing the signs of exploitation, and fear of the future. They probably did not imagine the type of globalised socialism, and the dismantling of current power structures as envisioned by Hardt and Negri. Subcultures were active at a time when hybrid identities were less common, when the difference between economic production and cultural production were more distinct. This threw the styles of ted, mod, goth and punk into greater contrast with the rest of society. However, most of the social issues that preoccupied subcultures were the result of changes and conditions brought on by the globalisation of capital-Empire. The style and music of the various social movements frequently illustrated how interconnected personal, gender and racial problems were, and traceable back to problems in economic production. They demonstrated the importance of subverting and appropriating signifiers that govern society in order to express resistance in late capitalism. Considering that the connection between signs and referents is still strong enough to facilitate domination in Empire, then rebellion through style is not insignificant. Although scholarship on subcultures has sometimes made too much of the participants as consumers, they did bring a passion to their art, fashion and music that foregrounded and celebrated its affective content while downplaying its status as commodities. The emotional intensity of the art kept important ideas in the consciousness of the participants and brought them together in a way that demonstrated Hardt and Negri's point that 'our innovative and creative capacities are always greater than the productivity of capital' (2004: 146). In that sense the passion of subcultures was just as important as their expressions of refusal in their foreshadowing of Multitude.

The music associated with British subcultures does point to another way that music could help bring Multitude into being. The way that goth bands, for example, drew inspiration from horror films and gothic literature shows how popular music might present new possibilities for collaboration between creative artists in order to signify immanence and to create more powerful and critical products of affective labour. In Multitude what artists signify to their audience must

---

struggle rather than by skin colour. This provided another point of commonality between black and white subcultures in Britain (2004: 104).

strike a balance between producer and transformer. Ideally the romantic notion of the artist as an inspired creator would need to be maintained in some fashion to remind people of their 'divine spark', their unique individuality that contributes to the whole rather than being swallowed up by it. Celebrating the individuality of creative artists of all types would need to be considerably different from the way that the romantic view of the artist has been used by capital to promote an individualism that alienates and weakens the whole. At the same time the Marxist view of the artist as a transformer of ready-made materials into values, myths, forms and ideologies (Eagleton 1976: 69) must also be foregrounded in the music and image of recording artists to signify Multitude and the interconnectedness of different forms of labour.

The music must be created in close collaboration 'with the past and present thought of others' so that each new idea, sound or image will invite new collaborations. Hardt and Negri write:

> the production of languages, finally, both natural languages and artificial languages [music as well] and various kinds of code is always collaborative and always creates new means of collaboration. In all these ways, in immaterial production the creation of cooperation has become internal to labour and thus external to capital. (2004: 147)

If subcultures can be considered part of the first embryonic step toward Multitude then it is clear that popular music and style cultures can continue to play a role in the transformation of consciousness necessary for this new formation to take place. Joel Bakan believes that musicians and subcultures need to become more radical, and express refusal based on a deeper and more informed analysis of social problems:

> The question to ask however is not what can popular music or popular culture do to facilitate social change, but what can we do to help popular music and popular culture bring about a more developed social conscience. (Personal telephone conversation 23 June 2010)

During the 1970s and 1980s British subcultures often expressed hostility against each other because they allowed themselves to be divided by issues of sexuality, race and lifestyle, largely ignoring how they were united by the same set of concerns for their future and for British society. The various subcultures in Britain did not, as Hardt and Negri might say, fully appreciate the common that they produced and its productive potential. Future subcultures and social movements cannot make this mistake. Expressing an awareness of immanence must remain their main focus.

PART II
Utopias, Dystopias and the Apocalyptic

Chapter 4
The Rock Counterculture from Modernist Utopianism to the Development of an Alternative Music Scene

Christophe Den Tandt

Overcoming Rock's Resistance to Academic Enquiry

Academic rock criticism struggles with a perennial paradox: it targets an object that draws its legitimacy from rebellion and therefore resists academic enquiry (Glass 1992: 94–8). In *The Blackboard Jungle*, a film that served as promotional vehicle for Bill Haley and the Comets' 'Rock around the Clock', rebellious students shatter the jazz records of a teacher who misguidedly seeks to connect to their popular-music interests. Similarly, rock has generated anti-school anthems – Chuck Berry's 'School Days' or Alice Cooper's 'School's Out'. Such songs pre-emptively disqualify observers who claim to view the music with critical distance or who avail themselves of a theoretical apparatus external to it. Nevertheless, academic studies devoted to rock have developed since the 1970s, particularly in the Anglo-American world. Yet, compared for instance to film studies, their methodology remains tentative: there is no consensus about the aesthetic function of the practices they study or about the latter's social role. Artistic excellence is still an object of internal debate within rock itself. For a limited period of rock's history – the late 1960s and early 1970s – musicians made technical and aesthetic achievement a requirement for rock musicianship, thereby laying the foundations of a culture of professionalism. Still, numerous fans, musicians or academic pundits privilege the opposite option: they single out non-art and raw entertainment as the proper terrain for rock music (Shumway 1990: 122). It is therefore difficult to elaborate a critical discourse about rock whose legitimacy is anchored in the analysis of musical codes and techniques of artistic production.

Similar uncertainties affect the music's social impact. While rock's definition always includes the display of rebellious behaviour and values, the nature and social function of the rebellion thus implied are not easily circumscribed. Rock has admittedly been a catalyst for political and social movements with an emancipatory momentum: anti-Vietnam war protests, the construction of new gender roles or the struggle against segregation (Pratt 1990: 1–3). Counterexamples abound, however. Feminist critics have pointed out that emancipation in rock music mostly fulfils the aspirations of a predominantly masculine audience. Angela McRobbie and Jenny Garber point out that rock marks itself out from pop according to a gender barrier. Rock fans and critics predictably favour the masculine pole of this binary – rock itself (1976: 220). Simon Reynolds and Joy Press underscore the misogyny of rock lyrics (1995: xiii–xvii), a phenomenon also expressed, as Sheila Whiteley indicates, in the phallic display of instruments (1997a: xix). Beyond sexism, rock has also served the needs of extreme-right-wing cultures (the racist component of Oi! and of the skinhead subculture). As Michael Moore points out in *Fahrenheit 9/11*, it can act as a soundtrack for military operations (2004). Above all, rebelliousness itself might only be a smokescreen concealing a tacit assent to capitalist mass culture. The music would in this case be a mere propaganda channel. It would deserve the stringent criticism Theodor Adorno, the leading figure of the Frankfurt School, targeted at the musical idiom he derogatorily called 'jazz' (1994: 206).

From the perspective of cultural studies, the semantic instability of rock rebellion is symptomatic of the music's wavering between several modes of social insertion. Rock hesitates between three planes of social practice: its capacity to act as the voice of counterculture, as the fabric of subcultures and, less glamorously, as purveyor of standardised mass entertainment. Counterculture, Andy Bennett writes in the present volume, promises 'a fully-fledged alternative lifestyle' leading for instance to the creation of a 'physical, alternative community' (Introduction 'Reappraising "Counterculture"': 18). Subcultures have a more limited scope: their social base is narrower and their practices, however oppositional, cannot define an alternative to dominant society able to confederate substantial segments of any given population. Ironically, the limited ambitions of subcultures have made them more compatible with academic study than counterculture. Researchers who offer a sympathetic account of counterculture must endorse a political programme whose legitimacy lies beyond the supposedly neutral scope of the social sciences: the sweeping change promised by counterculture is more the object of a teleological philosophy of history than of sociology. Worse, since the hippie movement serves as anchorage point for the rock counterculture, researchers in this field act as covert champions of a revolutionary agenda that, contrary to their own methodology, disregards rational argumentation. Subcultures, on the contrary, are manageable research objects in so far as they can be documented without subscribing to the group's own aims. Still, rock academics – in particular the neo-Marxists who pioneered the scholarly study of this mode of expression (Simon Frith, Dick Hebdige, Angela McRobbie, Lawrence Grossberg, Andrew Goodwin) – seldom settle for this distanced approach. They entertain the hope that rock might play a role similar to proletarian struggles: it should rank among the modes of expression carrying out, to paraphrase the title of a famous collection of the Birmingham Centre for Contemporary Cultural Studies 'resistance through rituals' (Hall and Jefferson 1976). In other words, academics' relation to rock is informed by the implicit hope that, 'depending on local socio-economic, cultural and demographic circumstances', the music may turn out to be countercultural after all (Bennett, 'Reappraising': 22). Beyond the plurality of subcultures, there is the lingering hope that counterculture might coalesce again, endowed with the momentum attributed to previous revolutionary movements.

The present argument re-examines these issues along two interrelated axes. On the one hand, it situates rock rebellion in the framework of twentieth-century modernist artistic protest and on the other it specifies how rock's countercultural aspirations have in spite of their ostensibly ephemeral nature durably reconfigured the social field. Against the temptation of rock musicians, fans and reviewers to confer to music an aura of exceptionalism defying academic rationality, it is indeed useful to point out that comparable forms of cultural rebellion have been attempted earlier, both within popular culture and outside of it. Secondly, one must determine how even practices that disown any social and aesthetic appropriation prove meaningful. Rock's anti-theoretical gestures, however resilient, cannot help generating socially significant behaviours and codes. The topic of the present chapter is therefore the swing of the pendulum between the rejection of any mode of social inscription and the construction of a field of alternative practices: one must think out how rock's centrifugal gestures leave their mark in the cultural field in the form of musical pieces, but also practices, territories and institutions. The corpus on which these reflections are based stretches from the 1950s to the 1980s, comprising early rock and roll, classic rock (psychedelic and post-psychedelic music), punk and post-punk.

The Transfiguration of Everyday Life: Rock's Utopian Discourse

In order to carry out the theoretical agenda outlined above, I anchor counterculture in the concept of utopia as it was elaborated by (post)modernist theoreticians Fredric Jameson and Ihab Hassan. Utopia, in this logic, refers to the desire to transfigure everyday life. The present argument builds on the premise that, in the field of rock, the refusal of co-optation (social, academic, even artistic) gives voice to the resolution to transcend alienation, thereby opening a perspective that is utopian in the literal meaning of the term. Several academic critics have given heed to this aspect of rock music (Grossberg 1983–84: 111; Pratt 1990: 21). Even 1950s rock and roll nurtures ambitions to go beyond mere entertainment: the affective intensity surrounding this music suggests that it carries the hope to access a field incommensurable with past or present. Chuck Berry claims that rock and roll must 'deliver [us] from the days of old', and lead us to the 'promised land' (1957, 1964); Eddie Cochran states that the music opens the gates of a 'teenage heaven' (Cochran and Capehart 1959). This teenage mythology prefigures the central utopian moment of rock's counterculture – late-1960s psychedelic music. At that time, the hope to transcend everydayness was voiced through images depicting the end of alienation as a magical metamorphosis – a 'secular illumination', to take up the term used by Walter Benjamin in reference to surrealism (Benjamin 1986: 179). In George Dunning's *Yellow Submarine* cartoon (1968), the Beatles' beneficial influence restores the colourful scenery of Pepperland, a country that had lost all pigment when it came under the sway of a caste of music-hating dictators – the 'Blue Meanies'. Joni Mitchell's 'Woodstock' utters the hope that the collective fervour of the famous festival might turn US Vietnam War bombers into 'butterflies' (1970). In 'Purple Haze', Jimi Hendrix claims he can 'kiss the sky' in a mist of dreams and hallucinogenic drugs (1967). Like many of his contemporaries, Hendrix implements thereby the programme previously sketched out by the members of the Beat movement (Allen Ginsberg, William Burroughs) or by Aldous Huxley, Timothy Leary and Carlos Castañeda – authors who looked to drugs for a shamanistic transcendence of everyday experience. Beyond their glowing accents, these emancipatory visions are apocalyptic in the religious meaning of the term: achieving revelation requires the annihilation of the present. Rock's utopian discourse therefore develops a darker side, more obsessed with destruction than with the hopeful outcome of transfiguration. In the late 1960s, the latter accents were sounded in the music of the Doors and the Velvet Underground (see Warner in this volume), and worked their way into late-1970s punk and post-punk. Punk's nihilism as well as post-punk's apparent surrender to alienation give voice to utopian desire by some sort of mirror logic: they gesture toward the possibility of a non-alienated existence by highlighting the latter's absence from the actual state of society (Reynolds 2005: xxi).

Ironically, if utopian desire legitimises fans' and musicians' distrust of all co-optation, it also enables academic researchers to position the rock counterculture within twentieth-century art: utopian aspirations have their own ascertainable history. Taking this historical narrative into account makes it possible to analyse rock in a broader frame than the customary US or British context. In so far as it seeks to transfigure everydayness, rock appropriates a key component of the aesthetic programme of modernism (Bradbury and Macfarlane 1976: 13). Egyptian-American theorist Ihab Hassan – who was with Leslie Fiedler, Charles Jencks and Daniel Bell one of the first to elaborate the concept of postmodernism – ranks among the definitional features of early-twentieth-century art the desire to free oneself from a round of life perceived as inauthentic (Hassan 1987: 35–7). Hassan's reading grid is representative of the analysis of modernism developed by Anglo–American critics: as far as artistic and literary production goes, some of the most influential figures of Anglo-American modernism – W.B. Yeats, T.S. Eliot, Ezra Pound, Wyndham Lewis – were innovative in the field of aesthetics yet fiercely critical of the social reality of modernity – a stance that drove them paradoxically toward political conservatism. As they lived in a world subjected to what Marxist theoreticians such as Georg Lukács and Theodor Adorno call reification and alienation, high modernist artists tried to reach for aesthetic absolutes outside of everyday life – in fields such as the unconscious, archaic civilisations and geometrical abstraction (Hassan 1987: 36; Lukács 1971: 110; Adorno 1984: 39). Hassan adds that, with the advent of postmodernism in the late 1950s, the aesthetic rejection of the social world lost its radicalism. The artistic practices that emerged at that point – the neo-romanticism of the Beat movement, John Cage's happenings, Pop Art – no longer disown everyday life but greet it instead as a field of artistic experimentation (Hassan 1987: 91). In our perspective, what Hassan interprets as an artistic about-turn – the passage from modernism to postmodernism – only designates a shift in the initial modernist project: the aspiration to emancipation is voiced as clearly in the newer as in the older movements, yet in a more pragmatic and optimistic fashion.

It is not necessary in these pages to determine how exactly the labels modernism or postmodernism apply to rock music. Suffice it to note that rock has its place in this cultural grid. It is crucial, however, to take stock of the fact that the struggle against alienation has been as relevant to mass culture as it has been to canonical art: this existential issue manifests itself in total disregard of barriers of cultural capital. Utopian desire, shared by both modernist art and rock music, has informed phenomena as diverse as all variants of the star system – nineteenth-century operatic divas, the Wagner craze, Hollywood films – or, in less commendable fashion, sectarians cults and the collective spectacles of totalitarianism. Each of these movements gives voice to the aspiration to transfigure and transcend modernity.

Admittedly, the above list mentions cultural practices alien to the supposedly emancipatory impulses of counterculture. Utopianism can, however, be defined so as to negotiate this paradox. American neo-Marxist critic Fredric Jameson, taking his cue from German philosopher Ernst Bloch, contends that the term utopian may designate cultural phenomena that are nefarious in appearance, yet that still give expression to legitimate aspirations if they are given their righteous place in the history of human emancipation (Jameson 1992: 30; 1971: 133, 156). If we follow Jameson's argument, the counterfactual claims of occultism must, for instance, be weighed against the laudable aspiration to a holistic world view informing the latter doctrines. Likewise, rock's violence may be interpreted as an alienated expression of the desire to cope with the industrial environment, which sets similarly violent energies in motion. On this basis, Jameson demonstrates that mass culture, contrary to what Frankfurt School theoreticians alleged, manifests a desire for emancipation comparable to what Bloch calls the 'Principle of Hope' (Bloch 1976: iii; Jameson 1992: 31). In this light, the most objectionable aspects of the politics of rock – sexism, extreme-right-wing sympathies – amount to signs of an unfulfilled project. They are symptoms, to take up Jameson's terminology, of the impact of 'symbolic containment structures'; concessions to hegemonic social discourses that artists simultaneously contest (Jameson 1992: 25).

The Practical Legacy of Utopia: Rock's Field of Restricted Production

Under the term 'containment', Jameson designates both explicit censorship procedures as well as structural constraints interiorised by cultural producers. Typically, containment manifests itself within works in the form of contradictions expressing the conflict between emancipation and repression. One thinks for instance of the last scene of Ridley Scott's *Thelma and Louise* (1991), where the two heroines enjoy their first homosexual kiss at the very moment when their car flies off the road and tumbles into a canyon: no sooner does the emancipatory gesture flicker on screen than it is annihilated, sparing the director the task of representing a lesbian relationship of long standing in an everyday context. However productive this reading method, it has to be completed with an approach that takes into account containment factors unrelated to conservative cultural politics. Overall, rock's momentum is bounded by the horizon of social reality – by the various obstacles (empirical, political, social) against which aesthetic projects contend. One must reckon with the fact that utopian impulses only enjoy partial fulfilment in the field of practice. They must therefore be evaluated as a function of the residual accomplishments they leave in their wake – the practices, works and social changes their empowering momentum makes possible.

Pierre Bourdieu's sociology of the cultural field does justice to the double movement depicted above – the centrifugal, utopian momentum and its residual sedimentation. As he investigates modern art, Bourdieu focuses less on what creators sought to achieve in purely aesthetic terms than on the social changes issuing from their practice. Bourdieu's admiration for Charles Baudelaire, for instance, does not target the poet's idealistic aestheticism: the latter only fuels what Bourdieu calls 'charismatic ideology' – the parasitical worship of great artists (1993: 34). Baudelaire's genius, according to Bourdieu, resides instead in his capacity to remodel the social field: the poet inaugurated a new space for artists, which Bourdieu calls the field of 'autonomous' or 'restricted production' (ibid.: 53, 58). This space obeys a paradoxical logic, opposite to that of the economic field. Against the bourgeois criteria of social ascension, the prestige afforded by restricted production is measured not by the pursuit of, but by the degree of autonomy achieved with regard to financial success – by 'disinterestedness' (ibid.: 40). Only recognition by one's peers – respect among the community of artists – provides validation for success (ibid.: 116). The legacy of artistic utopianism is therefore not to be found in artistic works themselves: it manifests itself in the emancipatory gestures that redraw the social and cultural field – gestures made possible by artists' capacity to evaluate the 'system of *objectively possible cultural positions*' available at a given period (ibid.: 385, emphasis in original).

Bourdieu's model, which was elaborated for the analysis of canonical modernism, seems difficult to transpose to mass culture. In Bourdieu's perspective, commercial art is by definition 'heteronomous' (1993: 129): it subjects its practices to economic imperatives alien to autonomous creation. But in the same way as Jameson discerns utopian aspirations in commercial art, an observer intent on broadening the scope of Bourdieu's theory will discern in rock music practices equivalent to restricted production. The development of a field of artistic autonomy – indeed of a popular avant-garde – within American music is admittedly older than rock and roll itself: it dates back to 1940s and 1950s experimental jazz (Charlie Parker, Miles Davis), which served as soundtrack for the Beat movement (Stowe 1994: 224–6). A similar phenomenon within rock emerged in the mid-1960s, when Bob Dylan chose to go electric, the Beatles progressed toward psychedelic music, and Jimi Hendrix released his first recordings. Mid-1960s rock musicians created a field of restricted production through their claims to musical excellence, originality and radical behaviour (Walser 1993: 61). By rejecting the censorship bearing upon commercial music, they traced out the line between autonomous and heteronomous practice. As in the avant-garde, the divide between leisure music and rock was defined by a constant struggle pitting musicians and fans against production companies and the media – conflicts over songwriting, sonic texture or the artwork of LP covers (Scaduto 1975: 220). What Andrew Goodwin calls the artists' 'star text' (1993: 98) – the narrative out of which their public image is constructed – feeds on this struggle, and makes it possible to position musicians in the cultural field, or to sketch out their itinerary towards a higher or lower level of autonomy (Walser 1993: 61–3). One of the durable achievements of this bid for empowerment exactly fulfils the criteria of restricted production defined by Bourdieu: as of the late 1960s, rock developed its own culture of professionalism, generating a specialised media sphere that confers to musicians, fans and journalists the prerogative to act as arbiters of musical autonomy (Frith 1981: 228; Théberge 1991: 272).

To most rock historians, the mid-1960s artistic shift evoked above marks the birth of the rock counterculture: rock and roll's naïve celebration of teenage pleasure gave way to politically resonant, artistically ambitious 'progressive' rock (Frith 1981: 21). Yet in the present perspective, the field of restricted production taking shape at this landmark moment overlaps with, yet does not entirely merge with counterculture itself. It constitutes instead the fabric of practices out of which a countercultural moment may emerge when artistic choices interlock with counter-hegemonic determinants from outside the musical field. This implies that rock's field of restricted production obeys principles of development partially distinct from the concerns of counterculture. On the one hand, the scene of restricted production is stabilised by a utopian thematics mostly compatible with countercultural values – an agenda of empowerment kept alive within rock even during periods when the countercultural moment is played out. On the other, the dynamic of restricted production is determined by the urge to foreground cultural autonomy by means of variable and mutable practices, sometimes reaching beyond the commonly accepted range of countercultural protest.

Giving due attention to the variability of the claims to autonomy is essential because rock's utopian project does not express itself through one single, stable gesture of rebellion. Out of personal preferences, I would be tempted to conflate autonomy with rock musicians' claims to artistic excellence and professionalism – with the elaboration of a popular form of art for art's sake that manifested itself in *Sgt. Pepper's Lonely Hearts Club Band* (1967) or *Electric Ladyland* (1968). Yet I would thereby ignore one of Bourdieu's most important caveats – the realisation that artistic autonomy is conquered differently in different contexts (Bourdieu 1994: 28; 1993: 58). The metamorphoses of the cultural field obey a dialectic of defamiliarisation and standardisation whose paradigm Bourdieu derives from the Russian formalist theoretician Yuri Tynjanov (Bourdieu 1993: 180).

Tynjanov's thesis corroborates one of Bourdieu's key assumptions: the same social function manifests itself through different practices at different historical periods and in different geographical areas; conversely, the same practice may be endowed with variable functions in different contexts (Bourdieu 1994: 20). On this view, rock's struggle for autonomy must have assumed various guises in the music's history, giving rise to conflicts among the practices endorsed by various generations of musicians.

Markers of autonomy in rock music have indeed followed an itinerary made up of successive reversals. Empowerment in 1950s rock and roll was voiced through the celebration of rhythm and blues sensuality, but also through the flaunting of consumerist pleasure. Appearances notwithstanding, the latter claim was in the 1950s context not a sign of commercial co-optation (of heteronomy, to take up Bourdieu's terminology). When Eddie Cochran includes in his teenage heaven the ownership of 'a house with a pool' and when Chuck Berry sings the praise of the Cadillac Coupe de Ville (1955), they make a bid for a mode of empowerment American teenagers (in particular African-Americans) had only recently secured. On the contrary, as of the Vietnam War and the hippie movement, autonomy is signalled through opposite channels – through the satire of conspicuous consumption voiced in Janis Joplin's 'Mercedes Benz' (1971), for instance. Similarly, musical excellence served as a marker of autonomy for a limited period only. When late-1960s musicians chose to produce music with a degree of cultural capital comparable to that of classical music, they carried out a gesture suited to their own context: their aesthetic ambitions made possible the conquest of a field of restricted production within a musical medium hitherto deprived of this prerogative (Walser 1993: 61–3). This gesture gave rise to artistic successes such as the Beatles' 'Eleanor Rigby', yet also led to the rigid professionalism of the post-psychedelic era, generating in the best of cases concept albums such as Pink Floyd's *The Dark Side of the Moon* and, at worst, Emerson Lake and Palmer's aimless virtuosity. Post-psychedelic music therefore laid itself bare to an iconoclastic rebellion: mid-1970s punk rock, with its genuine or feigned ethos of musical crudeness, reinscribed rock's autonomy through cultural means opposite to those developed 10 years earlier.

Beneath this shifting trail of emancipatory gestures, rock's enduring thematics define areas of cultural intervention within which the practices depicted above are acted out over long periods of time. One of these themes – arguably not the most familiar to the rock audience – is discussed in the third section of the present chapter: an examination of rock's capacity to depict musicianship as a field of non-alienated labour. Far more visible have been rock's contribution to the construction of an autonomous sphere of adolescence and its development of culturally hybrid musical idioms, transgressing ethnic boundaries and distinctions of cultural capital. The teenage sphere, I point out above, was staked out by the bid for sexual freedom, access to consumption and, in more negative terms, the celebration of violence. Whatever the fans' actual age, the space thus created served as psychological and social buffer area – a space of latency allowing fans to distance themselves from a world bearing the negative marks of adulthood, or, in the hippie project, to secure the groundings for a radical alternative (Grossberg 1983–84: 112). The social changes effected by rock's construction of adolescence may be gauged by the fact that, before the Second World War, young people were offered leisure opportunities mostly within youth movements structured according to a military model (boy scouts, leisure camps, the socialist Red Falcons or, in the worst of cases, the Hitlerjugend).

The second thematics – the cultivation of musical hybridity (tapping the resources of black music, in most cases) served as a rallying sign of teenage rebellion in the 1950s and acquired an autonomous existence as of the 1960s. One of its landmark moments was the development of soul music, where black and white musicians collaborated for the creation of the same musical corpus (Gillett 1983: 233). This crossover thematics also experienced its own reversals: rock has gone through moments of cultural resegregation: it occasionally turned its back on interethnic exchange (punk, hardcore heavy metal) (Reynolds and Press 1995: 80) or foregrounded a non-ethnic type of hybridisation, as in the appropriation of classical music by post-psychedelic musicians. Overall, the field of restricted production has had to balance the perpetuation of its long-term thematics with the preservation of the music's autonomy. This has given rise to apparently incompatible gestures: early-1960s British rhythm and blues musicians (the Rolling Stones, the Who) appropriated black idioms nearly unknown to European audiences in order to distance themselves from commercial teenage-oriented rock and roll (Cliff Richard or even the early Beatles). (Post-)punk, on the contrary, discarded blues out of disgust for the trivialised appropriation the latter had been the object of in early-1970s heavy metal and pub rock.

In a materialistic perspective, rock's field of restricted production has maintained its stability by developing its own production and distribution structures: in its bid for autonomy, music sets up an alternative scene. From an economic point of view, rock's history unfolds as a competitive process pitting independent producers against the corporate giants of the culture industry (Peterson and Berger 1990: 156). In this logic, corporate conglomerates are constantly driven to appropriate the novelties introduced by their smaller competitors. Elvis Presley and Jerry Lee Lewis started recording with Sam Phillips's Sun label whose headquarters fitted in a modest-sized building in Memphis (Gillett 1983: 92). Chuck Berry and Bo Diddley were signed by independent label Chess, where they enjoyed a working environment comparable to that of early-1950s rhythm and blues artists. Black music in the 1960s developed in comparable structures – Tamla Motown in Detroit, Stax in Memphis. Early-1970s post-psychedelic rock was hatched in small or medium-sized structures – labels such as Island, Virgin, or Brian Eno's Obscure records. Punk and post-punk witnessed the development of a permanent alternative scene possessing not only its own record producers – labels such as Stiff (the Damned, Elvis Costello), Mute (Depeche Mode), Fast Product (Gang of Four), Fiction (the Cure), or Factory Records (Joy Division) – but also independent distribution networks – Rough Trade, Play It Again Sam

(Reynolds 2005: 92–108; Taylor 2010: 5–7). Those smaller structures fitted in the margins of a record industry that, in the 1980s, enjoyed the most profitable decade of its history (Goodwin 1993: 38). The later evolution of the music scene, as it was remodelled by digital technologies and computer networks, has unfolded according to a similar topography: on the one hand, new means of production – home studios and the exchange of digital files – confer to musicians a higher control over creation and distribution, fostering the perpetuation of the scene of restricted production (Den Tandt 2004: 145); on the other, the works thus produced reach a sizable audience only through the intermission of large-scale corporate actors, whose role is sometimes exclusively limited to online distribution.

Musicians and fans often perceive the distinction between independent producers and corporate conglomerates – the so-called majors – from the perspective of romantic rebellion, locking these two poles in a stable opposition: the status of independent producer is viewed as a natural attribute of counterculture, whereas corporate structures are synonymous with commercial co-optation. When Siouxsie and the Banshees signed with a major (Polydor), they had to placate their sceptical fans, claiming that their contract safeguarded their creative freedom (Thrills 1978: 16). Before them, the Sex Pistols had on the contrary loudly slammed EMI's door in order to sign with Virgin, still an alternative label at the time (Reynolds 2005: 10). For academic researchers, it seems less simple to distinguish autonomous from heteronomous practice: a few small labels (Motown) pursued similar ambitions as their corporate competitors; several bands created their own record companies (Apple, Rolling Stones Records, Swan Song) in order to maximise their profits. On the contrary, a major (Columbia) offered Bob Dylan the opportunity to record his first songs – a gesture that from the company's perspective had the value of a low-budget experiment (Heylin 1991: 46). Overall, the stability of creative autonomy exists at a more abstract level: it resides in the very possibility to carve out within the cultural field the status of restricted production. The latter exists as a virtuality that manifests itself through various practices at different periods.

The Utopia of Non-Alienated Work: Rock Music as a Meta-Industrial Practice

Among rock's thematics, I mentioned above the culture of professionalism aiming at a mode of social integration characterised by non-alienated labour. As it evokes this utopian possibility, rock avails itself of the meta-industrial or meta-professional dimension of mass culture. The latter is often blamed for foisting on its audience escapist fantasies obscuring social realities. However, instead of encouraging its audience to ignore everyday conditions, mass culture has paradoxically elaborated narratives and characters depicting the subject's anchorage in the professional world. This thematics has often been investigated in studies on crime fiction: Sherlock Holmes, Philip Marlowe, Hercule Poirot and Jules Maigret are figures of identification for readers subjected to the constraints of industry and bureaucracy (Kracauer 1981: 53; Denning 1987: 14; Mandel 1986: 49). Similarly, the Hollywood western, in spite of a fictional context seemingly remote from the twentieth-century job market, develops what Will Wright calls 'professional plots' – narratives depicting possibilities for autonomy offered by various labour environments (1975: 85).

Wright's analysis suggests that westerns are informed by the utopian logic sketched out above: they give voice to the desire for a professional life freed from capitalist alienation. Similarly, hard-boiled detectives – Philip Marlowe, Sam Spade – preserve their economic and existential autonomy with regard to political and economic authorities. Yet, in accordance with the logic of containment outlined by Jameson, this utopian promise is counterbalanced by concessions to conservatism: the endorsement of upper-class norms (Holmes, Poirot), the celebration of aggressive masculinity, homophobia and racism (hard-boiled novels, the western). The gendered discourse developed in the framework of this thematics constitutes indeed one of its most visible strategies of containment – also one of the most relevant to rock music. The figures of identification offered by these popular fictions have with only few exceptions been masculine. The rebellion against professional subordination and regimentation they express is portrayed as resistance against feminising constraints: the rationalised economy appears as an environment that restricts an inherently masculine mode of freedom (Rotundo 1993: 251–2).

Rock and roll in the 1950s revolved almost exclusively around teenage leisure, and therefore excluded any positive representation of work. It took the mid-1960s reversal evoked above for rock to venture into this thematic field. The genres now lumped together as classic rock – folk rock, British rhythm and blues, psychedelic and post-psychedelic music – developed not only the practices that make up the material basis of musical work (multitrack recording, extended studio sessions) but also the media tools that confer public visibility to this labour (sleeve notes, specialised press, documentaries). The figure of the rock musician thereby gained a public presence it had hitherto been deprived of. Up to the early 1960s, the place in the spotlight was reserved either to individual performers (Elvis Presley, Eddie Cochran) supported by anonymous musicians or to bands (the early Beatles) profiled according to the promotional strategies of teenage pop, namely as objects of desire for a female audience (Frith 1981: 227). By the mid-1960s, a new set of stereotypes was deployed. In this new configuration, a contrast opposes, on the one hand, a front man whose provocative behaviour perpetuates the stardom function on the mode of transgression, and, on the other, the person guaranteeing the band's technical and musical integrity. The Jim Morrison/Ray Manzarek binary is the clearest illustration of this pattern. The pairing of Mick Jagger and Keith Richards or of John Lennon and Paul McCartney-George Harrison obeys the same logic. Sometimes, the polarity cuts across one single musician: on the cover of *Highway 61 Revisited* (1965), Bob Dylan appears as a haughty, intellectual front man; on the back cover he is the musical expert, playing piano and guitar. Similarly, there are two sides to Keith Richards: on the one hand, the rock and roll outlaw, on the other, the rhythm and blues erudite, passing on the traditions of black music to white musicians.

The classic-rock musical expert is a figure of emancipation in so far as he or she perpetuates the ideal of the autonomous craftsperson. In this logic, photographs on LP sleeves featuring musicians, roadies and gear – the back cover of Pink Floyd's *Ummagumma* (1969); the inner sleeve of Joe Jackson's *Night and Day* (1982) – are comparable to photos of craftsmen in their workshop. This iconography is reminiscent of the Arts and Crafts movement of socialist aesthete William Morris, who opposed craft to industrial practice. Classic rock is therefore bound to a nostalgic utopia – a feature defining both its attractiveness and its limits. It pits against the corporate context a craft-based countertype anchored in an economic model that might already be obsolete. In this, it follows the logic of crime fiction: the latter celebrates the private investigator's individualistic ethos – a profile that may already have been marginalised by the development of bureaucratic structures.

The evolution of the music market and the inherent limitations of classic rock's craft-based utopia have generated more oblique professional profiles. One of them expresses aspirations to creative and economic invisibility. Its logic is evocatively depicted in William Gibson's post-cyberpunk novel *Zero History*. In this work, the Canadian writer describes fashion designers who, even though they work at the heart of the consumerist apparatus, produce utterly anonymous avant-garde creations marketed through clandestine channels (Gibson 2010: 337). As of the late 1960s, rock music has developed comparable strategies. One thinks of record sleeves featuring little if any information about musicians or product – the Beatles' so-called 'White Album' (1968), Led Zeppelin's fourth album (1971), or Pink Floyd's early-1970s albums, which featured particularly austere art work (1973, 1975). Post-psychedelic musicians such as Robert Fripp and Brian Eno explicitly advocated this interstitial positioning (Eno 2009, Fripp 1979). In so doing, they laid the foundations for a central tendency of post-punk. The Cure's first four albums only feature blurred photographs making it impossible to identify musicians visually (1979, 1980, 1981, 1982); alternative label Factory Records privileged anonymous designs in dark colours, sometimes only featuring a serial number. These gestures express the refusal of personalised stardom. They foster the creation of paradoxical products eschewing the music market's customary markers: there is up to this day no consensus about the title of Led Zeppelin's fourth album.

A third professional profile implements a strategy comparable to what postcolonial theoretician Homi Bhabha calls tactical 'mimicry' (Bhabha 1994: 265): instead of opposing a counter-model to the music market (classic rock's craft-based practice, for instance) or to seek to vanish from its radar (post-punk anonymity), musicians mimic its strategies with some degree of ironical distance. Musicians from the electronic scene as of the 1980s have cultivated this gesture. They no longer use the means of production of classic rock, whose craft-oriented configuration foregrounded an anchorage in working-class labour. On the contrary, they handle computer tools whose basic operations are similar to gestures of bureaucratic management: their musical practice is anchored in the white-collar world. In technical magazines intended for musicians, this corporate profile gives rise to a utopian discourse offering the prospect of incorporating obsolete modes of production by computer technology: the gestures and sounds of the past are simulated by means of digital sampling or software-generated sequences. In so doing, corporate musicians avail themselves of the prerogatives of managers mastering a multitude of resources and interfacing systems (Den Tandt 2004: 150).

With this corporate profile, one fears that the internal dynamics of musicianship may drive rock's scene of restricted production to separate off from counterculture altogether. Performers simulating technocapitalist procedures to the point of identifying with corporate culture (DJs such as David Guetta and Martin Solveig, say) seem unlikely to perpetuate rock's critical dimension. These concerns are worth bearing in mind: it would be naïvely non-historical to assume that rock will indefinitely maintain its emancipatory momentum, let alone its central role in youth culture. Still, it is equally rash to pin rock's whole utopian project on its single meta-industrial thematics, ignoring thereby that recent musical movements adjacent to rock (world music, electro dance music) have remained faithful to other countercultural themes inherited from the 1960s (ethnic and gender equality, particularly). Similarly, the present argument is to a large extent pegged to the hope that the material configuration of the rock scene may act as custodian of the countercultural moment. If the autonomy of distribution networks is maintained, the possibility of oppositional gestures is preserved. Foregrounding a corporate musical profile amounts in this case only to an ironical postmodern gesture with a critical edge, exposing market practices. On this reading, the creation of a popular field of restricted production ranks as one of the most valuable legacies of rock's utopian discourse.

Chapter 5
'Helter Skelter' and Sixties Revisionism

Gerald Carlin and Mark Jones[1]

'Helter Skelter' and the End of the Sixties

In late August 1968, within a few days of each other, new singles were released by the Beatles and the Rolling Stones. The unusual proximity of release dates by the world's two most significant rock bands was echoed by the congruity of the songs' themes: the Stones' 'Street Fighting Man' and the Beatles' 'Revolution' were both responses to the political unrest and protest which characterised the spring and summer of 1968. Their topicality was obvious and much commented on, even though 'Revolution' was ostensibly the B-side to 'Hey Jude', and 'Street Fighting Man' was only released in the United States. The heightened anxiety in both the mainstream and the counterculture of the period led to polarised assessments of the tracks' political positions, in which they were judged as manifestos promoting action, rather than rock posturing. *Time* magazine contrasted the Stones' call in 'Street Fighting Man' for 'change, wildness, rebellion against civil authority' with the Beatles' pacific quietude (Anon. 1969). San Francisco underground newspaper the *Berkeley Barb* saw 'Revolution' as 'a clear unmistakable call for counter-revolution', while 'Street Fighting Man' 'lives up to its title' (Anon. 1968a). Britain's most politically radical underground publication, *Black Dwarf*, nailed its colours firmly to the Stones' mast:

> Now it seems that what was in the past simply an aesthetic preference for the Stones, now emerges as a part of the struggle for the hearts and minds of youth ... Although I've liked the Beatles in the past I hope that they get so fucked up with their money making that they become as obscure as Cliff Richards [sic] and on the debris they leave behind I hope we will see a new pop-group emerge – a 'street-fighting' pop-group committed to the movement. (Muldoon 1968)

What the establishment feared and the revolutionaries anticipated in late 1968 was that rock music would imminently become the cultural vanguard of a political revolution. The boundaries between the discourses and praxis of politics and the pop counterculture would be effaced in a utopian imaginary where 'the poetry of politics is rock music' (Gleason 1972: 146).

---

[1] The authors wish to thank their colleague Alan Apperley for his useful comments on this chapter.

While an enthusiastic music press, blind to the album's dubious sexual politics, proclaimed that the Rolling Stones' *Beggars Banquet* released in December 1968 'derives its central motive and mood from the theme of "revolution" ... [and] ought to convince us all that the Stones are right' (Landau 1972: 331), *The Beatles* (aka the 'White Album'), released only a few weeks earlier, had a more ambivalent reception. There was general agreement amongst reviewers that the album was fundamentally grounded in homage, pastiche and parody. For some, this was a sign of its musical intelligence: Tony Palmer in *The Observer* claimed that '[r]eferences to or quotations from Elvis Presley, Donovan, Little Richard, the Beach Boys, Blind Lemon Jefferson are woven into an aural fabric that has become the Bayeux Tapestry of popular music' (Palmer 1968). Others saw its evasion of contemporaneity as political disengagement: Jon Landau in a *Liberation News Service* dispatch wrote, 'The Beatles have used parody on this album precisely because they were afraid of confronting reality. It becomes a mask behind which they can hide from the urgencies of the moment' (Wiener 1995: 65). The album's few ostensibly engaged tracks tended to receive short shrift. Having already dismissed 'Revolution' when released as a single, the more politically ambivalent 'Revolution 1' was largely passed over by reviewers. Similarly, the album's greatest claim to experimentation, 'Revolution 9', later described as 'the world's most widely distributed avant-garde artefact' (MacDonald 1995: 230), was almost universally despised. Amidst the album's bricolage of musical styles and genres, one track in particular seemed original enough to evade denigration as simple generic refashioning. Tucked away near the end of the third side, sandwiched between the lilting 'Sexy Sadie' and George Harrison's low-key 'Long, Long, Long', 'Helter Skelter' surprised critics by its fusion of a solid rock momentum with whirling chaotic energy. Recognised by *The Times* as 'exhaustingly marvellous' (Mann 1987: 154), and moving at 'a pace that goes so fast they all only just about keep up with themselves' according to the *New Musical Express*, the only ascertainable meanings of the song were related to its '[f]renetically sexual' energy (Smith 1968: 5). Critics struggled to categorise it, reaching for terms from an emerging discourse which distinguished and defined stratifications of significance between pop and underground music. Nik Cohn in *The New York Times* utilised the neologism 'hardrock' (Cohn 1968: 8), and Barry Miles in underground newspaper *IT* called it 'probably the heaviest rocker on plastic today' (Miles 1968: 10). While 'hard' clearly aligns the track with contemporaneous rock innovators such as Cream and the Jimi Hendrix Experience, the term 'heavy' has a wider signification, connoting countercultural profundity and relevance (Landy 1971: 101) as well as beginning to be attached to a nascent musical form. For Jann Wenner in *Rolling Stone* 'Helter Skelter' was central to his presentation of the Beatles as 'sensitive like all others in McLuhanville, they are of course caught up and reflective in their music of what's happening around them, especially the recent scenes they have been through' (Wenner 1968: 13). Caught on the cusp of emergent heavy metal, and with its ambiguously frivolous/ominous 'coming down fast' lyric, 'Helter Skelter' perhaps seems far more synoptic of the slide from revolutionary optimism to disillusionment and crisis than other, more overtly political, tracks of the period.

The song's confrontational discordance was intended. Paul McCartney stated that 'Helter Skelter' resulted from his reading

> a review of a record which said that the group really goes wild with echo and screaming and everything, and I thought 'That's a pity, I would have liked to do something like that.' Then I heard it and it was nothing like, it was straight and sophisticated. So we did this. I like noise. (Anon. 1968b)[2]

In order to achieve this apparently simple aim, 'Helter Skelter' uses a range of musical and technical strategies. The song is in 4/4 time, and after an introductory descending riff on guitar, mirrored by an ascending vocal, the basic rhythm of the verse is in the root chord of E major, but the force with which the open bottom E string is hit at the start of each bar causes it to bend and raise its pitch almost a semitone – a dissonant position between E and F. This sustained droning power chord is a key ingredient in the overdriven feel of 'Helter Skelter', and it exists in tension with the bluesy major root chord. The chord sequence in the verse moves to a flattened position III (G, in the key of E major) and finally moves to position IV (A) in an ascending pentatonic scale, which creates a further tension between a hard rock and a blues structure, as the 'turn' or resolving V chord position (B) that features in blues and rock and roll is absent. The guitar in the chorus, which has a much 'cleaner' rock-attack sound than the guitar(s) in the grungy verses, follows a major key rock and roll boogie A5 A5 A6 A6 for a bar with a descent down the scale from a flattened A7 position for the second bar, repeating this climb and fast descent in E, returning to A, and finally ending on the root E major chord. In utilising the boogie riff the chorus alludes to rock and roll (specifically Chuck Berry) rather than the blues or hard rock, but again there is no position V chord which would 'resolve' a conventional blues or rock and roll stylisation. Despite the major root chord and the rock and roll allusions of the chorus, the song remains in pentatonic mode and suggests minor keys, giving the song a frustrated, contained or 'primitive' feel. This is intensified by the one instrument which stands out and drives 'Helter Skelter' forward: the bass. It has a gnarled timbre, is mixed to the fore and is characterised by a lot of treble and percussive attack – probably achieved by striking hard with a plectrum and at times forcing the strings to slap back onto the frets. It is played fast (always more strikes of a note than beats in a bar) and takes on something like the role of a second (or third) rhythm guitar or even a basic lead instrument – frequently dropping down to D to allow a hammer-on or slides to the root E note for example and moving between octave notes towards the end. The vocal delivery is cranked up and erratic and, again, exists in a strained relation to the smoothly precise 'pop' sound of the

---

[2] McCartney later identified the ur-text of 'Helter Skelter' as the Who's 'I Can See for Miles' (Miles 1997: 487).

backing vocals. Stylistically, the song is a hybrid, gesturing towards several genres simultaneously. The musical irresolutions of the song are finally manifested in its sequence of phased discordant endings, in which the song rejects obvious and acceptable forms of closure, returning repeatedly until it eventually collapses in exhaustion. Despite the manic energy which sustains the body of the track, nearly half of its duration is taken up by its increasingly entropic ending.

The abrasive 'heaviness' and unevenness of 'Helter Skelter' probably contributed to its early unpopularity with Beatles fans. In a 1971 poll in *The Village Voice* it was identified as the fourth least favourite Beatles track – 'Revolution 9' topped the list (Schaffner 1978: 217). A contributory factor, though, may have been the notoriety it had accumulated by its bizarre implication in a series of brutal slayings over two days in August 1969. Sharon Tate (film director Roman Polanski's pregnant wife) and six others were murdered in the Hollywood hills by Charles Manson and his 'Family' of young, mainly female followers. In 1971 assistant district attorney Vincent Bugliosi convinced a jury that the murders were part of an attempt to bring about an apocalyptic race war, fulfilling a communal mythos derived from Manson's exegesis of 'The Book of Revelation', and the Beatles' 'White Album'. 'Helter Skelter' was apparently the term used by Manson to refer to the impending period of anarchy and social collapse, similar to the Tribulation in millenarian Christianity. 'Healter [sic] Skelter' appeared written in a victim's blood at one of the murder sites, and it was later also found painted on a door at the Spahn ranch near Los Angeles where the Family were living when the murders were committed. This connection would prove crucial in the prosecution's case against Manson and the Family, and thus 'Helter Skelter' has become inextricably associated with the Manson murders. This was reinforced by the publication of Vincent Bugliosi's *Helter Skelter: The True Story of the Manson Murders* in 1974, frequently claimed to be the best-selling work in the true crime genre, and its subsequent highly successful television adaptation in 1976. The latter would prompt the re-release of the Beatles' 'Helter Skelter' as a single – originally conceived as an A-side to capitalise on the broadcast of the miniseries, it was relegated to a B-side when its tastefulness was questioned (Stannard 1983: 150).

The Manson murders have become an iconic marker of the 'end of the 1960s' – one of a series of events which are popularly considered to close the decade (*Witness* 1994), along with the violence at the Altamont Free Concert in December 1969 (Russell 2009) and the break-up of the Beatles in 1970 (Gitlin 1993: 429). While historians more generally utilise a variety of political and economic phenomena – including dissent and its suppression (ibid.: 407–19), developments in the Vietnam war (Burner 1996: 217–24), changes in governments (Kaiser 1988: 245–53, Sandbrook 2006: 741–7) and the oil crisis (Cairncross and Cairncross 1992) – in the popular memorialisation of this period of cultural revolution and mass mediatisation, it is pop culture which is mined for historiographic symbolism. The more salient and immediate relationship between these events and the end of the 1960s, though, is the wedge they drove at the time between mainstream popular culture and the political counterculture. After the

Manson Family murders and the violence at Altamont, the supposed communal project that united pop aristocracy, the underground, and the radical left, suddenly evaporated. The counterculture, particularly in America, was fatally divided over its assessment of the Manson Family. In 1969, the newly formed Weathermen, the extremist vanguard of the new-left Students for a Democratic Society, embraced Manson as society's victim and a revolutionary hero (Barber 2008: 209–11). This celebratory rhetoric disturbed and appalled much of the rest of the counterculture. While historians might balk at the idea that Manson contributed to the end of the '1960s', it is undeniable that he catalysed the splintering of the decade's countercultural coalition.

A Hard Rock Classic

The dispersal and depletion of the 1960s' radical energies was manifest in the diverging musical landscape of the early 1970s. Rock, considered in the late 1960s the soundtrack to the liberatory struggle, 'turned out to be a by-way in the development of twentieth-century popular music, rather than, as we thought at the time, any kind of mass-cultural revolution' (Frith 1988: 1). The diversity of styles and genres on the Beatles' 'White Album' proved to be a prophetic index of early 1970s pluralistic musical trajectories. The Rolling Stones continued to plough an increasingly lucrative hard rock furrow, and carried in their wake a plethora of novitiates similarly exploiting the commercial potential of rock posturing's rebellious heritage. One of the most successful of these has proved to be Aerosmith, dismissed in their early career as Rolling Stones clones, who have covered songs by the Beatles, Kinks and Yardbirds, and might best be located as American inheritors of the 'British invasion' (Campbell and Brody 2008: 33). These covers, the earliest being 'Helter Skelter' which the band has performed live regularly since 1976, mark a musical and cultural continuity with the 1960s rock scene. Aerosmith's 'Helter Skelter' is very close to the Beatles', remaining faithful to the rhythm and featuring a lead guitar solo and fills which are almost note-for-note renditions of the original. Apparently minor differences include the rhythm guitar's more regularised and faster rock attack, a simplification of the chorus's rock and roll boogie, and two dramatically punched bass-drum-guitar punctuations on the first and third beats of the final chorus when the song's title is vocalised. Together with a vocal performance featuring the high-pitched posturing characteristic of stadium rock, and the absence of the disconcertingly melodic backing vocals in the Beatles' version, these nuanced modifications subtly transform 'Helter Skelter' into a rock standard. Early Aerosmith's notoriously derivative stage demeanour, aping the Rolling Stones and sounding like Status Quo (Charone 1976), signals an attempt to fuse the fractured musical landscape of the early 1970s. Performing 'Helter Skelter' in the style of the Stones effaces the rift in the counterculture that the Beatles and Rolling Stones had symbolised in 1968, effectively replacing political engagement with rock heritage.

Aerosmith's recording of 'Helter Skelter', during the *Toys in the Attic* sessions in 1975, is the earliest recorded cover that we have been able to trace, though it was not released until 1991. The first to be issued was by Diamond Reo, a hard rock group from Pittsburgh, on their 1976 album, *Dirty Diamonds*. Here, the song becomes a frame for lead guitar display, featuring wailing guitar fills and an extended solo, continuing the song's progression towards hard rock standard. Diamond Reo were identified in *Billboard*'s review of *Dirty Diamonds* as 'uncompromising hard rock along the lines of a Led Zeppelin or Bad Company' (Anon. 1976). Also unmistakably 'good pre-punk heavy rock' (Field 1978) is the next released cover, by Don Harrison on *Not Far from Free* (1977); he had previously worked with members of Creedence Clearwater Revival in the Don Harrison Band. This association of 'Helter Skelter' with the various types of hard rock prevalent in the 1970s American music industry was reinforced by the next North American cover, by Canadian singer Dianne Heatherington, which was recorded in 1978 but not released until 1980, on *Heatherington Rocks*. Heatherington had previously worked with members of the Guess Who, a band which also later spawned Bachman-Turner Overdrive. As might be expected from their musical associations, both Harrison's and Heatherington's versions of 'Helter Skelter' can be squarely placed in the 'AOR' ('Adult Oriented Rock' or 'Album Oriented Radio') genre, partaking in particular of the epic rock treatment that Led Zeppelin had made a central aspect of the format. Both covers are more blues based than Aerosmith's and Diamond Reo's, slowing the song down and making the dominant key E minor. In Harrison's version the verses contain an octaval pulse between bottom and top E twice in each bar, until the final bar of each verse line, where a double hammer-on from D to E occurs on the last two beats. This gives the song a ponderous progression; combined with strings which accompany the rhythmic pulse and its expansive arrangement it recalls Led Zeppelin's then recently released 'Kashmir' (*Physical Graffiti* 1975). Also drawing heavily on a Led Zeppelin blues rock formula, Dianne Heatherington's 'Helter Skelter' foregrounds a dampened chug on the rhythm guitar which is punctuated on the last two beats of the final bar of each verse line by a shrill string bend to top E. The rhythm is regularised, but the vocal is drawn out, improvisational and highly eroticised; Heatherington goes so far as to modify the lyrics, repeatedly demanding 'Give me helter skelter, baby' during the extended orgiastic lead out, making the song unambiguously and wholly sexual. Though sung by a woman, this 'Helter Skelter' is easily aligned with late-1970s' 'cock rock', the hedonistic inheritor of 1960s sexual permissiveness after it had been drained of its ostensible liberatory agenda (Frith 1983: 240–43).

Manson's Looming Figure: Goth Covers and Shlock Horror

A somewhat different US 1970s is evidenced by the only other American version of 'Helter Skelter' that has emerged from the period, by the short-lived Detroit punk band, the Ramrods. Part of a live medley from 1977 with the Who's 'My Generation' and the Stooges' 'Search and Destroy', 'Helter Skelter' is retrospectively inserted into a genealogy of youth rebellion and punk attitude (*Gimme Some Action* 2004). While US punk looked to 'buried productions of a few cult prophets' from the 1960s for inspiration (Marcus 1997: 39), and acknowledged their genealogical roots (McNeil and McCain 1997: 3–104), punk in the UK was more musically nihilistic. At Siouxsie and the Banshees' first gig in 1976 they performed only covers, including 'The Lord's Prayer', 'taking the piss out of all the things we hated', asking each other 'What would you like to throw in as a shock tactic? What can we mutilate and destroy?' (Savage 1991: 220). By the time their first album *The Scream* was released in 1978, the only cover which remained was 'Helter Skelter'. The Banshees' adaptation is a radical destruction and reconstruction of the song which strips away its blues and rock and roll elements, turning it into a basic garage punk track, albeit with a gothically menacing extended opening. It starts with a regular but very slow isolated bass note in A, subsequently joined by a trebly dissonant guitar riff. When the vocal eventually begins, it is similarly slow and deadpan, accompanied by discordant guitar riffs which speed up through the major chord sequence A-B-C-D. The body of the song is faster than the original, and coloured by guitar vamping in major keys around the root A chord of the verse. Where the original moves to a flattened position III, the Banshees move to an E for the third line of the verse – the resolving position V, which is sustained for four bars, then slides down through E♭ to D and finally returns to the A root, signalling a much straighter rock I-IV-V stylisation. The chorus is introduced by a climb from A to D, the rock and roll boogie is replaced by straight chords and the accompanying run-down in the major scale is vocalised la-la-la-la-la-la-la on a single G note, with the refrain 'helter skelter' being chanted rather than sung, and again moving to chord position V for the final phrases.

The Banshees drain away the subtle allusions to rock structure that characterise the Beatles' carefully crafted original, and expose the almost banal barre chord architecture that underlies the song. Their 'Helter Skelter' resembles one of the offhand rockers that the Beatles may have performed and McCartney may have written in 1963. Its refusal to engage with the pretensions of late-1960s rock reflects punk's recognition of the self-delusions of countercultural politics – 'never trust a hippie' (Reid 1987: 103). The bleak energy that builds in the Banshees' version, and its disdainfully abrupt ending on the line 'then I stop', is in stark contrast to the artfully phased coda of the original, and is the parodic antithesis of the indulgent climaxes of the American hard rock covers of the 1970s. The dry cynicism displayed by the Banshees in ending the interminable 'Helter Skelter' by simply stopping presents an asymmetrical counterpoint to their version's protracted, ominous and discordant opening. The instrumental first 50 seconds of the song invoke a gothic nightmare which acknowledges the song's murderous accretions: indeed, in live performance Siouxsie has been known to dedicate the song to Roman Polanski (Baddeley 1999: 178). In this reference to the dark finale of the 1960s, the Banshees were signalling an emerging fascination with Manson amongst elements of the underground avant-garde on both sides of the Atlantic, exemplified in particular by Throbbing Gristle (Ford 1999: 6.30–6.33) and Boyd Rice (Schreck 1988: 125). The ambivalent Family-fixation demonstrated by select punks, provocateurs and poseurs – sometimes revelling in extremity, sometimes utilising Manson to critique the countercultural project *in toto* – is displayed in the Banshees' 'Helter Skelter', which combines existential threat with a parodic dismissal of 1960s rock.

In the United States, most rock music remained wedded to its 1960s legacies. While Black Flag would exploit Manson iconography for its shock value, naming their 1981 tour 'Creepy Crawl' after the Family's recreational housebreaking (Tonooka 2011: 75–6), mainstream American covers of 'Helter Skelter' seemed unable or unwilling to follow the informed example of the Banshees. Pat Benatar's 1981 version, on *Precious Time*, treads faithfully through the song, even incorporating the original's overdriven E–F semitonal bend into its rhythm section, duplicating the backing vocals, and following the blueprint of the brief guitar solo. The song tidies the Beatles' phased ending with a chorus of well-defined descending guitar riffs, contributing to the smooth power pop production qualities of the whole. Wilfully ignoring the song's cultural accretions, and the original's countercultural context, Benatar's 'Helter Skelter' is rendered palatable – suitable for the corporate 1980s' commodification of the 1960s. Hers was the first commercially successful rock rendition; from the evidence of official and bootleg live recordings, Benatar performed the song regularly at the time she recorded it, and it has since reappeared on several of her 'best of' compilations. Even more successful in appropriating 'Helter Skelter' as their own were Mötley Crüe, who released the song as a promotional 12-inch single and on the album *Shout at the Devil* in 1983. Subsequently re-appearing on several of the band's live and compilation albums, it has also been 're-covered' on a Mötley Crüe tribute album, and the score for their version presented in a 'hair metal' songbook (Anon. 2001). Recasting the song in the mould of heavy metal, Mötley Crüe join the Banshees in being the only artists to have successfully prised the song away from the Beatles.

Although Mötley Crüe's structural departures from the original are limited, they are enough to complete the generic transformation of the song through hard rock and into heavy metal. This recasting is apparent from the outset, where midway through an extended introduction of eight bars the chorused guitar is accompanied by a single heavy pulse on the bass guitar and drum every first and third beat. The song is grounded on a fast, dampened power chord guitar chug in E, but a squealing note bend to top B is introduced in the first verse, recurring intermittently throughout the song, and the final beat of each second bar of the verse is an abrupt and precise power chord in flattened III position (G). Such features produce a machined, tightened rhythm and structure, removing all suggestions of the expansive blues feel of the original and its standard rock versions. The position III G chord contains a chugging riff and is held for four bars as opposed to the original's two, and the position IV A chord is stifled in order to foreground the vocals and drums before a return to the root E chord and the squeal of the recurring high B lead guitar note. The chorus follows the same boogie and declining run of the original, but on the last note the fast opening riff of the introduction is abruptly reintroduced for two bars, obliterating the final 'yeah', and the next verse starts immediately afterwards – this eruption of the introductory guitar riff becomes a feature of the chorus throughout the song, even in its final repetitions, reigning in any potential expansion. The guitar break is prefaced by four bars of drum and vocals which usher in a 'shredding' 10-bar solo featuring hammer-ons, pull-offs, bends and runs which segue straight into the repeated introductory guitar and drum riff. What in the Beatles' version is the last appearance of the chorus before the extended, uneven outro, becomes here the first of three sharply defined repetitions, with the brief feedback of the concluding single chord the only allusion to the original's frame-breaking terminus. Just before the final chord Vince Neil screams 'comin' down on you', followed by 'it's helter skelter', menacingly whispered over feedback.

In ex-Deep Purple vocalist Ian Gillan's version, recorded around the same time as Mötley Crüe's cover, it is the opening eerie fairground sounds which produce the track's uncanny resonance. The main body of the two versions share several key features, including the move to a flattened III position during the verse, though in Gillan's the punctuating chords are delayed and rendered on keyboards. These methods of tightening and clarifying the song are typical of the performative and production approaches in heavy metal covers of 'Helter Skelter', of which there are many – including versions by Vow Wow, Trouble, Bon Jovi, Soundgarden, Joe Lynn Turner, Dimension Zero, Celtic Frost, Carnivore, Spite Extreme Wing, Sunday Fury and Caliban. The song has, perhaps, become something of a heavy metal exhibition piece; each revisiting of the track reinscribes the original – as some critics have claimed – as a metal ur-text (Blake 1997: 143). The covers achieve this by recasting the song using specific generic techniques which foreground its energy and attack, but which work to efface the original's nuanced references to its musical antecedents. This is characteristic of heavy metal, which seems to wish to concrete over its own musicological pre-history, to destroy its roots in the blues and rock and roll. Heavy metal takes a scorched earth approach to musical history, proclaiming 1969 or 1970 to be, in effect, year zero (Weinstein 1998: 143).

This musical breach is a reflection of the near-simultaneous collapse in the countercultural project. Heavy metal is typically characterised as a nihilistic response to the failures and revealed elitism of the 1960s' radicals (Weinstein 2000: 18). Black Sabbath's Ozzy Osbourne recalled the band's beginnings in the late 1960s: 'we lived in a dreary, polluted, dismal town and we were angry about it. For us the whole hippy thing was bullshit. The only flower you saw in Aston was on a gravestone. So we thought, let's scare the whole fucking planet with music' (Cope 2010: 30). However, while much of heavy metal's atmosphere of menace derives from its aural dissonance and aggression – the annihilation of the transcendent promise of 1960s rock – its theatre of horrors, combining violence, madness and the occult, is rooted in elements of the earlier decade's popular and exploitation culture. The 'dark' 1960s – gore films, bad trips and Satanism – was never entirely dispelled by the enlightenment ideals of the counterculture, and they would flourish in the 1970s mélange of paranoia and camp (Lachman 2001). A key and continuing figure in this resurgence of the sinister 1960s was Manson, tabloid bogeyman and the subject of numerous pulp treatments in various media. In popular music, Manson is a commonplace reference in songs across a range of genres: in rap, he provides a benchmark for homicidal achievement; alternative and industrial artists typically recapitulate details of the Family saga; heavy metal songs use Manson to invoke the devil or to herald the apocalypse.

Such an invocation occurs at the menacingly whispered end of Mötley Crüe's 'Helter Skelter', in which the Los Angeles heavy metal band implicitly realign the song with the murders committed in its name. Manson's cultural cache continued to rise throughout the 1980s, which saw a marked increase in songs about the Family and the murders, and a series of high profile television interviews which contributed raw audio for numerous subsequent samplers (Bugliosi 1994: 651). With Manson's ever increasing profile, reinflected covers of 'Helter Skelter' began to proliferate. Hüsker Dü's 'alternative' version from 1986 is structurally faithful, but its maniacal vocalisations and frenetic instrumentation give it the character of a crime scene recording; its dangerous immediacy binds it to its near contemporary Mansonic artefact 'Death Valley '69' by Sonic Youth. Also in 1986, 'deathrock' band Mighty Sphincter released a pounding horrorshow 'Helter Skelter'; its appearance on the album *The New Manson Family*, a collection of hardcore punk murder songs and pastiched horror clichés, made its associations transparent. Again in 1986, Secession's synth-gothic version ends with a sample from the Manson Family chorus of 'I'll Never Say Never to Always', a track from Charles Manson's *Lie*. It was becoming impossible to cover 'Helter Skelter' without Manson's shadow falling over its performance or reception; in the battle for the legacy of the 1960s countercultural project, 'Helter Skelter' had become ammunition for the sceptics.

Recovering 'Helter Skelter'

It was this cultural repositioning of 'Helter Skelter' which must have prompted U2's intervention at the opening of *Rattle and Hum* in 1988 when Bono famously introduced their live cover with the announcement, 'This is a song Charles Manson stole from the Beatles. We're stealing it back.' What follows is an imitative and somewhat insipid cover, lacking any recognisable U2 signature elements such as the Edge's guitar harmonics and layered delay, or the band's characteristic atmospheric expansiveness. *Rattle and Hum*, apparently a musical road trip into the roots of American music, is actually fixated on the late 1960s, the brief period when rock and revolution seemed to fuse. Quotes from the Rolling Stones, Van Morrison's Them and Jimi Hendrix at Woodstock supplement the album's two covers – 'Helter Skelter' and a version of 'All Along the Watchtower' which retains Hendrix's rearrangement of Dylan's song but loses his articulate guitar passages. These two songs have arguably become emblematic of the dark side of the 1960s –

played over clips of iconic 1960s events and images, as they frequently are, they inevitably darken them, evoking violence and degeneration rather than revolution and liberation. U2's versions of both apparently attempt to remove these accreted associations by reinserting them into the vocabulary and canon of 'classic rock'. In taking back 'Helter Skelter', U2 are attempting to negate Manson's appropriation of the song and its subsequent Mansonian reinterpretations; for U2 the song exists in a late-1960s depoliticised rockutopia.

Immediately following U2's undertaking to remove 'Helter Skelter' from its contextual contaminations, the original was sampled back into the late-1980s mediatised morass by Negativland in 'Helter Stupid'. This 18-minute long sampled montage – redolent of, and briefly sampling from, 'Revolution 9' – splices elements including the Beatles' 'Helter Skelter' and an interview with Manson with numerous contemporaneous fragments from a sensationalist and superficial media landscape. *Helter Stupid* is part of Negativland's assault on a gullible culture which is in thrall to fundamentalist religion and lurid headlines. Less analytical, and more exhibitionist, is the same year's 'Worlock' by Skinny Puppy, which samples Manson singing lyrics from 'Helter Skelter' over a fragment of the Beatles' guitar introduction. Charles Manson exerted an unusual fascination over the industrial music scene of the 1980s and 1990s. Post-punk band Cabaret Voltaire used several Manson interview samples on their 1985 album *The Covenant, the Sword and the Arm of the Lord*; My Life with the Thrill Kill Kult sampled Family member Lynette 'Squeaky' Fromme on 'After the Flesh'; but the most Manson-obsessed of the electro-industrial bands is Electric Hellfire Club, with several songs about the Family and the murders amongst their eclectically macabre output. Closer to heavy metal is Nine Inch Nails' *The Downward Spiral*, recorded in the house on Cielo Drive in which Sharon Tate and her guests were murdered, and featuring several oblique references to the killings and to the 'White Album' (Udo 2002: 209–10). The video for the earlier 'Gave Up' was filmed in the house, again with arcane references to its history as a crime scene, and featured Trent Reznor's new signing, Marilyn Manson. While the latter's appellation is itself a sardonic critique of the American media's obsession with celebrities and murder, Reznor's cryptic allusions to the Manson Family, refracted through veiled references to significant tracks on the 'White Album', work to augment Manson's mystique. The metonymic chain that leads to the end of the 1960s, through 'Helter Skelter', Cielo Drive and Manson, is used here to symbolise the protagonist of *The Downward Spiral*'s psychodrama. While Manson is not explicitly evoked as an iconic representation of the murderous conclusion to the counterculture, the album does cement the identification between 'Helter Skelter' and the Manson murders, and does so in order to turn the complex and highly politicised late 1960s into a metaphor for individualised trauma and victimhood.

In contrast to the cryptic invocation of Manson by Nine Inch Nails, industrial metal contemporaries White Zombie, and their founder Rob Zombie, have consistently advertised their Mansonian interests, expressed through song titles, sampling and imagery (Udo 2002: 163); the conjunction of 'Helter Skelter' with the Manson murders would reach an apogee with their live performances of the song in the early 1990s. White Zombie's version seems to draw on the heavy metal signatures established by Mötley Crüe, featuring a heavy drum beat in an extended introduction, and an abrupt move to a flattened III position on the final beat of each second bar of the verse. In common with the other heavy metal covers, the musical historiography of the original is overwritten; but White Zombie go further in firmly attaching 'Helter Skelter' to its Mansonic mythography. This 'Helter Skelter' partakes of heavy metal's *grand guignol* traits, which, spliced with Zombie's fascination with 1960s exploitation cinema, transforms epoch-ending murders into the material of schlock horror movies. The legacy of the 1960s counterculture would be refigured not in terms of its radical politics but through the display of its deracinated image.

Throughout the 1990s 'Helter Skelter' mutated and proliferated, as dozens of artists seemed to challenge U2's late-1980s bid to impose a singular and secure performance style on the song. While White Zombie attempted to exploit and intensify its sinister aura, for a plethora of other artists the song and its associations were material for ironic refashioning. Generic adaptations included jazz and rock instrumentals (Heavy Tuba, Mika Yoshida, Gamalon, Alice Donut), swing (Honk, Wail and Moan), psycho/rockabilly (Mad Mongols, the Ubangis), international punk (Idora, SexA, Mamá Ladilla), indie and goth (That Petrol Emotion, Rosetta Stone), bluegrass (Armchair Radicals), funk (Hoo Doo Soul Band), rap/metal (Urban Dance Squad), lounge (Necro Tonz), chamber pop (Lamé Gold) and stoner comedy (David Peel and the Lower East Side). Amidst the torrent of 1990s versions – which has accelerated in subsequent years – what seems to be absent is 'straight' rock covers of 'Helter Skelter'. Apart from bootlegged live performances by Trouble and Bon Jovi, and a handful of releases by tribute bands, only Skrew's 1997 recording approximates a rendition respectful of its rock origins; even here, though, several false starts and an incongruous piano accompaniment add a layer of frame-breaking irony. Detached from the rock moment of the late 1960s, it is no longer inevitable that 'Helter Skelter' signifies its originary contexts and countercultural conflicts.

'Helter Skelter' exhibits an unusual musicological hybridity which has allowed its mutation into a wide range of generically diverse covers.[3] In 2009 alone, there were at least 20 versions legitimately released, and a simple YouTube search will reveal numerous further amateur realisations, in addition to live performances, talent show broadcasts and mash-ups. Largely cut free from its unfortunate associations, as well as from its position at the apex of countercultural rock, it now requires an act of wilful provocation to reinvoke the auratic power of 'Helter Skelter'. Bonemachine's 2003 recording dispels any ambiguity by subtitling their cover – an 18-minute ambient industrial track, with a short looped guitar sample from the original – 'A Tribute to C. Manson'. When taken with the appearance of other tracks by the artist behind Bonemachine on a tribute album to the Chilean neo-Nazi philosopher Miguel Serrano, this is a reminder of Manson's continuing

---

[3] Details of the many covers of 'Helter Skelter' can be found at http://helterskeltercovers.wordpress.com/.

appeal to extremist ideologues, and an indication of the often overlooked roots of contemporary white nationalism in 1960s libertarianism. Manson also continues to exert a morbid fascination for those exploring the violent depths of contemporary urban society. Underground rapper MF Grimm's 'Karma' namechecks Manson, along with notorious Mafia hitman Roy Demeo, over a looped sample of the rhythm guitar track from 'Helter Skelter'. Only when mixed with the potency of Manson's name can 'Helter Skelter' still signal the authentic paranoia of the millenarian 1960s.

Paul McCartney's 'Helter Skelter', however, has had a different fate to Charles Manson's. McCartney began playing 'Helter Skelter' live for the first time in 2004, performing it at Glastonbury that year, and at the Live 8 concert in 2005; it continues to feature in his live set. In 2011 his performance on the 2009 live album *Good Evening New York City* won the Grammy for Best Solo Rock Vocal. The song now seems free from its historical taint, exorcised of its demons through McCartney's reclamation, and the marker of his rocker credentials. McCartney's performances are acts of radical forgetting, though the song's deviant frisson must still be present for many listeners. After over 40 years in which 'Helter Skelter' has variously signalled the failure of the 1960s, a hard rock heritage, metallic origins, schlock horror and apocalyptic race war, it now communicates an institutionally respectable radical chic. As the 1960s turn from memory into history, 'Helter Skelter' remains one of the few cultural objects which can still summon forth its revolutionary spectre.

Chapter 6
Apocalyptic Music: Reflections on Countercultural Christian Influence

Shawn David Young

Jesus Freaks

During the late 1960s, there was a revival of conservative, evangelical Christianity among youth in the USA. While this included youth from a number of backgrounds and traditions, hippie Christians entranced media to the point of making headlines with major publications such as *Time* and *Life*. Commonly referred to as the Jesus Movement, the revival challenged traditional Christian aesthetics while embracing a conservative understanding of the Bible. Dubbed 'Jesus freaks', hippie converts represented a group of Christians who displayed similar qualities endemic to converts during the Great Awakenings. Historian Donald E. Miller has considered the impact of the Jesus Movement, arguing that it had the makings of a second Reformation: 'Many of the principles of the Reformation were reborn as ordinary people discovered the priesthood of all believers, without ever reading Martin Luther' (Miller 1999: 11, 12). Similarly, Jesus freaks questioned the authority of the church and reinstated biblical authority while simultaneously retaining what was widely considered a countercultural aesthetic, often sporting the hippie image while using popular music for Christian proselytising. The fact that these converts rebelled against the Church (initially) within a conservative 'grid' is not without historical precedent. In considering the Second Great Awakening and new paradigm Christianity Miller notes, 'in both instances, establishment religion is rejected' (ibid.: 11, 12, 13, 67, 180–85). As Jesus freaks became the 'new paradigm' for many young evangelicals, a new norm was established, one which co-opted the tools and expressions common to other cultural revolutionaries. For Jesus freaks, the rejection of 'establishment religion' had less to do with theology and more to do with using the cultural vernacular as a way of creating distance from the parent culture – though the eventual goal would be to reform the establishment.

The reverend Billy Graham made the Jesus Movement viable, offering a bridge for countercultural youth to return to evangelical Christianity (Eskridge 1998: 106). Eileen Luhr argues that campus movements during the 1960s were actually about the 'existential search for self-meaning and only secondarily as a leftist attempt at structural change'. If the period is recast in this manner, she argues, the Jesus Movement becomes 'a critical part of the decade rather than an aberration'

(Luhr 2009: 74), allowing certain hippies to be 'reintegrated into the "continuing American consensus"' (ibid.: 68).

For youth, evangelism (proselytising) surfaced in mediums such as publishing, film, television, festivals and music, becoming a powerful force within American popular culture. This continued the historical lineage of American evangelicalism, affirming what historians such as David Bebbington and Nathan Hatch consider a complex, growing movement.[1] Donald Miller adds to the growing consensus surrounding the movement's place in history. Specifically, Miller's treatment of the movement's ecclesial legacy (new paradigm churches) demonstrates how Jesus freaks institutionalised their attempts to counter mainline liberalism's 'inability' to deal with existential anxiety. Noting the cultural impact of the Jesus Movement, historian Larry Eskridge (1998: 104) underscores the reciprocal element (religion influencing culture and vice versa) common to early Jesus freaks who made use of and benefited from American popular culture: 'Indeed, the Jesus Person "style" continued to prosper as a distinct evangelical youth culture with concerts, coffeehouses, newspapers, bumper stickers, crosses, and Bible studies ....'

The movement's countercultural roots (in the narrower example of the hippie movement) have been well established by historians of religion in the USA. However, the connection between the Jesus freaks, music and apocalypticism remains largely under-researched. To better understand the significance of

---

[1] David Bebbington has argued that that the principles of the Enlightenment made the rise of individualistic evangelical Christianity possible. Bebbington's 'quadrilateral' (conversion, biblicism, crucicentrism and activism) crystallises his conception of both the heritage of the Reformation and the growth of holiness and pietistic movements in eighteenth- and nineteenth-century American society. Bebbington provides a definition from which I can compare others. Mark Noll prefaces his definition of 'evangelical' by suggesting a difference between historical definitions and categorical definitions. The 'historical' simply refers to the genealogical organic lineage of any group which can be traced back to figures such as Jonathan Edwards, George Whitfield or John Wesley. He considers the Reformation and Martin Luther's criteria for Christianity, but uses American revivalists as catalysts for what reformed leaders regard as a movement – evangelicalism as popular conservative Protestantism within the American context, later diverging from reformed theology. Evangelicalism is a complex network of bible colleges, publishers and parachurch organisations, which hold to common traits. Thus the movement ('ISM') is somewhat nebulous; D.G. Hart and Jon R. Stone argue that evangelicalism is not a true movement. The 'categorical' refers to five categories Noll uses to define evangelical belief: scripture (divine authority and foundation for faith and practice), experience of God (emphasis on encounter and heart-assurance), rejection of institutions (priesthood of all believers, personal hermeneutics), flexibility (evangelicals adjust to culture) and discipline (piety, holiness, tenacity). Nathan Hatch positions evangelical Christianity within the American context, arguing that both the revolutionary spirit of early America and the democratic impulse created a form of Christianity which valued free-will (a departure from Calvinism), anti-clerical and populist hermeneutics. Thus, a rupture between cleric and commoner created a populist pope, each person their own theologian.

'countercultural Christian music', one must look to the political 'personality' of the movement, despite its own self-proclaimed apoliticism.

To the Left or the Right?

Throughout the 1970s and 1980s, evangelical activism was, for the most part, confined to a war over family values. Despite this, Jesus-freak veterans identified social causes that aligned with their own cosmology – but first they had to perceive the original attempts of the counterculture as flawed, particularly the New Left. What made new forms of activism necessary was the failure of the New Left. Todd Gitlin (1993: 436, 437) writes that 'The New Left, like its predecessors, failed to create lasting political forms; when SDS [Students for a Democratic Party] was torn apart, so was the chance for continuity.' Consequently, 'the New Left failed to produce the political leaders one might have expected of a movement so vast', writes Gitlin. 'The millennial, all-or-nothing moods of the Sixties', he contends, 'proved to be poor training grounds for practical politics.' Similarly, many Jesus freaks of the 1970s were ill prepared to organise sustained efforts toward projects dedicated to social justice. Furthermore, post-Jesus Movement evangelicals during the 1980s (many of whom were part of the Jesus-freak exodus from culture) translated activism in service of the Religious Right during the Reagan years (Eskridge 2005; Balmer 2006; Shires 2007; Stowe 2011).

The co-optation of the Jesus Movement by the Religious Right has been well documented.[2] Rightist affiliation, however, did not extend to aesthetics. Rather, the power of aesthetics was harnessed to serve evangelical Christianity, a movement that grew increasingly conservative throughout the Reagan era. If nothing else, the hippie aesthetic was sutured to Biblical literalism, an approach to exegesis that has long been the hallmark of Christian fundamentalism. In *Hippies of the Religious Right*, Preston Shires argues that both Christian fundamentalism and liberal Christianity alienated youth throughout the 1960s (Shires 2007). Fundamentalism was anachronistic. Liberalism was fraught with endless theological uncertainty. Thus a hybrid (of sorts) was needed. 'The eventual unity and common purpose shared between countercultural Christianity and evangelicalism', writes Shires, 'surpassed that shared by the Beats and the Old Left ... so much so that whereas the Old Left and the New Left disagreed on the means and purpose of reaching a non-capitalistic manner of life, countercultural Christianity [hippie Christianity] and evangelicalism eventually became unified both in goal and practice' (ibid.: 113). He maintains that the inability for the Old and New Left to agree on social strategies actually proved advantageous for 'conservative' evangelicals, particularly during the rise of the Right in the 1980s.

The move rightward for Jesus freaks was multifaceted. Although early hippies have often been depicted as apolitical, early Jesus freaks (to some extent) balanced

---

[2] See Shires, Eskridge, Stowe, Miller and Luhr.

their skyward gaze with a form of practical politics nuanced by dedication to a specific brand of eschatology, most notably dispensational premillennialism, a doctrine fleshed out by the nineteenth-century minister John Nelson Darby. For many hippie converts this eschatological position connected global events to the doctrine of the Rapture, an event many evangelicals believe a seminal moment in history: Christ will secretly gather those who have been 'born again' skyward, leaving the 'unsaved' to endure a tumultuous world governed by the antichrist.

It was believed that global events portended things to come. 'Part of the reason countercultural Christians would move rightward in their political orientation', argues Shires, had little to do with domestic policies, but 'a great deal to do with world affairs' (Shires 2007: 153–5). Unconditional support for Israel was 'perhaps the first shepherding of Jesus Freaks toward a political position' (ibid.: 108). Simply put, Jesus freaks were wooed by mythologies of the apocalypse, not unlike their secular counterparts.

Connecting doomsday to the Middle East was stylish throughout the 1970s and 1980s. Author Hal Lindsey's epic *The Late Great Planet Earth* (1970) ushered in a new generation of doomsday disciples as global events all appeared to confirm what both secularists and religionists suspected – the end was near. It is within this milieu that Lindsey's novel, writes David W. Stowe, 'popularized and condensed a body of thought about the end of the world that reached back over a century' (Stowe 2001: 70, 71).

Jesus Freaks and Rightist Affiliates

Pastors trained within the context of the Jesus Movement often maintained the hippie aesthetic. However, they tended to shed the more radical political notions previously held by affiliate countercultural movements: for example, Beats, Diggers, the Black Panthers, Weathermen, Motherfuckers, hippies, yippies and SDS. Despite any attempt to construct an ideological distance from secular counterparts, Jesus-freak pastors remained wary of a 'plastic' America as they simultaneously decried the excesses of reactionary moralities, which typified the now-romanticised 'seeker' of the 1960s and 'hedonist' of the 1970s.

For the Jesus Movement, a growing amorality appeared antithetical to the original intent of the hippie quest for enlightenment. Thus, many rallied around the growing Religious Right. Duane M. Oldfield writes that 'the New Right is seen as a status-based reaction against the trends of modernisation and the social elites who embody those trends' producing anxieties, which produce reactions 'against the complexities of the modern world' (Oldfield 1996: 38). Ironically, this is a similar social critique held by those in the New Left. Oldfield differentiates between the various expressions of the Right: New Right, Religious Right, Christian Right, Moral Majority and the Christian Coalition. Hoping to find a common ground (the culture war), some of these umbrella organisations affirmed an ecumenism – that created a coalition of politically and culturally like-minded constituents – regardless of theological orientation. Others particularised their agendas. But overall, social issues that involved faith-based interpretations of 'morality' trumped concerns for social justice as personal 'encounters' with Jesus (or faith-based family values) took priority. Organised efforts to avoid (or at the very least, minimise) social justice/activism was linked to millenarian expectancy; evangelists sought to convert people before the End of Days or to re-establish a Christian nation before the end. But what sort of action does this involve?

The millennialist vision often produces both action and apathy. Martha Lee and Herbert Simms (2008: 112) argue that within the North American context 'a group's orientation (religious or secular) is a stronger predictor of [millenarian-based] violence [or social apathy] than the socioeconomic factors that contribute to the initial development of millenarianism.' While the context used by Lee and Simms applies to violence it is conceivable that those apathetic to social justice – poverty, war, the environment and so on – are involved in a direct form of inaction (action by negation). Put another way, when matters of social justice are de-prioritised due to millennial expectancy (as was the case with evangelists such as D.L. Moody and Billy Sunday), what is otherwise a passive millenarianism becomes ironically active as leaders and parishioners allow suspicions of government and science – because of eschatological assumptions – to overwhelm any sense of objectivity concerning social causes linked to state and federal funding. Active inaction (or conscious social apathy) is evidenced in various Christian rock songs popularised during the 1980s (discussed later). Thus any attempts within conservative evangelicalism to engage social issues (those deemed important by establishment evangelicals) are often blunted as the End of Days remains ever on the horizon for the millenarian. The most noteworthy example of social apathy remains environmentalism.

Post-hippie Jesus freaks quelled any former urge to support environmental causes (as one example) thus countering their original parent (counter) culture. According to Frank Schaeffer (son of Christian apologist Francis Schaeffer), Richard Cizik, former vice president of the National Association of Evangelicals, 'had almost been forced out … when James Dobson [*Focus on the Family*] wrote to the NAE [National Association of Evangelicals] board demanding Cizik's dismissal for saying that he thought global warming was real' (Schaeffer 2009). There are certainly those who oppose this issue based on a perceived lack of scientific evidence or the fiscal effects of environmental activism and industrial overhaul – the loss of jobs. However, Dobson represents a continuum of evangelicals (which includes baby boom, Jesus Movement veterans) who affirm the doctrine of human depravity and view suspect any attempt to 'engineer' divine plan. The moratorium placed on environmentalism has been cloaked (at least in the past) in a shroud of religious determinism. Put another way, while conservative evangelicals have often opposed government regulations on economic grounds, the spectre of eschatology, I would argue, fuels economic theory – at least for those who have maintained a commitment to theologies associated with the Rapture and the Middle East.

This brand of evangelicalism has often characterised social justice as a mere bandage on a wound that yields to divine plan, only healed after a quite specific cosmic story unfolds. If this were otherwise – if Dobson's call for Cizik's resignation were merely a difference of opinion on matters of science or fiscal responsibility – he would not have called for the resignation of a position that represents spiritual leadership. Was Dobson's problem theological? Although James Dobson also represents a tradition of evangelicals who seek to (ironically) Christianise society, the millenarian impulse remains a powerful influence over biblical literalists. But this impulse does not negate the need to Christianise society. On the contrary. The apocalyptic tradition has many facets, two of which have thoroughly defined conservative, American evangelicals since the nineteenth century.

Many Jesus freaks were strongly influenced by Hal Lindsey's popular reiteration of dispensational premillennialism. However, for the postmillennialist, Christ will only return to a well-kept planet, one peopled by believers awaiting God's kingdom to come on Earth – literally. The result has been an increase in Christian Dominionism, a belief that Jesus will return and establish his kingdom on Earth after Christians have occupied positions of power. Contemporary Dominionism can be seen in the movement led by C. Peter Wagner's New Apostolic Reformation, a push to '"reclaim the seven mountains of culture": government, religion, media, family, business, education, and arts and entertainment' – a countercultural act if there ever were one (Burke 2011)!

Exceptions to the Rule

As has been established, early Jesus freaks (and music associated with the movement) engaged in a revival of a more conservative version of evangelical Christianity. But despite the near ubiquity of pop forms of Christian revivalism throughout the 1970s and 1980s, other expressions existed. Although common historical narratives about the West Coast Jesus Movement often portray communities such as the Vineyard Church and Calvary Chapel as co-opted arms of the Religious Right, little attention has been given to the left wing of the movement.

Throughout the 1960s and into the 1970s a great number of Jesus-freak communes developed, each with very different agendas. In considering a number of countercultural communal experiments of the time, Timothy Miller has observed that 'so many of them erupted that the Jesus movement communes may have been, in terms of sheer numbers of communes and of members, the largest identifiable communal type during the 1960s era' (Miller 1999: xxiv). Although these were all communally based and evangelical, they were not necessarily left-leaning in political identity.

After the initial movement's late 1960s' genesis in southern California (Eskridge 2005) a parallel story developed. In the winter of 1972 the seeds for a very different expression of evangelical Christianity and music formed out of Milwaukee, Wisconsin's Jesus People Army (JPA). Out of this community sprang a collective articulation of evangelical Christianity that was wholly counter to its predecessors. A handful of JPA members were sent out as the Jesus People U.S.A. Traveling Team, a folk-rock style 'Jesus music' group. This travelling community gave rise to a new communal experiment known as Jesus People USA (JPUSA) and evangelicalism's first official hard rock group, the Resurrection Band (also known as Rez).

The fledgling community settled in Chicago's Uptown neighbourhood with hopes of providing aid to local low-income families and the homeless. JPUSA's commune continues as a group of aging Jesus freaks and young punks and 'goths'. Considered a significant development for any evangelical community – particularly in the shadow of American individualism and capitalism – this inner-city commune's choice to live out of a common purse serves as a counterpoint to what has historically been viewed as the Republican base – at least within recent years. With an annual average of 400 members, this left-leaning community complicates assumptions about evangelical ideology and music. Along with other members of the 'Evangelical Left' – such as Brian McLaren and Jim Wallis, Shane Claiborne and Sojourners – this community serves as the exception to a once widespread conservatism among American evangelicals. But as we shall see, the Christian version of the countercultural 'impulse' – the need to challenge the hegemonic structure of the more dominant forms of Christianity (in this case, evangelicalism) – continues to inspire converts influenced by cultural radicalism, specifically the kind nurtured by early hippies and beatniks (Young 2011).

Songs of the End

Throughout the 1960s and 1970s there was a growing fascination with the Apocalypse. Barry McGuire's classic 'Eve of Destruction' (1965) gained notoriety within the context of radicals, revolutionaries and those who were convinced the world was on the brink of either cosmic or physical annihilation. Along with Bob Dylan, McGuire's conversion to Christianity gave credibility to the rising Jesus-freak revolution. As celebrities such as Johnny Cash and Eric Clapton converted, revivalistic Christianity found entry into the entertainment industry, launching a groundswell of activity. Paul Stookey preached at Berkeley's Sproul Hall. Kerry Livgren ended his search in the early 1980s, espousing Christianity openly through his rock group Kansas. And Fleetwood Mac's Jeremy Spencer joined the rigid and controversial commune the Children of God, a notable doomsday group.

Secular rock groups also explored religious themes, adding to the already enigmatic culture of Christian hippies. The Byrds' version of 'Jesus Is Just Alright' (1969), Ocean's 'Put Your Hand in the Hand' (1970), Creedence Clearwater Revival's 'Bad Moon Rising' (1969), and Norman Greenbaum's 'Spirit in the Sky' (1969) all implied that some expressions of the Cultural Revolution were beginning to change focus – to a point.[3] A paradigmatic shift occurred as young people wove tales of doomsday and sought absolutist resolve within a postmodern milieu. The result, however, was not merely the quieting of existential angst. Rather, this new movement gained hegemonic power as minstrels of the apocalypse found cultural traction within the religious mainstream.

Early converts knew the power of rock and roll. Hoping to garner a following, they chose to employ tools with which they were most familiar. In 1971, *Time* magazine said of the music that it was the 'special medium of the Jesus Movement'. Musicals such as *Jesus Christ Superstar* and *Godspell* added to a growing interest in hippie Christianity (spirituality more generally), bringing what was, to some extent, a vestige of Christian thinking into every sphere of pop culture. Christian rock emphasised a cosmology that was both triumphalist/postmillenialist (God's kingdom can be realised on earth as Christianity gains global influence) and premillennialist (Jesus would return in the Rapture to escort believers to Heaven). Now a powerful force in the music industry, Christian rock still retains elements of the eschatology that defined early Jesus freaks. As a result, fans often maintain a skyward gaze, looking for what humans have sought for centuries – signs of the end.

While Jesus freaks were largely apolitical, their fascination with the end of time – evidenced by their music – underscored the ways in which they viewed and engaged society. In *Children of Doom*, John W. Drakeford (1972: 36) refers to the phenomenon of this fledgling movement as a 'strange shotgun marriage of conservative religion and a rebellious counterculture'. Young converts simply expected the imminent return of Christ and the battle of Armageddon – and they viewed global events as predictors of things to come.

As established earlier, the millennial fervour that seemed to affect various expressions of the Cultural Revolution was already evident in pop music. McGuire's 'Eve of Destruction' painted a cynical picture of a hypocritical, violent world contributing to its own demise. But the immediate concern over catastrophic events such as the Vietnam War faded as Jesus freaks turned their attention to what they perceived as the big picture.

In the early 1970s Jesus rocker Larry Norman warned of the coming Rapture of the church. Others followed, proclaiming the advent of the apocalypse. Songs of doom and glory went beyond mere hokum escapades by hopeful minstrels seeking a better world. Music influenced by any 'politics of the end' was grounded in a deeper, populist response to a chaotic world. But it also represented a particular interpretation of historic events related to biblical prophecy. David W. Stowe (2011: 71) has argued that through the teachings of various Jesus Movement leaders, 'the theology of Rapture and Armageddon [became] one of the central threads in the music and belief of baby boom Christians, touching the music of everyone from [Jesus rockers] Larry Norman and Keith Green to Bob Dylan.'

---

[3] 'Jesus Is Just Alright' was written by Arthur Reid Reynolds and first recorded in 1966. 'Put Your Hand in the Hand' was written by Gene MacLellan.

Norman's classic song 'I Wish We'd All Been Ready' (1972) – part of the track to the film series that mirrored author Hal Lindsey's *The Late Great Planet Earth* – highlighted the sense of urgency with which evangelicals dealt; it was the anthem of the Jesus Movement's rapture theology throughout the 1970s and formed the seedbed for what would come to define evangelical pop music throughout the 1980s.

Jesus music gained cultural traction, giving rise to a formidable niche genre known as contemporary Christian music (CCM). Throughout the 1980s Christian rock emerged into an expression of Christian conservatism on par with the political agenda of the Religious Right. Bands and songs evinced an historical connection with Jesus-Movement predecessors and Reagan-era evangelicalism. As such, CCM – seated in Nashville, the epicentre of the Bible Belt – eventually became associated with political positions that were nationalistic, anti-abortion, pro-military and, to some extent, anti-gay. In this sense, the brand of CCM endemic to Reagan-era evangelicalism worked to operate as a contrary to many of the cultural values established during the Cultural Revolution.

Eileen Luhr offers an analysis of this cultural moment and its subsequent impact on American youth. Throughout the 1980s, argues Luhr, parents 'aggressively sought to reclaim the category of youth' hoping to restore meaning, purpose, and 'traditional authority in both public and private spaces' (2009: 33). The perception of cultural threat warranted new ways of viewing culture, thus continuing the evangelical heritage of cultural activism. Contrary to the Old Right, these families believed they could co-opt converts to '"restore" Christianity to the dominant spaces of suburbia' (ibid.: 101). For conservatives, young people represented a new hope to challenge issues considered detrimental to traditional values. The elimination of school prayer and the legalisation of abortion mobilised a new generation of culture-savvy evangelicals. Couched in the rhetoric of war, these issues were presented (via Christian rock) in a way that tapped youth rebellion, thus serving the purposes of conservative organisations such as the Moral Majority and the Christian Coalition. Moreover, Christian metal bands, writes Luhr, were 'an integral part of the cultural work of the Christian Right which comment[ed] on contemporary society' (ibid.: 136).

This new form of socio-cultural activism also served 'Middle America' by exploring 'suburban revivalism', a development Luhr links to baby boom evangelicals and the various cultural possibilities established during the Jesus Movement. Her study of the 1998 Harvest Crusade – an evangelical outreach event held at the Anaheim Stadium in Anaheim, California – offers a glimpse into a quintessential example of post-Jesus Movement, baby boom evangelicalism. The crusade exemplified how evangelical Christianity absorbed popular entertainment and later came to define 'third-wave' evangelical conservatism at the turn of the century.

Suburban revivalism during the 1990s went beyond simple proselytising, going on to serve as a platform for conservative responses to the 'culture war'. Viewed as an affront to 'family values', issues such as gay rights continued to galvanise social conservatives, providing impetus for a newer, revised activism as evangelicals offered crusades, Christian rock festivals, and developed business relationships with amusement parks. Moreover, 'evangelicals tried to buttress conservative values by making consumer culture – from bumper stickers to contemporary music to a ballpark atmosphere – a starting point for restoring biblical values to the suburbs', providing evangelicals with important acts of 'sacralization in which public space was claimed for Christ' (Luhr 2009: 177). 'In 2004', writes Luhr, 'concerts and benefits became part of a broader infrastructure for locating conservative voters' (ibid.: 197).

Beyond the battle for culture, a number of music groups remained apocalyptically-minded, often depicting their 'brand' as rhetorically combative in both name and lyric: Stryken, Bloodgood, Gardian (later Guardian), Rage of Angels, Sacred Warrior and Holy Soldier. Song lyrics portrayed a universe embattled with the forces of darkness, emphasising a world on the brink of nuclear, cultural or spiritual holocaust. The doctrine of the Rapture continued to be proclaimed in song throughout the 1980s and 1990s. Christian rock warned of the impending close of history. Petra's 'Grave Robber' (1983) and 'Not of This World' (1983), as well as Mylon Le Fevre's 'Crack the Sky' (1987) all portrayed a transitory world for those who had been 'born again'. Those who were 'lost' would endure the antichrist and hell.

Post-Jesus Movement converts continued to look skyward for the Second Coming. Christian rockers echoed a similar message: the world was evil and would soon be judged by God. While not entirely xenophobic, these groups have been categorised by sociologist Jay R. Howard as 'Separational CCM', a model that characterises the artist as one who is wholly counter to mainline culture and is wholly separate from what is perceived as evil (Howard and Streck 1999).

While standard 'mainstream' Christian rock continued to mirror separational tendencies (a product of Cold War evangelical tension), heavy metal brought with it the headiest representations of human anxiety. Metal came to dominate much of the 'arena rock' genre of the 1980s. Not unlike accomodationist methods of early Jesus rockers, metal heads and punk rockers applied a biblical worldview to musical forms once deemed subversive by mainline evangelicals, gesturing toward a different version of social inversion (Hebdige 1979). Despite this, notes historian Eileen Luhr, the burgeoning new styles were given the green light as parents and churches seized the opportunity to use metal and punk to invert 'sinful' messages portrayed by their secular counterparts. This co-optation (if we can call it that) allowed evangelical youth to engage in social and cultural resistance – to both the secular and CCM mainstream. The metal group Stryper's *Soldiers Under Command* (1985) capitalised on teen angst, encouraging listeners that they were part of God's army – which would vanquish the forces of evil. Even mainstream CCM groups such as Petra contributed to the milieu with songs that portrayed either cultural embattlement or apocalypticism: 'This Means War' (1987), 'He Came, He Saw, He Conquered' (1987), ending the decade with 'Armed and Dangerous' (1990).

Christian heavy metal music has played a significant role in dichotomising the world and inspiring the apocalyptic imagination. As a genre, heavy metal (regardless of religious affiliation) often constructs lyrics and imagery around apocalyptic scenarios, couching terrestrial life in clear binaries of good and evil, notes Jason Bivens. Emphasising the darker side of life, many expressions of metal articulate

> alternate social worlds; these worlds may consist of sword and sorcery valour (Dio) or socio-political criticism (Napalm Death or Lamb of God), but they all bear traces of what [musicologist Robert] Walser identifies as metal's key elements – its rebelliousness, its promise of an alternative identity and community, and its discourse of alienation and nihilism … (Bivens 2008: 107, 108).

Perry L. Glanzer argues that heavy metal music often draws from 'Dionysian and Chaotic strands of pagan myth' (2003). Glanzer cites sociologist Deena Weinstein who writes:

> Dionysian experience … is embodied in the unholy trinity of sex, drugs and rock and roll. The Dionysian is juxtaposed to a strong emotional involvement in all that challenges the order and hegemony of everyday life: monsters, the underworld and hell, the grotesque and horrifying, disasters, mayhem, carnage, injustice, death and rebellion. Both Dionysus (the Greek god of wine) and Chaos (the most ancient god, who precedes from itself) are empowered by the sonic values of the music to fight a never-ending battle for the soul of the genre and to join together in combat against the smug security and safety of respectable society. (Weinstein 1991: 35)

Glanzer draws on Weinstein's work to demonstrate how various Christians have appropriated the heavy metal genre, which actually compliments Christian millennial-apocalyptic mythology. Using Weinstein's argument that metal largely draws on rhetorics of chaos rooted in Judeo-Christianity, Glanzer makes evident the connection between Christian heavy metal music and doomsday scenarios. He suggests that for a particular heavy metal church known as Sanctuary – an evangelical gathering that has encouraged the development of Christian metal – 'apocalyptic images from Daniel and Revelation and references to the battle between good and evil, as well as Ecclesiastical allusions regarding hopelessness and meaninglessness of life, were prominent' (Glanzer 2003).

Evangelical musics have often underscored the dire nature of the world, as we have already established. Luhr's account reinforces my own suspicion that fans of these genres adopted their own subversive messages in the interest of countering the secular mainstream:

> The Christian punk and metal scenes often offered contradictory messages that illuminate the contested nature of Christian and rock culture and that defy

attempts to oversimplify what 'conservatism' offered to young people. Christian youths in the late twentieth century redefined true rebellion in a post-Christian (and post-1960s) world as obedience to biblical authority and resistance to a sinful world. In this interpretation, religious devotion and personal holiness allowed Christians to lay claim to being mavericks of popular culture. (Luhr 2009: 27)

Popular Christian music has often highlighted the human condition, the hope for a divinely orchestrated cataclysm, and even the macabre. Yet the forces of pluralism have begun to redefine ontological boundaries long cherished by evangelical musicians, allowing dialogue for ecumenical conversations pertaining to how the end should or ought to be perceived and represented in pop culture. To a certain extent the turn of the millennium ironically brought with it more nuanced interpretations of the end of time.

Changes

Although CCM of the 1990s remained overtly Christian, many artists began to emphasise uncertainty about cosmic events. The Rapture had not occurred. And despite the emergence of new ventures into the apocalyptic – such as the *Left Behind* series, by Tim LaHaye and Jerry B. Jenkins, and spiritual thrillers penned by Frank E. Peretti – a new generation of evangelicals proceeded judiciously. Employing lyrical metaphor and seeking cultural relevance and authenticity, Christian rockers engaged postmodern evangelical culture throughout the 1990s and beyond. A new breed of culture-savvy evangelicals – who tended to avoid topics such as spiritual warfare and the End of Days – replaced bands like Holy Soldier and Bloodgood. Jars of Clay and Sixpence None the Richer emphasised meekness, bringing kinder, gentler 'culture warriors' into the social conversation. This 'integrational' model of CCM, notes Jay R. Howard, best typifies those who seek to transform culture covertly. Put another way, while groups such as Jars of Clay steer far from the 'Jesus is returning soon' approach of the 1970s and 1980s CCM, they are, nevertheless, exacting in their evangelical message.

Throughout the 1970s and 1980s contemporary Christian musicians such as Larry Norman looked skyward – and their legacy continues to influence even artists who resist biblical literalism. But the paradigm appears to be shifting. Stephen Prothero has noted Christian musician Steve Camp's call for the Christian music industry to repent collectively for its drift toward anthropocentrism; Camp argued that the industry has lost its Christocentric (even Heavenward) emphasis. Unlike early 'Jesus musicians' of the 1970s, modern Christian rockers (at least in lyric) remain more focused on this world rather than the next. Along with Hal Lindsey's work, Tim Lahaye's widely successful book series *Left Behind* (1995–2007) titillated rapture-minded believers throughout the 1990s. But today's evangelicals are – in some ways – inured to any claims about the end of time, particularly those rooted in certainty. Moreover, while a number of evangelicals of the past would have gladly basked in the possibilities associated with a doomsday orchestrated to favour the 'chosen', today's evangelicals – even the Rapture-minded – appear to exhibit a balance between cosmic hope and social justice.

Although Christian relief organisations such as Compassion International and World Vision have been long associated with the CCM universe, there is now a growing emphasis on humanitarianism, which evidences a fundamental shift in how eschatology is applied in daily life. In other words, the immediacy of the apocalyptic is placed squarely on the now rather than the later. But even though CCM has evolved over the years (now deemphasising eschatological immediacy) the apocalyptic impulse still remains. In its simplest form the meaning of the word 'apocalyptic' is far more basic. Apocalyptic literature merely reveals 'the hidden'. But in the United States, the term has been broadened and deepened, its roots traced to Judeo-Christian deterministic beliefs about teleology. As a result, the term is often associated with global events connected to the cosmic, its actual meaning relegated to a pedestrian lacklustre signifier. More to the point, music with roots in evangelical Christianity has always been 'revelatory', whether fantastic accounts of doomsday are discussed or not. Christian pop music is often used for the worship of God, instruction on biblical narratives, or for unveiling or revealing the Christian message. Thus CCM is always about the apocalyptic.

Perhaps one of the more noteworthy examples of the changes taking place in the world of evangelical music – and its relationship to the apocalyptic imagination and music – is the Cornerstone Music Festival, an annual event sponsored by Jesus People USA (JPUSA). Edgy, subcultural, multicultural, even pluralist, Cornerstone signals changes in evangelical Christianity (Young 2011) and changes in Christian rock, providing a gathering that 'has absolutely challenged the CCM industry', according to historian Mark Allan Powell.[4]

While Jesus Movement veterans remain respectful – even ecumenical – when considering the church universal, many have been vocal about the failings of the 'traditional' church. JPUSA and Christian leaders who attend Cornerstone have noted festivals that simply mirror the cultural mainstream – even when those festivals purport to counter mainstream society. Certainly those who represent both subcultural and mainstream expressions of the evangelical universe attend this event. However, at Cornerstone the net is cast wide as staff members seek to include as many forms and expressions as can be managed, to include a strange coexistence between punk rockers, metal heads and 'straights'. When considering the parent culture (establishment evangelicalism), Cornerstone can certainly be viewed as countercultural. But what is the festival countering? Are participants changing society, being changed or simply experiencing something, if only briefly – that which they do not and cannot experience in the workaday world? Evangelical Christianity is built on a lengthy history of experiential religion, cultural accommodation and acculturation. So what is the festival opposing?

---

[4] Email correspondence, 24 October 2006.

According to sociologist Doug Rossinow, when one considers the 1960s and 1970s, 'a counterculture was, by definition, both marginal and oppositional' (1998: 251). Cornerstone is both.

Conclusion

Apocalyptic music comes in many forms, and it will perhaps never lose its lustre or its socio-cultural appeal. Tensions pertaining to the purpose of 'sacred' musics of any genre notwithstanding, CCM has begun to fade into the grey of pluralism. Despite the fact that there exists a near recidivistic quality about the American millennialist, there remains a continued ecumenical effort, a collaboration to join with other persons of faith to realise the end of war, hunger, AIDS, and a new push toward environmentalism. And while there *was* a concerted effort in the past to demonise global humanitarian efforts as being futile at best or antichrist at worst, even Rapture-minded evangelicals admit – unlike their evangelical forerunners – that they simply do not know when 'the end' will come.

Chapter 7
Nobody's Army: Contradictory Cultural Rhetoric in *Woodstock* and *Gimme Shelter*

Gina Arnold

The epoch which displays its time to itself as essentially the sudden return of multiple festivities is also an epoch without festivals. What was, in cyclical time, the moment of a community's participation in the luxurious expenditure of life is impossible for the society without community or luxury. Mass pseudo-festivals, parodies of the dialogue and the gift, may incite people to excessive spending, but they only produce disillusion – which is invariably offset by further false promises. In the spectacle, the lower the use value of modern survival-time, the more highly it is exalted. The reality of time has been replaced by its publicity. (Guy Debord 2006: para. 154)

The genesis for this project occurred late on a summer evening in the last part of the last century, during a massive summer rainstorm that drenched an Ohio-area concert bowl during a stop on a tour called Lollapalooza. As thunder and lightning battered the concert-goers and the band Soundgarden churned up an equally riotous noise, the crowd took to wrenching the metal folding chairs that were bolted to the earth and hurling them like sleds down the hillside which the venue occupied. Before long, the lawn area had become a mudslide down which audience members were travelling on their stomachs, landing in a heap of flesh and hair at the bottom, tangled up like giant snakes. When the concert came to its premature end, Chris Cornell, the lead singer of the band, surveyed the bespattered scene. 'You guys look like somebody's army out there'. he said ruefully. 'The question is, whose army are you going to be?' (Arnold 1993: 202).[1]

That was in 1992. Since then, it has become clear that those kids were nobody's army. As a group, the 18–34-year-old white males that made up a large part of that crowd and others much like it have floated through the ensuing decades, more like a gaseous emanation than a cohesive demographic force. This chapter, excerpted from a larger work, interrogates the genesis of the powerlessness and lack of direction that rock crowds represent. While concert-goers at Lollapalooza and other large festivals invariably define themselves as rebellious, countercultural and liberal, they are in fact largely docile, passive and conservative. I argue here that this misperception stems in part from earlier misperceptions formed through

---

[1] The damage caused the cancelation of that week's Natalie Cole concert.

specific discursive rhetorics and constructions circulated in the film documentaries about Woodstock and Altamont.

I am focusing here on the documentaries for several reasons. First, as a former rock critic, I know how different individual perceptions of concerts can be from media consensus. More importantly, though both concerts have been written about and analysed at length, the films have been examined less frequently, particularly in tandem. Finally, while those concerts may have much to tell us about the counterculture, music, performance, spectacle and the 1960s, their legacy and role in shaping the ideology of the rock festival *qua* rock festival has been left largely unexamined. For example, Simon Frith's foundational essay '"The Magic That Can Set You Free": The Ideology of Folk and the Myth of the Rock Community' (1981) discusses how rock falsely sees itself as creating community, but does not focus on festivals *per se* as sites of cultural production. Andy Bennett's excellent book of collected essays *Remembering Woodstock* (2004) adds many insights to important aspects of the festival. Memory, representation, nostalgia, aesthetics and the popular are all discussed, but most of the chapters concentrate on the festival itself, not on the film (the exception is Bennett's own chapter, which addresses the film and nostalgia). Braunstein and Doyle's collection *Imagine Nation: The American Counterculture of the 1960s and '70s* (2002), as is the case with a number of other books on countercultural history, refers to Woodstock in a larger context, but is not primarily about music or music audiences. Finally, Dale Bell's collection of essays on the making of the Woodstock film, *Woodstock: An Inside Look at the Movie That Shook Up the World and Defined a Generation* (1999) adds insight into the actual making of the film, but never steps outside that vantage point to observe how the film affected ideology.

By contrast, my work takes a broader view of Woodstock's role as a purveyor of ideology. In it, I suggest how such historic rock festivals worked ideologically to legitimate the highly contradictory beliefs and actions of rock fans at present day concerts. From a contemporary standpoint, Woodstock and other free (or quasi-free) festivals of the late 1960s and early 1970s are often seen as the most visible flowerings of the term 'counterculture'. They were countercultural in the sense that, as Bennett describes it in this volume, they were 'a means of articulating aspects of counter-hegemonic ideology, practice and belief' (Introduction 'Reappraising "Counterculture"': 17). Although there is little doubt that Woodstock et al. were countercultural in the sense that they at least superficially challenged the norms of dominant, mainstream culture, this chapter questions whether such festivals were in fact ever counter-hegemonic. I suggest instead that many aspects of them and especially of their mediations – specifically the massively popular films *Woodstock: 3 Days of Peace and Music* and *Gimme Shelter* – were the opposite, working to reinforce hegemonic values of democracy, capitalism and the utility of a free market. Today, rock festival attendance is very much part of a supercultural experience, and I argue that the seeds of reappropriation were tucked into their genesis and displayed via their filmed depictions. In his introduction to this volume, Bennett suggests that in recent years 'counterculture' has become a less historically contingent term, one that refers less to ways of furthering social change or identity formation, and more towards a range of lifestyle choices made between people with similar sensibilities. Here, I locate that shift in the discourse to much earlier in history.

This misunderstanding between countercultural and counter-hegemonic behaviour may be tied to early notions of freeness, as opposed to freedom; that is, the idea that music should be delivered for free. This concept has regained currency today in debates about peer-to-peer file sharing. But the notion was always based on a misconception: Woodstock was not intended as a free festival, though it became one (as did a number of other festivals, including the Isle of Wight Festival of 1970). Altamont, on the other hand, was intended to be free, but may not have initially been intended to be a festival, following more in the tradition of the free Rolling Stones concert in Hyde Park in July of 1969 that served as a memorial for founding member Brian Jones.[2]

What it clearly *was* intended to be was a film, thus creating a doubly confusing narrative. Indeed, Woodstock, Altamont, the Isle of Wight Festival and the Hyde Park concert all could serve as a sort of matrix of festival-type shows from which today's more codified version of a rock festival has emerged. Woodstock itself was the outgrowth of a series of free festivals in northern California, as well as a history of non-classical (mostly country, folk and bluegrass) outdoor music festivals in the US stretching back to the early twentieth century (of these, the annual Newport Folk Festival is the best known). In the early 1960s there were also a series of inexpensive festivals preceding Woodstock, especially in California, including the vastly influential but much smaller-scale Monterey Pop. Tickets to this festival cost from $3 to $6, and the arena held 6,000. In the UK, there were the Beaulieu Jazz festivals (1956–61), which were significant to the origins of pop festival culture in Britain (see Laing and McKay in Bennett 2004: 4–5 and 91–107).

Although it is difficult, if not impossible, to taxonomise the history of free festivals and concerts, the motives driving the promotion of each are especially important when considering events held in the 1960s. The obvious motive is profit – which, in the 1960s, was considered crass or worse. It is the great unspoken evil, and no wonder: even today a festival or concert which is provided at no cost has a

---

[2] The difference between a festival and a concert is difficult to define, but if a concert is described as the performance of a single act, though perhaps augmented by a lesser-known opening act, then Altamont – a singular event of its kind – was probably closer in spirit to a festival. Although the only known poster for the event calls it a 'free concert', it was promoted elsewhere in everything written about it as 'The Altamont Raceway Free Festival', and featured performances by Santana, Crosby, Stills and Nash, the Flying Burrito Brothers, Jefferson Airplane, all of whom were nationally acclaimed acts in their own right (the Grateful Dead were also scheduled to perform, but left the site due to the violence). The poster, which now sells for $5,000 on ebay, must have been printed up in the 24 hours after the venue was changed from Sear's Point, and, previously, Golden Gate Park. It is not, in other words, an official document.

measure of power over its audience that fee-driven concerts do not. For that reason alone, the 1960s abounded with free festivals, especially in northern California, but Woodstock was the largest and most mediated, thanks to the success of the documentary account of it and its soundtrack, *Woodstock: 3 Days of Peace and Music*. It holds iconic standing as a historical moment. Gustav Le Bon famously called the twentieth century 'the era of crowds', stating further that 'the power of the crowd is the only force that nothing menaces and of which the prestige is continually on the increase' (1897: xv). Woodstock proved once and for all that Le Bon was right.

Since Woodstock, rock crowds have been formed and joined by literally hundreds of millions of people. Every summer they gather in fields across the planet.[3] But unlike other types of crowds, such as protest crowds, football crowds or famine crowds, they do not evoke a sense of fear or danger. The rock crowd, however large, is largely considered a benign gathering, eagerly joined by young and old alike.

This newfound twenty-first-century trust in the crowd – and the sense that the crowd is peaceful, righteousness and essentially passive – can be traced through its depiction on film, specifically in the documentaries *Woodstock: 3 Days of Peace and Music* (Wadleigh 1970) and *Gimme Shelter* (Maysles Brothers 1971). It is a depiction that may have little to do with the actual experience or meaning of attending Woodstock or Altamont, but a lot to do with how a young person today attends Roskilde, Glastonbury, Rock in Rio or Bonnaroo.

Since 1969, there have been thousands of rock festivals similar in nature to Woodstock all over the world, many of them gathering together hundreds of thousands of people. But appearances to the contrary, this doesn't mean that these rock festivals have provided coherent and decisive communities. As Simon Frith has written, although rock music, like folk before it, articulates communal values, the idea of a cohesive rock community springing out of it is a myth:

> Sociologically, rock's account of community has always been unsatisfactory. Reference is usually made (in Belz's book, for example), to the 'community of youth' but as youth is described only in terms of musical taste, the resulting concept of community is vacuous – we are left only with windy phrases like 'the Woodstock Generation.' This is not, in fact, how the myth of community works in popular music. The music (whether rock or pop or folk) is not made *by* a community, but provides certain sorts of community *experience*. (Frith 1981: 164)

As he points out, what is important about a rock festival isn't any of the music or messages one receives there, the importance is *participation*.

---

[3] The yearly Roskilde Music Festival, in Denmark, routinely draws 160,000 people per day. Hardly Strictly Bluegrass, held in San Francisco's Golden Gate Park each autumn, draws 750,000 across three days. These are just a small sample of audiences.

This is why in one sense, the rock festival provides a powerful mimetic force able to replicate cultural memes, although I would argue that despite the false consciousness surrounding it, it does so only in order to (as Debord noted, above) 'incite people to excessive spending'. What I want to suggest here is that the power to replicate cultural memes originates not in the concept of the rock festival itself, or in any individual experience of it, but in the way that certain cultural rhetorics about festivals were circulated via two specific films, *Woodstock* and *Gimme Shelter*. My analysis of these films shows how they were able to translate a chaotic and multi-dimensional event into a particularly appealing fairy tale.

Today, Woodstock is generally portrayed as a spontaneous emanation of, as the title of Barbara Ehrenreich's 2007 book on rituals, dancing and the counterculture would have it, 'collective joy'. But this is the first of the misconceptions around Woodstock et al., since spontaneity is not really a hallmark of festivals, rock or otherwise. In actuality, rock festivals take years to organise and are in fact highly administrated events. In this way, if not necessarily in others, rock festivals are inevitably outgrowths of the culture industries. Supporting this claim, in his critical essay 'Culture and Administration', Theodor Adorno questioned the idea of spontaneous mass behaviour, calling such actions a part of the 'administrated' nature of modern life. Music festivals in particular, he said, were like 'a gypsy wagon ... roll[ing] about secretly in an enormous hall, a fact which they do not themselves notice' (1991: 118).

And yet, the festival has always been an administrated event, in ancient Greece and Rome as well as in medieval times. Indeed, the most direct precursors to the rock festival were surely the fairs and carnivals that were a major feature of pre-capitalist life. Fernand Braudel's historiography, *Civilization and Capitalism, 15th–18th Century*, not only describes these festivities but provides a useful framework for how to interpret the meaning of such celebrations economically, that is, outside the confines of mere religious rituals. Braudel describes how these early fiestas allowed ordinary citizens to participate in revelry in ways that gave them not just a religious jolt, but also a ringside view of the emerging market economy. As he writes, 'As the proverb rightly said, "Coming home from the fair is not the same as coming home from the market"' (Braudel and Reynolds 1982: 245).

In the same vein, coming home from the rock festival is not the same as coming home from the record store. Particularly in the age of mechanical reproduction, going to a rock festival is not primarily a way of hearing music, but a portal through which middle-class Americans are able to experience the same three attributes that made medieval fairs so appealing (and which allowed for the hegemonic stranglehold of the Doges): in Braudel's words, 'entertainment, escapism, and worldliness' (ibid.: 245). Worldliness is a particularly apt word to describe participation in a rock festival experience, for Woodstock and its precursors were the province of the informed, the educated, the politically minded and the liberal elite. Moreover, participating in them is not cost-free, even when the entrance fee is waived, but requires access to transportation and equipment. Finally, although festivals often champion rurality and nature, participants are drawn to festivals in places which enhance their cosmopolitan credentials.[4]

Despite early historical parallels, however, the modern rock festival is in many ways a unique form of gathering, and its crowds differ from those who gathered in Saint-Germain, Bayreuth or Sensa. The most obvious difference is technological. Amplification changed the way that gatherings like these could be experienced, by increasing the centrality of music as a focal point, and decreasing the sense of the individual as a reveller. Other technological innovations, like those that transformed mass media and allowed news and images of festivals like Woodstock to be transmitted to the masses, have had more lasting effects, as audiences are incited to gather through reports seen on television, heard on radio or experienced in the movie theatre. Walter Benjamin's famous ideas on the concept of aura apply forcefully to attendance at the rock festival, for it is the festival's presence in time and space, its unique existence at the place where it happens to be (1968: 220) that gives it value over other ways of experiencing music.

That value resides not only in the music, but in the less tangible notion of participation. In most observable ways, the rock festival crowd is racially and politically homogenous, socially conservative and wedded to mainstream musical aesthetics. The only thing that differentiates them from fair-goers is that rock festival constituents believe themselves to be at odds with societal norms. Unlike medieval crowds, who went to the fair as part of a normative social ritual, members of rock crowds see going to the festival as a way to make themselves social transgressors. Moreover, since their association with the anti-war movement in the mid-1960s, rock crowds are usually depicted in the press and in the public sphere as liberal, emancipatory, resistant and political in nature, even when these are traits that the festivals do not explicitly claim for themselves. This emancipatory element, however imaginary, is clearly one of the rock festival's biggest selling points, and accounts in part for its longevity as a cultural form.

One reason that large rock festivals were able to successfully configure themselves as discursive sites of social and political discourse to their audiences is because they are begotten from a historical genesis – the 1960s – that is even more fraught with conflict than public memory invests them. The anti-war movement, Civil Rights Movement, and the conflict known as the generation gap are all aspects of the era that rock festivals purport to speak about. However, some of the conflicts inscribed in these festivals are not of the struggles for which we'd like to remember them. Indeed one of the things my work reveals is that while such concerts – both past and present – frequently represent themselves as sites of hegemonic struggle and resistance, they also work as ideological state apparatuses, inscribing conventional values in their attendees. This shouldn't be

---

[4] This is particularly true today, when what promoters call 'destination festivals' occur in tourist Meccas like Rio and Sydney, inviting urban enclaves like Austin and Chicago, or, most tempting of all, out of the way destinations. In 2011, Iggy Pop headlined a festival in Corsica, and plans are currently underway for a rock festival in China for 2013.

surprising when one notes that these festivals invariably (if largely unconsciously) catered to a white, middle-class elite.

The misconception that Woodstock was a site of resistance surely arose not at the festival itself but through its film. *Woodstock* consolidated the public consensus that Woodstock was (as the film is subtitled) *3 Days of Peace and Music*. The glow was so strong that even direct evidence to the contrary – such as a disastrous festival on the Isle of Wight in 1970 – did nothing to diminish the future popularity of such festivals, which have only grown in popularity ever since. The early 1970s were particularly rife with Woodstock-styled festivals, especially in England, as Glastonbury Fayre and the three Isle of Wight festivals attest.[5] Indeed, the final Isle of Wight Festival drew an astonishing 600,000 people, or 0.1 per cent of the population of Britain at the time (although the Isle of Wight Festival had been in the works for several years, the enormity of its success that year may in part be a testament to the excitement generated around the film, which was shown for the first time in Europe at the Cannes Film Festival in June of 1970). The film *Message to Love* (Lerner 1996), which documents that festival, ends with the promoter, Ron Foulk, saying, 'this will be the last event of its kind'. Foulk is completely off base.[6]

Woodstock

Woodstock's importance as a nonfiction film, as a vision and as a marketing tool for rock cannot be overstated: it is the mainstay of the rock business's sense of cultural relevance and its supreme self-confidence in its market. Joe Boyd, then manager of a band called the Incredible String Band, categorically believes that if his band had played in front of the cameras in the rain on Friday night, they'd have become the stars that Melanie – who took the Incredible String Band's time slot and is a central figure in the movie – became: they opted to take a later slot, weren't filmed, and flopped. 'We knew we had blown it', Boyd writes in his memoir *White Bicycles*. 'The extent of the error became clear in the months to come as the Woodstock film reached every small town in America and the double album soared to the top of the charts' (Boyd 2007: 223).

One reason that Woodstock's vision had such impact was simply that the film was the most popular documentary of its era. Richard Barsam called *Woodstock: 3 Days of Peace and Music* 'a lavish, lyrical poem to the green and grassy splendours of a pastoral event' (1973: 288). It is, Barsam also notes, 'a subjective

---

[5] The film *Glastonbury Fayre*, directed by Nicolas Roeg (1972), documents the 1971 Glastonbury festival. As that festival follows the wide release of *Woodstock*, it would provide an excellent counterpoint as to how the films *Woodstock* and *Gimme Shelter* may have shaped future festivals – and future films on festivals – rhetoric. Unfortunately it is outside the scope of this chapter.

[6] Due to ownership disputes, the film *Message to Love* wasn't released until 1996, thus placing it outside the lens of this chapter.

record – a traditional non-fiction film', which, he claims, has much in common with Leni Riefenstahl's *Olympia* (about the 1936 Olympics). Barsam means this as a compliment: he characterises *Woodstock* as 'a newsreel of a documentary event'. But this is a naïve assessment of how films are assembled. In *Woodstock: An Inside Look at the Movie That Shook Up the World and Defined a Generation* (Bell 1999), various producers of the final product describe how they assembled the film with limited financial resources, film stock, cameras or man power, in addition to logistical problems, rain and sonic difficulties such that sound had to be overlaid or used diegetically.

This description of how the film *Woodstock* was made clearly points to a creative process of assemblage, rather than to what Barsam was pleased to call a 'newsreel'. But I'd argue that *Woodstock* goes even farther in adding a narrative and even an ideology to the event in question. In fact, it owes its success to its canny use of Hollywood tropes, to its anointing itself with the weighty title of historical document, and to the way it flatters its audience, who are told over and over again that *they* are stars of the event.

Simply put, Woodstock's director Michael Wadleigh has crafted much more than a record of a concert here, as can be seen by the ever-widening effects that it has had on popular culture. First, it has long served as a redemptive vision for a counterculture which might otherwise have to think badly of itself. Second, it has helped to popularise a number of bands and styles of music that might otherwise have had rather short cultural stays. And finally, it has inspired almost a half century's worth of similarly organised rock festivals, drawing the youth of three continents into their experience. In addition, *Woodstock: 3 Days of Peace and Music* allowed its promoter, Michael Lang, to recoup his losses. Prior to its release, Lang had lost an estimated million plus dollars, but the film earned $13.3 million in wide release, and much more in its repertoire after life, as well as in its recorded form as a soundtrack album.[7] By 1979, it had earned $50 million (Bell 1999: 10).

Woodstock's most important function, however, was discursive. Far more than the film *Monterey Pop* (which came out a full year earlier and was a considerably shorter film) *Woodstock* cast a spell on those who saw it – a spell that caused them to long to go to rock festivals. Prior to its release as a film, the days-long rock festival was a curiosity, attended only by a moderately well-off urban elite cadre of young people hooked into the media and the moment. After the release of the film, potential festival-goers began to include members of other social classes eager to experience Woodstock's notion of 'collective joy', with or without its political and social implications. By 1975, the rock festival was no longer tied to a particular

---

[7] This can only have been seen as an incentive for future festival promoters: today, many enormous rock festivals are sponsored by communications companies, whose financial backing keeps consumer costs relatively low while boosting sales of synchronous markets in film, music and beer sales.

political movement or collectivity, but merely served as a smorgasbord of pop for consumers to experience cheaply.[8]

To do all that, it stands to reason that the film of Woodstock was really much more than just the visual record of a concert. It is a *Bildungsroman*, with the festival itself standing in as young Werther. In other words, it is the festival, rather than the festival-goer, that will grow and change and find itself, as the film wends its way to its finish. But this is not the only way in which the film frames itself as a novel of discovery. Many of its images are directly linked to fictional devices, particularly the appreciation and worship of nature and the way that nature is linked in every frame to a teleological view of American history.

Consider, for example, the first 25 minutes of the film, which are devoted to shots of the pristine empty green fields of Max Yasgur's farm in upstate New York. These shots are full of shimmering distant lakes and amber waves of grain. The camera lingers on the fields, only gradually depicting a slow invasion by handsome, shirtless young men on horses and tractors. It is as if western expansion occurs right before our eyes. A brief scene of these young men communally erecting the stage, lifting its framework high over their heads, is highly suggestive of barn building or roof-raising: the entire scene implies that what is being built is not a stage, but a church, underscoring the sense of Manifest Destiny. Hence, rather than hippies, the men in these scenes appear to be something with more gravitas: Quakers, or pioneers, creating a foundation for America. The men in these scenes are depicted as movie star handsome, strong and rugged, while the women in these shots (and in the film as a whole) are invariably shown as domestically contained vessels, fulfilling conventional female roles. In one brief shot, a beautiful young woman rides behind a craggy, bearded frontiersman on a horse. In another, a heavily pregnant woman tends children.

Presently, the scene shifts to the arrival of the 300,000 concert-goers who will fill the fields over the course of the weekend. The pace of the scene implies that Wadleigh is reimagining them as settlers, repopulating a continent – although such a vision paints an unusually benign view of the coming of Europeans to the New World. Here, no Native Americans are driven cruelly off their land, no slave labour is used to cultivate or build, and no questions of ownership mar the pristine landscape. Instead, they arrive on foot, riding bicycles and motorcycles, on horseback, via helicopter, and by car. They come as pilgrims – the word used later by *Time* magazine to describe the scene – to set up camp in ways that, as pictured by the film, are natural, communal and friendly.

Interestingly, an enormous amount of this footage is presented in split screen, a technique that will be much copied in rock films which then 'quote' Woodstock. Bennett says that the split screen effect has two purposes, to intercut between the artists and the audiences, thus giving both equal weight, and 'to provide extra

---

[8] That would be the year I attended my first Day on the Green, a mid-decade iteration of Woodstock held in American football stadiums nationwide. It featured the Beach Boys, Linda Ronstadt and Eddie Money.

visual commentary on points and observations made by those interviewed in the film' (2004: 48). I would add that the technique also calls attention to Woodstock's duality. On the one hand, the concert is spoken of as an organic, beautiful celebration of nature – of 'going back to the garden', as the film's theme song put it (the song, 'Woodstock', by Joni Mitchell, was recorded a month after the concert. It is sung here by Crosby, Stills and Nash, and then overlaid on the scenes of arrival, the first and most egregious instance of how non-diegetic sound is used here). On the other hand, the split-screen emphasises that the concert is a highly technical and technically mediated event. In addition to the split screen, which in itself highlights technology over nature, the film shows this mediation explicitly via complicated aerial shots which capture the traffic jams, through shots of the stage and of the amplifier towers, and through many film-within-film scenes of the media interviewing people on the site. These reflexive moments allow the audience to see the concert as newsworthy and historic. But at the same time, the film's clever split screen gimmickry and its use of non-diegetic music serve to distance the film-makers from mainstream media.

Another duality that is often brought to the fore in the movie is the one between 'the squares' and the 'freaks' – that is, the townspeople and the hippies, the *artistes* and the *bourgeoisie*. Again and again the film calls attention to the two 'nations' that are merging here at Woodstock, as when townspeople praise the hippies and the hippies behave nicely back. This is another fictional cliché from the western genre: the stranger comes to town; at first he is looked at askance, until finally he is accepted and his difference assimilated into the culture (see *Shane, Stagecoach, True Grit*, and so on). Over and over again, duality is on display, both of the conventional and the unconventional, and of technology and nature, as when a shot of the moon is paired with a shot of the klieg lights, or when a shot of the vast crowd as seen from a helicopter is paired with the close-up of the face of an individual. The scenes appear to be dominated by the memory of Richard Brautigan's notion of a 'cybernetic meadow' from the poem 'All Watched Over by Machines of Loving Grace' (Brautigan 1968).

Woodstock reaches its climax during memorable concert performances by artists like the Who, Santana and Jimi Hendrix. But throughout it continues to purvey themes of duality, difference and tolerance. The split screen continues to emphasise the size of the crowd and the duality of that size with individual moments: for a movie of a concert, there are few live shots and quite a bit of the music was re-recorded. The weather comes in for a lot of air time, as does female nudity. Most of the performers play second fiddle to these shots: much of the music is used as background music for shots of concert-goers swimming, smoking, sleeping, talking dancing or doing yoga. The first performer, Richie Havens, is given an enormous amount of screen time, and at the end of his set says, 'This concert is about you … tomorrow people will be reading about you tomorrow all over the world.' This is the first sense that the audience gets that it, itself, is the star of the show, that they have been invited into this space to perform as a rock crowd. It is an invitation they will continue to accept for the next 40 years.

Yet another important visual argument which *Woodstock* (and to some extent *Gimme Shelter*) makes to viewers can be detected in its depiction of geographical space. In addition to addressing the more normative 'back to the land' narrative which the counterculture was highly invested in at the time (see Turner 2006), *Woodstock*'s images of crowds in nature may well have addressed and even assuaged the public's growing fear of overpopulation. The idea of a population explosion was very much in the *Zeitgeist* at the time, thanks in part to Paul Ehrlich's enormously influential book *The Population Bomb* (1968). *Woodstock* calms these fears by showing a crowded world where everyone is still having a good time; a world where resources are shared and nature (in the form of the rain storm which drenches the crowd on Saturday night) is benign. The aerial shots of upstate New York (and, in *Gimme Shelter*, rural Livermore) also assure viewers that the land is not under siege: over and over again we are visually reassured that it is endless, pristine and there for the taking, once again evoking the epic American ideal (or idyll) of the west. Hence, the scenes of crowds are invariably overlaid with a sense of happiness, mellowness and joy to reassure viewers that overpopulation and its attendant problems are nothing more than a myth.

The most important assurance that Woodstock gives, however, is of America as a united nation. This is most evident in the final and most canonical scene in the film (a scene recreated in Ang Lee's 2009 film *Taking Woodstock*). In it, an older, white, male sanitary worker, clearly standing in for conservative blue-collar America, is interviewed about the concert. 'I have two sons, one here and one in Vietnam', he says. It is a comment which is explicitly meant to unite the two sides of debate – the counterculture and its opposition. That it worked is attested to by the wild success of the film, its longevity as a cultural referent, and the hundreds of recreations that take place every summer.

Gimme Shelter

The film *Woodstock* opened one year after the festival, in 1970, and was immediately embraced by the public. The film *Gimme Shelter*, which chronicles another free concert of 1969, did not receive nearly as much love. As Barsam has pointed out, *Gimme Shelter* is *Woodstock*'s Manichean rival, both in popularity and in spirit. 'The two films', he writes, 'represent polarities, not only in the festivals themselves and their significance to the so-called counterculture, but also in the approaches the film makers take to them' (1973: 287). *Woodstock* relied on filmmaking gimmickry and an underlying narrative point of view, while *Gimme Shelter* is a triumph of *cinéma verité* filmmaking. *Woodstock* both assumes and uses news documentary techniques, while *Gimme Shelter* attempted to 'live' the film: at the concert's height, the filmmakers deployed 35 camera people in the field (one of whom was a very young George Lucas) to capture crowd moments.

On the surface, *Gimme Shelter* is the yang to *Woodstock*'s yin, an unblinking depiction of the dark side of crowd gatherings, the concert that ended the Age of Aquarius and which ushered in the tainted 1970s. In fact, a close reading of *Gimme Shelter* shows that it uses similar rhetorical strategies to make a similar point to that of *Woodstock*. Both would have it that rock's effect on a crowd is so soul-shaking and spell-binding that it overrides any danger or violence. Both reinforce the idea that attending rock concerts is a form of taking part in history. Both films valorise the idea of being part of a rock crowd, but *Gimme Shelter* goes further. Sheila Whiteley has argued that the Stones' role at Altamont brings up 'the question of the relationship between performer/audience, the performance, and the musical text itself', adding that 'the unmitigated violence at Altamont suggests that for many the songs were interpreted as inciting brutality, that they provided a model for behavioural patterns' (1997b: 84–5). While most agree that the reason for the violence at Altamont – which began well before the Stones took the stage – had more to do with the hiring of Hells Angels as security, few would argue that the menacing subject matter and sound of songs like 'Sympathy for the Devil' and 'Midnight Rambler' would, as Whiteley puts it, 'hardly calm the already explosive atmosphere' (ibid.: 84).

Gimme Shelter opens with a shot of Rolling Stones drummer Charlie Watts sitting on a donkey. He is wearing a top hat and is draped in a cape, and he is brandishing a rifle. The absurdity of this image – taken for the cover of the Stones' 1970 live album *Get Yer Ya-Ya's Out* – is well in keeping with the film's overall themes of chaos, crowds and culpability: indeed, filmmaker Albert Maysles has stated that the image is reminiscent of the opening scenes of *A Tale of Two Cities* which are intended to portend the coming French Revolution (in fact, the eventual image that was used is inspired by a Bob Dylan song, 'Visions of Johanna', which reads in part, 'jewels and binoculars hang from the head of a mule').

Like *Woodstock*, *Gimme Shelter* has a paradox at its core: it wants to be the conventional concert documentary about the Stones' 1969 tour that the Maysles Brothers were originally hired to produce. Thus, for the first half of the film, we see the Stones performing at Madison Square Garden to rapt (and peaceful) masses – ecstatic crowds upon whom lead singer Mick Jagger literally showers rose petals. Later, we see the band recording at Muscle Shoals recording studio in Alabama, and the camera lingers on them lovingly, depicting them as zonked on their own talent. Finally, we see them back stage, behaving like rock stars, but by this time, the power of the earlier scenes has made us complicit in this vision of them as bohemian *artistes*. Thus, the horrifying end to *Gimme Shelter* is mitigated by our sense that the band is above reproach.

About half way through the film, the mood darkens as we begin to see scenes of live performances intercut with scenes of people attempting to set up the free concert which will later be dubbed Altamont. The arrangements for this concert – which first has to be moved 34 miles north from Golden Gate Park in San Francisco to Sears Point Raceway in Sonoma and finally 56 miles east to the Altamont Speedway, in a part of unincorporated Livermore now known as the Altamont Pass – are portrayed as embattled, chaotic and possibly not even in the band's best interest.

In these scenes, they are surrounded by lawyers and the media, and there is a lot of incomprehensible shouting. The chaotic nature of these interludes serves to heighten the viewer's sense that this movie is an unbiased document, that is, a real piece of *cinéma verité*, with no directorial intervention.

But that's nonsense, of course. The Maysles Brothers, like other proponents of the contemporary direct cinema movement (notably the directors/auteurs D.A. Pennebaker, Ricky Leacock and Robert Drew) were adept at creating moods, which become more sombre in this case, with the Altamont footage.[9] To begin, in a sequence that echoes *Woodstock*, we see people setting up stages, arriving at dawn and partying.[10] Gradually, however, the images of peaceful attendees degenerate: there are a lot of clearly drug-induced freak-outs, many naked people and other ugly images. Eventually, we see the murder. Intercut throughout this footage, we are sent back to a studio where the filmmakers David and Albert Maysles are observed showing the footage of the murder to the Stones themselves. An inordinate amount of time is spent watching the Stones' faces as they are confronted with the film's 'truth'. In this way, the film evades condemning the Stones: by allowing us to see them confronting the crime itself as it happens, there is a sense of expiation.

Gimme Shelter has gone down in history as a dark film about a murder. But in the end, as Whiteley suggests, what is upheld by the entire film is the Stones' *mystique*. Whereas *Woodstock* argued that there, power is vested in crowds, *Gimme Shelter* argues that the power in these events lies with the rock stars. Although it prides itself on its objectivity, the Maysles Brothers film is clearly sympathetic to this vision of the Stones and follows a similar line of reasoning. The movie neither condemns nor praises the Stones or the violence it depicts at Altamont. Instead, it presents the Rolling Stones as atavistic romantic heroes from another age, and then exculpates them. The final image – of the Stones performing (indoors) in Maryland – leaves one thinking not, 'Gee I'm glad I skipped Altamont', but 'If only I had been there'! As with Woodstock, to have attended was to have become worldly. It was to have participated in the world.

The Maysles Brothers' film, though vilified at the time, has ultimately made for a compelling viewing experience. But it can't be called historical truth. Instead, despite the stated precepts of direct cinema and in the same spirit as *Woodstock*, *Gimme Shelter* takes familiar narratives from Hollywood and fiction – in this case, the myth where the powerful piper pipes the children down the canyon to their death – subjectively depicts it, and then dubs it historical documentary. By so doing, *Gimme Shelter* argues that despite the violence at its core, attending festivals like Altamont is a crucial way of participating in the history of the era. To have been there is to have been an actual actor in the scene: it is to have taken part in the shaping of a cultural moment of great importance – the 'revolution'

---

[9] For an excellent overview of how this occurs, see Dave Saunders, *Direct Cinema: Observational Documentary and the Politics of the Sixties* (2007).

[10] The sequence echoes *Woodstock*, but can not be influenced by it: these two films were in production at the same time.

alluded to in the image at the start of the film. *Gimme Shelter* portrays the horrors of Altamont starkly.

This, then, explains the film's genius: that nothing about its portrayal of Altamont has prevented generations of rock fans from going to equally dangerous and chaotic scenes. Despite the different modalities of the two films (one dark, one light) there is a core of similarity between *Gimme Shelter* and *Woodstock*. Perhaps this accounts for the odd fact that critics have compared both films to the work of Leni Riefenstahl, generally considered to be the finest producer of twentieth-century political propaganda. That, despite the clearly shown downside of each event – the rain, the loss of money, the murder – thousands of similarly-styled festivals have been crafted, attended and succeeded in their wake is another strong case for their lasting power as generational touchstones.

Conclusion

The fact that the Woodstock experience is entirely imaginary is perhaps not that surprising. A more problematic absence in the discourse surrounding it is discussion of the fact Woodstock's audience was almost universally white. African Americans are relegated to the role of performers, specifically Richie Havens, Sly Stone and Jimi Hendrix, whose otherness is made explicit, particularly in the case of Hendrix as he performs a mesmeric and transformative version of the *Star Spangled Banner*, complete with sounds of gunfire, evoking protest of the Vietnam War. Meanwhile, the camera's male gaze roams freely over the fields, picking out naked women from the crowd. This gesture is clearly meant to enhance the discourse of free love which *Woodstock* works hard to uphold, and which has always represented one of its main appeals to mainstream audiences. These two tropes – free love, and the African American as transgressor and dangerous disturber of national security – have persisted well into the present day, as have the rock festival's contrary rhetorical appeals of expensive discomfort and elegiac emotional release. Both are specious.

In this chapter I have shown how two films re-imagined rock festivals as a powerfully enticing new crowd formation and then disseminated that vision. I argue that by so doing, they allowed concert-goers to feel as if they were participating in civic discourse while in fact they were doing nothing of the sort. Today's rock festivals, which explicitly relate themselves to these early sites, also situate themselves as discursive sites of political and social meaning-making, but, as was the case at Woodstock and Altamont, the meanings that they are making are not the same ones that they say they are. Instead, I would like to suggest that these festivals may also serve to make visible the new market economies of late capitalism (for example social networking), allowing a space for citizens to understand the shifting ways that post-industrial society might be used to their own advantage.

In his book *Worlds Apart,* Jean Christophe Agnew has suggested that Elizabethan theatre helped make the emerging market relations of nascent capitalism visible to play-goers. Both *Woodstock* and *Gimme Shelter* reveal a new way of viewing democracy, such that the pursuit of pleasure, in the form of music, drugs and sexuality, becomes political and hence almost a moral imperative. At the same time, the films also suggest a new relationship between consumers (concert-goers) and vendors, artisans and musicians which allows the market economy to seem moral. This is a relationship that has been upheld on the festival grounds the world over.[11]

Finally, both films reveal to viewers a reshaped idea of the commodity as something not necessarily material, but something intangible – an aura, a feeling, 'an experience'; all the trademarks of late capitalism. In these films, celebrity, experience and presence are seen to be more valuable than commodities. The mental transformation that these depictions allow for – the transformation of the free market into a supposedly moral space and of the commodity into something more invisible – may go a long way toward explaining the disjunction between rhetoric and reality that haunts rock festival grounds today.

---

[11] Elsewhere in my work, I explore a 1983 festival sponsored by Apple cofounder Steven Wozniak which showcased the relationship between computer technology and music 20 years before the invention of the iPod.

PART III
Sonic Anarchy and Freaks

Chapter 8

The Long Freak Out: Unfinished Music and Countercultural Madness in Avant-Garde Rock of the 1960s and 1970s

Jay Keister

The avant-garde – understood in its most provocative sense as an aesthetic attack on prevailing institutions and stylist conventions of art – altered the course of art history in the twentieth century and continues to influence critical discourse in the twenty-first century, but to what degree has the avant-garde affected rock music? Writers on popular music have demonstrated various ways in which the avant-garde has contributed to the common historical narrative of rebellion in rock by examining subjects such as the development of art rock out of English art schools (Frith and Horne 1987), the Situationist strategies of the Sex Pistols (Marcus 1989), and the interaction between artists and musicians in the New York post-punk scene (Gendron 2002). One might presume that aggressive sonic features of musical attack, such as chaotic sounds, absurd lyrics and amateur musicianship, would be as widespread in rock as aggressive visual aesthetics are in painting and sculpture. But this is clearly not the case as many critics and fans typically dismiss recordings by rock musicians who overstep the boundaries of acceptability in rock music with extreme avant-garde recordings.

This chapter examines avant-garde approaches to rock music by focusing on what can best be described as the 'freak out' – recordings of chaotic sounds and free form improvisation that reject conventional notions of song structure, lyric meaning and technical competence. From the title of the first album by the Mothers of Invention, this term that has come to mean 'madly panic' in contemporary English aptly describes the atmosphere of madness and irrationality evoked by these extreme recordings that began to appear on record albums in the 1960s. Freak outs were usually cast as oppositional statements against mainstream culture by embodying the unstructured and unbridled freedom called for by the post-war counterculture, generating what Lochhead calls 'liberatory chaos' in music that 'conveys a human condition of freedom by setting itself up directly against social and intellectual structures that are comprehended as constricting' (2001: 217).

While it is tempting to view such experiments merely as attempts by pop musicians to gain cultural capital by appropriating the language of the avant-garde, a closer look at these recordings and their reception reveals no such gains on the part of musicians who have gone to such extremes. Given that 'aural sculpting of sound without a beat or melody is not accepted as music' by most rock fans (Gracyk 1996: 100), these risky, fractious works often alienate fans and even jeopardise careers in keeping with the avant-garde's 'built-in tendency ultimately to negate itself' (Calinescu 1987: 124). Such self-destructive attacks on the emerging music business in the 1960s and 1970s echo the Dadaist and Surrealist impact on art institutions earlier in the century and invoke similar apocalyptic aesthetics of death and madness. Whether created by hippie-era musicians invoking countercultural ideals of social and aesthetic revolution or by post-punk musicians reacting to a decadent music industry, these recordings constitute a distinctive type of rock music that negates all manner of oppressive structure, even at the cost of alienating listeners with unlistenable noise. As such, the freak out suggests a kind of madness, either invoked by musicians as a countercultural weapon against the sanity of mainstream culture or perceived by listeners who sometimes explain away such unlistenable records as temporary madness by their favourite musicians.

In addition to the overarching theme of madness conveyed by freak out recordings, I have identified three characteristics that most of these recordings have in common: anarchy, absurdity and amateurism. First and foremost, anarchy predominates in the way sounds seem to be erratic and uncoordinated, producing an overall sense of chaos or of being out of sync. There is no clear sense of song form and these tracks are often overly long, sometimes taking up an entire side of a vinyl record album. Secondly, absurdity is often pushed to the point of complete irrationality, either non-teleological in that these recordings seem to go nowhere or, if they have a goal, it is based on an irrational belief that the sounds can work some kind of magic. Defying meaning, rather than making meaning, freak out tracks feature vocals that seem to be utter nonsense, either fragments of recognisable language or unrecognisable gibberish chosen more for sound quality than semantic meaning. Thirdly, while performers of freak out recordings evoke amateurism, this is clearly by design. Whether musicians lack conventional technical skills or simply give the appearance of incompetence by making music that sounds disjointed, this valorising of amateur performance values is in line with hippie ideals of open participation and punk ideals of DIY musicality. The freak out affirms the notion that anyone can do it.

The Unfinished Music of John and Yoko

John Lennon is the most well known pop musician to be thoroughly condemned for extreme avant-garde recordings and his work with Yoko Ono during the late 1960s provides some insights about the use of avant-garde strategies and techniques in popular music. *Unfinished Music No. 1. Two Virgins* (1968), the first album collaboration by the couple commonly referred to as 'John and Yoko', is infamous for completely alienating a mass audience and attracting widespread condemnation from its initial release to the present day. Yoko Ono has offered her own explanation for the concept of 'unfinished' music:

If you listen to it, maybe you can add to it or change it or edit or add something in your mind. The unfinished part that's not in the record – what's in you, not what's in the record – is what's important. (Yoko Ono cited in Rockwell 1982: 275)

This pleasant, if naïve, invitation to participate in utopian idealism belies the harsh sound of a record that readily evokes harsh criticism and scatological insults from Beatles fans. For many rock fans and critics, *Two Virgins* was seen as a nadir in the career of John Lennon and evidence of the follies and failures of rock musicians whenever they stray too far from the accepted conventions of rock and into the realm of high art. But a brief consideration of the contents of the album and the context in which it was made reveal an expression of resistance to making a commercial product and a deliberate refusal to construct a cohesive work of art.

'Unfinished' accurately describes this album that presents the couple as literally raw, with its naked cover portrait and two extended tracks improvised and recorded in one night, consisting of fragments that never coalesce into anything more than discrete momentary sounds. While Yoko wails, sings and makes animal-like noises, John occasionally shouts while maintaining a background of disconnected sounds using guitar, piano, organ, tape recorded sound effects and fragments of old records from a turntable. Snippets of conversation between the two of them give it a real-time feel and an air of domesticity, with what sounds like a tea break coming at the end of Side One that is almost inviting to the listener. But Side Two continues relentlessly as Lennon spins short bursts of old jazz records on a turntable, refusing to give the listener the satisfaction that normally comes from the passive listening experience so antithetical to their album's concept. In the final moments John engages Yoko in an intimate piano-vocal duet that ends with Lennon chanting 'Amen', but the record ultimately remains unfinished. Presenting music as a perpetually incomplete process, *Two Virgins* is the antithesis of the high-toned art rock that the Beatles had perfected the previous year with the album *Sgt. Pepper's Lonely Hearts Club Band*.

Extreme recordings like *Two Virgins* and 'Revolution 9', John and Yoko's contribution to the Beatles' 'White Album' released just a week earlier in that November of 1968, are typically dismissed by critics as pretentious folly or bad taste (Spitz 2005: 795) and hated by fans as a kind of temporary insanity from their heroes. Following the avant-garde ethos of rejecting all convention and institutions, such recordings seem designed to deliberately confound all listeners, even critics who try to be open-minded and seriously consider such works. Critic John Rockwell, for example, grants John and Yoko much more leeway for their experimentation than the average Beatles fan, but miscasts the purpose of rock musicians who experiment:

For all their eagerness, however, rock experimenters lacked roots, in that they weren't always aware of the spiritually similar experiments that had taken place in earlier decades among the literary, and even musical, avant-gardes of Europe and America. And they often lacked the craft to shape their newly liberated imaginations. Too much art rock became clumsy imitation of the classics or shallow vulgarization of real avant-gardists or cynical exploitation of teenagers' seemingly endless capacity to be blown away by the obvious. John Lennon was too clever to be that crude. But it took Yoko to bring out his tendencies fully for both liberated expression and primal self-indulgence. (Rockwell 1982: 273)

This concern for a lack of 'roots' – certainly not true in the case of Yoko Ono or Frank Zappa – reveals Rockwell defending a hallowed tradition of 'classic' artists and 'real avant-gardists' who possessed talent as opposed to 'clumsy' and 'shallow' rock musicians who lack 'craft'. Not only does Rockwell take an aesthetic position that seems awkward for a rock critic, he also underestimates the power of rock music that is inspired by art. While more virtuosic rock musicians' 'clumsy imitation of the classics' may have had a more insidious agenda of criticising society than they are typically given credit for (Keister and Smith 2008), the more chaotic and raw 'vulgarization of real avant-gardists' as found in John and Yoko's work reveals an iconoclasm with which rock musicians are particularly well-equipped.

Rock music in the most extreme form of raw, chaotic experimentalism considered here shares similar goals with the most radical artists of the avant-garde who attacked art as an institution, something to be despised for valuing bourgeois notions of craft and beauty at the expense of spontaneity and truth. In John Lennon's case, his experimental works were more than just an ideological quest for spontaneity and truth. Beyond the utopian concept of the album, *Two Virgins* was a very direct attack on the Beatles in 1968, by that time a fully developed musical and financial institution built on craft and beauty, as well as an oppressive pressure-cooker of a business that damaged relationships between long-time friends. As Lennon felt increasing hostility from his band mates toward Yoko, his collaborations with her became more than just new avenues for liberated expression – they became aesthetic weapons. *Two Virgins* met with resistance from many in the Beatles organisation who tried to delay the release of the album and, with even Ringo Starr voicing his concern that the album could damage all their reputations (Spitz 2005: 796–7), it is hardly surprising that Lennon persisted in further 'primal self-indulgence' with Yoko Ono during the final years of the band.

Considering Lennon's awareness of his position in an organisation that many believed was leading the countercultural charge during the late 1960s, his avant-garde works with Yoko Ono at the time were as perfectly placed as Marcel Duchamp's infamous urinal in an art gallery about 50 years earlier. Just as the early twentieth-century Dadaists attacked an art institution that had developed a business out of commoditising bohemian self-expression, John Lennon's attack went to the heart of a music industry that was just then discovering the economic gains to be made from marketing rock music as high art. But unlike Duchamp's urinal, which by the 1960s had fully transformed from prank to masterpiece and earned its reputation as high art, there was no such pay-off for John and Yoko as their avant-garde albums seem to resist such canonisation. During the 1960s when highbrow culture was bemoaning the death of the avant-garde because it had actually sustained the very system that it was supposedly trying to destroy (Mann 1991), the avant-garde was very much alive within popular music as rock musicians began employing similar strategies of resistance to – and exploitation of – the culture industry.

Freaking Out in the 1960s: From Countercultural Events to Rock Albums

In what may have been the first freak out of the post-war counterculture – Allen Ginsberg's legendary reading of the poem *Howl* in 1955 at the Six Gallery in San Francisco – Ginsberg showed that the madness that he claimed was so destructive of the post-war generation was both the symptom of a disease and its cure. In the poem Ginsberg urged Carl Solomon, whom he had befriended during his brief stay in a psychiatric ward, to 'accuse your doctors of insanity', evoking madness as a weapon to be used against Moloch, his metaphor for the Western society that he felt was sacrificing the minds and bodies of the young (Ginsberg 1956: III). Ginsberg's method of embodying madness and projecting it back at society was rooted in nineteenth-century French writers Baudelaire, Rimbaud and Lautréamont and early twentieth-century artists associated with Dada and Surrealism such as Schwitters, Dalí and Artaud, who practised an art of insanity that could be seen as the only sane way of dealing with an already insane society. 'Openly declaring one's insanity', as Donald Kuspit describes it, is a quest for authenticity necessary for artistic growth and 'the only genuine authenticity in an insanely inauthentic world' (Kuspit 2000: 153).

Many in the counterculture eagerly embraced the utopian promise of creative madness as a way of overcoming personal alienation, as well as instigate radical political change. In his 1968 countercultural diatribe, *Bomb Culture*, Jeff Nuttall quotes an anonymous poster hung on the doors of the Sorbonne: 'The society of alienation must disappear from history. We are inventing a new and original world. Imagination has seized power' (Nuttall 1968: viii). Adding that 'the root of political development is creative and irrational' (ibid.: ix), Nuttall outlines in his book a number of tactics that call for a hallucinatory insanity that could spread 'an ego-dissolving delirium' and 'release forces into the prevailing culture that would dislocate society' (ibid.: 264). In *The Making of the Counterculture*, Theodore Roszak attacked what he called the technocracy and how it curtailed human creativity, citing the mad visions of William Blake, whose work had been reduced by civilisation to the sober respectability of art, passively consumed and completely divorced from the ecstasy of experience that had generated the poet's original visions (Roszak 1969).

In the early 1960s, those in search of profound, Blake-like mystical experiences that could cleanse the doors of perception sought their inspiration in a combination of psychedelic drugs, Eastern spirituality and radical psychology, and portrayed society's version of sanity as a public health problem. 'No one is more dangerously insane than one who is sane all the time', proclaimed popular philosopher Alan Watts who advocated an environment of complete spontaneity 'for dancing, singing, howling, babbling, jumping, groaning, wailing' in which 'nonsense may have its way' (Watts 1962: 88). Watts created just such an environment in a freak out session that was recorded and released as an album called *This Is It!* (1962) in which Watts and collaborators chanted and babbled nonsense words in faux tribal rituals accompanied by acoustic instruments. Although similar to the audio anarchy explored by John Cage during this time period, *This Is It!* was presented not as art music, but as a kind of audio prescription for mental health. As this idea of invoking experiential madness as therapy and resistance began to motivate similar underground gatherings in the 1960s, rock music began to play an important role in countercultural events.

Ken Kesey and his Merry Pranksters pursued freaking out with an evangelical fervour in California in the mid-1960s. Armed with a plentiful supply of LSD and bolstered by the idea that collectively freaking out could therapeutically bring about Buddha-like enlightenment in any participant, Kesey created the Acid Tests, a series of about a dozen multi-media events designed to get young people to take acid and dissolve their egos in hopes of transforming society. Like Alan Watts' freak out session, these events documented in Tom Wolfe's *The Electric Kool-Aid Acid Test* (1968) were conceived more as rituals than performances with the only goal being to 'mess up the minds' of those in attendance and ensure they 'go nowhere' (Sculatti 2005). The temporary insanity instigated by Kesey was meant to be a kind of rite of passage in which the individual, provided with free LSD, would become immersed in an alternative environment of free expression, interaction and experience without boundaries, and could eventually return to everyday life a newly enlightened person.

Audio fragments of Kesey and his Pranksters freaking out in a recording studio in early 1966 appeared on an album called *The Acid Test* in which Kesey described the events as 'open circles' of participatory possibilities as opposed to the 'closed circles' of everyday reality:

> Everything is closed circles between people. When you get an open circle it's dangerous, it's like children or animals. It means they demand you doing weird things like playing a harmonica that is going nowhere, that at any moment you can add to it your own kind of noise and it's part of it. This is different from Beethoven's Fifth which is finished and there's no place for me in it except as an audience. (*The Acid Test* LP, 1966)

Music in this environment was not intended to be a performance for an audience, but a spontaneous interaction between all participants, like John and Yoko's unfinished music in a communal setting. Although the house band for the Acid Tests was an early incarnation of the Grateful Dead, the sound of these events was a chaotic blend of Grateful Dead music, the amateur Prankster band and anyone else who felt like making noise. 'None of us are musicians', said Kesey proudly, 'we are all completely bumbling amateurs' (*The Acid Test*, 1966). Although some of the later acid tests took on the atmosphere of concert performances by the Grateful Dead and other nascent psychedelic groups, until the last such event in 1966 Kesey worked to keep the events as disorganised as possible, describing them as 'deliberately self-defeating' and trying 'to achieve nothing at all times' (ibid.). Kesey's disorganisation by design rejected the idea of finished work in favour of a participatory experience of failure and crisis somewhat akin to Artaud's theatre of cruelty.

Even closer to Artaud's concept of an overwhelming style of theatre was Andy Warhol's *Exploding Plastic Inevitable* [hereafter *EPI*], a series of performances that occurred at about the same time as the Acid Tests. A multi-media freak out with connections to the New York neo-avant-garde art scene and the happenings that had become fashionable at the time, *EPI* was a series of multi-media events delivering sensory overload and, like the Acid Tests, featured a legendary house band, the Velvet Underground, to guide the trip. But unlike the Acid Tests, there were few traces of optimism and critics viewed the trip as a bad one. Lacking any promising concepts such as Kesey's 'open circles' of free expression or possibilities for accidental discovery, *EPI* was essentially an audio-visual attack in what seemed at the time to be a more dangerous environment. Reviewers described being 'brutalized, helpless' and 'ducking in the midst of shrapnel' in an event that 'vibrates with menace, cynicism and perversion' (Joseph 2005: 250–51). Although in retrospect, these shows were perhaps no more assaultive than typical rock concerts or dance raves today, they sharply contrasted with the peace and love philosophy then promoted by the counterculture.

The intensity of freak out events like *EPI* or the Acid Tests was difficult to capture on record, but going mad in the recording studio eventually became a method for bands that emerged out of these underground scenes, each exhibiting varying levels of skill in creating the raw atmosphere of freaking out. With impeccable musical skill, the Grateful Dead, on their album *Anthem of the Sun* (1968), blended excerpts from live shows with studio recordings to create sound collages on songs like 'Caution (Do Not Stop on Tracks)' and 'That's It for the Other One', the latter song paying tribute to Kesey's Merry Prankster activities. Much more raw by comparison, the Velvet Underground brought their high volume noise into the recording studio for their first album, *The Velvet Underground and Nico* (1967), with the feedback-drenched final track, 'European Son' being the closest audio approximation of Warhol's *EPI* at the time.

The album that most successfully captured freaking out in the recording studio in the 1960s was the appropriately titled *Freak Out!* (1966) by the Mothers of Invention led by Frank Zappa. The album package itself was an image of sensory overload, blasting a message of radical social critique that resembled a Dadaist manifesto. The liner notes included relevant quotes, names of influential artists, as well as everyone who played a part in the Los Angeles freak scene documented by Zappa, and even included a map to 'freak out hot spots'. Most importantly, in the liner notes Zappa defined freaking out as a process whereby an individual casts off outmoded and restricting standards of thinking, dress and social etiquette in order to express CREATIVELY his relationship to his immediate environment and the social structure as a whole ... when any number of 'Freaks' gather and express themselves creatively through music or dance, for example, it is generally referred to as a FREAK OUT. The participants, already emancipated from our national social slavery, dressed in their most inspired apparel, realize as a group whatever potential they possess for free expression. (Zappa 1966, caps in original)

With gratuitous use of capital letters and italics, Zappa invited his listeners to freak out and become members of what he called 'The United Mutations' (ibid.).

On the extended tracks that made up Sides 3 and 4 of this double LP, Zappa displayed his 'united mutations' – the freaks of the Los Angeles scene – who he invited into the Hollywood recording studio to 'freak out on $500 worth of rented percussion' on a Friday night in March, 1966 (ibid.). 'Return of the Son of Monster Magnet' [hereafter RSMM], the 12-minute track that concludes the album, captures the raw sounds of that late night collective freak out, but ironically – and there is always irony with Zappa – the entire track is meticulously structured. In the liner notes it is listed as an 'Unfinished Ballet in Two Tableaux' in a nod to Stravinsky's *Le Sacre du Printemps* with the first part subtitled 'Ritual Dance of the Child-Killer' and the second part subtitled 'Nullis Pretti (No commercial potential)'. As Watson interprets the track, the reference to ritual is more than just a parody of Stravinsky, but a symbolic sacrifice of the character Suzy Creamcheese who represents innocence deflowered and corrupted (Watson 1997: 157). But deflowered and corrupted by what? The conventional society attacked in Zappa's manifesto? Or the hedonistic, drug taking, free love counterculture that he seemed to be celebrating?

The 'Ritual Dance' begins with a brief dialogue between Zappa and the character Suzy Creamcheese, in which he asks her, 'what's got into you', implying anything from a drug to a penis to self-realisation, all potentially corrupting influences common at the time. This is followed by a slow build-up of orgasmic panting by the voice of Suzy Creamcheese, accompanied by Zappa's freaks vocalising non-melodic sounds, faux jungle calls and occasional screams over repeating drum patterns and a siren sound. As Suzy's orgasmic panting builds, the drums speed up and the accompanying voices increase in density with a chorus of males mimicking excited animals. The first section concludes with the instruments in rapid tempi fading behind several voices saying hippie expressions such as 'flashing', 'oh wow' and 'happening, man', suggesting that the conflation of music, drugs and sex has killed the innocent child. The shorter second part, 'Nullis Pretti (No commercial potential)', is more playful as the voices, including Suzy's, continue to chant and the phrase 'cream cheese' is subjected to multiple vocal variations. As the tape speed of the voices increases, the final vocal sounds evoke the laughter of children, perhaps suggesting that the sacrificed child has been reborn.

Although such an interpretation may be reading too much into this audio celebration of anarchy, the freak out of RSMM is clearly a highly structured work that is much more finished than either Kesey's Acid Tests or John and Yoko's first album, resulting in several ironies. While his invited guests freaked out in the studio, Zappa was the control freak, carefully organising these sessions in advance (Walley 1972: 61) and manipulating them in the editing process. The collective free expression that Zappa championed in his manifesto was perhaps less about emancipation from social slavery than a way to add tone colours to his individual compositional palette, enabling him to better critique society and even the counterculture itself. Perhaps the greatest irony was that while RSMM and the entire album seemed to celebrate psychedelic drugs, Zappa was fiercely opposed to all drugs and even published a public statement that year denouncing all forms of drugs (ibid.: 64–5). Zappa soon expanded his critique beyond mainstream culture to attack the counterculture's gleeful indulgence in dangerous drugs and simplistic rock and roll with naïve messages of peace and love as heard on the Mothers' 1968 album, *We're Only in It for the Money*. While it is open to question whether or not Zappa was representing the counterculture or simply exploiting it, Zappa was clearly employing avant-garde technique not for the kind of experience advocated by Kesey, but for the purpose of making art.

Zappa's transformation of that late night freak out is what Peter Bürger would call a 'non-organic work' of avant-garde art in that it is built on principles of chance and montage as opposed to the structural integrity of 'organic' modernist works:

> Artists who produce an organic work ... treat their material as something living. They respect its significance as something that has grown from concrete life situations. For avant-gardistes, on the other hand, material is just that, material. Their activity initially consists in nothing other than in killing the 'life' of the material, that is, in tearing it out of its functional context that gives it meaning. Whereas the classicist recognizes and respects in the material the carrier of a meaning, the avant-gardistes see only the empty sign, to which only they can impart significance. The classicist correspondingly treats the material as a whole, whereas the avant-gardiste tears it out of the life totality, isolates it, and turns it into a fragment. (Bürger 1984: 70)

This transformation of material in order to make art explains a great deal of Zappa's montage style of which his first album was just the beginning. Throughout his career Zappa was always a realist, not a madman, and constantly responding to current affairs that provided the impetus for his work. Yet Zappa's transformations of popular culture, whether the disco satires of the late 1970s or the PMRC hearings of the 1980s, were always directed at subduing the forces he opposed and make them serve his purpose as an artist.

Psychedelic Party Tracks and Freak Out Failures

The freak out may have appeared to support countercultural revolution, but its self-destructive death instinct – as suggested by Zappa's cynical RSMM – worked against any hopes the counterculture may have had for building an alternative community through rock music. Activist John Sinclair declared rock music to be 'one of the most vital revolutionary forces in the West' precisely because it made people feel 'alive again in the middle of this monstrous funeral parlour of western civilisation' (Sinclair 1995: 301). But freaking out, like avant-garde actions that die 'consciously and voluntarily' (Calinescu 1987: 124), had a built-in tendency to negate itself, and was perhaps more about death than life. Strategies of instigating a delirium of the senses through media overload, dissolving egos, and messing up minds with chemicals to circumvent any goal are linked to a death obsession in rock that is hardly limited to the psychedelic era, but seemed to be everywhere in the late 1960s. Themes of death permeated psychedelic rock from the Mothers and the Velvet Underground to the Beatles, the Stones and the Doors, and for a brief moment freaking out was a fashionable expression undertaken by many musicians in mainstream pop music that seemed to be leading nowhere.

One manifestation of rock and roll's capacity for celebrating life was the 'party track', a type of recording that includes sounds of people shouting and making noises as if at a party. As explored by the Beach Boys on the album *Beach Boys Party*, the party track created the illusion of people seemingly enjoying a party with the band in which anyone could participate by clapping, banging on bottles or playing bongos. Party tracks went psychedelic in 1966 with songs such as the Beatles' 'Yellow Submarine' and Bob Dylan's 'Rainy Day Women #12 and 35' in which the parties became wilder under the apparent influence of drugs and began to carry a distinctive countercultural message: not only was everyone invited to the party, but everyone listening was implicated in the counterculture – 'we all live in a yellow submarine' and 'everybody must get stoned'. Conceived this way, the party track seemed to offer the promise, or at least the illusion, of a unified counterculture.

But as party tracks became a type of freak out this approach led to creative dead ends for some bands. The competitive Brian Wilson continued with the party track technique to salvage the Beach Boys' aborted Smile project that ended up as the album *Smiley Smile* in 1967. Featuring several stoned party tracks with giggling voices spouting nonsense that are sometimes sped up, *Smiley Smile* has since become a cult favourite and even praised for pushing the boundaries of conventional song form, but this disturbing version of the ordinarily squeaky clean Beach Boys alienated their fans and was a commercial failure at the time (Harrison 1997). The Beatles' other competitors, the Rolling Stones, with their more decadent, Dionysian image, were perhaps more convincing at freaking out, but they also failed. The album *Their Satanic Majesties Request* (1967), widely considered a failed imitation of the Beatles' successful psychedelic pop, was an erratic, stoned-sounding record in which the band explored unusual and eclectic instruments such as recorders and Indian percussion. The eight-minute 'Sing This All Together (and See What Happens)' featured meandering jamming complete with snippets of conversation intended to recreate a drug party and is critically viewed today as a blemish on their recorded output.

If freaking out on record albums was unwelcomed by listeners, it also met with animosity from audiences of the more adventurous live acts that attempted them onstage. The Syd Barrett-led Pink Floyd, the darlings of the London psychedelic scene, favoured free form, pan-tonal jams such as 'Interstellar Overdrive' and, when playing at venues outside the underground London scene, were often met with openly hostile audiences expecting their current hit songs (Mason 2005: 67–9). The band did record a shorter, nine-minute version of 'Interstellar Overdrive' for their 1967 album, *The Piper at the Gates of Dawn*, which became the raw blueprint for the more controlled, extended progressive rock pieces by the reformed group following Syd Barrett's legendary collapse from what appeared to be drug-induced madness. Also on the London scene was Soft Machine, a band that explicitly cited the Dadaist pataphysics of Alfred Jarry in their music. Soft Machine's most notorious song in concert, 'We Did It Again', was a single 4-beat-measure-long riff played over and over again along to a repeated vocal chant of '*we did it again*'. While extended versions of this minimalist joke were embraced as hip Dadaism in France, it generated hostility among audiences in the UK (Bennett 2005: 110). Like their colleagues Pink Floyd, Soft Machine soon underwent personnel changes and began developing multi-movement progressive rock suites in a more listener-friendly and professional style that dispensed with Dadaist pranks.

With the lack of audience and critical support, it seemed that freaking out was not particularly revolutionary nor was it entertaining. More of a party spoiler, freaking out helped bring an end to the party of psychedelic pop just as it was getting started, making the genre one of the shortest historical periods in rock (Borthwick and Moy 2004: 42). The demand for immediate and total transcendence in psychedelic rock – what Russell Reising calls 'psychedelic carpe diem' and 'psychedelic apocalypse' (Reising 2009: 528) – could not possibly be sustained. In a music industry that began marketing rock as an art form, rock musicians in the late 1960s either looked backward, as in the return to roots for the Rolling Stones, or looked forward, as in the development of progressive rock by Pink Floyd and Soft Machine. Rock music of the new era would not be based on audience participation in a wild freak out, but on audience consumption of music made by professionals who carefully controlled their craft. As for the San Francisco bands associated with Kesey's Acid Tests, several of these groups were signed to CBS Records and marketed using countercultural rhetoric. The resulting advertising slogan, 'The Revolution is on CBS' (Harron 1988: 184), ironically proclaimed the advent of the real revolution of the psychedelic era: a newly revitalised music industry.

The most destructive avant-garde attack on the burgeoning rock music industry of the late 1960s was the self-destruction of the Monkees, a prefabricated teen idol band that was one of the entertainment industry's most successful appropriations of late 1960s counterculture. After nearly two years of a successful weekly television series, their feature film *Head* (1968) was essentially an extended freak out that can be seen as an attempt either to gain countercultural acceptance or to terminate the band's career. Although this Hollywood-created band had fought for artistic control over their product and eventually obtained it by playing their own instruments and writing their own songs, the irony of this foray into art filmmaking was that the group once again became, in the words of singer Davy Jones, 'pawns in something we helped create but had no control over' (Lynskey 2011). Created by the Monkees' producers with a script by Jack Nicholson, *Head* satirised war, the entertainment business, and the Monkees' own commercial enterprise. Like the satirical works of Zappa – who has a cameo appearance in the film – *Head* is another example of a 'non-organic' work that uses montage to kill the life of the material and expose the façade of the band. The death of the Monkees as an entertainment commodity is made explicit in the film's opening sequence of drummer Micky Dolenz leaping off a bridge in an apparent suicide and the final scene in which Dolenz and the rest of the band make the same leap only to become trapped in a giant aquarium that thwarts their ultimate act of freedom. The commercial failure of the Monkees' final freak out may have been its only success in that it helped to euthanise this band that was viewed as inauthentic, not only by rock fans, but by some members of the band themselves.

Freaking Out in the 1970s: For Some the Revolution Never Ended

At the end of his 1968 book on countercultural revolution, Jeff Nuttall declared that the 'freak out is over' and, retreating from the sensory delirium he advocated throughout the book, called for artists to 'turn away from the Nothingness' and give 'power and body to the true music of the gods by cultivating the craftsman in us' (Nuttall 1968: 268–9). While many rock musicians of the 1970s proceeded to develop their craft in a thriving music industry, some rock musicians continued dabbling in absurdist anarchy despite critical and public antagonism toward avant-garde gestures. John Lennon, the most high-profile rock musician of the time, continued his extreme collaborations with Yoko Ono, leading some critics to question his sanity, but what many saw as Lennon's folly was part of a larger, more calculated Dadaist protest against war (Wiener 1998: 8). Much less calculated and far from the media spotlight, Detroit-based band the Stooges experimented with psychedelic drugs during recording sessions, concluding their album *Fun House* (1970) with a song titled 'L.A. Blues', a formless noise jam originally titled 'Freak' (Matheu 2009: 61) that cast freaking out as a raw, punk gesture stripped of the customary countercultural statements.

For many German underground rock musicians in the early 1970s, in a genre known today as 'krautrock', freaking out was an essential part of a radical approach by bands that operated as musical collectives dedicated to avant-garde approaches to music making. Long freak out tracks were the norm for commune bands such as Amon Düül, its spin-off band Amon Düül II and Ash Ra Tempel, a band that recorded an actual 1960s style 'acid test' with countercultural guru Timothy Leary leading a large group of amateurs in an LSD ritual documented on the album *Seven Up* (1972). Even the more sober-minded, Cologne-based group Can experimented with extended jamming in the studio to capture spontaneous freak outs with eccentric and unstable lead singers such as Damo Suzuki and Malcolm Mooney babbling nonsense lyrics. The German commune band most dedicated to Dadaist anarchy was Faust, a band formed by impresario and journalist Uwe Nettlebeck with a manifesto proclaiming the therapeutic properties of the absurd (Koch and Harris 2009: 586). Faust's disorienting, non-organic collages of sound attacked all conventions of popular music with mad laughter the most frequent recurring motif on their records.

In contrast to the outsider approach of commune bands from Germany, former Velvet Underground guitarist Lou Reed used his insider position as an established artist with RCA Records to directly attack the music industry with his album *Metal Machine Music* (1975). This double disc of continuous guitar distortion and feedback has become one of the most infamous albums in rock history and an avant-garde prank that mocked the music industry's marketing strategies by creating an ambiguity as to whether the work is highbrow art music, lowbrow rock or an elaborate joke. Lester Bangs portrays Reed as delighting in a sadistic relationship with his fans, his critics and his record label, as he reports Reed trying to convince RCA to release it on their classical Red Seal label, insisting that references to Beethoven were hidden within the impenetrable walls of feedback on the record (Bangs 1987: 189). While many record buyers demanded refunds shortly after it was released, Bangs celebrated the album as one of the greatest of all time, thus canonising it as a landmark punk album, but undoubtedly one with as few listeners as *Two Virgins*.

Extreme recordings by Lou Reed, Faust, Can and the Stooges reveal continuities between the countercultural anarchy of the 1960s and the punk rebellion of the mid-1970s that encompassed music more diverse than three-chord rock songs. The punk revolt against a music industry dressed in countercultural disguise spawned numerous post-punk bands who created freak outs that refute the punk cliché of 1976 as a 'year zero' for rock and supports the notion that 'the punk and hippy eras were much closer to each other than to what came before or after' (Harron 1988: 205). Like the 1940s bebop movement that can be seen as both an evolutionary and a revolutionary force in jazz history (DeVeaux 1997), 1970s punk reveals just as many continuities as disruptions if one looks at bands involved in avant-garde experimentation (see Reynolds 2005 and Hegarty 2007). Public Image Limited (aka PiL), Throbbing Gristle, Psychic TV, Nurse With Wound, Coil and Current 93, are a few of the UK post-punk, industrial and post-industrial groups that celebrated destruction of song form, amateurish values of musicianship and conceptual absurdity, demonstrating that the freak out was not over.

John Lydon of the Sex Pistols and PiL is the central conduit through which hippie avant-gardism passed through punk into post-punk avant-gardism (see Albiez 2003). The sloppy performance of conventional song forms by the

Sex Pistols may have been homologous to the social anarchy behind the UK punk movement, but Lydon – a record collector with a taste for rock avant-gardism – explored sonic anarchy further with his group PiL that developed a distinctive style of ineptitude. Unlike many punk musicians for whom ineptitude is a virtue that connotes authenticity (Hegarty 2007: 94–5), the more skilled musicians of PiL, such as guitarist Keith Levene, exaggerated amateurishness by intentionally playing 'wrong' notes (Reynolds 2005: 20). Like Zappa's counterattack on hippie culture, the early PiL albums were counterattacks on punk orthodoxy, each LP veering further away from punk and toward krautrock eclecticism that alienated many fans (Hegarty 2007: 97). John Lydon's self-destructive tendencies were, like John Lennon's, partly a reaction to his position as the most prominent figure of a powerful youth movement within a revitalised popular music industry.

With the late 1970s punk DIY philosophy encouraging young amateurs to create their own musical enterprises, freaking out could prove just as useful as three-chord simplicity, as was the case for Steve Stapleton, founder of the band Nurse With Wound. An obsessive record collector and devotee of krautrock, Stapleton and his friends set out to collect as many freak out records as possible and followed three basic guidelines: long tracks, no songs and drug-related album covers (Stapleton 2001). When a friend of Stapleton's who worked at a recording studio offered him free studio time if he had a band, Stapleton lied, telling him that he was in a band and immediately bought some instruments and invited his record collector friends to the recording studio. Having never touched musical instruments before, the three novices went into the studio with no rehearsal and recorded the album *Chance Meeting on a Dissecting Table of a Sewing Machine and an Umbrella* (1979) as a spontaneous freak out, becoming the band Nurse With Wound. In punk DIY fashion, Stapleton packaged the album himself and created a lifelong career for himself independently selling his surrealist-inspired music.

For groups like Nurse With Wound and related post-punk bands, as well as bands such as Faust that continued into the twenty-first century, it seems as if the revolution never ended and psychedelic apocalypse is perpetually looming. Since the 1980s, the band Coil have treated their recordings more as magic rituals than as musical works – as in their extended track 'How to Destroy Angels' – and the group's use of psychedelic drugs to achieve altered states in the recording studio was a common method for the group up until their dissolution in 2004. Genesis P-Orridge of Psychic TV and David Tibet of Current 93 have both expressed fondness for the consciousness-altering spirit of 1960s psychedelic rock and have expanded on its darker side in their own music. This ongoing obsession with the 'Six Six Sixties' – a song title by Throbbing Gristle – suggests the dark side of the long sixties. Whereas mainstream absorption of countercultural values, as argued by Tom Hayden in his book *The Long Sixties* (2009), have helped drive cultural change, evidenced socially by President Obama's election and musically by the political activism of rock groups such as U2, among some underground musicians there is a more apocalyptic spirit that continues as well. No longer part of any countercultural movement, the 'long freak out' continues a discourse of anarchy in which musicians flail at instruments and shout against meaning in pursuit of chaos, irrationality and notions of revolution that may not be collective, but are individualised and desperately solipsistic.

Conclusion: Unfinished Music as Resistance

Yoko Ono's notion of unfinished music offers a useful way to understand how freak out recordings function as a strategy of resistance by rock musicians. The recordings included here range from the unfinished rawness of *Two Virgins*, to the more intentional chaos of drug party tracks, punk noise jams and krautrock tape collages, to more finished, cohesive works such as Frank Zappa's freak out ballet. But all of these recordings are unfinished in the sense that they deny completion. Freak out tracks resist becoming rock songs by rejecting beat, melody and song form, and in their fragmentation they also resist becoming organic musical objects for aesthetic contemplation. Deeper readings of *Two Virgins* or *Metal Machine Music* might reveal further insights – perhaps identify specific avant-garde source works or an aesthetics of audio madness – but such detailed analysis, like analysing the elegant contours of Duchamp's urinal, risks misrepresenting as art objects what are essentially raw and noisy acts of resistance. Such sonic attacks should not be misinterpreted as poor imitations of avant-garde tradition or efforts to gain highbrow cultural accreditation (see Gendron 2002), but as attacks that are immediate and of the moment in their lack of any clearly defined goals.

The idea of madness that runs through all of these recordings is problematic as it is feigned in almost every case and for this reason needs to be understood as a conscious act of provocation. Whether it is a broad, utopian attack against what Kesey called the 'closed circles' of society or a focused attack on record executives or demanding fans, the avant-garde strategy of pushing an art form to its deepest point of crisis in a self-destructive manner can only be seen as madness in the competitive business of popular music. One explanation for this madness might be that musicians use it as a pose of authenticity, still regarded by some scholars as an essential part of the aesthetics of rock (see Moore 2002 and Gracyk 1996). Allen Ginsberg declaring his authentic insanity against a sane world certainly helped make him a countercultural hero, but the Monkees declaring their authentic selves trapped within an inauthentic music industry left them as sacrificial victims of the marketplace. Whether a rock musician's experiment in avant-gardism destroys an existing career or, if they're lucky, creates a new one, the consumer plays a participatory role, ultimately completing these works either by buying into utopian ideals, expanding their own listening habits or demanding refunds for albums of unlistenable noise. Such are the perils of Kesey's dangerous, open circles designed to go nowhere.

Ironically, the marketing of countercultural revolution by the music industry during the late 1960s allowed musicians this freedom to go 'beyond music' and engage in precisely the same participatory aesthetics practised by neo-avant-garde artists at that time. Just as avant-garde aesthetics in the art world had empowered artists with the ability to transform anything they touched into art (Rosenberg 1972: 11), the music industry endowed charismatic rock stars with a similar artistic license and at the height of the counterculture some rock musicians and artists seemed to share similar goals. The marriage of pop star John Lennon and Fluxus artist Yoko Ono symbolised the mutual efforts by rock musicians and avant-garde artists to integrate art and daily life through collective creation and reception of music unhindered by any boundaries between performer and audience. But whereas the avant-garde had obliterated the old hierarchy of values in art, generating new styles of conceptualism incomprehensible to the mass audience, yet recuperated by museums (see Calinescu 1987: 144–8), the rock experimentalists can claim no such triumph within popular culture. The raw, anarchistic nonsense of the freak out seems designed to resist coming to fruition as either a successful work of art or slice of entertainment that could serve any function in the marketplace of popular music.

In the twenty-first century countercultural madness is no longer the preferred method of resistance to the culture industry. While the romanticised battle between creative freedom and corporate domination continues in the narrative of rock, the very notion of resistance has become a cliché in which just about anyone can declare their independence as an artist and gain points for authenticity. Alongside this still-thriving romantic model of the 1960s and 1970s – what Frith and Horne call 'rock bohemianism' – is the more self-conscious 'pop situationism' that emerged in the late 1970s when musicians began to apply cool-headed, neo-avant-garde theories of pop art to their work and its marketing (Frith and Horne 1987). From this perspective, marketing what Bloomfield calls 'resisting songs' – pop songs that subtly disrupt the conventions of pop song form – is seen as a way of resisting commodification while avoiding the avant-garde 'cultural ghetto' (Bloomfield 1993: 28) where rock extremists like Steve Stapleton reside, even though his music seems more effective at resisting commodification by resisting conventional song form itself. Compared to the soft sell pop resistance of today – if such pop is indeed resistant – the extreme freak out records of the past still scream and spark more controversy than the Dadaist readymade objects that quietly reside in art museums. While the Beatles remain the most iconic symbol of the romantic ideal of the rock band, creating authentic art and selling it – still today – within a commercial music industry, albums like *Two Virgins* are still actively engaged in resistance. As long as there are Beatles fans outraged over albums like *Two Virgins*, John and Yoko's music will remain unfinished.

Chapter 9
The Grateful Dead and Friedrich Nietzsche: Transformation in Music and Consciousness[1]

Stanley J. Spector

When the original five members of the Grateful Dead first started playing together, they performed from April 1965 until December 1965 as the Warlocks. They then discovered that there was already another band called the Warlocks, so they changed their name and played as the Grateful Dead for the first time on 4 December 1965, at the San Jose Acid Test at Big Nig's house. From their first gig as the Grateful Dead, they were already in the centre of a counterculture, sharing space with Neal Cassady, Allen Ginsburg and Ken Kesey. While Kesey and the Pranksters were experimenting with different forms of art, the Grateful Dead were experimenting with different forms of music, primarily a new genre of music, 'psychedelic' or 'acid' rock, and a unique style of playing, 'jamming' or 'collective improvisation'. The Grateful Dead clearly were successful. The band played 2,314 concerts over 30 years at over 500 different venues, all the while integrating elements of folk, bluegrass, blues, rhythm and blues, jazz, classical and rock and roll into their distinctive sound and way of playing. A much larger project than what is appropriate here would be to show the dynamic interrelationship among all of these factors: the band's success at musical experimentation, their commercial success in terms of their fan base, the kind of consciousness required by the band members to play the way they did, and the kind of consciousness presupposed by the legions of fans who have been incredibly receptive, encouraging and forgiving of the band as together they continually took new chances musically. My goal here is more modest. After differentiating modes of improvisation and delineating Grateful Dead psychedelic explorations from Grateful Dead jamming, I conclude by suggesting that the mode of consciousness presupposed by Grateful Dead jamming exemplifies Nietzsche's emphasis on the 'present moment' as he formulated it in the principle of the Eternal Return of the Same.

Bill Graham, the San Francisco rock promoter, expressed the sentiment that many Grateful Dead fans have when he put on the Winterland Marquee: 'They are not the best at what they do; they're the only ones that do what they do' (Hunter et al. 2003: 253). Graham was not alone in his assessment that the Grateful Dead were offering something no one else was. Consider this comment by Kesey:

---

[1] I thank my colleagues in the Grateful Dead Caucus for their kind support, generous feedback and enthusiastic encouragement.

> Anybody who's been on acid and has felt Garcia reach in there and touch them, all of a sudden they realize, 'He's not only moving my mind. My mind is moving him!' You'd look up there and see Garcia's face light up as he felt that come back from somebody. It was a rare and marvelous thing. Whereas the Doors were playing at you. John Fogerty was singing at you. When the Dead had a real good audience and the audience began to know it, they were playing the Dead. Which meant the Dead didn't have to be the leaders. They could let the audience play them. (Greenfield 1996: 76)

No one else was playing this way. Other bands were not encouraging the same kind of audience participation; Grateful Dead audiences were participating, and by virtue of their participation, they were encouraging the band to continue with its free form improvisational musical explorations. The band would often explore various musical possibilities within the context of a chord, or a time signature, or even a single note, always improvising spontaneously during a performance, listening to the ideas of their band-mates, responding and introducing ideas of their own. Collective musical explorations would often result in a musical climax, and in the case of the Grateful Dead, that climax is the moment of collective improvisation, the same style of improvisation that characterises the jams that occur in the middle of fairly structured tunes.

Taking their cue from John Coltrane, who often played improvised solos within a context established by his rhythm section and who also might have responded to musical suggestions made by the other members of his quartet, the Grateful Dead's innovation was to take the possibility of a single musician's soloing within an ensemble and transform it into a new musical space which both allowed and encouraged each musician in the band to solo simultaneously. By playing this way, the Grateful Dead pioneered a new type of music – 'psychedelic' or 'acid' rock. Neither ballad, blues nor traditional rhythm and blues, and certainly not jazz, folk or bluegrass either, some of the songs the Grateful Dead introduced into the musical expression of the mid-1960s could be described as attempts to explore musically both the inner and outer spaces of the musical structures themselves, as the band members along with the audience explored new dimensions of consciousness. It seemed a natural development for the band to play this type of music as it afforded them the maximum freedom for improvisation.

Two salient features of most musical improvisation are the spontaneous creation of something that had not been played before and the primal element of conversation inherent in the structure of all music. Both elements are evident in Grateful Dead music. The Grateful Dead's music was also highly structured, and it was in the context of that structure that they were free to play extemporaneously. That is, while they did in fact make something up on the spot, they always played within a context provided by the musical structure they were exploring. Even when they were exploring musical ideas in between actual songs, they were still playing together as an ensemble within a structure.

Most improvisation, while both spontaneous and conversational, is also usually a blend of both hierarchical and associative modes (Pressing 1988). Hierarchical improvisation occurs whenever musicians play spontaneously in the context of the structural framework of the composition. This framework is often held in place by the rhythm section as it expresses the established boundaries of a song while allowing for intermittent spontaneous explorations of the soloist. On the other hand, when the dominant song structure is largely abandoned, associative improvisation occurs as the musicians in the band each suggest new ideas. They listen to each other and respond, all the while building a new collective framework for their free-form musical conversations.

To be sure, the Grateful Dead improvised in both hierarchical and associative ways. They were improvising hierarchically any time a single musician played a solo within a song framework established by other musicians in the band. Traditional blues tunes, cowboy songs and numerous 'cover' tunes allowed the various band members to improvise independently. At other times, the band's extended jams or segues between structured tunes brought out an associative dynamic, with each musician suggesting and responding to musical ideas in conversation with other members of the band. But in addition to these two modes of improvisation, the Grateful Dead also performed a third style of improvisation, manifesting what David Malvini termed a 'transformational' quality, which he traces to 'the space and tension' between the hierarchical and associative (forms of improvisation) (2007: 5).

All musical improvisation requires a certain level of musicianship and skill, not just in the individual but also within the ensemble. Players need to be proficient with their instruments, but they also need to be able to participate in a musical conversation with their band mates. They need to listen to the statements of the other players and then respond with a musical statement of their own. Grateful Dead performances presupposed both hierarchical and associative modes of improvising, but also an additional skill: each musician performed spontaneously without having to track consciously or respond to what the others were playing.

The band recognised the tremendous effort it takes to play this way. As Jerry Garcia once remarked in conversation with David Gans, 'you can't play the way the Grateful Dead plays without working at it. It's not something that just happened to us' (Gans 2002: 68). They had to practice: first to learn the structure of the songs; then to learn how each player could solo within the structure of the song (hierarchical improvisation); then to learn how each instrument and player could participate in a free flowing musical conversation no longer tethered to the structural framework of the song (associative improvisation); and finally, to make a musical statement not so much in *response* to another player's statement as in *relation* with it – that is, musically dancing within the phase space of the improvisational journey.

Phil Lesh has described this phase in the band's development as a lesson learned by going 'back the woodshed'. The goal, in his words, was:

> ... to learn, above all, how to play together, to entrain, to become, as we described it then, 'fingers on a hand'. [In the process,] each of us consciously personalized his playing: to fit with what others were playing and to fit with who each man was as an individual, allowing us to mold our consciousness together in the unity of a group mind. (Lesh 2005: 56)

In other words, each band member while transforming his own individual consciousness to allow for a group consciousness was simultaneously developing a new mode of playing making it possible for the band as a whole to improvise transformationally.

In Michael Kaler's analysis of the band's music from 1966 to 1967, he described how they were learning to improvise. He argued that as the band was developing its own jamming sound, their:

> ... real innovation, their distinctive approach, (was) in their determination to show the potentialities that lie hidden within the structures and codes that make up normal lived experience. What the Grateful Dead do is not so much to change these codes and structures – the song remains a song, the band remains a band – but rather to crack them open and show the freedom at their heart. (Kaler 2011: 97)

The Grateful Dead did not abandon structure and form. The first stage of their transformative innovation in jamming, Kaler explained:

> ... can be likened to that of a jazz rhythm. The parameters (tonal, rhythmic, melodic, etc.) of the piece are understood, the feel is broadly expressed, but within that context the players are free to play as they see fit, continually adjusting their lines and phrasings to express their take on what is happening at any given moment or to respond to what the other players are doing – and also, potentially, to aspects of the song's harmony or rhythm. (ibid.: 101)

At this point in their transformation as musicians they were still playing predominately in the hierarchical and associative improvisational modes. As they became more comfortable playing this way, they pushed themselves in different directions and began consciously working in the transformational mode. With this next phase in their development as musicians and members of a band, they began to abandon dominant structures and forms, while also beginning to play what would become the quintessential 'psychedelic' composition of their songbook – 'Dark Star'.

This stage in their musical development also saw the addition of two new band members, Mickey Hart and Tom Constanten. During the three years that the original Grateful Dead musicians, Jerry Garcia, Phil Lesh, Bob Weir, Bill Kreutzman, and Ron McKernan, played together before Hart sat in with them in September 1967, they had become a seasoned performing band, having played 102 concerts in 1966 and another 101 thus far in 1967. Also, they were still exploring musical modes and styles just as they had been during the Acid Tests, and so by September 1967, they had written songs whose lyrics suggested a psychedelic world-view while simultaneously allowing places for improvisational experimentation. They also rearranged standard tunes to open possibilities for jamming. The songs they performed in 1966 were all covers, and the band played both 'Viola Lee Blues' and 'Cold Rain and Snow' eight times each. In 1967, in addition to these two tunes ('Viola Lee Blues' 10 times and 'Cold Rain and Snow' eight times), they composed and performed two new tunes: 'Alligator' and 'Caution: Do Not Stop on the Tracks', playing the former 12 times and the latter seven times while adding 'Good Morning Little Schoolgirl' also at seven shows. Grateful Dead concerts were still not as structured as they came to be post-1978, but they still included fairly short songs that had places for solos or jams and longer exploratory pieces. Three weeks after Hart joined the band, they played the 'Cryptical' 'Other One' suite and just less than two months later, they debuted 'Dark Star'. Clearly the moment that Hart joined the band, he added another dimension to their playing, but it was not until two months later, after his meeting with the Indian tabla player Alla Rakha in New York, that Hart's contribution to the band's psychedelic musical exploration in terms of polyrhythmic rock and roll took place. Hart introduced the rhythm games he had learned with Alla Rakha to the rest of the band, and 'For months', Hart remembered, the band 'spent all day, every day, except when there was a show, practicing, just laying sevens over fives and elevens over nines ... It was during these months of experimentation that we ceased being a blues band and began mutating into our present form' (Hart, Stevens and Libermann 1990: 143).

Phil Lesh claimed that 'Dark Star' was the band's 'signature space-out tune'. It was, significantly, the only tune crediting every band member in its composition. When Lesh reflected on the development of the song, he wrote:

> As we played around with it, it started expanding itself into a flood of endless melody, and from there into some scarifying, chaotic feedback, and back to the original theme, almost of its own accord – as if the music wanted to be expanded far beyond any concept of song. (Lesh 2005: 191)

With the addition of Tom Constanten on keyboards in November 1968, the 'Dark Star' unit was in place. Blair Jackson described the band during the 'Dark Star' period this way:

> This is the Dead at the height of their improvisational powers, with Garcia and Lesh alternately charging through fantastic musical worlds, sometimes following a similar course, at other times trying to lead the jam in two different directions at once. The addition of Tom Constanten's organ to the fray provided a new texture to the Dead's extended pieces during this period: on 'Dark Star' he manages to weave in and out of the other musicians perfectly, working

simultaneously as a lead and rhythm player. Also notable ... was Weir's new maturity as a guitarist. He had never been a conventional rhythm guitar player, but (during this period) he opened up his playing in a hundred new directions, unleashing glistening series of odd chords, or attacking a jam with quicknote filigrees that resembles mini leads. Hart and Kreutzman helped keep it moving, following the leads of the other players or making insistent statements with their drums that would drive the music in another direction. (Jackson 1983: 97)

As the song progressed into its 'scarifying, chaotic feedback', and moved 'beyond any concept of song', it abandoned its original structure and form. This movement from form to un-form, or chaos, was actually a liberating moment for the musicians and a reminder of their formative experiences with the Acid Tests. When asked about the effect of the inherent chaos of the Acid Tests, Jerry Garcia remarked:

Formlessness and chaos lead to new forms. And new order. Closer to, probably, what the real order is. When you break down the old orders and the old forms and leave them broken and shattered, you suddenly find yourself a new space with a new form and new order which are more like the way it is. More like the flow. And we just *found* ourselves in that place. We never decided on it, we never thought it out. None of it. (George-Warren 1995: 95)

In exploring the musical possibilities afforded by 'Dark Star', the band was actively breaking down the old forms and old orders of music simply by disregarding them. Nonetheless, the band never completely abandoned the overall structure of the song, even with its inherent musical ambiguity in what Graeme Boone called the basic 'Dark Star progression'. Moreover, Boone identified nine coordinated structural elements that make up the song and allow for separate musical explorations during the playing of the song:

Beginning of song
Beginning of the first instrumental episode
Climax of the first instrumental episode
Beginning of verse 1
Text of verse 1
Beginning of second instrumental episode
Climax of second instrumental episode
Beginning and text of verse 2
Ending of song and segue into next tune. (Boone 1997: 173)

Within the structure of this song, we can easily identify the places where the entire band would improvise associatively, namely, during the instrumental episodes. Here the musicians were in conversation with each other while they were playing the song. Any one of the musicians could lead with the introduction of a new musical idea that the other band members could develop or ignore as the band ventured into new musical spaces. Most of these musicians, though, had already played together for almost three years; consequently, they already had an idea of what and how their bandmates would play, and they trusted their understanding. As the music transformed from the conversation and exploration of the musical episode to the climax, the band members were no longer in conversation with each other; they were not listening the way they did while they were exploring. Now each of them was independently exploring the space and the tension between the two traditional modes of improvisation. At this point in the song, no one was stepping forward to play an associatively improvised solo against the background groove established by the rest of the band, nor were they exploring together the possibilities of new forms and structures as if they were in an hierarchical mode. The possibility of transformative improvisation emerges where the space and tension between these other modes occurs, and it is precisely that moment when the band has found its new groove together, allowing each musician to play in the context of listening to the implied and understood groove rather than to what each player was playing at that moment.

'Dark Star' became the Grateful Dead's signature 'psychedelic' tune, as they played it 29 times in 1968 and 65 times in 1969. It was not their only 'psychedelic' tune though, as songs like 'The Other One', 'The Eleven', 'Cryptical' and 'Caution' fulfilled the same function for them during this era. Later, tunes such as 'Playing in the Band' or 'Help on the Way > Slipknot' also had formal structures designed to open up spaces for explorations around and in those very structures. In addition to playing these other 'psychedelic' tunes, the Grateful Dead incorporated this style of playing with many of their other songs, even traditional ballads and blues, always first exploring musical possibilities associatively and eventually segueing into collective, transformative improvisation. As Lesh described the process of playing 'Viola Lee Blues':

> we tried to take the music *out* further – first expanding on the groove, then on the tonality, and then both, finally pulling out all the stops in a giant accelerando, culminating in a whirlwind of dissonance that, out of nowhere, would slam back into the original groove for a repetition of the final verse. (Lesh 2005: 59)

One philosophical issue that emerges from this analysis is that of consciousness and its possible states. To improvise in any mode at all presupposes a different kind of consciousness than one who does not improvise. That the Grateful Dead band members improvised in a new transformative mode indicates that they were already open to the possibilities of different kinds or states of consciousness than what is required for mainstream and traditional musical forms. Similarly, their fans, simply by participating with the music, likewise presupposed such open possibilities. Too often, LSD and other psychoactive substances are given sole credit for this transformation in consciousness, and while it may be true in many cases these substances might be a sufficient cause for this shift in consciousness, they are not a necessary cause, for it is possible to experience the shift in consciousness without the drugs. Of course, even though we know that the Grateful Dead were immersed in the LSD culture, this particular problem of consciousness remains centred around the element of conversation in musical improvisation.

Whether it is composing, uttering, bringing about or performing, improvisation is an activity that takes place 'on the spur of the moment' or 'extemporaneously', as the spontaneous aspect of the activity always takes place in a context. In traditional jazz improvisation, the spontaneous expression takes place within a structural tension at work in the ensemble, usually between the rhythm section and the soloist. Ingrid Monson describes this structural tension in terms of the individual and the group:

> ... there are two levels on which the individual-versus-group tension operates: the relationship of the soloist (who may be a rhythm section member), and the relationship of each individual to the remainder of the rhythm section. (1967: 67)

Her general argument in *Saying Something: Jazz Improvisation and Interaction* is that it is not only the soloist who improvises against the groove of the rhythm section, but that it is the rhythm section as well which is improvising in establishing that groove. In either case, it is essential that each of the players has something to say and that the music played and heard is in fact an extemporaneous conversation that they are having with each other.

This conversational aspect of improvising music was also emphasised by Bruce Ellis Benson in *The Improvisation of Musical Dialogue: A Phenomenology of Music*. Arguing from a perspective informed by twentieth-century Continental philosophy, he claimed that all music is improvisational in so far as it 'depicts composers, performers, and listeners as partners in a dialogue. From this perspective, music is a conversation in which no one partner has exclusive control' (2003: x). Benson's argument and examples are not specifically about the Grateful Dead, although they could be. His primary emphasis was on classical music where the roles of composers, performers and listeners are clearly delineated. He also applied his analysis to jazz music with just a brief comment about rock and roll. Nonetheless, his analysis is germane to our discussion of the Grateful Dead, who, while on stage, both composed and performed their music. For Benson, their dialogue is not so much between different sets of composers and performers as it is a conversation among themselves as they composed and performed.

As the band learned to play together, the musical conversation of improvisation took place during rehearsals when they were learning to play as a band. It was during rehearsals that each musician listened to what the other was playing and adjusted his playing to fit in the whole. Garcia echoed this thought when he said 'when you're working in a band, you have to try to let everybody have his own voice the way he best sees it' (Gans 2002: 39). In that interview, Garcia emphasised the art of listening to the other players in order to have a meaningful conversation in a band. But when the Grateful Dead performed, there were times when they did not alternate solos, first hearing what the other players were playing and then responding.

The jazz model of improvisational conversation, both hierarchical and associative, does not explain how the Grateful Dead played collectively in a jam, if we maintain, as that model would suggest, that the members of the band were conversing with each other. In performance, when exploring musical spaces between structured songs or when exploring musical possibilities within the song space itself, once all of them were committed to the same tune or fell into the same groove, they were no longer in a listen-respond mode of conversation anymore, even though, according to Monson and Benson, they were still in conversation and dialogue; now the dialogue was just not with each other. I have argued elsewhere that they were in conversation with the un-played song itself (Spector 2009: 195–205).

What kind of a conversation that could be still needs to be articulated. Before looking at the details of that conversation though, it might be useful to consider a theoretical framework formulated by Friedrich Nietzsche where he suggested possible strategies for overcoming the cultural malaise of his contemporary culture. Nietzsche argued that one of the primary problems with the Western intellectual tradition that has contributed to the cultural malaise has been its incredible emphasis on rational consciousness, even though, as Nietzsche observed, consciousness is not only our most recently developed organ but also our most fallible one as well. Philosophically, consciousness is defined in terms of intentionality, which is to say that it always intends an object, that is, thoughts and beliefs are always about something. For example, if you pay attention to it, you can be conscious that you are reading the words on this page right now. This kind of awareness forms the baseline understanding of consciousness as we have ordinarily objectified the world. The subject-object structure of consciousness is also an expression of a temporal horizon. To think of something is both to impose a temporal structure on the act and a gap between the thinker and the object thought about. When the members of the Grateful Dead jammed and played solos simultaneously, that temporal horizon had to disappear as they were all playing in the same present moment. Garcia once described the times when transformational improvisation really worked as 'those moments when you're playing and the whole room becomes one being – precious moments, man. But you can't look for them and they can't be repeated' (George-Warren 1995: 64). As the whole room is one being, there is no gap between subject and object, and you cannot look for those special moments, for if you try, you will firmly situate yourself in a subject-intended object structure of consciousness, and those special unified moments will elude you. To experience those moments, you have to be present for them; if you try to think them, you will not find them. Lesh said something similar when discussing the way the band played: 'If you're playing along, all of a sudden you find yourself thinking about what you're doing, thinking the notes as you ... play them. In my experience, when I do that, it means I'm not listening' (Gans 2002: 162). If he is thinking about the notes that he or the others are playing, then he is not listening to the song as he plays but what the other players are playing. In those thinking moments he is an active subject intending the objects of the notes and sounds. As such, the kind of listening that Lesh has described is an awareness of what the other musicians are playing in the context of his own playing and in the sense of allowing the sounds to be heard as a complete relational whole rather than actively trying to hear them particularly or individually. To listen this way means that each musician is in an independent conversation with the song, while simultaneously hearing each other's conversation, none of which can happen within the temporal framework of consciousness' intending an object; they must be present, and presence presupposes a consciousness predisposed to a non-dualistic, non-intentional structure.

Nietzsche is a useful philosopher to invoke here. He was the first in the Western philosophical tradition to recognise that the framework driving this tradition that has so valued reason to the exclusion of other human drives and passions is fraught with difficulty. In his delineation of some of the elements of what he called the Western cultural malaise, Nietzsche uncovered fundamental structures of mainstream culture that members of the 1960s counterculture were trying to transform, and in his projection for the future of humanity, he indicated possible strategies for bringing about that transformation.

Already in Nietzsche's first work, *The Birth of Tragedy*, he identified the temporal boundaries of Western culture and indicated its internal contradiction. Beginning after the fall of Athens with the ascendancy of Socrates and Plato as cultural forefathers and continuing through the end of the nineteenth century with Nietzsche himself proclaiming the end of that tradition and the possible beginning of a new one, Nietzsche indicated that the legacy left by Socrates and Plato was the elevation of reason as a function of consciousness as the dominant drive in human experience to the exclusion of other more natural drives and instincts situated in our bodies. What has held this tradition together through its various permutations of Rome, Christianity, the Scientific Revolution and the Enlightenment is precisely what is problematic for Nietzsche, namely, the tenacious grip that rationality as a function of consciousness, along with its presupposed metaphysical dualism, has had for two millennia. Nietzsche argued that by emphasising reason, the intellectual and religious traditions had essentially not only denied the reality of lived experience but also shown that lived experience stood in contradiction to the supposed 'truths' discovered by reason. In *On the Genealogy of Morals*, Nietzsche described the consequences of being overly rational. As human beings neglected or subordinated natural drives and impulses, Nietzsche observed:

> They felt unable to cope with the simplest undertakings; in this new world they no longer possessed their former guides, their regulating, unconscious and infallible drives. They were reduced to thinking, inferring, reckoning, coordinating cause and effect, these unfortunate creatures; they were reduced to their 'consciousness', their weakest and most fallible organ. (1967: 84)

For Nietzsche, the cultural malaise infecting Western culture resulted from an overemphasis on reason and reliance on thinking, or consciousness, to the exclusion of lived experience and instinct. In other words, thought had trumped life.

That is, thinking about life became more important than living a life. Or put another way, life was to be lived rationally, or according to how consciousness determined it should be lived, and if consciousness determined that there was more reality in an unchanging form than in our experience of change, then we were mistaken about our experience. As philosophers have been reflecting on the nature of consciousness, they eventually agreed that the defining characteristic of consciousness is *intentionality*. To say that consciousness is *intentionality* is to say that consciousness always *intends* an object, that is, it is always directed to an object in that consciousness is always about something. Thus, one essential characteristic of consciousness is a metaphysical dualism of subjects and objects. Nietzsche's critique can now be reformulated in terms of what the 1960s counterculture was trying to overcome: mainstream culture accepted the faith in reason promoted so successfully by Plato, and so those living in accord with mainstream culture lived their lives and understood their experience as if there exists a static grid of truth that can be discovered by a thinking subject who stands in opposition to the grid. Most music has been exempt from this charge because it is in the very nature of music to indicate the edges of order rather than the order itself. But the history of music is rife with examples of innovations that challenged the status quo. The Grateful Dead appropriated the innovations of Coltrane and Ives, for example, applied it to rock and roll, and gave it a special Grateful Dead psychedelic twist.

Playing the way the Grateful Dead did cannot be accounted for in terms of this culture of reason and dualism, just as the music of John Coltrane defies categorisation through the grid established by that culture. Nietzsche's critique identified two interrelated problems of the role of consciousness in that grid: the overemphasis of rational consciousness in the living of a life and the defining of consciousness in such a way that it excludes certain experiences. As we return to 'Dark Star' we can see how even lyrically, the role of reason is being challenged.

The first verse of 'Dark Star' expresses poetically what Nietzsche expressed philosophically about the first problem of rational consciousness, that is, the supremacy of reason at the expense of other drives and impulses. Robert Hunter, the Grateful Dead's primary lyricist wrote:

> Dark star crashes, pouring its light into ashes
> Reason tatters, the forces tear loose from the axis
> Searchlight casting, for faults in the clouds of delusion. (Hunter 1990: 54)

When the supremacy of reason is reduced ('reason tatters'), the grid determined by axis is shown to be an illusion ('forces tear loose from the axis'), or in the language Garcia used to describe 'Dark Star', reason had imposed an arbitrary form on the underlying dynamic un-form, or chaos. Once the forces are torn asunder and the grid is shown to be arbitrary, the human endeavour shifts from discovering predetermined truths to navigating through the openings that shift in the un-form ('searchlight casting, for faults in the clouds of delusion').

The second problem of consciousness, that is, defining it in terms of intentionality is brought to the forefront when we try to explain how the musicians were conscious, but not of an object, when they jammed. Put another way, if improvisational music is understood in terms of conversation, what kind of conversation is the band having when it jams, since the conversation is no longer of a listen-response mode, for clearly in the jam, they are not playing in response to what their band mates are playing. In other words, the temporal horizon allowing for a succession of listening and then responding has been abandoned. Here again, Nietzsche can be helpful, for his concept of the eternal recurrence of the same, which for him is the fundamental aspect of a strategy for overcoming the current cultural malaise with its super-emphasis on rational consciousness, can account for the experience of presence in the context of jamming.

The idea of the eternal recurrence is unique to Nietzsche, but it is also problematic since Nietzsche formulated the principle differently in different contexts. Even so, as he himself noted, this insight into human experience is central to his philosophy. He wrote in *Ecce Homo*: 'The idea of the eternal recurrence ... the highest formula of affirmation that is at all attainable' (1966b: Z1). A full interpretation of the concept of the eternal recurrence requires that it be situated in the context of a discussion of the will to power and self-overcoming, a task that is beyond the scope of this chapter. Nonetheless, we can gain a preliminary understanding of what Nietzsche may have meant and its relationship to the experience of the presence required to improvise transformationally through a reading of the following passage from *Thus Spoke Zarathustra*. In the speech, 'On the Vision and the Riddle', Nietzsche wrote:

> Behold this gateway, dwarf! ... it has two aspects. Two paths come together here: no one has ever reached their end. This long lane behind us: it goes on for an eternity. And that long lane ahead of us – that is another eternity. They are in opposition to one another, these paths; they abut on one another: and it is here at this gateway that they come together. The name of the gateway is written above it. (1954a: III.2)

With each event, action, or moment, the horizon of temporality with its structures of past and future disappears as we live each of those moments in the present. It is this sense of the eternal recurrence that speaks to the presence required for Grateful Dead improvisation.

The formula of the concept 'eternal recurrence' itself is problematic; the juxtaposition of the two words could express a contradiction. Clearly the word recurrence is indicative of a process in time; however, it is not so clear what the term eternal signifies. In the passage above, the paths stretch beyond in both directions for eternity, and we understand eternity there in the sense of an everlasting duration. But there is another sense to the word eternal, one that is the opposite of temporal. In this sense, to say something is eternal is to say that it is not in time at all. It has no beginning, middle or end; it just is. It does not stretch across time, and it has no duration. So, the concept of the eternal recurrence could mean that we return to a state of a-temporality; that is, it is not the events that recur over and over again, but rather it is we who return to those moments when the horizon of temporality has disappeared.

We are not normally aware of this experience in our everyday lives, since so much of our experience is marked by beginnings, middles, ends and the intentionality of consciousness with its subject-object structure. But, it is not impossible for us to have experience that is a-temporal, and I think we have them more often than we realise. My suggestion here is that there is the possibility of human experience that is conscious but non-intentional. An experience in which we are aware of being conscious, but are not conscious of any object. When the Grateful Dead jammed, they were playing music in the moment; they were also aware that they were playing music in an ensemble. In terms of the Gestalt theory of perception, there were no figures emerging from the ground, not themselves, not their bandmates, not the stage and equipment and not the audience. Everything constituted ground, or as Garcia described it, 'the whole room becomes one being' (George-Warren 1995: 64). Their goal as musicians was to be conscious of what Garcia called the flow. Or as Lesh characterised it: 'Those moments when you're not even human anymore – you're not a musician, you're not even a person – you're just there' (Gans 2002: 110). It is not just in playing that both the subject-object structure of consciousness with its accompanying temporal horizon can be replaced by a consciousness in presence, but in listening as well. There are moments when we are with the jam, when it is possible for us to experience consciousness in presence as well – when we are not listening to the music in a subject-object mode, but when we are also in conversation with the song as we dance with the band who also is in conversation with the song. In playing and listening to Grateful Dead music, both the musicians and the audience have been transformed musically and consciously.

Chapter 10

Scream from the Heart: Yoko Ono's Rock and Roll Revolution

Shelina Brown

In her 1972 feminist anthem, 'Sisters, O Sisters', Yoko Ono calls upon women to stand up and vocalise their resistance against patriarchal oppression, declaring, emphatically: 'it's never too late/ to shout from the heart.' While most academic scholarship on Yoko Ono focuses on her work as a pioneering conceptual and performance artist, little has been devoted to her accomplishments as an experimental rock vocalist who revolutionised women's vocal practice in the late twentieth century. In this chapter, I will discuss Yoko Ono's searing vocalisations, or *screams* – for lack of a more refined terminology – as politically charged instances of abject sonic art,[1] situated within the tumultuous socio-political context of 1960s US counterculture. As a feminist performer, Yoko Ono's revolutionary impulse to 'shout from the heart' will be treated as a move to redefine musical expression through gendered processes of abjection and cultural resistance – her vocal performances constituting an impassioned response to contemporary movements in art and politics.

Whether working in the media of conceptual art, performance art or popular music, Yoko Ono's creative output reflects one woman's drive to challenge the socially constructed boundaries that prescribe and delimit the acceptable parameters of artistic experience.[2] To this end, the impetus behind Ono's subversive work is

---

[1] The term 'Abject Art' is typically employed to refer to a tradition of radical performance art that involves the use of bodily fluids and excretions as a means of conveying the often disturbing processes of abjection. Julia Kristeva's *Powers of Horror: An Essay on Abjection* (1982) articulates a theory of abjection that gained prominence within academia and experimental fine art scenes throughout the 1980s and 1990s. To briefly capsulate Kristeva's psychoanalytic perspective, abjection refers to the cultural and linguistic processes of exclusion that function to expel and marginalise that which cannot be symbolised within a paternalistic economy of signification. In my discussion of Yoko Ono's extreme vocalisations, I hope to demonstrate that the unsettling 'screams' that Ono unleashes can be interpreted as abject vocal emissions that both disturb and challenge the listening audience.

[2] As a pioneering conceptual artist active within both Japanese and New York art worlds, Yoko Ono's works aimed to challenge conventional notions of art and artistic experience. One of her most renowned feminist art works, *Cut Piece* (1964), required audience members to cut off a piece of the artist's garments, gradually exposing her

in part derived from her early involvement in avant-garde art scenes, primarily the Fluxus movement in 1950s and 1960s New York. During this period, New York was emerging as the centre of what would later come to be termed conceptual art and performance art – art forms that disputed the humanistic ideal of 'art as historical object', demanding that art be redefined as a processual encounter unfolding between a work and its audience.

This radical reconceptualisation of art was nothing less than revolutionary. Susan Sontag, in her influential essay, 'One Culture and the New Sensibility', rightly observed a drastic 'transformation of the function of art' occurring throughout the 1960s (Sontag 1966: 296). According to the identified 'new sensibility', artistic praxis was to be (re)conceived as an extension of life rather than a detached commentary upon life. As an artist who actively established herself as a leading international figure in the art world during this time period, it follows that Ono's own works espouse this revolutionary 'new sensibility' – infusing a life-affirming energy into the rarefied world of 'high' art.

A key aspect of the 'new sensibility', as defined by Sontag, was the move to include all art forms, both 'high' and 'low', within an egalitarian, inclusive definition of 'art'.[3] Exemplifying this practice of the 'new sensibility', Yoko Ono, the avant-garde conceptual artist, opened herself to the possibility of carrying out her artistic experimentations within the world of rock and roll. Through her creative partnership with John Lennon, Yoko Ono gained access to some of the most influential popular musicians of the 1960s. Her arrival on the rock and roll scene was welcomed by the more discerning, forward-thinking recording artists of the time. Throughout the 1960s, there was an increased interest in avant-garde or 'high' art musical experimentation amongst popular musicians, two notable examples of this phenomenon being the influence of Stockhausen's tape compositions upon the Beatles' studio practices, as well as Robert Scheff's noise experiments at the Ann Arbor ONCE festivals taking hold of a young Iggy Pop. Prior to joining forces with John Lennon, Yoko Ono was involved in avant-garde, Cagean experimental music circles, and her familiarity with electroacoustic music contributed to her unique interpretation of rock and roll according to a 'new sensibility'. Ono's experimentation in popular music was thus initiated at

---

nude body. *Cut Piece* invited audience participation in its realisation, and evoked a powerful feminist message concerning the role of women in society as objects of a male visual hegemony.

[3] Sontag distinguishes 'high' and 'low' art in terms of the uniqueness of the art produced. In Sontag's view, traditional 'high' art was characterised by the artists' expression of their individual perspective, whereas 'low' art was marked by mass production and impersonality. Matthew Arnold's seminal work on 'high' art, *Culture and Anarchy* (1869), defines 'high' art as that which serves the purpose of elevating the morality of society. In contrast to Arnold's thesis, Sontag observes that the increasing tendency to incorporate modern technologies into all forms of art has resulted in a blurring of the boundaries between 'high' and 'low'. As avant-garde musics come to be more specialised and scientific, popular musics, too, seek inspiration in technological innovations.

a time when the socio-cultural function of rock and roll was shifting from that of 'relaxation and diversion', towards fulfilling a more artistic, reflexive and often overtly political function (Sontag 1966: 303).

By the late 1960s, Yoko Ono thus occupied a borderline position within the US cultural sphere, working coterminously within the realms of avant-garde conceptual art and rock and roll. Embracing the transformative 'new sensibility' of the era, Ono's musical experimentations were undergirded by her countercultural political convictions, particularly her commitment to the Women's Movement. Throughout her extensive career, Yoko Ono has constituted a powerful feminist voice within global popular culture. Her musical output often deals explicitly with themes of gender inequality, oppression and the need for feminist cultural resistance. According to art historian Midori Yoshimoto, Ono has repeatedly claimed that for her, 'art is a means of survival' (Yoshimoto 2005: 79). Ono's creative urgency thus points to a wider political aim of employing artistic processes as a means of 'surviving' within the world at large. As a Japanese woman active in white male-dominated avant-garde art circles as well as the notoriously androcentric world of rock and roll, Ono was faced with the challenge of inserting herself into powerful, hegemonic cultural milieux that discouraged the participation of independent, creative women – and moreover, women identified as racially 'other'. Indeed, Ono's will to 'survive' through art was initiated in response to the oppressive forces that sought to silence her creative voice, and relegate her to the margins.

In response to such silencing forces, Yoko Ono's feminist anthem, 'Sisters, O Sisters' (1972), calls for women to vocalise their demand for equality – to 'shout from the heart'. Given Ono's native Japanese cultural background, her usage of the term 'heart' can be interpreted in terms of the Japanese Buddhist notion of *kokoro*, an expression encompassing Western conceptions of heart and spirit, pointing to the deepest reaches of human feeling and interiority. According to the revolutionary sentiment expressed in 'Sisters, O Sisters', then, the most effective expressions of feminist cultural and political resistance emerge from the 'deepest reaches' of the gendered, female body. In her more experimental musical works predating 'Sisters, O Sisters', such as the searing 'Why?' (1970) and 'Don't Worry Kyoko (Mommy's Only Looking for Her Hand in the Snow' (1969/1971), Ono's screams emerge from the depths of her body, unleashing a subversive vocality that threatens to destabilise not only the boundary between music and noise, but also the gendered and racialised sonic codes that delineate acceptable modes of vocal musical expression. In their politicised interpretation, Ono's unruly vocalisations thus point back to the deepest reaches of her own unique, albeit gendered and racialised body.

In this chapter, Yoko Ono's extreme vocalisations will thus be treated as revolutionary cultural expressions that constitute visceral responses to 1960s and early 1970s political movements and countercultural practices. Taking as a starting point the assertion that the power of Ono's 'scream' lies in its violent, jarring evocation of an intense bodily immediacy, I would like to argue that this 'bodily immediacy' that is produced by her 'scream' is also bound to paradoxical process of bodily abjection. My central contention is that in the context of Yoko Ono's vocal performances, the scream functions as an act of sonic abjection, and brings to the fore a marginalised body negotiating, and defying, its own liminal borders within the wider socio-political formation. The following discussion is structured in two parts: first, it provides a psycho-social interpretation of Kristeva's theory of abjection as a means of understanding the scream as an embodied, revolutionary vocalisation and a politicised mode of artistic expression; second, it contextualises Yoko Ono's screams as extreme vocalisations that straddle the liminal boundaries of numerous contemporary, revolutionary and countercultural discourses and practices. Each section will integrate interpretive musical observations; Yoko Ono's extreme vocal works from the albums, *Yoko Ono/Plastic Ono Band* (1970) and *Fly* (1971) will be considered as evocations of an immediate, revolutionary, abject body politics.

The Scream as Sonic Abjection

In the field of academic musicology, Tamara Levitz stands as one of the few scholars to date who has engaged with the music and revolutionary vocal practices of Yoko Ono. In her article, 'The Unfinished Music of John and Yoko: Imagining Gender and Racial Equality in the Late 1960s', Levitz provides an insightful, even poetic, interpretation of the musical nuances of Ono's oeuvre, taking into account the gendered discourses of Eastern philosophy and Cagean avant-gardism that come to be challenged and reinterpreted through Ono's performances. In her discussion of Ono's work, Levitz puts forward the notion that Ono's extreme vocalisations give rise to an increased awareness of the performer's body – in Levitz's view, Ono's 'screams' thus constitute extreme acts of corporeal expression that cannot be achieved through more conventional, lyrical practices of 'singing'. Levitz writes:

> [Ono's] voice is not beautiful, lyrical, or accompanimental, and thus does not inspire daydreaming or nostalgia. Rather, it forces an awareness of Yoko's very real existence, as it relates imaginatively with listeners' own inner sounds and the emotions attached to them. (Levitz 2005: 223)

For Levitz, Ono's vocal performance communicates a sense of her bodily interiority that in turn resonates with listeners' own experience of their bodies. This visceral, embodied connection between performer and listener is thus distinguished from the wistful 'daydreams' inspired by lyrical singing. Following Levitz's interpretation, we might infer that in order for a vocal performance to inspire a 'daydream', or any form of escapist fantasy, it must follow an established semiotic code that in turn garners a pre-conceived aesthetic response in the listener. Ono's performance of her sonic bodily interiority, however, gives rise to a shared experience of the 'inner sounds' that precede symbolisation. Further, Levitz proposes that these 'inner sounds' are tied to 'emotions', thereby implying that it is possible that human affective experience *precedes* the codified realm of semiotic abstraction. Such an affective experience would no doubt be distinguished from the codified affects transmitted through standardised musical practices.

As a means of theorising Levitz's above-mentioned proposition, I will turn to the work of French revisionist psychoanalyst, Julia Kristeva, whose work provides a critical exploration of the embodied aspect informing linguistic and artistic processes. Kristeva's *Revolution in Poetic Language* (1984) offers a psychoanalytic perspective on the embodied, material processes that undergird discursive formations and the development of human subjectivity. Within this influential work, Kristeva develops a unique mode of semiotic analysis, identifying two oppositional yet coterminous properties of discourse: the symbolic and the semiotic. While the 'symbolic' refers to all extant linguistic and cultural systems that construct meaning, the 'semiotic' points to the sonorous qualities of language, and the material, embodied experience that lies beyond (or within the fissures of) the 'symbolic'. According to the Kristevan model, a 'revolution' in language occurs in the enunciative moment when the semiotic collides with the symbolic – that is, when language assumes its embodied manifestation. According to a Kristevan perspective, the revolutionary potential of artistic practice lies in its capacity to bring about such a collision within a politicised context; the artist's 'semiotic disposition' thus enables 'the critique and renewal of discourse' (Barrett 2011: 13). Turning to the realm of musical practice, then, one can say that Levitz's identified modes of acceptable singing – 'beautiful, lyrical, accompanimental' – each conform to abstract, 'symbolic' systems and standard conventions that guarantee and maintain musical 'meaning' within a given social order. On the other hand, Ono's 'inner sounds' suggest a semiotic disposition dangerously encroaching on the threshold of the 'symbolic' – embodied, visceral vocalisations that promise a Kristevan revolution in 'musical language'.

The Kristevan model of the 'semiotic' and the 'symbolic' is not a dialectical binary, but rather marks an attempt to formulate a relational dynamic that accounts for the often conflictual relationship between the materiality of human lived experience and the abstractions of human consciousness that forms subjectivity, language and discursive meaning. While Ono's 'screams' thus occupy a Kristevan 'semiotic disposition', it is also true that her 'semiotic' vocalisations often simultaneously occupy a liminal space both *within and without* a 'symbolic', codified range of vocal expression. Ono's extreme vocalisations often slip into ranges of codifiable musical expression, sometimes even pronouncing discernible words and phrases, or repeating melodic patterns – but Ono refuses to linger in the realm of the symbolic.

Listening to a piece such as 'Why?', the opening track from Yoko Ono's first solo record, *Yoko Ono/Plastic Ono Band* (1970), the listener is assaulted with a series of brutal 'screams' presenting a fraught imbroglio of bodily 'noises' that disrupt, defy and ultimately transfigure various musico-symbolic codes. Interpreted solely in terms of its lyrical 'symbolic' content, this piece consists of a repetition of the word 'why'. While the contour of the word 'why' is repeatedly conjured, however, the searing ebb and flow of screams brutally deconstruct the word to the point of collapsing its symbolic manifestation. The choice of the word 'why' is significant in that it constitutes a highly polysemous utterance. Based on the inflection of the speaker/singer's voice, as well as the semantic context, the meaning of 'why' changes drastically. 'Why' might alternately function as a question, an answer ('that is why'), a demand, or as an expression of insurmountable grief or rage. In the course of Ono's performance, the many meanings of 'why' are rendered and rent in turn, giving rise to a vocal persona in conflict with a verbal symbolic order.

Although academic musicology has yet to fully explore the implications of applying a Kristevan conception of the 'symbolic' and 'semiotic' to a musical context, in the context of my interpretation of 'Why?' I propose that the 'symbolic' musical content can be heard in the performance of the rhythm section. After a chaotic intro of merely 17 seconds, Ringo Starr settles into an almost ironically regular 4/4 beat, and Klaus Voorman grooves on an ascending scalar bass riff. While the drums provide a straight rock and roll backbeat, the bass riff emphasises the first beat of the measure, suggesting a funk influence, linked together, these two highly repetitive rhythmic phrases construct a bouncy, driving cross-rhythm that sounds 'unbreakable', endlessly chugging along a steady course. A strong sense of rhythmic regularity is thus established early on in the piece, and it is against this order, a kind of musical 'symbolic', that Yoko Ono's vocal performance exerts a disruptive influence. Mimicking the timbre of the distorted electric guitar, Yoko Ono's maniacal vocal acrobatics compete with John Lennon's shrieking guitar slides. The vocal techniques that Ono employs in the performance are mainly derived from her avant-garde experimentations with the Nagra recorder. Utilising this technology, Ono would practise singing along to her voice played backwards, and at high frequencies (Woo 2006: 286). In liberating her singing voice from a linguistic intonation, Ono is able to veer into a liminal sonic space that is at once music and noise. Feminist rock historian Gillian Gaar describes the sonic context of this piece as 'a harsh, confrontational barrage of noise in which the instrumentation and vocals were just barely restrained from tumbling over into complete chaos' (Gaar 1992: 234).

Taking into account the often jarring juxtapositions that constitute any one of Ono's extreme vocal works, it is possible to consider these as expressions of a fragmented bodily interiority. While such 'screams' challenge the border between music and bodily noise, the disjunctive, jarring succession of vocalisations also simultaneously challenge the listener's ability to construe Ono's own performative persona as a unified subjectivity, and indeed, whether her bodily interiority is in fact a singular material reality, or a performed amalgam of *bodily interiorities*. Lennon's famous characterisation of Ono as 'the woman with the 16 track voice', indicates that her experimental vocal techniques had the effect of not only causing a rupture within standard musical practice, but also rupturing her own vocal subjectivity. Rather than a unified bodily interiority, Ono's vocal contortions point to a bodily interiority-in-process, that is, a body consisting of multiple, fragmented, often opposing material 'interiorities' vying for sonic existence.

Considering Yoko Ono's performance of 'Don't Worry Kyoko (Mommy's Only Looking for Her Hand in the Snow)' included on her 1971 album, *Fly*, her vocal subjectivity shifts radically, suggesting the presence of multiple 'voices' within the singing subject. In my interpretation, 'Don't Worry Kyoko' unfolds as a competitive timbral tug-of-war between at least three distinct voices: that of the kabuki vibrato, the alto voice repeatedly intoning the words 'don't worry', and a high-pitched, cyborgian vocality that suggests a machine-like, synthesised quality – one that vacillates between artificial and hyper-feminine. As an avant-garde artist who was interested in incorporating aural experimentation into her conceptual art throughout the 1960s, Yoko Ono was highly influenced by 'John Cage's decision to widen the range of sounds available for purposes of musical composition' (Danto 2005: 70). Indeed, Yoko's performances reveal a host of vocal influences, ranging from animalistic noises, to the highly refined art of kabuki, and Second Viennese School opera. Her ability to shift between these radical vocal subjectivities with such visceral power is a testament to Yoko Ono's early training in opera performance.[4]

Ono's subversive, transformative vocalisations thus resist categorisation according to the widely adopted musical 'symbolic' codes that would render them 'beautiful, lyrical, or accompanimental'; instead, Ono's 'screams' are violent, revolutionary expulsions emerging from an unstable body, an interiority-in-process. The 'semiotic rupture' that results as the visceral origins of the 'scream' collide with the threshold of the 'symbolic' can be understood as a subversive instance of border-crossing. As a mode of psycho-social critique, Kristeva's theoretical models thus enable a connection to be forged between embodied processes of artistic expression and wider political aims of socio-cultural subversion and revolt. In her influential work, *Kristeva and the Political* (2005), Cecilia Sjöholm provides the following assessment:

> The writings of Kristeva were, already from the start, politically motivated. Rather than wanting to formulate a theory of aesthetics and situating it in a political context, the project has consisted of a systematic displacement of politics from the public to the intimate domain of signification. (Sjöholm 2005: 2)

Always critical of second-wave feminist identity politics that put forward the individual as a unified subjectivity, Kristeva proposes a mode of approaching human expression and individuality as radically embodied, heterogeneous processes. In every instance of human expression, the 'semiotic' and 'symbolic' are brought into dialogue, resulting in a dynamic process of meaning formation whereby bodily noise, silence and non-language are expelled in order to re-establish symbolic codes that guarantee meaning. The political

---

[4] In her seminal article on Yoko Ono, 'The Spirit of YES: The Art and Life of Yoko Ono' (2000), Alexandra Munroe observes that Yoko Ono's foundation in classical training directly contributed to her later revolutionary vocal style.

dimension of artistic practice lies in its capacity to bring about a revolutionary reconfiguration of the symbolic order through creatively enacting moments of semiotic rupture.

The Kristevan theory of the abject, expounded in her 1982 work, *Powers of Horror: An Essay on Abjection*, thematically anticipates the concepts of border-crossing and liminality central to *Revolution in Poetic Language*. In *Powers of Horror*, however, Kristeva chooses to theorise processes of subject formation rather than linguistic expression, focusing on the negative drive to expulsion that undergirds subjective individuation. The trauma of birth, and one's separation from the mother's body, lies at the heart of Kristeva's psychoanalytic theory of abjection – and this fear-inspiring moment of expulsion is thought to form the basis of later psychological processes of subject formation.

Considered in the context of human development, the first experience of abjection occurs at the moment of birth: the child emerges as a discrete individual, while still maintaining a connection to the mother's body. In this scenario, the mother is not an 'object' distinguished by the child, rather, the maternal body is abject, occupying a liminal space that is at once self and other. Within a Western patriarchal context, as the child matures, the abject space of the maternal must be repressed in favour of the law of the Father, represented by the symbolic order. The unspeakable 'horror' that underlies abjection, and subject formation, can thus be interpreted, from a feminist perspective, as the horror of gendered repression. What renders this form of repression, or expulsion of the maternal, particularly unsettling is that it can never be complete. In Kristeva's words, 'the abject is something rejected from which one does not part' (1982: 4). The individuated subject always maintains an embodied connection with the pre-verbal authority of the abject maternal body.

Beyond the mother–child relationship in early developmental stages, considered within a broader context, abjection comes to signify all of the processes of expulsion that serve to maintain our bodily and subjective boundaries. According to Kristeva scholar, S.K. Keltner, 'abjection is an ambiguous threshold both essential to and threatening of the tenuous individuation of the subject' (2011: 45). The expulsions of our bodies, be they bodily fluids, or visceral 'inner noises', are thus 'birthed', or abjected entities that both challenge and (in their expulsion) serve to maintain the borders of the unified body and the unified subject. Our 'horrifying' bodily emissions are relegated to the realm of the abject, that ever present reminder of the uncertainty of our position within the symbolic order. The negative, foreboding affects evoked by the abject are closely linked with those fearful, threatening qualities associated with the feminine in Western patriarchal cultures – the power of this abject 'horror' lies in its latent potential to dismantle a symbolic order that is undergirded by a necessary expulsion of the feminine. In Kristeva's oft-quoted words, the abject 'pulls us towards the point where meaning collapses' (1982: 2). For Kristeva, then, the abject can be interpreted as the body's insistent presence revolting against a repressive symbolic order, threatening to rupture patriarchal 'meaning'.

Returning to the discussion of Yoko Ono's extreme vocalisations, I would like to interpret these as abject sonic expressions. As a vocal expulsion unleashed from the deepest reaches of Ono's body, the scream points to a violent abjection that conjures the pangs of birth. Indeed, Ono has been quoted as referring to her vocalisations as inspired by her experiences in labour. In the late 1960s and early 1970s, critics frequently referred to Ono's vocal performances in terms of 'sickness, suffering, and unintelligibility', responding to a particularly disturbing quality identified therein (Woo 2006: 280–81). Because of its subject matter that directly thematises motherhood, Ono's lament for her lost daughter, 'Don't Worry Kyoko (Mommy's Only Looking for Her Hand in the Snow)', provides an apt example of Ono's extreme vocal repertoire evoking processes of abjection. Ono's daughter, Kyoko, was abducted in 1969 by her father, art promoter Anthony Cox. While the moment of birth and the subsequent early stages of development might be considered to be the time when mother and child develop an awareness of their abject bond, the mother's loss of a child later in life could be said to constitute a traumatic, secondary abjection – the intense corporeal bond between mother and daughter still lingers despite physical separation. Through abjection of the maternal, the symbolic order, or the law of the Father is reinforced; or, in Ono's case, the division between mother and daughter is perpetrated by the illegal intervention of Kyoko's biological father. The multiple vocal 'interiorities-in-process' that were previously discussed in the context of this vocal performance also point to a ruptured maternal body in crisis. As the abject grapples for a 'voice', she is met with a symbolic order guaranteed by her exclusion. The wavering, maniacal scream that ensues is one of desperation, horror, trauma – but most of all, it suggests the radical possibility of a sonic 'other' finding expression.[5]

The horror of the scream thus alerts us to a body in crisis, a body being ruptured, fragmented – a pre-verbal, transformative body that resists co-optation within the symbolic order. As Ono's screams twist in and out of comprehensible semiotic codes, we hear a sonic breakdown of her performative subjectivity, and the emergence of a bodily 'interiority-in-process'. Given the fear of the feminine that comes to be ascribed to the abject, Ono's vocal performances can be interpreted as a direct sonic challenge to the boundaries that anxiously prescribe and reinforce patriarchal order – the scream in this context thus marks a revolutionary, abject vocal expulsion.

---

[5] In applying a Western feminist psychoanalytic framework to Yoko Ono's vocal works, one runs the risk of putting under erasure her unique cultural positioning as a borderline figure whose feminist music constitutes a response to both Japanese and Western forms of patriarchy. In order to augment my Kristevan analysis, in the context of my extended Dissertation project I will provide a cross-cultural, comparative interpretation of Japanese and Western context; in this chapter I have chosen to focus on these works as responses to a Western paternalistic economy of signification.

The Scream in Socio-Historical Context: 1960s Revolutionary Movements and Rock and Roll Counterculture

In my discussion of Yoko Ono's experimental vocal works thus far, I have offered a possible means of theorising her performances as 'revolutionary' from the perspective of Kristevan psychoanalytic critique; I would now like to take a step back from the more intimate processes of her vocal practice, to reflect upon her vocalisations as musical responses to the wider socio-cultural revolutionary movements of the 1960s. An avant-garde artist who crossed over into the world of rock and roll as John Lennon's musical partner, Yoko Ono assumed a highly public position in the late 1960s US popular cultural sphere, one that often resonated with the countercultural realms of underground music and youth culture. According to cultural historian and feminist critic Marianne DeKoven, the late 1960s socio-cultural landscape was a highly transformative, dynamic terrain, characterised by a shift away from modernity towards a postmodern, post-industrial social framework. For DeKoven, the emergence of the postmodern marked 'the end of modernity's totalizing, grandly synthesizing utopianism ... and the shift of modernity's democratizing, capitalist, and individualist impulses to a commercial, popular, populist, subjectivist, multiple and diffuse, unevenly critical or resistant, egalitarianism' (2004: xvi). Yoko Ono's entrance into the forefront of 1960s US music culture thus transpired at a time when the utopic, radical, revolutionary movements of the decade were at their peak – soon, however, these 'grandly synthesizing' modernist causes would give way to postmodern fragmentation and depoliticisation.

Initiating their experimental musical collaboration in 1968, the year that marked a critical, if not somewhat ominous turning point for 1960s countercultural movements, Yoko Ono and John Lennon emerged as a celebrity 'spokes-couple' for various contemporary causes such as the anti-war movement and the Women's Movement.[6] Considering the various human rights campaigns that surfaced during the 1960s, one can say that this era in US history marked the entrance of formerly marginalised peoples into the hegemonic realm of national politics – the onset of the 'populist, subjectivist, multiple and diffuse' postmodern political landscape characterised by DeKoven. It is fitting, then, that Yoko Ono, a Japanese woman, would surface as a powerful public figure in the US at this historical moment. As the voices of formerly silenced, marginal social figures encroached upon the dominant order of middle-class white culture, however, the year 1968 witnessed the violent aftermath of the Summer of Love – race riots broke out across the eastern US, and wide-spread mistrust in the US government grew amongst the youth of the nation in response to the intensification of violence in Vietnam.

---

[6] Yoko Ono and John Lennon released *Unfinished Music No.1: Two Virgins* in 1968. The work consisted of avant-garde tape music that was spliced together by Yoko and John over the course of a night-long LSD trip. This work stands as one of the first instances of avant-garde musical practice being made available to the general public.

In many ways the tumultuous political milieu of the late 1960s marked an historical moment of rupture. The fraught borderlines between self and other, centre and periphery, white and black, man and woman, were now being called into question on a larger scale than ever before. The revolutionary political movements of 1960s US thus opened up a host of transformative social spaces, many of which were shaped by unfolding processes of rupture and abjection.

A politically-charged artist active within such a tumultuous, transformative era, Yoko Ono occupied a liminal status as a woman who straddled two cultural spheres: that of avant-garde, or 'high' art, and rock and roll counterculture. To further complicate her position, Ono was often relegated to the margins of each of these disparate spheres of cultural production. As a member of the Fluxus conceptual art group in New York City, Yoko Ono faced a considerable amount of gender-based discrimination. In her own words:

> Being a woman and doing my thing in the [Fluxus] days was especially hard because I was a woman. Most of my friends were all male and they tried to stop me from being an artist. They tried to shut my mouth and tried to get me as an owner of the loft who helped in concerts. (Ono quoted in Woo 2006: 232)

In the context of Fluxus, Ono's male colleagues thus persisted in viewing her as a *salonnière*-type figure within their art world instead of a bona fide artist in her own right. As a *Japanese* woman, Ono also faced the additional burden of being type-cast as a 'Zen' artist by contemporary art critics, despite the critical distance that she carefully maintained from such an artistic disposition. While Yoko Ono was indeed instrumental in introducing John Cage to Zen philosophy, within her artist's manifesto, 'The Word of a Fabricator' (1962), she clearly distinguishes her own artistic project from that of the Cageian, Zen-inspired artist. Likening Zen enlightenment to a 'plant-like' state, Ono declares that she has no desire to attain such a stultifying mode of artistic 'being'; instead, she proclaims that she will remain actively 'groping in the world of stickiness'. This disquieting image of the 'world of stickiness' evokes a space of the abject, a womb-like world coated in the sticky residue of life, its viscous borders blurring the boundaries of self and other. As a doubly marginal figure within the world of 1960s art, facing discrimination as a result of her racial and gender-based difference, Yoko Ono no doubt sorely felt the 'stickiness' of her abject situation.

Upon entering the world of rock and roll, however, Ono experienced a host of antagonistic reactions to her person and her musical work. While rock and roll promised liberation from the oppressive socio-cultural milieu of the post-war era, it was still a highly androcentric cultural sphere, which allowed relatively few women into its folds. Throughout the 1960s, the majority of women musicians continued to be objectified within popular music genres, often relegated to the role of the highly commodified pop singer. The general public, and the media's backlash against Yoko Ono no doubt stemmed from gendered and racial anxieties that were evoked as a result of an independent-minded, Asian woman asserting herself as equal to her partner, John Lennon, the 'hero' of the counterculture. As is often the case in transformative historical periods, we see that despite the winds of change blowing in a new direction, certain key aspects of the former 'regime' still linger. Nonetheless, within this countercultural milieu, Yoko Ono managed to actualise her experimental musical projects. Her strongest advocate was of course, John Lennon, who was convinced of the revolutionary potential of Ono's music; John proudly proclaimed that Ono's music was '20 years ahead of its time' (Gaar 1992: 233). Notably, countercultural publications of the day such as *Rolling Stone* magazine also strongly supported Ono's avant-garde rock and roll experimentations. The overwhelming majority of media publications, did, however, promote a negative view of Ono, which caused the artist great anxiety, to the point where she claims she developed a slight stutter.

Yoko Ono thus occupied a contradictory position within the counterculture that was simultaneously both marginal *and* central. As John Lennon's collaborator, she was very much at the centre of the world of rock music; as an Asian woman whose musical practice was strongly influenced by the avant-garde, however, she remained a troublesome anomaly that could not be easily integrated into the androcentric, 'low-art' world of rock and roll. At a time when cultural and social roles were being challenged and redefined, Yoko Ono was a highly visible public figure who was simultaneously 'a part of' as well as 'expelled from' the identificatory categories of artist, musician and rock star. Her cultural positioning was thus abject – and through re-enacting processes of abjection in her musical output, she was able to transform the reigning symbolic order that denied her inclusion within its folds. In historical hindsight, then, it can be said that Ono's abject, borderline cultural positioning perhaps rendered her a figure that was most keenly attuned to the transformative *Zeitgeist* of the times.

Throughout the course of their highly public careers, Yoko Ono and John Lennon were noted for their passionate involvement in contemporary revolutionary political movements, publicly advocating the end of the Vietnam War, and penning countless songs thematising women's equality, social injustice and the need for social change. In the aftermath of the Free Speech Movement (FSM) of 1964, youth cultural protests of the 1960s placed a great deal of importance on 'raising one's voice' to bring about revolutionary change – in the context of late 1960s counterculture, *vocalisation* was thus considered a key means of social, cultural and, indeed, individual liberation. As popular recording artists whose works were informed by revolutionary politics, Yoko Ono and John Lennon's musical output from this time was largely driven by a need to vocalise their desire for a better world. In this sense, the success of the FSM forged a powerful link between the vocalisation and the actualisation of utopic ideals in the minds of socio-cultural activists and artists in the 1960s.

According to historian M.J. Heale, public life in the late 1960s was characterised by a 'pervasive activism, and this energy was grounded in part in the realisation that the country was being fundamentally transformed' (2001: 9). This 'activism' was not restricted to the realm of politics; rather, it infused many contemporary US socio-cultural discourses. The transformative 'new sensibility' that Sontag identified in the art world could be characterised as one aspect of the 'activism' that pervaded US culture at the time. As well, the newly emergent discourse of humanistic psychology had a wide-reaching impact on 1960s US culture, promoting a positive view of the transformative potential of the individual (ibid.: 15). The discourse of humanistic psychology no doubt influenced the youth counterculture of the day, for whom the desire for self-expression, and the expansion of one's consciousness, was paramount. In the 1960s US, the active drive towards social transformation was thus rooted in a widely held belief in the capacity for individual transformation.

The FSM can be considered a key, transformative historical moment that galvanised many US white middle-class youth to embrace political activism, and the power of political speech, or vocalisation. On 1 October 1964, a ban was enacted on political activity at the Telegraph and Bancroft intersection on the Berkeley campus. This relatively small area was the centre of political speech-making at Berkeley; on the afternoon of 1 October, however, a civil rights activist, Jack Weinberg, was arrested for violating the newly instituted campus ban. According to historian Max Heinrich, supporters of the FSM 'view[ed] the triggering events [of the student protests, such as the campus ban on political activity, and the arrest of Jack Weinberg] as a moment of "truth" when the exploitative nature of power alliances in higher education became visible – and intolerable to anyone with a sensitive conscience' (1968: 4). The police car holding Jack Weinberg was soon surrounded by a mob of non-violent student protestors, whose fervour was brought to a head by student activist Mario Savio's impassioned speech delivered atop the roof of the police car. Reflecting on the importance of Savio's speech, historian Robert Cohen states that Savio's address to the crowd 'not only set the tone for the non-violent occupation of the administration building – which culminated in the largest mass arrest of students in American history – but also became the most famous oration in the early history of the New Left' (2002: 1). Although the FSM began as a liberal movement aimed at '... restor[ing] the traditional political values that had been destroyed by bureaucracy, consumerism, and conformity', in the aftermath of the FSM, the late 1960s saw an increasing radicalisation of public speech (DeGroot 2008: 188). With the onset of the Vietnam War, and mounting racial tension within the nation, US students grew increasingly disillusioned with their government, and the establishment in general. At such a time, the success of the FSM inspired the hope of a youth cultural revolution. Most importantly, the power of youth culture was consolidated in a dramatic oration delivered by a young student activist.

Mario Savio, however, was not the only orator who bravely vocalised his political convictions atop a police car on 1 October 1964. Bettina Aptheker, a highly influential figure in the FSM protests, also mounted the historic police car on that day. Aptheker recounts her experiences as the only female student involved in the FSM: '[it] was a moment of great personal liberation for me. It gave me a taste of power – not in the sense of power over but in the sense of self-empowerment'

(2002: 131). The sight of Aptheker atop the infamous police car was broadcast across the nation, and had a powerful impact on many women viewers. Aptheker recalls that despite the progressive values espoused by the FSM, the movement remained male-dominated.

> [It] was men who dominated our meetings and discussions. Women did most of the clerical work and fund-raising and provided food. None of this was particularly recognised as work, and I never questioned this division of labor or even saw it as an issue! (ibid.: 130)

Aptheker's incredulous exclamation point reveals the enormity of the social change that occurred between 1964 and 2002, the publication date of her article remembering the FSM. Despite the male-dominated constitution of the FSM, in climbing the police car and having her voice heard, Aptheker inspired a generation of women to 'speak up and be heard' – her oration hence served as one of the many catalysts for the growth of the Women's Movement throughout the 1960s and early 1970s. The FSM thus laid the foundation for the successes of later political movements that gained momentum in the late 1960s; moreover, the FSM marked a moment of historical rupture characterised by the emergence of the 'voice of the youth'. The Berkeley student riots served to reinforce the importance of free speech – and the need for *vocalisation* as a means of liberation from social oppression.

Several years after the success of the FSM, US psychiatrist Arthur Janov published his influential work *The Primal Scream*, which spurred wide-spread interest in a unique mode of psychotherapy that hinged on the release of repressed feelings through the practice of screaming. Primal Therapy – or 'Scream' Therapy, as it came to be known – gained a great deal of popularity in the early 1970s, owing to the fact that numerous celebrities, including Yoko Ono and John Lennon, took part in this unconventional course of treatment. Janov's monograph, *The Primal Scream*, carefully outlines his mode of psychotherapy; his central contention is that neurosis is a side-effect of a culture that encourages its subjects to repress their emotions as a means of assuming the guise of controlled, adult social subjects. The release of the scream is thus an outpouring of unbridled feeling that Janov considers to be the dialectical opposite of neurosis and repression. Janov writes:

> Primal therapy is essentially a dialectical process in which one matures as he feels his childish needs, in which a person becomes warm when he feels coldness, in which one becomes strong when they feel weak, in which feeling the past brings one wholly into the present, and in which feeling the death of the unreal system brings one back into life. It is the reverse of neurosis, in which one is afraid and acts big, and continually acts out the past in the present. (1970: 412)

The dialectical binaries that Janov defines suggest a dualistic structure of human consciousness; liberation from repression – the ultimate 'maturation' of the subject, in Janovian terms – is brought about when the two oppositional states of mind are brought into conflict, and the subject is able to synthesise a healthy balance between the two. The stimulus for this dialectical process is the scream, a 'primal' vocalisation that opens the floodgates to our childhood, pre-neurotic state.

Just as the FSM advocated the need for public speech and political vocalisation as a means of combating social oppression, the contemporary psychotherapeutic practice of Primal Therapy also called for individuals to tap into an extreme, powerful vocality in order to ward off the strictures of a repressive social order. In the case of both the FSM and Primal Therapy, then, vocalisation is perceived as an extreme expulsion that holds the power to bring about the transformation of society as well as the individual psyche. Reframed in Kristevan terms, the transformative potential of vocalisation can be considered the enunciative moment that brings about a 'semiotic rupture' of the symbolic order. As Mario Savio and Bettina Aptheker shout out to the masses of protestors, and as Yoko Ono unleashes primal screams for her lost daughter, vocalisation assumes a meaning beyond 'giving voice to' the symbolic; rather, vocalisation serves the function of redefining the parameters of the symbolic. According to such a Kristevan analysis, the transformative potential of the extreme vocalisation is rooted in the persistent presence of the abject body. As the source of the revolutionary, semiotic content, the body lingers in the scream that it expels; Yoko Ono's extreme vocal music is a product of a cultural milieu that viewed vocalisation, and in particular forms of abject vocalisation, as a means of bringing about a more harmonious re-ordering of society and the individual.

Conclusion

Considering the many avenues of inquiry that have yet to be thoroughly explored in relation to Yoko Ono's musical oeuvre, my aim in this chapter is to raise certain key issues pertaining to her vocal performance, and the socio-historical context of said performance, in order to arrive at some useful insights for future feminist analysis. Abjection, in its Kristevan interpretation, is not a theoretical concept that can be explained in a few paragraphs; however, the enigmatic nature of this concept serves as a source of inspiration for those of us who are drawn to the more challenging pieces of music that colour the landscape of late twentieth-century experimentation. The power of horror – of that which disturbs and unsettles – ultimately rests in its capacity to suggest an alternative to the naturalised arbitrary, and in so doing, to allow us a momentary glimpse into (and respite from) the oppressive operations of a symbolic order. Because of her spirited urge to shout from the heart, in the late 1960s and early 1970s, Yoko Ono produced a series of screams that linger in the popular soundscape as abject expulsions of a woman's body. The horrors of this body come to symbolise 'unspeakable' aspects of material existence that tug at the boundaries of symbolisation, and thereby suggest the possibility of an alternate reality. As we engage with her vocalisations, and tackle the interpretation of that which defies meaning, is it possible that we, too, are transformed? In this way, Yoko Ono's rock and roll revolution can only gain momentum from this point onward.

Chapter 11
From Countercultures to Suburban Cultures: Frank Zappa after 1968

Benjamin Halligan

Suburbia would prove to be the terminus of Frank Zappa's satirical project. In the final analysis, the ringmaster of freaks, a mother to the North American counterculture and champion of outsiders would find himself outnumbered and outmanoeuvred by the rising tide of 'plastic people'. The nature and efficacy of Zappa's last formal political stand at this juncture is the concern of this chapter. It is the precise social and political moment of this juncture – as the 1970s turned into the 1980s, and the dawn of the Reagan era, perceived as the final routing of 'the long 1960s' – that lends a context to Zappa's seemingly reactionary sentiments, a framing which goes some way to recover Zappa's work from its detractors.

Those detractors typically admit to bafflement and frustration at Zappa's infantile and puerile preoccupations of these years. Despite the ingenuity and forensic textual analysis of those who would seek to defend Zappa against the serious charges arising from his recordings at this time (homophobia, racism, violent misogyny, red baiting), principally associated – in print, at least – with Watson and Leslie (2005), Zappa's cultural significance seems to have waned rapidly since his death. In his study of the music of 1989, for example, Clover quickly passes over Zappa: although his legacy is noted as central to Clover's concerns of the intermeshing of music, social upheaval and formal political change ('... despite his role as unofficial attaché to Václav Havel's government, and despite the memorial statue of Zappa to be found in Vilnius, Lithuania ...' (2009: 6–7)), Zappa's presence in the music scene of 1989 is considered marginal from Clover's 20-year perspective. At best, Zappa is indicative of earlier paradigms of music and change; at worse (and in a moment of the widespread infiltration and subversion of the mainstream: the second summer of love and early manifestations of grunge), irrelevant.

Indeed, at this rough point in Zappa's own career, after a run of albums that increasingly privileged instrumental music over satirical social content (a transition apparent in the Synclavier use of *Frank Zappa Meets the Mothers of Prevention* from 1985 and with the full shift to 'serious' and Zappa-executed compositions marked by *Jazz from Hell* of 1986), and with the data-dump-like release of a dozen or so official live double albums between 1988 and 1992, Zappa would seem to have abandoned any claim to contemporary and popular relevancy. The instrumental and compositional, of confounding complexity, with increasingly difficult challenges to live performance and appreciation, would preoccupy his remaining years, culminating in the collaboration with the Ensemble Modern and the density and freeform abstraction of what is typically held to be Zappa's farewell symphony: the composition 'N-Lite' on the posthumous *Civilization Phaze III* (1995). After 1989, when Zappa had mostly abandoned touring and even guitar playing, satirical music was an exclusively archival concern, and best framed via hours of live recordings. Frank Zappa, as he had been known, was ever-more historicised in this tendency: to paraphrase one live release, the question seems to have been posed, and answered in the affirmative: *did* humour belong in music?

And yet Zappa, as a contemporary composer, remained a diffident figure: wilfully obtuse, avant-garde to the point of delivering 'impossible' scores, difficult to take seriously by the Conservatoire (responses that Zappa certainly cultivated and actively courted),[1] and tedious and humourless for those who knew the Zappa of old. What change had speeded this process, so that the figure of Zappa as a countercultural gadfly, ferocious guitarist, scourge of Republicans, and fearless band leader, had faded into the background by the late 1980s?

It is difficult to avoid the conclusion that it was in Zappa's engagement with the idea of suburbia that his satire began to flounder and his political positions grew increasingly disorientated, and that this ultimately prompted Zappa's retreat from contemporary concerns in favour of a renewal of his lifelong objective to be taken seriously as a composer. However, an engagement with the idea of suburbia had been present throughout Zappa's career, and so connected the countercultural years to those of the onset of Reaganism. A number of Zappa's 'lesser' and often more problematic recordings evidence this connection, and so track a key aspect in the evolution of Reaganism and neoliberalism: the routing or dissipation of any latent countercultural sensibilities.

1968 and the Suburbs

Initially the homogenising mores, ambience and routines of suburbia were a target for the counterculture: that horizon of modest expectation for compliant, complacent and uncomplaining members of the workforce. The quiet boredom and desperation beyond the manicured lawns, the essential hypocrisy of the moralism of these mostly white, ex-urban middle classes, their seeming indifference to those outside or back home, those lacking financial security, and a fear of those who would erode financial and civil security, represented the order to be usurped. Timothy Leary's cry of 'tune in, turn on, drop out' was the invite to break free from this gravitation pull, and gain a subjectivity that would have been understood to be both the antithesis, and the breaking, of the suburban fate that awaited.

---

[1] See particularly the transcript of Zappa's 1984 keynote address to the American Society of University Composers, 'Bingo! There Goes Your Tenure', reproduced in Zappa and Occhiogrosso (1989: 189–94).

Zappa's entourage and acolytes, and his cosmology of, for Miles (2004: 282), that 'pantheon of anthropological discoveries' – freaks, mothers, hippies, groupies, including the GTOs, and outsiders such as Wild Man Fisher and Captain Beefheart – represented a society of difference and nonconformity: the alternative.

The success and duration of such a collective sensibility – this alternative: the counterculture – is identified by social historians of 'the long 1960s'. Within a decade of 1968, however, revolutionary impulses and radical subjectivities had been near-fully buffered by and absorbed into a new suburbia. Suburbia, once a target, was now a destination. And yet this counter-revolution was one that had also been achieved via an accommodation of the alternative: demands would be mostly met and freedoms readily granted. Boardrooms were thrown open and wealth moderately redistributed as the baby boomer generation – with force, through persuasion, via reassurance, and in the name of progress, after occupations, draft card burning, the full countering of the prevailing culture and, more problematically, à la Zappa, the trashing of its received values and its proposed futures – took the reins of power, and the keys to the institutions, from their parents.

Left critics of 1968 and, more specifically, left critics of the project of the 'soixante-huitards', tend to accept the success of the social, cultural and institutional upheavals but on specific grounds: demands were met but these demands were intrinsic to post-1945 society, to finesse the burgeoning service and tertiary sectors, as manufacturing resumed its decline, and to deinstitutionalise, socialise and modernise market relations. Régis Debray's 10-year anniversary reading of 1968 (1979: 45–65) advances just such an hypothesis: empowerment as having occurred at the behest of global capital, with 1968 as a kind of spasm internal to the bourgeois sphere and as necessary for a radical reorganisation of industry at the point of the dawning of new modes of production.

The long 1960s is a period which sits unhappily in Zappa's career: the trajectory from arch-satirist and avatar of the underground to Mother-less, berater of consumers – from *Freak Out!* (1966) to *Sheik Yerbouti* (1979). To track Zappa's concerns in these matters of social change is to find that the sociological meshes with the scatological. Sexual activity became, for Zappa, the continuum of, and echo-chamber for, post-1968 freedoms. Initially, such freedoms were enabled by free love and the availability of contraception and abortion, and a leisure sector further given over to facilitating sexual encounters rather than orientated to marriage, mortgage and monogamy. The achievements of communal living (multiple, simultaneous partners: the eradication of the call on or sole loyalty between one and the other), which itself would naturally arise from a culture that had called into existence the Woodstock event,[2] were parlayed into non-phallocentric / patriarchal / hetero-normative practices (dyke communes,

---

[2] For the integration, or partial integration, of communal living and open relationships into bourgeois society, see Roberts' field reports of commune life (1971). For a perspective from the other end of the decade, concerning post-Stonewall queer subcultures that emerged

cruising and early disco cultures, and Second Wave feminist separatism) and to BDSM cultural ghettos. Although much of this continuum revolved around – especially in Zappa's reading – a simple matter of fucking, and in this simple matter of fucking came the re-imagination of a Great Society, as comparable to Lyndon B. Johnson's. Marcuse, writing in 1969, could identify the coming sensibility of a '… negation of the entire Establishment, its morality, culture; affirmation of the right to build a society in which the abolition of poverty and toil terminates in a universe where the sensuous, the playful, the calm, and the beautiful become forms of existence …' (1973: 33). This is the attempted or assumed development of the long 1960s, from the counterculture and through the liberated cultures of the 1970s. But in the matter of fucking, or as reduced to the matter of fucking, the revolutionary impetus is also curtailed: sexual freedom is not anti-imperialism, libertarianism is not intrinsically pacifist, brotherly love is not necessarily socialist.

The battle for the maintenance of such freedoms after 1968 was not so much to be won in the urban centres – traditionally in advance when it comes to shunning morals and mores, and traditionally the point of origin of new forms of artistic expression, and their more liberated subjectivities – but in the suburbs. The outward spread of freedoms, decentred and diluted, corralled and atomised, in the guise of widened consumer and lifestyle choices, resonated deepest in the fertile grounds of the suburbs.[3] It is in this naturally conservative milieu – safely away from the new polarities of city existence in its asset-stripping phase of de-industrialisation – that change can be fully accepted and entrenched. The suburbs become the very vector for the 'normalisation' of alternatives and their embedding, and the location where time is available – away from the bustle and distractions of the city centre, and towards the stretches of commuter tedium so much in need of enlivening. Such an assumption lives on in the urban myth, and pornographic genre tropes, that equate wife-swapping with wealthy but dull suburban areas. Suburban culture requires enticements – the dividends of emancipation – to finesse the influx of the upwardly mobile from the city centres. So the suburbs become the loci of the very institutionalisation of the freedoms of the late 1960s.

If the suburbs, suburban life and suburban cultures became Zappa's primary concern during the years of Reagan's ascent, culminating at the point of Reagan's coming to office, it is firstly because in Zappa's conceptualisation of the suburbs is the hauntology of the dreams of 1968 in North America, and of freaking out, difference, opposition, outsiderism and dissonance. Secondly, it is because the West Coast suburbs, almost uniquely, represent future shock. Southern California,

---

along similarly open lines, see Edmund White's *States of Desire: Travels in Gay America* (1986). For a discussion on communes and the counterculture see Miller (2002: 327–53).

[3] Historians of suburbia find a strong correlation between isolation and the erosion of communities, and new housing sprawl – particularly at this time. See, for example, Putnam (2000: 204 and ff.). For Jackson, the balance that comes to favour the suburban over the metropolitan is apparent in the phenomena of the 'center-less city' as evolved in, or by, California, see (Jackson 1985: 265 and ff.).

Zappa's locale, increasingly also became his area of scrutiny, and its people his subject matter. Los Angeles, the largest Californian city, has traditionally functioned as a vision of the near or coming technocratic future for the West, in terms of architecture, technology and new paradigms of labour and leisure – with Hollywood cast as a propaganda machine in this respect. Hardt and Negri propose the region, and nearby Silicon Valley, as the most advanced sector of the seeming appearance of an imperial 'new Rome': after 'Washington (the bomb), New York (money) [comes] Los Angeles (ether)', where ether is 'communicative' – the immaterial essence of the virtual (2001: 347, 360).

London and Los Angeles

The suburbs of the West: metroland, commuterville, the dormitory village, bedroom suburbs, edgelands, the 'edge city', 'the Valley', the stockbroker belt, the hinterland, going 'upstate', 'retiring to' – an area of a negative definition whose denizens, suburbanites, are parochial and home-making rather than, as with the city-dweller, masters of their own location. Such geographic and social marginalisation, and a recalcitrant feminisation of a society increasingly associated with suburban home- and family-making (both the female hand in the making of the home, and the permanent re-location of the female to the home, as a housewife and mother, away from the city-centric professions and opportunities) are not typically considered to be matters for celebration, or naturally lending themselves to the concerns of popular culture. The contributors to *Visions of Suburbia* (Silverstone 1997) tend to eke out the sensibilities of a suburban culture in the changes in kitchen designs, lowbrow television comedies, gardening trends and run-of-the-mill advertising, and even then find the articulation of a deep ambiguity as to their suburban settings and locales.

A useful exception to this trend is found in Morrissey's work in the mid/late-1990s – that is, in journalistic opinion, at the point of his floundering at what was perceived to be a low-point in a formerly distinguished career. Morrissey's London suburbs are conceptualised in a way that is diametrically opposed to Zappa's LA suburbs although, crucially, both engage in a sexualisation of suburban existence. The difference is apparent in the way in which Morrissey's suburban music is elegiac, finding in the suburbs the ruins of the near-past, while Zappa's conception is prophetic, seeing in the suburbs a vision of the near future.

The sexualisation of suburban existence, for Morrissey, becomes an organising principle for both his imagination of suburbia and his entrée to suburban subjectivities. In suburban sex is the entropy of former aspirations for out, and this explains the persistence of drab, shabby suburban life, and the puzzling immobilisation of those characters encountered who seem too big and restless for these modest corners of the world. The promise of adventure is mapped onto, and crystallised in, the shadowy nature of suburban sexuality. And that adventure is invariably illicit: taboo-busting, class barrier-breaching or just straightforwardly illegal. In the forgotten hinterlands of suburbia – the abandoned futures of yesteryear – social and civic certainties have weakened to the point that diversion and experience and movement are vertical (upward and downward mobilities, and sexual conquests) rather than horizontal (sticking to your own class and wage bracket: an organising principle in the planning and political economies of suburban sprawls). For *Southpaw Grammar* (1995) and *Maladjusted* (1997) Morrissey left his native Manchester for the London suburbs – specifically those parts of Essex, such as Ilford, that remain part of the Greater London conurbation. Morrissey also shifted his focus of observation, from outsider to chronicler, or assumer, of the perspective of a cast of familiar suburban stereotypes rather than outsiders: a variety of proletarian wide-boys, blissfully unaware of their marginality, all of whom Morrissey seems to sexualise.

For 'Maladjusted', where Morrissey's declamatory singing veers from spiteful to pitying as he adopts the perspective of 'semi-perilous lives', the suburbs are formally named. The line of flight is 'around / SW6' and 'the Fulham Road lights' (an agreeable enclave of South West London) and 'a Stevenage overspill' (a London commuter town). Our underage callboy, peering at the 'lights in the windows / of all safe and stable homes', may tarry in to those homes and that suburban realm, but only ever temporarily. The song plays with an 'us and them' perspective, dividing those fascinated with the suburbs, but whose critical distance means they can never be truly suburbanite, from those who dwell in these dreary suburbs and get by as best they can (via, in this case, the use of callboys against the deadening hand of suburban and/or family existence). There is a sense that even the 'maladjusted' (both client and callboy) will find a function, and welcome, of sorts, and each other, in suburbia. What liberations occur do so privately and under a cloak of anonymity. Yet such goings-on represent an underground, or psychogeography, of sexual difference, intermingled with the white, working-class cultures that remained (despite, and even in the teeth of, Conservative rule), precarious and dangerous. These suburban stretches are a refuge or haven: the place where forgetting can occur. Signs of life, for Morrissey, signal an acquiescence to and accommodation of daily defeat.

Zappa's suburban sexuality is not furtive or discrete, and not class-ridden, since – only a decade after the radical sexual agendas of the Summer of Love – sex itself has been edged into commercial domains. What is underground for Morrissey has become overbearingly omnipresent for Zappa, and the results are a matter for ridicule. Sex has been feminised for Zappa – in the senses of becoming the preoccupation or pastime of the sexually aggressive female, '*pace*' feminism, and of the 'femininity' of the character of the passive male homosexual, receiver rather than giver, who now looms large. Rounding on sexuality in this way, with sex as the optic through which suburban cultures are presented, examined and decried, inevitably opened up common ground between Zappa and reactionary, moralistic elements then ascendant in the public and political spheres.[4] Zappa's

---

[4] The argument could be made – although it is beyond the scope of this chapter – that Zappa's attempt to block any such commonality and disavow such company resulted in the self-consciously outrageous strain in his work.

concern is not so much diagnosing mass sexual dysfunctionality (in the manner of Wilhelm Reich's writing of the 1930s) as spinning a Chaucerian picaresque, drawing on specific case studies of sexual bad practice.

Zappa's encounter with the suburbs is less passive than Morrissey's, and not at all celebratory. Zappa's suburbs remain cast as the locale of Pyrrhic victories rather than a defeat: the freedoms of 1968, as filtered through this strata, coloured by it, and giving rise to modes of life that would have been perceived, at the time of *We're Only in It for the Money* (1968), as the minority preserve of pop stars, hippies and freaks. So Zappa, whose relationship with 1968 was never as straightforward as the iconic use of his image at that time would have suggested, came to strike an ambiguous, even contradictory relationship with suburban cultures. They become a constant theme in Zappa's music from the mid-1970s onwards – gaining momentum especially (and overtaking concerns more centred on the mythology of the rock band on the road) at the point of the soundtrack to the suburbs engulfing the pop charts: the second wave of commercial (rather than underground and gay nightclub-orientated) disco.[5]

The 1976 album *Zoot Allures* concludes with the track 'Disco Boy', as if in response to Zappa's update of Dylan's 'Twenty years of schooling / And they put you on the dayshift' (of 'Subterranean Homesick Blues'): an update articulated in the opening track, 'Wind Up Workin' in a Gas Station'. The inexorable 9-to-5 fate of the protagonist is clear: 'your education won't help you ... / you're gonna wind up working in a gas station'. As with the protagonist of *Saturday Night Fever* (dir. John Badham, 1977), the worker's compensation comes in escapist weekends away from suburbia and in city centre discos. 'Disco Boy' is typical of a foundational concern of Zappa's, the commercialisation of countercultures, but beyond this, however, little coherent is said. The disco boy is derided for his effeminacy (referred to as 'honey') and yet his care over his appearance, the narrator seems to begrudgingly concede, leads to the promise of success with a woman he meets on the dance floor – albeit one who then elopes with the disco boy's friend. The very Zappaesque punchline is that the disco boy's dance floor dexterity is now needed for compensatory, masturbatory ends, once he has returned home alone. Auto repairs or autoeroticism – the choice seems ultimately only in respect of what

---

[5] For disco as the underground soundtrack to queer subcultures and the burgeoning New York gay nightclub scene, see White ([1980] 1986: 269–85). For the commercialisation of disco and the anti-disco backlash, see Shapiro (2005: 194, 226) who dates this phase as 1977–79. The release of *Sheik Yerbouti* in 1979 (the title a play on the disco classic '(Shake Shake Shake) Your Booty' by KC and the Sunshine Band), which contains the attack on the exclusivity of disco culture, 'Dancin' Fool', falls into this anti-disco timeline too. Zappa, in his autobiography, posits disco as only ever a sly disguise of '*corpo-rock*', enabling bar owners to replace live music with recorded music and, for those who 'sort of "looked good"', to take drugs and engage in casual sex (Zappa and Occhiogrosso 1989: 202). In his film *Baby Snakes* (dir. Zappa, 1979), Zappa also speaks approvingly of the 'Disco Sucks' T-shirts he spies in the audience in the 1977 concert footage.

the character is asked to do with his hands: be they gas-stained ('Let me see your thumb' is a refrain in 'Wind Up') or semen-strained ('thank the Lord that you still got hands / to help you do the jerking that'll / blot out your disco sorrow').

Other than an incorporation of disco-like, Bee Gees-esque alto voices in harmony, 'Disco Boy' evidences little comprehension of the sonic palette or even beat of disco. Rather, the song contains wildly off-the-mark synthesiser sci-fi rumbles, reminiscent of the threatening tympani bent notes of 'Who Are the Brain Police?' from *Freak Out!*, and which, in terms of a semiotics of sound, can be taken to connote disco as the then-coming sound: low supercomputer growls, as found in 1970s sci-fi dystopia/disaster films. This future world of disco only offers a prospect as sexually frustrating and spiritually bankrupting as the same old past. It is as if, within the space of a few years, the very inverse of the project of the communes beckoned: isolation over collectivism and hardened character armour (to use Reich's term) over the de-alienating experiences of nudity and nature. Even the qualified but radical potential of 'the freak', for Zappa, would have seemed to have been sublimated into this post-1968 culture of conformity, as represented by disco: in 1978, Chic's 'Le Freak' would be a disco anthem, with the instruction or social advice to 'freak out!' for this 'new dance craze', as happening in Studio 54, and with equation in the chorus of 'Le freak – c'est chic'. This cultural homogenisation, as exerting a centrifugal force on the suburban cultures, and which is established in a dialectical manner on *Zoot Allures* (gas station to discotheque), becomes Zappa's chief concern at the point of the ascendency of neoliberalism.[6]

Zappology and Reaganomics

Zappa's live popularity in the US began to wane in the late 1970s. Zappa claimed his initial fans had simply grown out of the more youthful pastime of the live concert ('... now that they have wives, kids, mortgages, day jobs ...'; quoted in Miles 2004: 277) and so geared his music to a younger audience, while Miles reasons that the shift occurs in respect to Zappa's falling out of touch with the younger audience, resulting in his touring more extensively outside the US (2004: 281). But looking to age disparities risks the danger of overlooking a socio-political change, and one that increasingly marginalised anti-establishment sensibilities.

---

[6] This neoliberal phase, discussed here in relation to Reagan, can be said to have been merely embodied in the figure of Reagan (a nightmare figure particularly for Californians of the 1960s), and identified with Reaganism. Neoliberalism itself is typified in post-Marxist critical thought as the time that had come, after the close of the long 1960s, for, in the US context, monetarists, the New Right, exponents of the Chicago School and Cold War Warriors now unencumbered by Nixon, etc. Bifo, for example, refers to 1977, as 'the year of the end of the twentieth century: the turning point of modernity' (Berardi 2009: 15).

The film *Baby Snakes* records Zappa's band and entourage of the *Sheik Yerbouti* period: the bunker mentality that Gray would rail against is apparent in the film's claustrophobia:[7] small studios, cramped backstage areas, airless audition rooms, the relatively tight space in which the band performs live, and with the indistinct audience area mostly a haze of bluish light. The effect, across the film's two-and-three-quarter-hours running time, is stifling. But in its final minutes – in a sequence positioned after the closing credits – Zappa is seen emerging from the concert venue, is walked through a scrum of fans, and whisked off in his car. It is a startlingly sudden ethnographic lurch into the world outside. Sartorially, the fans themselves can be identified precisely: children of '68, still living the counterculture, albeit confined to evenings and weekends, since their smart-casual clothes and hair (and uniform whiteness) speak of a creeping accommodation of professional life now that they are in their thirties. The glasses, and the air of the educated comfortably slumming it,[8] suggests positions in the ascendant information technology industries, university research and tertiary sector management. These are not the deracinated wasters of the mid-West who crowd the frame for Sex Pistols gigs in *D.O.A.* (dir. Lech Kowalski, 1980) or the appealing, healthy masses who pack the discotheques of *Thank God It's Friday* (dir. Robert Klane, 1978).[9] Rather, they are those whose imminent move to suburbia would mark the point at which they made their peace with the world – a truce dramatised in the suburban lifestyles and creative professions as awaiting this generation in the television series *thirtysomething* (ABC, 1987–91). This motley collection of weekend freaks, waiting to high five Zappa, were perhaps his last real live audience. And their innate, generational preference for difference would be so thoroughly marginalised by Reagan's coming to office that only one option would present itself at this crucial juncture: to settle down, come into their inheritance and so renounce earlier ways. Such youth excesses would be demoted to nostalgia and fetishism – for one protagonist of *thirtysomething*, an advertising executive, in his treasured collection of Haight-Ashbury posters.

---

[7] As well as being an unapologetically patriarchal, authoritarian bully, and essentially friendless and cold, Zappa is, for Gray, '... a man who spent most of his life locked away in a basement, inside a semi-fortified house ...' (1994: 238). This extraordinary outburst in the final pages of a relatively placid biography seeks to effectively undermine the high moral ground from which Zappa, for Gray, evidently found himself free to damn the wretches he encounters (see ibid.: 236–9).

[8] In the absence of any demographic data, the assumption that Zappa's sexual crudity played and appealed to blue-collar workers, found in much critical writing on Zappa, seems like straight class prejudice.

[9] And indeed Zappa here is a celebrity, kept apart from the crowds, rather than the ringmaster or MC figure of the burgeoning countercultural scene of his appearance in *Mondo Hollywood* (dir. Robert Carl Cohen, 1967), or for *Head* (dir. Bob Rafelson, 1968) in which he comments upon the scene in passing, rather than being seen as an A-list survivor, or product, or even purveyor of products, of that scene.

Despite Zappa's then focus on the suburban locale of this coming entrenchment, and the counterattack found in his work, his own marginalisation can be accounted for by this sea change too. The dissipation of emancipatory impulses of the 1960s, and the lack of empathy for dissident cultural projects of the 1970s (which would account for Zappa's animosity to disco, wariness of punk and lack of engagement with rap and hip-hop), would leave his oppositional politics high and dry and his confrontational, antagonistic tendencies with an ever-diminishing audience. Zappa would retreat, as Gray notes, to his basement.

Sheik Yerbouti, which is a last hurrah in terms of this timeline, was released in March 1979. The 10 subsequent sides of vinyl that constitute Zappa's journey through the suburbs coincide with Reagan's successful presidential campaign and ascent to office, in January 1981: the *Joe's Garage* albums were released September-November 1979 and *You Are What You Is* in September 1981. In these predominantly studio albums, the coming America – Reaganite, embourgeoisified, materialist, Puritanical (and its flipside: discourses of identity politics, feminism and gay rights in particular, as engendering new underground cultures of sexual emancipation) – is examined almost entirely in sexual terms.

Suburban Accommodations

Sheik Yerbouti initially dwells on the detritus of suburban existence, via a number of concerns, only to transcend them in its final 'movement'. The first of the album's four sides begins with a track that would reduce the romanticism and intimacy of Peter Frampton's popular hit 'I'm in You' (and 'sully' the innocence of doo-wop, which the song fondly parodies) to the simple boast and promise of repeated intercourse, made via mock-sleazy intonation, and with the proviso that the unpleasant experience of previous intercourse will not waylay or delay the coming intercourse ('I Have Been in You'). 'Flakes' has been taken as an attack on the sloth and criminal nature of union-protected blue-collar workers in a way that shares a sensibility with the pro-Reagan press of the late 1970s,[10] and includes a parody-cameo by the former poet of the 1960s proletariat: Bob Dylan. 'Broken Hearts Are for Assholes' seems to chart an odyssey through underground gay clubs, with the 'lonely guy' protagonist reduced to a literal 'asshole' for a series of anonymous sexual encounters. However, such sexual practices then seem to be imported back into heterosexual relations, with a female now promised anal sex and fisting. In the later track 'Bobby Brown (Goes Down)', which also parodies doo-wop, feminist aggression and the confusion arising from gender-bending sends an all-American-boy on a similar gay odyssey of S&M and wet sex.[11] The flatness of the lyrical imagination (the one humorous lyric

---

[10] A point of debate between Lowe (2006: 140 and ff.) and Watson (1993).

[11] Medhurst notes the particularity of homosexuality as a threat to the perceived calm of suburban life: the difference within the vistas of sameness and the ending of the conventional nuclear family unit – for whom the suburbs exist, (1997: 266). In this respect,

lamely attempts to rhyme 'afternoon' and 'tampon' by inserting an extra 'o' into the latter, although the spoken words of 'Assholes' record authentic gay slang of this period) are in profound contrast to the lyricism of the guitar playing, which is constantly surprising and inventive. The general rockist tone, and concert hall echo of the liveness of some of the recordings introduced into the studio material, lends an audio depth to the album.

This depth is found via Zappa's palimpsest 'xenochronic' techniques,[12] as utilised on *Sheik Yerbouti*, and its final movement is marked by a melancholic xenochronic timbre, as applied to a lament for the collective passions that used to drive free love ('Wild Love'),[13] and the fate of disorientated hippies. The album ends describing a retreat back to the familial home for such idiosyncratic, Syd Barrett-like characters ('You ain't really made for bein' out in the street / Ain't much hope for a fool like you / 'Cause if you play the game, you will get beat'), followed by a 'retreat', for Zappa, into extended, melancholic soloing ('Yo Mama'). In this soloing, in the rockism and the space of the production, and this concern with the diminishing legacies of 1968, which is also a concern with time passing and youth giving way to middle age, *Sheik Yerbouti* seems to mark the end of an era. Triple-album *Joe's Garage* strikes, in its penultimate track, an equally transcendent note: the extended soloing of 'Watermelon in Easter Hay', which marks the retreat of the protagonist (imprisoned, his pop star days well and truly over) into a world of fantasy: the track is introduced as the dream of an 'imaginary guitar solo'. In place of these fading embers of the counterculture seems to come its very antithesis: the San Fernando Valley over Laurel Canyon, and the commerce surrounding 'love', as commodity, over communal and free love.

Joe's journey begins in the suburbs and with a small town mentality: the album tracks band rehearsals in a parent's garage to the excesses of aspirant rock star life, and a series of flaky life-style concerns, including Scientology, against the backdrop of a creeping Big Brother state that seems as much totalitarian-left as dictatorial-right.[14] The path to stardom (soon curtailed by sexually transmitted disease, organised religion and gaol) is the exit from suburbia for Joe, and Zappa

---

Zappa's conceptualisation of the suburbs (and this analysis posits all these albums under discussion as 'concept albums') reproduces the stereotypical fears of what excessive things might be going on 'out there' – that is, in the environments of the everyman.

[12] The technique of splicing elements of live recordings into or (in absolute atemporal or polyrhythmic counterpoint) onto studio recordings. Xenochrony, in dissolving the studio/live dichotomy, results in music that can be seen as a total narrative (spontaneous/planned, contemporary/archived, found/recreated) of musical creation.

[13] Such collectivity is particularly apparent in the 1978 quadraphonic mix of 'Wild Love' with its multiple voices separated out into a call-and-response oratorio, released in 2004 on the album *QuAUDIOPHILIAc*.

[14] In the 'stage directions' supplied with the album lyrics, Zappa's vision of the future – which, he states, was inspired by the Iranian Revolution – is one in which everyone collects welfare payments and spends the money on the repair of broken consumer goods (in this respect, the song shares a concern with 'Flakes').

is precise about the locations and parochial locale in the stage directions: 'a boring old garage in a residential area' ('Joe's Garage'), '[a] festive CYO [Catholic Youth Organization] party with crepe paper streamers' ('Catholic Girls'), '[b]ackstage at the local Armory' ('Crew Slut') and The Brasserie nightclub in Miami for 'The Wet T-Shirt Contest'. This track, in particular, paints a depressingly mundane vision of suburban sexuality – of a type that would later be milked for pseudo-amateur softcore pornography (particularly the *Girls Gone Wild* series), and would lend Hollywood-filmed pornography a characteristic *mise en scène* (the fitted kitchens and airy living rooms of rented condominiums).

Mary, having abandoned Joe for a life of groupie-dom, is now down on her luck and so enters the wet T-shirt contest for the prize money she needs for the bus fare home. The MC, defrocked priest Buddy Jones, urges on 'the charming Mary from Canoga Park' (in the San Fernando Valley) and leers at both her and the audience (referred to as 'mongoloids squatting on the dance floor' in the stage directions). Jones is voiced by Zappa, and the track is not so different from the straight live recording 'Panty Rap', from 1981's *Tinsel Town Rebellion*, during which Zappa actually instigates a tamer version of such an event – inviting female audience members to throw underwear onto the stage for his inspection, something typical of his live shows at this point.

In Mary's performance comes an expression of the ambiguity of Zappa's take on suburban sexuality – both deriding the cultures of the commercialisation of sexuality, and yet seemingly finding in its practitioners an undeniable spark of humanity. Mary seems to remain blissfully unaware and colludes happily in her sexual exploitation, both here and at the hands of Catholic boys, Father Riley (the former Buddy Jones), the band members and crew of another touring rock group, and seemingly her biological father. As voiced by Dale Bozzio, Mary comes across as feisty and ready to party: an attractiveness that arises from an innocence and naivety that remains intact despite her dire history and situation. The exploitation does not impinge on a personality built on a willingness to please, and a lack of awareness of any other option. Even her lack of education ('Where ya from?', 'The bus!'; the giggling and squealing; 'Here I am!'; 'I'm dancing!') is winning. And, indeed, Mary triumphs in the competition: a validation of such an engaging persona in the commercial cultures of sexuality.

Certainly these characteristics represents a type and trope typical of pornographic models, and a female persona commonly dissected by feminists (the virgin/slut dichotomy), but in the context of encroaching and dehumanising state control, Mary stands out as – in Shavian terminology – an authentic life-force. The universal of music, theorised by Zappa as the foundational, youthful domain of authentic human expression (be it dancing, doo-wopping, guitar-playing, and so deserving of a rare dose of sentimentality, in the album's opening track) and thus to be censored, is embodied in the figure of Mary. And, reappearing in a vision later in the narrative (for 'Packard Goose'), she is given the somewhat Ruskinesque moral of the story to delivery: that music is absolute and transcends the relative values of information, knowledge, wisdom, truth, beauty and love.

The track that 'The Wet T-Shirt Contest' most closely resembles is another blast of mindless chatter: 'Valley Girl' (voiced by Moon Unit Zappa, on the 1982 album *Ship Arriving Too Late to Save a Drowning Witch*). And this time, despite the exaggerated nature of this pastiche of valley-speak, whatever its sociological pretentions, the traction was such that the song became a radio hit and, establishing an urban type, spawned a minor 'Valley Girl' industry in the early 1980s (which eventually included two feature films).[15] In that the focus of modernity in these two tracks is the valley girl, the question is not over the problematic of the commercial cultures of female liberation – a concern of Third Wave feminism which floundered on the matter of sexual self-performance, as in a wet T-shirt competition (with this 'raunch culture' identified by Levy (2006) as now virtually institutionalised). Nor is it a question of whether valley culture oppresses and retards (in the manner of survival of the stupidest) womankind, and degrades participants and observers. Rather, Zappa's presupposition – intentional or otherwise – seems to be that both these tendencies are in operation simultaneously. For this reason, the track – and much of the First Act of *Joe's Garage* – is caught between celebrating and condemning simultaneously. This ambiguity structures 'The Wet T-Shirt Contest', 'Valley Girl' and even (as the male subjectivity as conversant with such women) 'Titties & Beer' (from 1978's *Zappa in New York*), since all three contain dialogues between two voices and positions (Buddy Jones and Mary, Moon Unit and nondescript male singing voices, the unnamed protagonist and the Devil).

The future shock culture of these suburbs, as rendered and explored in sexual terms, explains why disco and valley girl cultures should be received by Zappa in such a negative way rather than just acknowledged or dismissed as passing trends. The imminent and place-specific nature of the promised freak explosion of *Freak Out!* presupposes an authentic culture that was anything but homogenising and mass-produced and was about to break surface. Now, where there were once hungry freaks, Zappa finds valley girls, and where there were once hungry esteemed musicians of the Magic and Mothers of Invention bands, Zappa finds soulless computer muzak. And love in the suburbs, in Lowe's analysis of Zappa especially, is the motor of this homogenisation, this pervasive blandness, now occurring in terms of romance and related feelings (sexual, sentimental, communicative) reduced to commodities and clichés, especially by record companies.

Zappa's cynicism in this regard is one that seeks to look beyond the façade, not so much to find the myths threadbare, but to find an unstable state of continual rupture in homogenising processes. Here Zappa's position becomes unclear. Sociological pretentions aside, where does he actually stand? For or against Mary and the valley girls? If there is no straight answer is it because there is a paradoxical and catholic irrationalism at work in Zappa's love for, and time spent with, the very figures he pities? The net result is the contemporary and typically

---

[15] Despite his strong distaste for the culture of the San Fernando Valley (see, for example, Miles 2004: 305, and Watson 1993: 397), Zappa's career received a considerable boost from its unwitting promotion.

postmodern actuality: irresolution as a state of constant weirdness, as amplified in the suburban margins. It is this position that is closest in Zappa to a critique of political economy, and can be placed in a more general strain in popular American culture, incorporating Matt Groening (who often cites Zappa's work as influential), the 1980s films of John Waters, Tim Burton and David Lynch, the re-imagination of suburban spaces enacted in the resurgence of skateboarding culture, and the room and building-splitting of artist Gordon Matta-Clark.

... What You Is

Only the constant manifestations of the biological nature of sexuality, its very materialism, and the extended and often dissonant guitar soloing in Zappa's music, seem to cut through this confusion. When love is reduced to mere bodily fluids and parts, and the cast silenced for Zappa's frequently hard-edged guitar-playing (where the plectrum is used in an aggressive manner on the strings, and the phrasing resolutely avoids repetition and familiarity, or even locking into a groove or given time-signature), the prurient framings, and uneasy preoccupations of his narratives, can be momentarily neutralised. Biological essentialism, and an essentialism or primacy of music and musicianship, are easier, and less disorientated, philosophical positions, and so plug the social and ideological lacuna that bewildered Zappa. And such essentialism is translated even into the tautology of the title of *You Are What You Is*.

Unlike *Sheik Yerbouti*, *You Are What You Is* offers very little musical respite. Drenching notes the 'stifling flatness' of the 'evenly-mixed palette' of the album (2005: 93, 98 footnote 10). The majority of the album is taken up with near-constant vocals, moving relentlessly, and with jarring speed (and often via segue rather than formal endings and beginnings as lyrics leak from one song to the next) across a succession of suburban targets. The attacks are unsparing and the sexual subject matter unremittingly joyless: idealist teenage rebellion enmeshing with stimulant abuse ('Teen-age Wind'), infidelity and relationship termination, with the object of lust seemingly acknowledging the male's abusiveness ('Harder Than Your Husband'), sexual frustration and pleading for intercourse ('Doreen'), 'cosplay' and/or fetishism and oral sex ('Goblin Girl'), and all within less that the first quarter of an hour. Thereafter the album returns to oral sex and female stupidity as the defining characteristic of a deceased character ('Charlie's Enormous Mouth'), a bungled suicide attempt by a character craving attention ('Suicide Chump') and the threat of violence to a groupie described as ugly, made once the narrator has tired of receiving oral sex from her ('Jumbo Go Away').[16]

---

[16] This last track seems to be the breaking point for Zappa apologists. Lowe, who feels obliged to perform interpretative acrobatics of the most impressive kind throughout his study, is finally defeated by 'Jumbo Go Away' (2006: 175–6). Likewise Watson, who breezily promises a robust defence of his subject at the outset of his study, comes to

Lyrics are often functional, repetitive during outros, and scan comfortably within their time signatures. And these character / event sketches, even if improvised by Zappa at speed or considered *a priori* to be secondary to the music, or as the vehicle for singing in character, or enabling riffing off a wide-ranging selection of musical genres, only reinforce a sense of pinched horizons.[17]

This wallowing in the enemy camp on the part of Zappa again presupposes a double determinant: both celebrating and condemning. And yet, in the sheer gusto and indestructibility of Zappa's array of emblematic types, the *personae dramatis* of the drama of this concept album, there is a vitality that is uncontained by conformity. Watson's claim for *You Are What You Is*, that the album 'remains one of the most ambitious public stands against Reaganism in the 80s' (1993: 395) – sketchy in Watson's appraisal – can be acknowledged in this context. Along with the absence of sonic depth is an absence of the hauntology of the dreams (if not the nightmares) of 1968. The contemporary sheen of the album, its speed and flash, its peppy, bubble-gum pop, and even its debt to punk (in its longueurs and repetitions) makes for the music of the new society that the album addresses.

In the album's concluding minutes, the dividend of Zappa's conservatism is apparent. Despite the preceding trawl through the detritus of modern society, an intrinsic, human, anti-Reagan sentiment emerges. 'I Don't Want to Get Drafted' speaks of a defiance (these individuals simply do not want to risk life and limb), as a totality (the lyrics are taken up by a chorus of innumerable voices), underscored by a fear as to where the Reagan years will lead. This sentiment is from one who knows. Zappa recalled the psychic disturbance of militaristic violence of the late 1960s, winding haphazardly and poisonously back into the counterculture, and his own midwifery of the resultant live 'happening':

> I handed them [three Marines in uniform] a big baby doll and said, 'Suppose you just pretend that this is a "gook baby".' They proceeded to rip and mutilate the doll while we played. It was *truly horrible*. After it was over, I thanked them and, with a quiet musical accompaniment, showed the ruined parts of the doll to the audience. Nobody was laughing. (Zappa and Occhiogrosso 1989: 94; Zappa's italics)

---

level criticism at the song – even directly, albeit tentatively, to a dying Zappa (1993: xxx and 548–9).

[17] At any rate, the precision and deftness of the lyrics of 'Heavenly Bank Account', concerning another Zappa bugbear, the televangelist (where the comically complex time signatures mimic the mystifications and confusions confronted by the IRS on inspecting this citizen's tax returns), and the fragmented existential flailings of 'You Are What You Is', concerning extremes of personality reinvention (in the MTV-banned promotional video applied to Reagan), which could be termed Beckettian, suggest that the lyrics were not necessarily prepared without due care.

The impression is given that the milieu upon which Zappa poured his scorn, the new suburbs of the ascendant 'plastic people', was not exactly unpleasant. Zappa is able to articulate, if not find a synthesis between, the enviable freedoms given to the common man while, at the same time, he attacks their misuses.[18] In the frescos of merrily fellating groupies and predatory disco dancers there is no sense of anything other than a collective, endemic stupidity – and one finessed by the trimmings of material wellbeing and sexual opportunities. Yet such a world view, prompting this misanthropy, can remain the foundation of celebration when the future anterior to these suburbs is suddenly so threatening: the return of the Old West, with all its militaristic hubris, chauvinistic righteousness and imperial violence. For an aside in 'The Blue Light', Zappa appropriates and subverts the title of Reagan's old cowboy show for a resounding warning: *'Death Valley Days – straight ahead!'*

---

[18] The populist forms of *You Are What You Is* raise a supplementary question: to whom is this satire usefully being addressed? One answer, albeit presumably beyond the intentions of Zappa, was East Bloc dissident music listeners. The album's position matches elements of a pre-1989 anti-Communism perspective: the notion of the excesses of consumer society as understood to represent a goal to be achieved nonetheless since excesses could then be moderated. In this respect, Zappa can be read in the cultural front of the war against the Soviet Union, also claimed (and claimed as successful, even if retrospectively) by the Reagan administration.

PART IV
Countercultural Scenes –
Music and Place

Chapter 12
Countercultural Space Does Not Persist: Christiania and the Role of Music

Thorbjörg Daphne Hall

Within human geography the study of countercultural space is well established, and the term 'counterculture' is used to describe the values and norms of behaviour of a social group that functions in opposition to the social mainstream of the day.[1] The term was first used in 1969 by Theodore Roszak (1970) and subsequently assigned more generally to 1960s political, social and cultural activities. Music is important in most writing about countercultural space. Regardless of whether the writer is a historian, journalist or sociologist, the significance of music within the culture is often highlighted. There may be two reasons for this. On the one hand, music has been seen as a mediating tool of the counterculture, because the message of the counterculture was communicated through music. It was by no means the only communicative tool, but it was an effective one. On the other hand, music from the time when countercultural space flourished in the 1960s has lived on and can now arguably be seen as its most potent legacy. It seems strange, therefore, that the subject has not been popular among music scholars.

The counterculture movements of the 1960s began in the US and have often been interpreted as the rejection of social norms of the 1950s by young people. Hippies were the most recognised and largest subgroup within this demographic. They upheld alternative ways of living and among their main issues were sexual liberation (including gay rights), free and new spirituality, relaxation of prohibition against recreational drugs and an end to the war in Vietnam. The hippie counterculture can be traced back to the Beats of the East Village in New York, who had 'removed themselves from the mainstays of dominant ideology' (Gair 2007: 57). Another important group of the 1960s counterculture, named the 'New Left', was regarded as a political movement and it focused mainly on social activism. There was some tension between the two groups, even though they both grew out of social restlessness deriving from cultural discontent (Breines 2004: 36).

---

[1] This chapter is based on my MA dissertation from the University of Nottingham, which was written under the supervision of Dr Daniel Grimley. I spent the summer of 2008 in Christiania doing field research. I would like to thank Helga 'Nova' Højgaard Jørgensen for all her help and insight into the community. Dr Gudni Elisson made helpful comments on the manuscript. All translations are mine and the translations of lyrics aim to be as direct as possible.

It is generally agreed that the counterculture, as defined above, was driven by a genre of new psychedelic rock and artists such as the Grateful Dead, Jimi Hendrix and Jefferson Airplane. At first sight music seemed to have purely entertainment value. However, Sheila Whiteley sees music as central to the counterculture and states that it was a common belief that rock music could communicate countercultural concerns, values and attitudes, thus 'providing a particular location for self-identity' (2000: 23). Waksman found that the countercultural community was defined through rock music (1998: 56–7) and he quotes Robert Duncan, a rock critic and editor, who observed that 'it is around the music that the [countercultural] community has grown and it is the music which holds the community together' (ibid.: 55). In addition, music was a way to fuel the economy of countercultural practices (Hale 2002: 143).

The counterculture movement spread to Europe, where London, Amsterdam, Paris and Berlin became centres of countercultural space. The student uprising in Paris in May 1968 and the 'Prague Spring' in the same year are manifestations of this dissemination of countercultural activity (Junker and Gassert 2004: 424). Another and less familiar countercultural space was 'Christiania' in Copenhagen, Denmark. Christiania was founded in 1971 and is still very much alive today. Its society, culture and alternative ways of living clearly derive from the counterculture of the 1960s and it remains an important centre for cultural resistance even today. Christiania thus offers an interesting case study in the broader topic of music and place, which has recently emerged in musicology. The hybridisation of musicology and cultural geography with urban space provides tools that enable the scrutiny of place and space through musical performance practice. Via this interdisciplinary methodology it is possible to shed light on the complex cultural and social formation of Christiania as a city within a city and to re-examine whether Christiania can today be considered a countercultural space opposed to 'normal' Danish culture.

Theoretical Background

The theoretical framework of this chapter is drawn mainly from the works of two scholars, Adam Krims and Sara Cohen. Both focus on music in urban space, and their approach provides a helpful starting point for the analysis. For both Krims and Cohen, music in the city operates within a 'post-industrial' context; however, Christiania does not easily fit such a profile or even a city at all. Hence, many of their ideas do not apply neatly here. Indeed, the study of music in Christiania seems to problematise many of the conclusions reached by Krims and Cohen.

Many of Krims' ideas are relevant to the study of Christiania, such as how music 'spatializes' (2007: xv) and the importance of music for place and the people who socialise there, how music 'can come to characterize space', how people can become an important factor in characterising space and its music, and how different socio-economic classes play a role in this characterisation (ibid.: xxxi). Krims sees contemporary cities as simultaneously both open and closed but, in many senses, Christiania seems to resist the binary models of openness/closure outlined by Krims, and it therefore offers an interesting case study in the analysis of music and urban space. Cohen discusses the interesting, but problematic idea of a 'local city sound' in Liverpool (ibid.: 68).

This chapter investigates the idea of a local sound in Christiania and the 'authenticity' of the music. It also asks whether music in Christiania sounds different compared to music in other places in Denmark and explores the role of tourism in this. Christiania can arguably be seen as a place containing different cultures. The chapter explores which musical culture, if any, is seen by Christianites as the most 'authentic' and true to their values, whether it is possible to trace a hierarchical structure through Christiania's cultural practices, and how people act within the community.

Christiania as a Countercultural Space

Christiania has clearly defined borders in a geographical sense, as a village in the heart of Copenhagen. However, as a social and cultural construction, it is ambiguous, as it remains central to the Danish discourse on democracy and freedom. Christiania has been described as an 'outdoor museum for the culture of the 1960's and 70's, which, because of a fence, has survived in a world that would otherwise have destroyed it years ago' (Kvorning 2004: 85). It goes without saying that things have changed in Christiania over the last 37 years, but because of its walls and the community created within them, Christiania has been able to maintain a certain uniqueness. It has been allowed to develop through the years as a 'social experiment' but in the light of recent political changes there are dangers that this experiment and the countercultural community might be coming to an end.

The army barracks, which now form Christiania, were built at the beginning of the twentieth century. The military moved out of the barracks in 1969 and, as the authorities had not made future plans, '*Slumstormere*'[2] ['Slum Stormers'] broke into the barracks in May 1971 (Christianias Baggrundsgruppe 2006: 34). The only member of the media that reported on this development was the alternative newspaper *Hovedbladet*, which encouraged people to move into the area (Ludvigsen 1971:10–11). The relative silence about Christiania at the beginning meant that when the public, media and politicians finally became conscious of the existence of Christiania at the beginning of 1972, between 400 and 500 people were already living in the area (Baldvig 1982: 11). Folketinget [The Danish Parliament] officially recognised Christiania as a 'social experiment' in 1973 (Davis 1979: 794). Its existence has caused political controversies over

---

[2] '*Slumstormere*' were a mixture of homeless people from Christianshavn and political activists that protested against the renovation that was taking place in the area and the lack of housing.

the years and it has always been on the verge of closing. But due to extensive protests among the general public, the experiment has been allowed to continue to the present day. Baldvig describes the original settlement pattern in Christiania as follows:

> The interesting thing is that it became an area which was populated both by representatives of the student revolt and by the weaker members of society, who, individually, had inter alia tried to improve their lot with the help of crime. Christiania's immediate function for these two groups was, of course, crucially different. The students, the activists, regarded Christiania as a challenge, an opportunity to realize some of the ideals they had with respect to an alternative society. For the dropouts, the weak, and the criminals, Christiania was, in the short-term, a refuge, an opportunity to escape from the problems which they had experienced in the metropolis. The activists thus went to Christiania, while the down-and-outs fled from Copenhagen. (Baldvig 1982: 11)

These two groups can perhaps be paralleled with the two different poles of the counterculture: the New Left and the hippies, or in other words, political and cultural rebellion. However, the Christianite Laurie Grundt describes the inhabitants of Christiania in the following way:

> Christiania er opdelt i tre dele ... En tredjedel af christianitterne (omkring 300) er 'de entusiastiske', det vil sige akademikerne og de intellektuelle. En tredjedel er medløbere, den "organiske del". Resten udgør den 'sovende del'.

> [Christiania is divided into three parts ... One third of Christianites (around 300) are 'the enthusiastic', i.e. the academics and the intellectuals. One third are the followers, the 'organic part'. The remainder are the 'sleeping part'.] (Hansen and Gonzalez 2004: 23)

Part of the enthusiastic section was a guerrilla theatre group called Solvognen [The Sun Wagon], which existed from 1969 until 1983 and who 'used their theatre activities both to criticize the rest of Danish society and to suggest new social, historic, and economic relationships' (MacPhee and Reuland 2007: 136).

In the first year, some of the more 'active' occupants summarised their vision of Christiania as a space for an independent society, economically self-sufficient where individuals are free, subordinate only to the community. Christianites should constantly strive to eliminate the negative influence of modern society; capitalism and stress (Christianias lokalhistoriske arkiv). Today, it is possible for inhabitants to live exclusively in Christiania – technically speaking. The residents can buy food, personal goods and materials to renovate their homes locally and there is a variety of restaurants and pubs for entertainment. However, the community does not provide social services, such as education and health care, and the residents therefore also rely on 'the outside world'.

The form of government or administration in Christiania has been called consensus-democracy and is built on the basic idea that all inhabitants are equal and have equal power. From the beginning the organisation of Christiania was also seen in a negative light where it's inhabitants were already falling into different groups:

> But the class system in Christiania – it would perhaps be better described as a caste system – is, if anything, more rigid than that in the outside society. By and large, the junkies are at the bottom of the pile ... This puts them at a special disadvantage, and has caused grave problems to the more idealistic social leaders in Christiania. The junkies, by virtue of their unwillingness and inability to contribute to the community effort of Christiania, have come to be regarded as 'leeches' on the community! (Davis 1979: 806)

In this light, Davis argues that Christiania's ideology is not an answer to the problems of modern Danish society. He also points out the 'failure of the economic ideal of Christiania. Far from rejecting capitalist values, the community has developed not only a petit bourgeoisie of restaurateurs and shop-owners, but also a definite upper-class leadership' (ibid.: 808). Despite the negative outlook on junkies in Christiania, drugs were a defining part of its life, just as they were in countercultures elsewhere. Today, even though drug use is prohibited in Denmark, 'pushers', who live partly outside the community, sell cannabis openly in Christiania. According to my informants, there have been problems with the 'pushers' as they were not willing to fulfil their social duties within the community and were therefore regarded as problematic. The only prerequisite for selling cannabis is to have lived in Christiania for two years and many of the 'pushers' employ outsiders as 'runners' who have no ties with the community.

Musical Spaces in Christiania

Over the main entrance into Christiania a large sign reads 'Christiania' (Figure 12.1), while on the other side it reads 'You are now entering the EU'. This indicates that Christianites perceive Christiania as both a physical area and an ideological one, which distinguishes itself politically and socially from the rest of Denmark.

The area offers a physical contrast to Copenhagen's busy asphalt streets and traffic as most of Christiania is green, and the roads are nothing more than paths or gravel roads, as the whole area is free of cars.[3] The urban area in Christiania or '*byen*', with its paved streets and ubiquitous graffiti, greets visitors who come through the main entrance on foot or bicycle. Soon a cosmopolitan market square appears in front of Pusher Street. This is the main street in *byen*, where vessels,

---

[3] This does not mean that Christianites do not own cars, but they keep them in neighbouring streets.

Figure 12.1   The entrance into Christiania. Photo: Thorbjörg Daphne Hall

filled with glowing coals, burning 24 hours a day all year around, are a prominent landmark. Here the pushers sell their cannabis, and tourists[4] are frequently offered hash whilst walking around.

Since its inception Christiania has had many musical venues. Den Grå Hal [The Grey Hall] has hosted many of the biggest festivals, concerts and meetings throughout Christiania's history, including various *Støttefest* [support festivals]. Månefiskeren [The Moon Fish] is one of Christiania's oldest musical venues and a home to Månekabareten [Moon Cabaret], 'authentic hippy music', reggae and hip-hop (Vesterberg 2007: 15). Another music venue, Operaen [The Opera], was originally called Det Gule Værtshus [The Yellow Pub], but received its present name in 1976 when the opera *Jensen på Sporet* was performed in the building (Martinussen 2007). Since then, it has been popular for performances of all kinds of music and cabaret (Madsen n.d.). Musik Loppen [The Musical Flea] opened in 1973 as The Viking Jazz Club (Lauritsen 2002: 62) but the name quickly changed to Jazzhus Loppen. Rock music arrived on the scene two years later when a rock band managed to sneak on stage. In 2002 the State Music Council declared it

---

[4]   The term tourist is used throughout the chapter as a collective term for all people who do not live in Christiania, including inhabitants of Copenhagen, Denmark and foreign guests, according to how the term was used by my informants.

Figure 12.2 The stage by Nemoland. Photo: Thorbjörg Daphne Hall

'a regional music venue' for showing new and experimental music (ibid.: 62). Woodstock and Nemoland (Figure 12.2) are pubs that frequently offer concerts during the summer on an outdoor stage.

In the summer of 2008 Nemoland was part of the Copenhagen Jazz Festival and was advertised as such in the jazz festival's brochure. Interestingly though, the venue had created its own poster, which didn't mention the Copenhagen Jazz Festival, thus separating itself from the mainstream events. Bars and cafés use different genres of music to characterise their space; Woodstock plays rock and Café Nemoland reggae. However, by looking at these two bars from the perspective of Krims' idea that people bring their own cultural preferences with them (2007: xxviii), it is possible to argue that the people who attend the different bars affect the music. The customers in Woodstock are mainly old men, and the music is often as old as Christiania, or in a similar spirit, thus suiting the customers.

Café Nemoland is mainly occupied by younger people, many sporting dreadlocks, which have often been associated with the 'Rastafari movement' and therefore with Jamaica, Bob Marley and reggae music.

One example of how venues change according to the surroundings and do not necessarily adhere to their own pattern became clear during a visit to Woodstock. As it represents the local culture, Woodstock was described by inhabitants as an old rock venue that would certainly not play commercial popular music.

However, I soon discovered that it happily played this kind of music, showing that nothing is set in stone, and that the expectations the inhabitants have for a certain venue reflect only how they feel it should operate.

It is clear that for a community of only around 1,000 inhabitants, Christiania is musically a very active place, and the number of music venues is uncommonly high. It can be argued, therefore, that music plays a large role in the way Christiania is experienced. In addition to performances at the traditional music venues, buskers can be found playing at the main entrance, in Maskinhallen [The Machine Hall] workers play music on a stereo system from dawn till dusk, Genbrugsstationen [The Recycling Centre] has hosted outdoor concert series – such as Dancing at the Trasher – and the market square, Carl Madsens Plads, can also be seen as a musical hot spot and is a point of cultural rendezvous with many of the booths or tables playing their own music: African drum music, hip-hop, reggae and rock, all mixed together, creating an exotic atmosphere. Just across the street a ghetto blaster plays gangster rap 24 hours a day – I experienced this as the music of the pushers, who work around the clock.

Clearly, contrasting musical 'hot spots' exist within the fairly small area of 'downtown' Christiania. Each of them creates a certain uniqueness for the space surrounding it. This can be compared to Krims' idea of 'music as interior design' (2007: 157). The different spaces offer their own perception of Christiania and can therefore attract or 'service' diverse consumers. Some spaces are obviously designed for tourists, such as the market, where the music can arguably be seen as a commercial phenomenon; other spaces are not considered 'tourist areas', and in these areas the music has a different function. However, for all of them, the music plays a role in characterising the space.

Sometimes music can be used to delimit a certain sphere within a larger space. Here, the role of the music is to create the 'right' atmosphere for the venue, thus creating invisible borders. For example, each booth in the market square had its own music to emphasise the products on offer, drawing the consumers into its 'exotic world' in order to make the product more appealing. Another 'world' is represented by the music of the pushers, and the music marks out the invisible borders of the pushers' territory – to me, it seems that the music created an atmosphere of danger and forced behaviour and accented illegal activities that require caution. This is largely due to the musical genre, especially gangsta rap, which often depicts such a situation. In Christiania, music consequently plays a major role in creating an atmosphere for different spaces. It can be used as a commercial ploy or purely for entertainment, but in either case, music generates a character for each space and affects how people experience it.

The Openness and Closure of Christiania

In a geographical sense, Christiania is a closed community, as it is contained within the walls surrounding former military barracks. A few years ago it was possible to take a bus labelled 'Christiania', but the service is now called 'Refshalevej', and the stop for the main entrance is 'Prinsessegade'. The route still exits, but for unknown reasons the name has been changed. Furthermore, while Christiania is one of the biggest tourist attractions in the city, and city authorities normally pave the way for tourists to main attractions, on several occasions, whilst walking in Christianshavn, I was asked directions to Christiania, suggesting Christiania is fairly difficult to find. Similarly, brochures, posters and information on concerts, events, shops and all imaginable things to do in Copenhagen often lack information on Christiania. Perhaps a conscious political decision has been taken by the city authorities to rebrand the city by excluding Christiania, especially since it is such a popular tourist destination. Christiania may not fit the image that the authorities are constructing for Copenhagen because it represents for them what is 'wrong' and 'problematic' with Danish society, for example alcoholism, drug addiction, unemployment and homelessness, and perhaps what is arguably worse: an area that the authorities struggle to control. Ironically, though, by excluding the village from the cultural map, the authorities might only be intensifying its countercultural status.

Musical activities can be one of the ways in which communities open their doors to the general public. Many people come to Christiania with the sole purpose of attending a concert, and others use the music as an excuse to come into the area and smoke a joint while a band plays on stage. People can enjoy a good concert despite their differences. By studying the programme at Loppen, Christiania's most famous and active music venue (Figure 12.3),[5] it is obvious that it does not clearly reflect Christiania, as most of the bands playing are foreign and the price for admission is much higher than many Christianites are willing to pay, according to my informants. This implies that part of the musical practice is intended for tourists rather than for local residents.

The general lack of information in the Copenhagen area on events in Christiania, as mentioned above, raises the question of how Christianites attract their audience. Loppen and Café Nemoland are the only venues that maintain an active webpage where concerts are advertised and hence where the venues actively try to attract people from outside the community. Venues in Christiania, therefore, appear to advertise their programmes selectively, in an effort to maintain control over their visitors and to preserve their space from invasion by the outside world. However, the relatively restricted way of advertising can also be read as a commercial ploy being made by the organisers in order to attract those who associate themselves with the countercultural image. The underground appearance of the venues thus intensifies the selectiveness of this demographic group. The venues obviously gain some significance from the location, but are otherwise musically no different from venues elsewhere.

---

[5] A programme can be found at Loppen's home page: http://www.loppen.dk/.

Figure 12.3   Outside Loppen. Photo: Thorbjörg Daphne Hall

Too much interest from tourists can also appear to 'spoil' events for Christianites. In July 2008 a concert was organised to entertain Christianites but also to attract tourists to Christiania in the hope of gaining their support for the community. The event was large, and boasted many popular mainstream Danish singers. It was advertised around Copenhagen, many people came, and it was a big success. At least that was how I experienced it. Later when one of my informants and I were walking around Copenhagen, she saw one of the posters for the event and became very irritated, explaining that she thought too many visitors had come to the concert, taking space away from the Christianites. Rather than being happy that so many people had attended, and that the concert had been a success, her feeling was that the concert had been a failure because it did not serve Christianites in the way she had envisaged. To my informant, the balance was not right, and the tourists took too much space away from the locals

All of these observations indicate a 'struggle of identity'. Christiania thrives on tourists coming into the area, using the facilities by shopping, eating and drinking. Moreover, Christianites serve tourists by publishing a guide book and offering guided tours around the area (Figure 12.4). Indeed, without tourists Christiania would cease to exist, at least in its current form, because financially, the largest percentage of the community's income comes from tourism. It has also been demonstrated over the years that Christiania would have closed down had it not

Figure 12.4 The tourist information hut where guided tours are offered.
Photo: Thorbjörg Daphne Hall

been for the support of the broader public in Denmark. Indeed, in difficult times, Christianites have opened up their homes and venues to outsiders in order to seek support from the public. However, by advertising selectively and not actively inviting people to the area – apart from when they really need the support – there seems to be a troubled relationship between the Christianites and the outside population, based on need and dislike. Comparing this with Krims' idea of the 'desirables' – that is, those who fuel the economy – in Christiania, the converse is true as the drivers of the economy are the tourists or the 'undesirables', while the 'desirables' are the Christianites themselves. Obviously this situation has created a strain or uneasy feeling among the 'desirables'.

Christiania is at the same time both open and closed and therefore, in some sense, it fits Krims' binary model of openness and closure. On the other hand, Krims' idea of desirables versus undesirables are reversed in Christiania. Consequently, because Christiania still relies on tourists/'undesirables' to fuel the economy, a strange love–hate relationship has emerged. Furthermore, within the society another layer of tension exists between the different groups of residents, as the society does not accept everyone equally. Christiania does not, therefore, altogether follow the same binary model of openness and closure as outlined by Krims.

The Expression of Locality

Cohen has 'critiqued the notion of a local, city sound for promoting an essentialist view of music, and for suggesting that cities can have a "natural", "authentic" sound that can be directly mirrored or expressed in music'. She states that 'the relationship between a city and a musical sound is not deterministic, organic or homological and it is difficult, if not impossible to identify within rock music sounds that are purely local'. However, similar to Cohen's experience, which found people who happily 'promoted familiar media stereotypes of Liverpool' (Cohen 2007: 68), people in Christiania were happy to point out to me 'typical' Christiania bands or music, and, in turn, denigrated the importance of other music that seemed equally, or perhaps even more 'typical' of Christiania. This raises the question of what qualities determine whether music is 'typical' or not. Perhaps it is not necessarily the sound of the music, but rather the local or historical connotation expressed that is important. From my discussions with Christianites, it is clearly important that a band or musicians 'are friends with Christiania'. Arguably, 'being friends with' must mean openly supporting the ideology behind Christiania. The music-making of the locals is also important, and Christiania promotes its 'own' musicians in their own events such as at 'Christiania – hvad nu?' and Christiania's annual birthday celebration. However, specific genres or people in particular seemed to be promoted. Here the idea emerges that some of Christiania's music is more 'real', 'true' or 'typical' than other types.

The idea of the construction of 'real' Christiania music seems to lie very much in the past. Thus, one way to gain an understanding of 'real' Christianian musical practice is to explore the early years of Christiania. '*Fællessange*' [Communal singing] is a deep-rooted Danish custom practised when people gather together, sometimes incorporating new lyrics written to a well-known melody to fit a special occasion. Christiania also embraces this Danish practice and *fællessange* have been written since the community's beginning. It has been stated that Christiania had even had a national song written in 1971 (Ludvigsen 2003: 183). This was set to 'Kongesangen' ['The King's Song'], a well-known Danish song, demonstrating that the lyrics mattered most for these *fællessange*, and that Christiania thus followed the Danish trend of writing new lyrics set to old melodies.

Tage Morten and *Fællessange*

Tage Morten was one of the more active *fællessange* composers. In a song book incorporating his songs, published in 1985, he is described as the city musician of Christiania, where he created a place for acoustic music, where all music-loving people and those active in acoustic music could find a musical sanctuary (Nielsen 1985, repr. 2004). 'Vore Drømme' ['Our Dreams'] was written in 1974 and was one of the first *fællessange* written in Christiania. In the song, Christiania is depicted as a part of Copenhagen, '*Vi er en del af byens miljø*' ['We are part of the town's surroundings'] (ibid.), where the residents live in close contact with others in the city, many of whom come for a visit. However, the final line expresses the view of the poet that some are bad, probably pointing to those who do not agree with the society and who therefore threaten it. Perhaps it is possible here, calling on Krims' binary model, to identify a group of 'undesirables'. The society is open to all, except those who do not agree with its ideology. The chorus then expresses a fairly typical hippie request, calling for peace and love: '*Vi vil ha'fred, så livet kan gro, omkring voldgravens høje*' ['We want peace, so the life can grow, around the high walls of the moat'] (ibid.). The song calls for peace around the high walls rather than within them, which means outside Christiania or throughout the whole Copenhagen area, demonstrating that Morten is concerned with society at large.

Morten not only wrote songs about Christiania, he also took a political stand and wrote songs about the housing in Christianshavn. The district's renovation caused problems for the poor who lived there, and in 'Christianshavn's Saneringshymne' ['Christianshavn's Renovation Hymn'], from 1975, Morten worries about the consequences of this renovation work for the people in the area. Morten also wrote about '*fællesskab*' [joint ownership], which had extended far beyond the limits of Christiania at the time (in 1976). He believes that this is a future arrangement that will be adapted by more and more people throughout the country. Again, here the voices of those who opposed these ideas appear, but as they are 'undesirable' their thoughts are not important: '*Kun de onde protesterer, deres tanker løber ud I sandet*' ['Only the evil ones protest / Their thoughts fizzle out'] (ibid.). In another song, 'Varme vibrationer' ['Warm Vibrations'], similar ideas appear, and Morten says that with belief, hope, smiles and encouragement, it is possible to live together and create '*nærdemokrati*' [participatory democracy]. Morten was clearly a political writer who addressed the problems of the society and offered solutions such as joint ownership, which were familiar to life in Christiania.

'*Slagsange*' and Support Records

From its inception, Christiania had to fight for its existence. Musicians took an active part in this battle and many '*slagsange*' [protest songs] were written for this purpose. One of the most popular is 'I Kan Ikke Slå os Ihjel' ['You Cannot Kill Us']. Written by Tom Lunden – leader of the rock band Bifrost – in 1976, it explains that Christiania cannot be destroyed. 'They', the government or the rest of Denmark, can use all available means to get rid of the Christianites, '*I kan sætte os i fængsel og fjerne os fra verden*' ['You can put us in prison and remove us from the world'], but it is not possible to kill the idea of Christiania, because it is a part of the larger society, '*I ka' ikke slå os ihjel, vi er en del af jer selv*' ['You cannot kill us, we are part of you'] (Various 1976). Moreover, since Christiania is part of the society at large, the song wonders what is causing the spite aimed at Christianites: 'Er os eller er det jer selv I er bange for at møde' ['Is it us or is it yourselves you are afraid to meet?'] (ibid.). Here the same idea appears as in Morten's song

'Vore Drømmer'; Christiania is a part of the city but at the same time it is a focal point for something different: a different community, different freedom, different democracy, separating it from the rest of the country. In spite of this, Christiania is not that far from the Danish mainstream as the song claims '*vi er en del af jer selv*' ['we are a part of you']. The song was originally recorded by Bifrost, Povl Dissing, Anissette and Sebastian with a choir called Det Internationale Sigøjnerkompagni [The International Gypsy Company], but subsequently many other versions have been made. Today the song is sung in demonstrations and 'where all good people gather', and features in the mainstream *Højskolesangbogen* [*The High School Song Book*] (Vesterberg 2007: 14).

This song appeared on the first Christiania record, made in 1976 when the community was in danger of having to close down. Apart from 'I Kan Ikke Slå os Ihjel' the record included songs written for it by many of Denmark's most popular rock musicians, including Gnags, Kim Larsen, C.V. Jørgensen and Røde Mor. Over the years, Christiania has appeared in popular songs, and musicians have written '*slagsange*' for the village. In the years after 2000, the government applied more pressure in their attempts to normalise the area. Pusher Street was cleared and relations with the police degenerated following prolonged debate with the authorities on the 'normalising' process for the area. During this period, three new support records were made, *Nye Christiania Sange* [*New Christiania Songs*], *Bevar Christiania* [*Preserve Christiania*] and *Christiania Forever*, offering many new songs on Christiania. Interestingly, though, big names in Danish music were not involved as they had been in the 1970s.

These support records are sold in a booth in the market square, which also sells the tourist guide, clothes and other products marked 'Bevar Christiania'. Inhabitants emphasised to me the triviality of these records and implied that they were only made for tourists and do not represent the 'real' music of Christiania. Perhaps, these records serve more as a commercial artefact for Christiania than a cultural one. This attitude is much the same as Cohen describes in her discussion on the music tourism centred on the Beatles in Liverpool (2007: 178).

Vesterberg, in his article 'Sangene Kan de Ikke Slå Ihjel', found many of the songs on these new records 'more strange than good' (2007: 15). He concluded that they mainly described the atmosphere and events in Christiania but the feeling of '*vi er en del af jer selv*' ['we are a part of you'] had disappeared (ibid.: 15). He took examples of songs from *Christiania Forever* that were produced by people from Christiania and released in 2004 by an old hippie, Tømrer Claus, and his company Karma Music. He claims that the song 'Christiania Mit Hjerte' ['Christiania My Heart'] by Zofia Hedvard[6] represents a self-centred statement offered to the rest of the Danish population that Christiania is a strong community that makes its inhabitants strong and that those who are on the outside look, perhaps longingly, to them. The void between the two societies and the tendency to simply depict

---

[6] The song can be found on Hedvard's homepage (http://www.zofiart.dk/) under the link: http://www.zofiart.dk/musik/solo/07-Track-07.mp3.

atmosphere can be found in more songs from the record (Hedvard n.d.). The song 'De Skæve Drømme' ['Skewed Dreams'] by the band Ache similarly praises life in Christiania as being close to paradise. However, the song by Tømrer Claus (the man who released the record), 'Christiania Sangen', has a very similar message to 'I Kan Ikke Slå os Ihjel'. The key line is *'Vi er en del af dem selv, og det kan de ikke holde ud'* ['We are a part of them, and this they can't stand']. Despite this particular song, it is fairly clear that the focus of the songs on the newer support records has shifted from the social awareness and political subject matter expressed in the old *fællessange* and songs on the first support records, to a more localised and atmospheric depiction of Christiania.

Perhaps this shift can simply be explained by the fact that the genre of the music on the new support records is more varied than on the early records for which the rock musicians themselves wrote the songs. On the newer records, in addition to the old 'hippie' rock like the music of Tømrer Claus, rap, metal, 'indie' rock and a combination of all these different styles appears. A look through Christiania's music history reveals how different types of music genres reflected contrasting views of the village. The old hippie musicians used Christiania to portray people who lived outside normal society and who were preoccupied with political activism, while the punks did not mention anything as mundane as a hippie enclave (Vesterberg 2007: 15). While the first generation of rappers were made very welcome in Christiania, they used the place mainly for consumption. When Christiania appears in a rap song, most references focus on it as a nice place to visit for a smoke rather than the political tensions discussed in the older songs.[7]

To summarise, the new records show a shift of emphasis away from political activism or an improvement of society[8] towards the consumption of Christiania and are therefore more aimed at tourists rather than Christianites. The records represent the local culture as it is seen from the outside, depicting either an idyllic place to smoke and relax or a place of violence and struggle with the outside world. The sense of unity or will to improve the world using the ideas of Christiania, as found on the early records, has been left by the wayside. The newer records are therefore arguably more commercial.

Locality

The varied approach to Christiania displayed in the music highlighted above can arguably be seen as representing groups of Christianites who have different

---

[7] For example see '28 Grader i Skyggen' ['28 Degrees in the Shade'] by MC Einar from 1989.

[8] Bear in mind that the politically and sociologically active people in Christiania are also those that organise events and concerts and see themselves as 'true' and 'typical' Christianites and therefore represent the group of people who have an opinion on what is 'true' or 'typical' Christiania music.

opinions on how the area should develop. The musician Helga Nova and the band Fri Galaxe base their music on the old 'hippie' music and the countercultural values of the 1970s. They often play at events organised in support of Christiania, and they represent the people in charge or the group of Christianites who in the introduction to this chapter were labelled 'the intellectuals' or 'the upper class leadership'. It was clear to me that they base their values and ideas on the old counterculture and, judging from their music, strongly emphasise society at large and how Christiania can be beneficial to Denmark. The new support records similarly represent a different group of people, such as those who live in Christiania for reasons other than political or idealistic beliefs. It is likely that a large number of the inhabitants of Christiania do not share the political interests of the 'intellectual' elite and live there only because it is convenient: the relaxed attitude towards cannabis and the very cheap housing.

Cohen lines up Liverpool against London as opposites in terms of independent practice versus commercialism, and localism versus metropolitanism, with Liverpool being seen as local, alternative and authentic. These ideas can be employed to explore Christiania's relationship with Copenhagen. However, I believe that a similar tension can also be found within Christiania itself, as it is a fragmented and complex community, and that this in itself is a more interesting subject matter in the present context. Comparing the artists behind the new support records with Helga Nova and Fri Galaxe, it becomes clear that both groups represent Christiania, and that their music is considered important in the locality. In one respect, the new support records rely more on the idea of locality, as they emphasise the idyllic nature of the place and rarely expand beyond that. They seem to be made mainly for tourists and can therefore be considered a commercial endeavour. The way they are presented and sold seems much more commercialised than is the case for the records by Helga Nova and Fri Galaxe. Their records are made independently by the artists themselves and rather than being sold in the tourist booth in the market square, they are found for sale only in the local shops.

All this creates an ambiguous construction of locality and the idea of independence versus commercialism. My informants steered me away from the support records, because they felt that they did not represent the 'true' Christiania. Perhaps the new support records can be seen as selling the Christiania atmosphere to tourists but not hoping to change society at large. Thus they can be seen as working against the counterculture of the place and, without meaning to, fuelling the normalising process. Rather than trying to 'recruit' people to the cause of Christiania, they represent its society as untouchable and separate from the mainstream and thus impossible for the general public to join in with. The play with alterity can therefore be seen as more harmful for this society than helpful, as it perhaps goes against what Christiania originally stood for.

This tension between the 'independent' and the 'commercial' evokes Cohen's discussion of Beatles tourism in Liverpool. Musical practice, both in Christiania and Liverpool, has generated debates about 'authenticity' and what represents the 'real' music of the place. This, in Cohen's view, typifies cultural tourism in general (2007: 178–9). Nevertheless, the relationship between commercialism and independence is perhaps more complex in Christiania. Cohen describes how government officials, including Liverpool City Council, some music entrepreneurs, musicians, bankers and individuals employed in higher education, joined in the policy-making of the Merseyside area in order to revitalise it as a thriving musical venue (ibid.: 133–8). The city of Copenhagen, on the other hand, as discussed above, has not taken part in promoting Christiania as a tourist destination. Without the interference of an official body, the appearance of tourism in the village seems disorganised. Certain tourist services are offered, such as the guided tour, the guide book and information offices, but they do not seem to work together to create a holistic experience for the tourists. The venues seem to be unsure of their purpose and embarrassed by their existence. Arguably, the reason for this is the complex relationship between the countercultural ideology of the village, which opposes commodification and commercialism, and its financial need for the tourists, who, in turn, are attracted to Christiania because of its image as a countercultural space.

Furthermore it is possible to see a hierarchical structure in the music practices that parallels the class division of the society discussed above. Both Davies in 1979 and Grundt in 2004 mention three class layers; the upper class/intellectuals, petite bourgeoisie/followers and junkies/sleepers. This can be matched with hippie rock at the top representing the old activists who created and now rule Christiania, the support records of the non-political inhabitants and the cover band culture of the dropouts.

Conclusion

Music is important to the way Christiania can be experienced and within the community various musical 'hot spots' create a certain atmosphere that is suitable for each space. The music is used both commercially, to attract people to the space in order to construct a fitting environment, and also as a way to pass time. Different kinds of music appeal to different groups of people, and different music genres play both a historical and a contemporary role in Christiania. The result is that some music is regarded as more 'authentic' than other. In the lyrics of the music created in and about Christiania, two different lines of approach can be perceived: one can be traced back to the early days of Christiania, and the other represents something new, perhaps a shift in outlook towards the original purpose of the village. The more politically active musicians write music containing ideas comparable to those in the old music. This obviously fulfils the expectations of the active part of the society for music representing the 'true' Christiania. These musicians also emphasise the localised aspect of their production, as the records are only sold in local shops, not in those intended specifically for tourists.

An analysis of openness and closure reveals that, on the one hand, Christianites are united against Denmark but at the same time rely on the outside world both for practical things and political support in order to exist. On the other hand such analysis also points to a difficult relationship between contrasting groups within the society. Music is a key to opening Christiania up to tourists, but sometimes the tourists can interrupt or 'spoil' events for the locals.

In its early days, Christiania was very much a countercultural space, similar to other enclaves. However, it soon developed away from the original vision. The musical practice shows that the old values are still important to many, but at the same time there is a struggle within this society to determine which direction should be taken for the future of Christiania. By assembling the evidence of how the society functions, my overall conclusion is that Christiania is no longer a countercultural space but bases its existence on a longing for the past. It is interesting that authorities continue to try to normalise the area, perhaps rather for financial reasons than to uproot countercultural practices. In many respects it is difficult to determine whether it would be possible to maintain a countercultural space at all, because the ideology behind it seems to challenge the fundamentals of every society.

Chapter 13
A Border-Crossing Soundscape of Pop: The Auditory Traces of Subcultural Practices in 1960s Berlin

Heiner Stahl

In 1960s Berlin young adolescents were not supposed be bored and annoyed, because this would have cast a damning light on the achievement potential of the opposing post-war German societies. Social institutions and youth associations providing options for (self-)entertainment and study were seen as key features of youth policies in East and West Berlin. But restricted access to cultural participation and distraction gave young adolescents a reason to hang about in parks or on street corners. These practices produced discontinuities in the state's institutional efforts to integrate, include and involve people by all means available. Experiencing entertainment in urban Berlin was thus an important aspect of a cultural sphere tightly linked to competing images of Cold War Berlin.

Cultural transfer is a multi-channelled process in which the signs, symbols and sounds floating around are rearranged in peer-group and media environments. These signifiers are filled with additional meanings and staged in public spaces. Pop is one such performative practice (Klein 2004: 48). Furthermore, public space is itself a fluid concept, in which social environments, discourses and narratives, infinite struggles to claim possession of space and the means to police crowds are enclosed (Lash and Urry 1994; Lefebvre 1996; Lindenberger 1995).

Sound and City: The Auditory Experience of Urban Clubbing in 1960s Berlin

Sensing past cityscapes, as Mark M. Smith has suggested, might well be a promising standpoint from which to detect traces of subcultural auditory experiences and to frame negotiating differences within constellations of cultural transfers (Smith 2008). Therefore, visibility and audibility may be understood as two main features of self-empowerment in public space. To be heard in public is a mode of generating attention. To be seen by others and to perform in front of others is a social practice that draws lines of aesthetic demarcation. Pop, in this respect, is a cultural technique bound to rituals (Hall and Jefferson 1976; Hebdige 1988; Bennett 2000), or to rather abstract cultural signs that are inscribed in acquirable cultural products. In the processes of transmission the past and contemporary usages of such signs are blended with additional content and meaning at a local level (Hannerz 1996: 67). Testing various cultural options, then, is an important feature of pop (Holl 1996: 59). A wider interpretation argues that pop, understood as a setting of multiple dispositions, reflects the notions of cultural boundaries and dominance by producing and enforcing counter-narratives and encouraging deviant behaviour (Barthes 1964: 85). Thus, public rejection of cultural dissidence is a mainspring of pop as a practice of self-empowerment (Thornton 1996; Middleton 2000; Svede 2000). In this respect, three modes of pop can be described: 1) official pop, which concerns the means and strategies of public institutions and private agents to transform popular music and the materiality of signs; 2) media pop, which refers to the policies of the printing press as well as public and private broadcasting stations in terms of coring the acoustic and aesthetic material to form a neat and clean version of pop; 3) subcultural pop, which comprehends the various modes of reclaiming streets.

Looking into the uses of signs and sounds in and off the streets, I intend to map public space by identifying the strategies of youths to become visible and audible. Giving public space an acoustic spin, I postulate that deviant behaviour and self-empowerment goes along with specific, temporarily stable mixtures of sounds. Despite this, the oral and mediated framing of sound, and of noise, stores information about practices of good taste, of engineering proper democratic or socialist citizens and of defending cultural territory. Auditory space is such a territory, in which the reformulated registers of senses and a different perception of the cityscape can be explored off the beaten tracks of conservative, middle- and working-class milieus. Consequently, traces of hearing and listening within processes of cultural transfers need to be identified in order to track down transitions from subcultural practices to countercultural social and cultural action becoming a signifier for change. Such an approach even fits the examination of non-liberal and democratic, authoritarian and repressive political systems such as socialist East Germany and the Eastern Bloc countries.

Taking inspiration from Raymond Murray Schafer's dazzling definition of 'soundscape' (Schafer 1973: 24) reveals that the acoustic dimension of everyday life conceals hidden layers of social, cultural and political power relations (see Corbin 1994; Smith 2001; Picker 2003; Thompson 2002; Rifkin 1993; Schweighauser 2006; Smith 2008; Müller 2011; Morat, Bartlitz and Kirsch 2011). Thus the sensory experience of audible cultural material leads to appropriation through communicative acts, selective insertion and intentional exclusion. Sound and noise, therefore, express notions of cultural diversity and dissidence, echoing previous strategies and codifications (Hannerz 1996: 60) While the aesthetic of noise could be read as an effect of technical and social progress, especially in a post-war socialist context (Guentcheva 2004), controlling auditory space is a powerful tool in consolidating communities (Attali 1977: 16). Creating noise is thus an aesthetic procedure that has the potential to subversively mirror existing cultural frames by accentuating anomalies and marginalities.

By focusing on auditory experience in the landscape of clubbing in 1960s East and West Berlin, I am connecting the sounds on the streets, in clubs and venues, as well as on pop music radio broadcasts, to a pattern of reinventing public space acoustically and of demasking the noises of repression. Writing about clubs, bands, broadcasting and pop music in Cold War Berlin needs an entangled perspective to rip through the media images and narratives of Berlin, that are consolidated as a multi-layered myth of the Cold War conflict in Europe. Although the acoustic space of broadcasting is limitless, such an approach proves valuable in providing flexibility to an analysis of the shifting constellations of politicised cultural codes and aesthetic practices across geographic boundaries. Referring to the claim that club cultures are taste cultures (Thornton 1996: 3) I want to compile an auditory map of venues and places in the sonic environment of 1960s Berlin's music subculture.

Framing the Auditory Field: The Beat and Skiffle Music Scenes in East Berlin

East Berlin's local heroes were the Telstars (who later became the notorious rock band, Phudys), Sputniks, Franke-Echo-Quintett and Diana Show-Band. The Beatlers, the Bottles, echo-team, the Brittles and Arkadia-Combo were from Berlin-Mitte, the Jokers, the Brightles, the Big Beats, the Five Stones, the Shouters and the Hot Five from Prenzlauer Berg, and the Cants,[1] Team 4, Atlantics and the Greenhorns played in the Köpenick and Treptow area.[2] These bands preferred rough music created with self-made distortion and delay effects or with smuggled devices bought on the black market. Listening to live broadcasts on the German programme of the private station, Radio Luxemburg, or the allied military stations, American Forces Network and British Forces Network, the musicians in these bands transferred what they heard into unique cover versions. Having poor English language skills, the young amateur artists adapted the lyrics while reproducing a similar auditory space with their instruments. As a consequence, pop music heard at live concerts in 1960s East Berlin was a brilliant mixture of excellent musical talent, misunderstanding the original lyrics and inventing words that sounded very British or American without making any actual sense.

After the Berlin Wall was erected in August 1961 the somewhat uncontrolled growth of youth clubs escalated in East Berlin. This was well in line with the Socialist Party decree on youth policy published in January 1961. The borough councils and socialist civil society institutions allocated spaces to create a sort of

---

[1] The band members were pupils of a secondary school named after the German philosopher Immanuel Kant. It is possible that the band intentionally made a reference to a vulgar swear word out of the name's sounding.

[2] Landesarchiv Berlin (LAB), C Rep. 121, Nr. 235 unpag. Magistrat von Groß-Berlin, Abteilung Kultur, Auszug aus Berichten der FDJ-Kreisleitungen über festgestellte Gitarrengruppen in den 8 Stadtbezirken, Berlin 29 October 1965, 1.

educational arena where youths could benefit from self-learning in their leisure time. However, this did not work out at all as planned. The clubs were run by kids from the neighbourhood who started to organise concerts, inviting different bands, and basically having alcohol-fuelled parties on the weekends. Youngsters had previously formed skiffle and guitar bands, and played wherever possible. East Berlin's pop-cultural sphere was thus a vibrating, noisy landscape of clubs where a distinct lack of repressive state control was evident.

The youth club, Freundschaft [Friendship], in Fredersdorferstrasse was located between East Berlin's main station and the tube station Marchelewskistrasse[3] on Karl-Marx-Allee. It was one of a number of underground pop hotspots in socialist East Berlin. Another, named Twistkeller, could be found in the basement of the Treptow council culture centre in Puschkinallee (Rauhut 1993: 104). This venue provided space for amateur bands, concerts and parties, and was located just a few footsteps away from the Berlin Wall.[4]

The kids running youth clubs like Ernst Knaack in Greifswalderstrasse, Kuba-Klub in Bötzowstrasse or Kosmos in the Helmholtzplatz park area were proficient when it came to increasing attendance at the clubs by organising music events and making additional money by selling beer, wine and schnapps. As a consequence the cultural branch of the Prenzlauer Berg borough became rather dissatisfied with the situation at the clubs. As five out of seven venues were managed by youths without any kind of control or regulation, in May 1965, the functionaries argued that the borough was displaying an example of best practice regarding integrating urban teenagers, and showing confidence both in their capacity to self-organise and in their willingness to be responsible in their leisure time activities.[5] However, administrative bodies were not convinced because the youths did not spend their time voluntarily educating themselves and instead were simply organising and promoting guitar-band shows so that they could meet, chat, dance and drink large quantities of beer. Moreover the youths cared nothing for the laws aimed at protecting minors. Consequently, over the years, these venues and sub-cultural places earned a bad reputation. Many of the young men, when very drunk, would soon start to throw chairs and tables around the rooms, urinate against the walls of neighbouring buildings, or steal bicycles. From an administrative point of view, mouldy walls, stale smoke from too many cigarettes, glue-repaired windows, broken chairs and mismatched tables, pop music from Western broadcasting stations and excessive noise did

---

[3] [Online] Available at: http://www.alt-berlin.info/cgi/stp/lana.pl?nr=22&gr=7&nord=52.526098&ost=13.430859 [accessed: 21 March 2012].

[4] [Online] Available at: http://www.alt-berlin.info/cgi/stp/lana.pl?nr=22&gr=7&nord=52.498647&ost=13.453563 [accessed: 21 March 2012].

[5] Stiftung Archiv der Partei- und Massenorganisationen der DDR im Bundesarchiv Berlin (SAPMO-BArch), DY 30 IV A 2/16/123 unpag., Rat des Stadtbezirkes, Prenzlauer Berg, Abt. Kultur, Analyse Jugendklubs, Berlin 12 May 1965, 1–5, 1.

not contribute to creating the kind of environment needed to foster socialist morality and decency.[6]

Taking an ideological stance on pop music and its sounds as cultural and political issues, the secretary of the Central Committee's office, Erich Honecker, cleverly positioned his argument. The capitalist evil of beat music and an insufficient focus on education provided by the Free German Youth, the Ministry of Culture and socialist media had opened the gates to ideological diversion from the West. The claim was supported by representatives of the regional Party bodies who could tell their own stories about juvenile deviance linked with concerts and venues.[7] Honecker thus successfully slowed down the somewhat progressive spin put on the current youth policy by Kurt Turba, a journalist who had been installed by the first secretary of the Socialist Party, Walter Ulbricht, in June 1963 (Schuster 1994; Kaiser 1997).

In this respect, socialist media – in particular Berlin Radio and its youth programme – was heavily criticised. Jugendstudio DT 64 reportedly played too many dance and pop titles from the West and showed a rather uncritical, and therefore 'decadent', approach towards the issue. In a briefing to Honecker, the music expert in the cultural branch of the Central Committee confronted the Deputy Director of the State Broadcasting Committee and the propaganda branch of the Central Committee regarding not making significant efforts to influence their subordinates to change the sound of the youth broadcast.[8] The ideological dimensions of beat and pop music had been underestimated and what were considered the 'false' practices of DT 64[9] had encouraged amateur bands to follow suit.

Moral Panic Across Town: The Rolling Stones Play West Berlin's Waldbühne, 1965

High-ranking Party officials adjusted quickly. As long as new rhythms were staged in a calm and cultivated atmosphere, as head of the cultural branch of the Central

---

[6] Ibid.: 3.

[7] SAPMO-BArch, DY 30 J IV 2/3/1.129 foliert, Protokoll der Sitzung des Sekretariats des ZK Nr. 89 vom 24 November 1965 – Auswertung des Beschlusses des Politbüros vom 23 November 1965 zu ideologischen Fragen auf dem Gebiet der Kultur. SAPMO-BArch, DY 30 J IV 2/3A/1.243 foliert, Sekretariat des ZK, Arbeitsprotokoll Nr. 89 vom 24 November 1965, Bl. 1. 6. Tagesordnungspunkt 2: Auswertung des Beschlusses des Politbüros vom 23 November 1965 über ideologische Fragen auf dem Gebiet der Kultur, Bl. 2–3. SAPMO-BArch DY 30 / IV A 2/9.06/4 unpag. [ZK Kultur] Entwurf für den Abschnitt, Probleme der ideologischen Arbeit der Partei im kulturellen Bereich, Berlin, o.D., 1–12. [an Gen. Honecker und Gen. Hager gegeben, 2 December 1965].

[8] SAPMO-BArch DY 30 / IV A 2/9.06/4 unpag. Abteilung Kultur, Peter Czerny, Wie konnten sich dekadente Tendenzen im Big Beat ausbreiten? (o.D.), 1–3. 2.

[9] Ibid.: 3.

Committee and chair of the ideological commission of the Politbüro, Kurt Hager, argued, the groups assured decent dancing. Although he stated that the Socialist Party should not ban beat music completely, Hager suggested that such music could unleash the beast of the masses, and would inevitably lead to hysteria and the breaking into pieces of stages and venues.[10] In referring to the Rolling Stones concert at the West Berlin outdoor venue, Waldbühne, on 15 September 1965, Hager reproduced the populist media image fostered by the conservative West Berlin press. He then gave the story another spin: the young adolescents drawn to this music might, when they become adults, or even earlier, be capable of destroying the new socialist society if the autocratic system proves to be immobile in tackling the challenge. Waldbühne thus became a code and signifier for Party officials and bureaucrats' general paranoia towards youths and their cultural practices. It also yielded an argument that flattened internal disputes on badly governed youth and the cultural field.[11]

Linking the Waldbühne event to a manifestation of juvenile discontent in the city of Leipzig on 31 October 1965[12] regarding the official banning of well-known guitar bands like the Butlers,[13] Hager expressed his thankfulness to the police forces and the supplementary activists of the youth association for instinctively taking strong measures to disperse the crowd.[14] Beat music fans had gathered at Leipzig's Hans-Leuschner-Platz, reclaiming the city centre, wearing olive-coloured US-army anoraks and parkas, and singing deviant chants. Between 800 and 1,000 youngsters strolled about the inner city, expressing their annoyance regarding the decision made by the cultural branch of the local Socialist Party (SED) to ban beat bands like the Butlers. Records reveal that the police and the Ministry of State Security noted that about 2,000 people attended the demonstration and threatened socialist order.[15]

---

[10] SAPMO-BArch, DY 30 IV A 2/9.01/21 unpag. Ideologische Kommission beim Politbüro, Kurt Hager, Protokoll über ein Seminar der Ideologischen Kommission mit den Sekretären für Agitation und Propaganda der Bezirksleitungen und den Leitern der Abteilung Kultur der Bezirksleitungen zu ideologischen Fragen auf dem Gebiet der Kultur 7 December 1965, 1–176, 56.

[11] LAB, C Rep. 902, Nr. 2118 unpag. Leiter der Jugendkommission der SED BL-Berlin, Harry Smettan, Betr.: Information über eine Aussprache beim Genossen Kurt Turba 5 October 1965, Berlin 6 October 1965, 1–3.

[12] See the original leaflets [Online] Available at: http://engelsdorf.net/images/Flugblatt.jpg [accessed: 21 March 2012].

[13] [Online] Available at: http://www.ostmusik.de/butlers.htm [accessed: 21 March 2012].

[14] SAPMO-BArch, DY 30 IV A 2/9.01/21 unpag. Ideologische Kommission beim Politbüro, Kurt Hager, Protokoll, 7 December 1965, 47. Concerning policing thugs in the GDR see Lindenberger (2003: 397–448) and Korzilius (2005).

[15] SAPMO-BArch, DY 30 / IV A 2/16/171 unpag. Abteilung Sicherheitsfragen, Borning, an Abteilung Jugend ZK, Dr. Naumann, Betr.: Information über das Auftreten von kriminellen und gefährdeten Gruppierungen Jugendlicher in der DDR, Berlin 5 July 1966, 1–12, 2.

What had actually happened at Waldbühne when the Rolling Stones and several support acts performed? On 15 September 1965, a journalist from the conservative populist yellow press paper *BILD* reported that she found herself in a hell where 21,000 concert-goers had gone mad, dancing aggressively and smashing wooden seats.[16] The conservative Christian Democratic Union (CDU) faction of the West Berlin assembly questioned the governing Social Democratic Party/Liberal Party (SPD/FDP) coalition on how the mass riot at the show actually happened. The delegates stated that only a few youths had been responsible for the scenes of riot and the destruction that followed. Due to the hard and monotonous rhythm of the music, a number of kids had run wild, while the majority reached a state of mere ecstasy. Pictures taken at the event were published on the front page of *BILD* the next day. The Free Berlin Station broadcast and televised reports and held furious discussions on this display of juvenile deviance, which, as the CDU faction claimed, every Berlin citizen had come to learn about.[17] Moving forward, the conservative delegate, Siegmund, attacked the liberal and more open-minded youth policy of Senator Ella Kay, noting that listening to beat music and playing in guitar groups was gaining ground in youth clubs and other public premises financed by the Senate's administration of youth. A number of delegates were heard to express their indignation, shouting 'unbelievable'.[18]

Siegmund claimed that staff at these facilities were unable to cope with the problems and obviously did not have the required means to assert control. The CDU politician added that his party would not dictate what kinds of music should be listened to, or what kinds of clothes should be worn, because West Berlin lived in the free and liberal West, and he knew that these kinds of things were happening in the Soviet zone. Nevertheless, the Senate and social workers in the youth clubs had to deal strictly, albeit carefully, with the new trends to keep them on a reasonable and publicly acceptable track.[19]

For more details see Rauhut (1993), Ohse (2003), Liebing (2005), Fenemore (2007) and Wierling (2008).

[16] Rauhut (2008: 30). [Online] Available at: http://www.morgenpost.de/multimedia/archive/00177/mim_w_stones60er_BM_177598b.jpg [accessed: 21 March 2012].

[17] Abgeordnetenhaus von Berlin, IV. Wahlperiode, Band 4, Stenographischer Bericht, 46. Sitzung, 23 September 1965, 367–411, Große Dringlichkeitsanfrage der Abgeordneten Amrehn, Dr. Riesebrodt, Dach, Wolff, Siegmund und der übrigen Mitglieder der Fraktion der CDU über Verhinderung von Rowdyszenen und Zerstörungswut in Berlin, 404–11, 404.

[18] Ibid.: 404.

[19] Ibid.

'Then We Take Berlin': Clubbing and Pop in 1960s West Berlin

In West Berlin, from time to time, Cold War conservatives across party lines attacked the Senate's youth policies – the notorious Waldbühne incident was one such occasion. In response, Senator Ella Kay and the Head of Youth Services, Ilse Reichel, outlined the comprehensive success of their strategies to positively integrate youths. Finally, implementing the concept of youth clubs in 1961, Kay and Reichel looked to offer respectable, modern and accessible spaces in venues like the Jazz Saloon (Steglitz), Dachluke (Kreuzberg) and Haus Metzler (Spandau).[20] Obviously, the intention behind this effort was to offer decent and morally harmless distractions in direct opposition to pubs, gaming halls and basement clubs.

The Jazz Saloon opened on 30 April 1960 after only a few months of preparation and planning (Müller 1961: 164). Although the idea was copied from a youth service initiative in the West German city of Mannheim, the Berlin launch was expedited when the West Berlin branch of the Socialist Party announced that it would buy the whole Haus Breitenfeld property to build a cultural centre on the site (ibid.: 165; Poiger 2000: 210). British beat music, however, did not reach Berlin via the Jazz Saloon, but via the Hermsdorf Star-Club located in the northern outskirts of West Berlin, named in homage to Hamburg's notorious Star-Club (Klitsch 2001: 133–78). In the suburban venues, the mod style ruled in opposition to the physical violence of rockers.

In the emerging landscape of clubbing, restaurants and pubs like Seeschloß Hermsdorf – also known as the Hermsdorf Star-Club – Festsäle and Dorfkrug Lübars or the Sport-Kasino Spandau – a pub linked to a local rowing club – gained importance (Nimmermann 1966: 496). Decorated in a petit bourgeois late-1930s and 1940s style, the infernal noise of the beat bands produced an acoustic space opposed to the aesthetics of sound created in previous venues. Compared to the Jazz Saloon or Dachluke, these suburban pubs offered relatively unrestricted and uncontrolled spaces. Young women wore short skirts combined with tight-fitting jumpers and haircuts seen in women's magazines (ibid.) or polyester blousons tagged with beat group names. Some wore dirty fur coats and pelt boots, wide slop trousers and lumberjack shirts. Wooden chains, wrist bands and fake silver rings were the accessories to this new kind of body politics, while green military jackets and anoraks protected the clothes.

Pop Takes to the Air: Youth Radio Programmes in West Berlin

Alongside this, two youth-orientated radio broadcasts – Wir-um zwanzig in October 1965 and S-f-beat in March 1967 – were launched by the Free Berlin Station. Reading news that concerned teenagers, presenting music, and talking

---

[20] LAB, B Rep. 013, Nr. 434 unpag., Berliner Jugendclub e.V., Antrag Einrichtung von Jugendtanzstätten, 1.

about various issues between tracks built up an acoustic and auditory texture that contested the well-balanced sound identity of the whole station. Citations, references, comments and acoustic flashes were mixed in sequence to create a somewhat chaotic flow. The sounds, the musical styles and the hosts' voices, audiotakes and self-made jingles – for example screaming 'Oh no!', beating drums or playing recorded canned laughter – were so far from the regular radio soundscape that adults, school headmasters and social workers became alarmed and put off. Adults did not get the joke of hearing a howling siren jingle[21] on the radio – probably because it recalled a certain sonic experience from Second World War bombings and subsequent shelter-seeking efforts.

The soundscape of S-f-beat mixed up the auditory identifiers of the white, US middle class (Beach Boys, the Mamas and the Papas, Bob Dylan etc.) and the Afro-American counterculture (the Raelettes, Martha and the Vandellas, Sly and the Family Stone etc.) with English beat, psychedelic and hard rock music. S-f-beat's music programming was tied to underground music, and step by step it started to neglect releases that proposed nice melodies and catchy tunes. Songs were meant to have something special – original and stand-alone features – not just powerful guitar riffs and loud drums.[22] Journalists admitted that Pink Floyd's *The Piper at the Gates of Dawn* (1967) and *A Saucerful of Secrets* (1968), the Beatles' *Sgt. Pepper* (1967) or Frank Zappa's productions with the Mothers of Invention had stunning musical arrangements and smart melodies fitted into three-minute tracks, but entertaining listeners meant playing 'easy listening' pop music like *El Condor Pasa* and *Bridge over Troubled Water* (Simon and Garfunkel 1970) or Mungo Jerry's *In the Summertime* (1970), and not torturing listeners with pure noise.

Focusing on contemporary and trendy pop music,[23] S-f-beat's programming was distinct from the mainstream music played on air. Indeed, it traced out the high-cultural auditory framing of German broadcasting from the late 1960s to the early 1980s. Besides playing music from the extreme border areas of conventional popular music, S-f-beat also illuminated the boundaries of reporting. In the wake of the late 1960s, a younger generation of broadcast journalists understood themselves as embedded commentators on youth culture, student protests and issues of higher education or squatting in inner city areas. They communicated these minority positions with rhetoric fervour, and as such questioned authority

---

[21] Deutsches Rundfunkarchiv (DRA) Potsdam-Babelsberg, Schriftgut Hörfunk, Bestand Sender Freies Berlin, Nr. 3712/47, s-f-beat am Dienstag 10 October 1972, 1404. Sendung. [1. SCHREI, Oh, no!, 3s; 2. Trommel 5s].

[22] DRA, P.-Bblg., Schriftgut Hörfunk, Bestand Sender Freies Berlin, Nr. 3686/20, s-f-beat- Sendung Nr. 917 vom Mittwoch 4 November 1970, 18.30–19.30 Uhr, Ulrich Herzog: Live-Sprecher, Musikauswahl. Hans-Rainer Lange: Aufnahmeleitung, Selbstbeschreibung von s-f-beat, o.D. (Nov. 1970), o.A., 1–2, 1.

[23] DRA, P.-Bblg., Schriftgut Hörfunk, Bestand Sender Freies Berlin, Nr. 2668, Abteilung Familienprogramm, Susanne Fijal an Programmdirektion, Herr Döring, Betr.: Musiktitel in 's-f-beat', Berlin 27 November 1970, 1–3, 1.

and order. The new investigative approach to journalism produced long-lasting conflicts with the decision-makers in broadcasting stations and the (pre-)political establishment of Cold War West Berlin. By reporting from investigation panels on repressive policing in West Berlin, or reporting live on the conditions of youths in prisons and approved schools, S-f-beat was fostering a bold auditory presence[24] and challenging the harmonic orchestration of images, narratives and success stories of proper, clean and liberal West Berlin that the Free Berlin Station was so keen to present.

By announcing music events at Deutschlandhalle, Waldbühne, or in venues like Neue Welt, Dachluke, Pop-Inn, Star-Club Hermsdorf,[25] Tuesday Club[26] in the borough of Schöneberg, or the notorious jazz club Quasimodo in Charlottenburg,[27] youth club parties or book readings and discussion sessions, the youth programme S-f-beat acted as a broker of subcultural news. Local Berlin bands and domestic groups from West Germany like the Petards,[28] Cologne-based krautrock pioneers Can (1970) or the more advanced West Berlin bands the Gloomys[29] or the Lords (1970)[30] rarely got airplay, though others, like the local the Safebreakers, the Outs

---

[24] DRA, P.-Bblg., Schriftgut Hörfunk, Bestand Sender Freies Berlin, Nr. 3686/11, s-f-beat, 8 October 1968, 398. Sendung, Hans-Rainer Lange: Live-Sprecher; Wolfgang Kraesze: Musik & Aufnahmeleitung. s-f-beat-Meldung.

[25] DRA, P.-Bblg., Schriftgut Hörfunk, Bestand Sender Freies Berlin, Nr. 6041/10, s-f-beat, 20 September 1967, Mittwoch 18.30–19.30 Uhr, 133. Sendung, Hans-Dieter Frankenberg: Live-Sprecher & Musikauswahl. Hans-Rainer Lange: Aufnahmeleitung.

[26] DRA, P.-Bblg., Schriftgut Hörfunk, Bestand Sender Freies Berlin, Nr. 6041, s-f-beat, 4 April 1967. 20. Sendung, 18.30–19.30 Uhr. Tipps für 4 April 1967.

[27] DRA, P.-Bblg., Schriftgut Hörfunk, Bestand Sender Freies Berlin, Nr. 3686/30, s-f-beat, 10 September 1970, 878. Sendung, Hans Dieter Frankenberg: Live-Sprecher & Musikauswahl. Ulrich Herzog: Aufnahmeleitung. Tipps für heute: Im Quartier von Quasimodo, Kantstr. 12a, 22.00 Uhr, 'The Peter Brötzmann-Group' (FREE JAZZ).

[28] DRA, P.-Bblg., Schriftgut Hörfunk, Bestand Sender Freies Berlin, Nr. 3686/5, s-f-beat, 17 July 1968, 18.30–19.30 Uhr, 340. Sendung Joachim Pukass: Live Sprecher & Musikauswahl. Hans Dieter Frankenberg: Aufnahmeleitung. The Petards, Pretty Miss, Horst Ebert, A-Side: Baby, run, run, run, 7", CCA 5021, 1966. [Online] Available at: http://www.twang-tone.de/babyrun.jpg, http://www.thepetards.com/songs.htm [accessed: 21 March 2012].

[29] DRA, P.-Bblg., Schriftgut Hörfunk, Bestand Sender Freies Berlin, Nr. 3686/7, s-f-beat, Freitag, 9 February 1968, 232. Sendung, Hans-Rainer Lange: Sprecher. Wolfgang, Kraesze: Musikauswahl & Aufnahmeleitung. The Gloomys, Calling Mayfair, Ralf Siegel/Michael Kunze, A-Side: Daybreak, 7", Capitol C 23694, [Online] Available at: http://www.gloomys.de/ [accessed: 21 March 2012].

[30] DRA, P.-Bblg., Schriftgut Hörfunk, Bestand Sender Freies Berlin, Nr. 3686/6, s-f-beat, 22 January 1968, 218. Sendung, 18.30–19.30 Uhr, Ulrich Herzog: Livesprecher & Musikauswahl. Hans-Rainer Lange: Aufnahmeleitung. The Lords, John Brown's Body, Claudio Szenkar, B-Side: Cut my hair, 7", Col. C. 23549, 1967, 2'30. [Online] Available at: http://hitparade.ch/cdimages/the_lords-john_browns_body_s.jpg [accessed: 21 March 2012].

or the Bus Stop Four received some radio promotion, when information was provided on upcoming gigs in youth clubs across the West Berlin boroughs.[31]

The pop news on S-f-beat promoted a completely different lifestyle: talking about record stores with posters and underground music in Charlottenburg, or a local branch in the district of Steglitz furnished with cushy armchairs, Lenco Stereo Systems record players and light displays,[32] or giving notice of an independent swinging London-style fashion shop named Market opening at Uhlandstrasse, cornering Kurfürstendamm, offering barrels of free beer before noon and with the progressive rock band Murphy Blend performing live.[33]

Conclusion

Performing acoustic deviance in public spaces and especially listening to Western pop music on Radio Luxembourg's German service, Radio (East) Berlin's Jugendstudio DT 64 (June 1964), the S-f-beat broadcast Station of Free (West) Berlin (March 1967) or on Radio in the American Sector's RIAS-Treffpunkt (October 1968) with the volume turned right up were the preferred cultural practices of 1960s East Berlin youth who cared little for the extensive administrative measures.[34] The entrance to the SKALA cinema (Prenzlauer Berg) was one such public meeting place, as was the Helmholtz park area where some 30 adolescents hung about every evening, brawling. Similar situations and practices could be seen at Kollwitzplatz, or at the crossing of Hufeland and Esmarchstrasse in the Bötzowstrasse neighbourhood. The youth did not invent these meeting places, but they did reclaim them (Lindenberger, 2003: 423–32). Leaving acoustic traces in this urban soundscape was an important thing to achieve, with noisy pop

---

[31] DRA, P.-Bblg., Schriftgut Hörfunk, Bestand Sender Freies Berlin, Nr.6041/9, s-f-beat, 15 September 1967, 18.30–19.30 Uhr, 130. Sendung, Gesine Frohner Live-Sprecher & Musikauswahl. Wolfgang Kraesze: Aufnahmeleitung.

[32] DRA, P.-Bblg., Schriftgut Hörfunk, Bestand Sender Freies Berlin, Nr. 3686/17, s-f-beat, 16 September 1970, 882. Sendung, 18.30–19.30 Uhr, s-f-beat Meldung: 16 September 1970. Zu Lenco Plattenspieler: [Online] Available at: http://www.zwillingssterne.de/images/LencoL70_kpl.jpg [accessed: 21 March 2012].

[33] DRA, P.-Bblg., Schriftgut Hörfunk, Bestand Sender Freies Berlin, Nr. 3686/16, s-f-beat, 25 September 1970, 889. Sendung, 18.30–19.30 Uhr, Hans-Rainer Lange: Live-Sprecher & Musikauswahl, Rolf Seiler: Aufnahmeleitung. See [Online] Available at: http://www.market-berlin.com/ [accessed: 21 March 2012]. Please listen to Murphy Blend [Online] Available at: http://www.myspace.com/murphyblend1970 [accessed: 18 June 2012].

[34] Bundesbeauftragter für die Unterlagen des Staatssicherheitsdienstes der ehemaligen Deutschen Demokratischen Republik (BStU), MfS, HA XX, Nr. 11635 foliert, Präsidium der Volkspolizei Berlin, Präsident, an Verwaltung für Staatssicherheit Groß-Berlin, Leiter, Dokumentation über Tendenzen der Fehlentwicklung jugendlicher und jungerwachsener Bürger der Hauptstadt der DDR–Berlin, 10 June 1969, Bl. 1–96, 12.

music being a distinctive feature of this act of self-empowerment. The border-crossing community of listeners in East and West Berlin correctly guessed and understood the references, but the representatives of the Free Berlin Station's broadcasting commission were repeatedly appalled when they, by chance, tuned into this constantly changing auditory map and West Berlin's pop soundscape. On the other side of the wall, the same procedure emerged. The auditory presence of Jugendstudio DT 64 constantly conflicted with an idealised approach to socialist cultural politics.

Popular dance music, the so-called *Unterhaltungsmusik*, played by dance orchestras, constituted the soundscape of 1960s broadcasting on East as well as West Berlin stations. Indeed, all across Europe, this aesthetic was favoured by those people who compiled music for entertainment broadcasts. American and British pop music was the outright opposite, an alien and unfamiliar auditory experience. However, the emerging sounds of beat, soul and rock music were gradually inserted into the acoustic space of radio, first by being actively refused and disapproved of, and secondly by the creation of slots to accommodate the sounds within the programme flow. This integrative approach was more targeted towards reaching younger prospective audiences in a competitive mediascape (Appadurai 2000: 33), rather than aimed at being in accordance with the politicised framing of cultural transfer in Cold War Berlin. By introducing American and British pop music into the local constellations of divided Berlin, original content, references and meanings were transformed into hybrid cultural forms. These hybrids stored the tensions concomitant with renegotiating cultural identities. New auditory experiences became possible through multiple channels – attending live concerts, forming a band, listening to broadcasts via mobile transistor radios, recording those broadcasts or listening to records in shops or on personal record players.

Pop culture as a specific cultural and social practice evolved into a constellation that might be labelled 'triadic' (Giesecke 2006: 284–9). As highlighted in this text, *subcultural pop* is generated at the level of users, customers and cultural pioneers combining different visual, acoustic and aesthetic materials to infuse additional social and cultural meaning opposing mainstream society. In East Berlin, youths switching between different acoustic spheres were testing options that the Socialist Party's cultural policies did not fully provide. Opting to not take part in the socialist acoustic space – in the youth organisations or the Party – was read by functionaries as a form of deviance that would lead to opposition of the regime. In West Berlin, accessing pop culture was far easier, but the cultural connotations were also in opposition to middle-class ideas of aesthetic superiority. By actively grabbing 'foreign' acoustic and aesthetic influences, West Berlin youths contested liberal rhetorics of Cold War democracy, and mirrored the mainstream strategies of cultural and social exclusion by challenging the tales of cultural openness. Basement clubs, untenanted flats, street corners and suburban beer halls were an integral part of the 1960s subcultural sphere. *Official pop* was the practice of youth service representatives and political functionaries being concerned with protecting minors and providing opportunities for teenagers to come to terms with adult society. The notions of pop created by journalists and by radio DJs, on the other hand, could be considered *media pop* because it mediated cultural styles by adding them to a given framework. *Media pop* also contested the acoustic space of broadcasting itself and challenged the sound identities of the stations as internal contenders. Therefore, making audible processes of cultural transfers means broadening the perspective on how media shapes cultural codes at a local level. *Subcultural pop* and its practices left auditory traces in the public space, mirroring and opposing what mainstream society had agreed on as a cultural code and a proper mode of public behaviour.

Chapter 14
Music and Countercultures in Italy: The Neapolitan Scene

Giovanni Vacca

Following the Second World War Italy slowly recovered democratic life after 20 years of fascism. Despite this, in cultural terms, only the elites who lived in big cities like Rome, Turin and Milan could fully taste the openness brought about by democracy: the rest of the country was split between a Catholic conservative stance, with the Christian Democrats (DC) in power, and the strong influence of the Italian Communist Party (PCI), notably the biggest communist party in the Western world. During the 1960s Italy lived the so-called 'economic boom' and became an affluent society: mass production and mass consumerism expanded enormously, the circulation of ideas and cultural products reached an intensity never experienced before and the Italian way of life, still largely provincial in many areas, was totally upset by this revolution (Ginsborg 1990).

In music, after the war, jazz had returned to radio programmes but the Italian traditional song descending from the 'romanza' was still at the forefront, receiving the seal of approval of a popular national song contest, the 'Festival di Sanremo'. Then in 1958 Domenico Modugno shocked the audience with 'Nel blu dipinto di blu' ('Volare'), a song new in form and content, which was destined to become one of the most famous Italian hits in the world. At the beginning of the 1960s the first seeds of rock and roll began to take root in Italian popular music with the first beat groups ('complessi', as they were called). Moreover, in the wake of what was happening in the United States and in other European countries, the counterculture was also beginning to make a mark. After 1968, a crucial year in many places, youth culture and music in Italy took a giant leap: from that year onwards, British and American rock stars started to include the country in their tours and Italian rock bands found a more well-defined identity as beat declined in favour of progressive rock. At the time, though, Italy experienced the development of a grave social conflict that would reach its height in 1978 with the tragic outbreak of terrorism. During this turbulent period, a new radical political culture emerged outside the Communist Party that began to appeal to students and young workers, with criticism addressed to 'the system' in all its articulations: family, education, politics, work, entertainment – in short, what Louis Althusser called 'ideological State Apparatuses' were all strongly questioned (Balestrini and Moroni 1997). Against what was considered the official discourse of the establishment (not only the conservative Christian Democrats in power, but also the traditional working-class culture of the Italian Communist Party), a more politically militant stance emerged, marginalising what had been the creative and visionary alternative thought of the 1960s. In this new political climate, a rediscovery of folk music represented a renewal of class culture and an explosion of the political song genre indicated the development of an engaged popular song to suit the times. Among the galaxy of ideas floating around in those years, often in conflict with each other but sometimes forming original combinations, many of the ideas aimed to be complete visions of the world and hence also aspired somewhat to take on the mantle of 'counterculture'. The term 'counterculture' will here be used in a wide sense, without splitting hairs over the difference between 'countercultures' and 'subcultures', accepting that, generally, 'subcultures' are oriented more towards a symbolic rebellion through 'style' (Hebdige 1979), while 'countercultures' are more inclined to active political protest (Maffi 2009). In Italy the former frequently slipped into the latter, particularly in the 1970s and in the 1990s, primarily due to the morass caused by the heated political climate.

Music was obviously a privileged vehicle for countercultures: functioning as a marker of identity, acting as a powerful means of collective aggregation and benefiting from a growing technology that allowed unprecedented circulation, music found itself in the contradictory position of being a much longed for agent of real social change and, at the same time, a virgin and potentially gigantic market into which the cultural industry could expand. Such a contradiction exploded, more than anywhere else, in the widespread idea that music had to be 'free', liberated from the tentacles of the industry and available to everybody. For a long period rock concerts in Italy were often the scene of riots with the police, with demonstrators protesting against ticket prices (or just because tickets were required), clashing outside, and sometimes inside, the venues. The disorder began in the early 1970s (for example at Led Zeppelin, Milan, 1971; Jethro Tull, Bologna, 1973; Soft Machine, Naples, 1974; Lou Reed, Rome, 1975), becoming more and more frequent such that, after 1977, the most popular foreign acts left Italy out of their itineraries for years. Many Italian musicians, on the other hand, were involved in political militancy and in countercultures; they can be roughly divided into two categories: 'cantautori' (singer-songwriters) and 'gruppi rock' (rock bands). Singer-songwriters exist everywhere but the Italian 'cantautore' was a very peculiar figure for the social role that the more politicised audience attributed to him (female singer-songwriters – 'cantautrici' – were rare): that of being a sort of lay saint, expected to be uninterested in success, transparent and ideologically coherent, only dedicated to his art and to its social role and, most of all, prepared to undergo periodical 'ethical examinations' by his audience. Rock bands, on the other hand, were expected, by the same audience, to be 'experimental', not commercial and, obviously, politically committed. 'Cantautori' were meant to be more valuable for their lyrics, 'gruppi' for their music.

Naples, in all this, found itself in a very peculiar position. In a nation full of evident regional differences, the late unification of the state, the economic distance between North and South, and the geographical influences caused by the North being closer to Europe and the South nearer to the Mediterranean areas, a great variety of specific cultures have been produced. Yet Naples is probably the only Italian city in which its traditions and history are almost impossible for local artists to ignore or avoid. As the capital of a kingdom before the nation came into being, Naples was home to rich traditions in music, theatre, the visual arts and literature. Moreover, these traditions were about to become powerful symbols of the whole Italian culture, but Naples was deprived of the role of nation's capital in favour of Rome. As the largest city of southern Italy at the time of unification, Naples was also the main city of a largely depressed area. It was big, overcrowded and had a vast subproletariat without any kind of stable employment, somewhat the legacy of the *Ancien Régime* of the Bourbon monarchy.[1] In the 1950s Naples found itself in the hands of a highly reactionary middle class of *parvenus* who elected as mayor the ship-owner Achille Lauro, a demagogue who gave the green light for gigantic urban speculation that devastated the city. In the 1960s the city came under the rule of the Gava family, a local conservative Christian Democrat power group that continued Lauro's urban politics, creating a much tighter connection with the central government in Rome (Allum 1973).

Song has a central place in Neapolitan culture, and although the city was considered one of the capitals of opera, it is here that Italy can boast its most famous repertoire of modern songs. Born between the nineteenth and the twentieth centuries as the product of a bourgeoisie of continental taste, the Neapolitan song was a product of a massive project of modernisation involving culture as well as city planning: the latter set the streets free of the local folk culture in order to transform Naples into a proper capitalist environment, while the former provided the new social scenario with its own form of entertainment. Neapolitan song thus grew up as an important part of the identity of the local emerging middle class, but at the same time was taken up and continuously revisited by the lower classes, for example by itinerant musicians known as 'posteggiatori' (Artieri 1961), who adapted the songs to folk styles thus making them immediately recognisable to the common people. Through the charm of the Neapolitan song, the conservative values of the bourgeoisie became locally hegemonic, creating the so-called 'napoletanità' (a sort of 'Neapolitan vision of the world') – an amalgamating ideology that upheld internal cohesion, prevented class conflict and generated a sort of inter-class city pride. Nevertheless, as remarked by writer Raffaele La Capria, it is 'napoletanità' that has given the citizens of Naples, even those of the lowest classes, their European spirit, sense of humour and typical sense of irony (La Capria 1986).

Neapolitan song, although always sung in the Neapolitan dialect, is now considered the 'classic' Italian song and one of the foremost repertories of popular music in the world, widely recognised as one of the most relevant components

---

[1] The philosopher Antonio Gramsci, in his *Prison Notebooks* observed the peculiarity of Naples, which appeared to be reluctant to adopt any kind of rational organisation of work (Gramsci 2007, III: 2142).

of Italian culture. Neapolitan song has also always pervaded the city: whistled on every street, reproduced through records heard from the windows of the buildings in the streets (particularly in popular areas), performed in restaurants and at every ceremony (private parties, especially marriages) and mentioned in everyday conversation. But in the 1960s, when its creative cycle seemed to have come to an end, it was employed more and more as an ideological tool by the most reactionary forces active in Naples, so that it weighed like a stone on the creative potential of Neapolitan musicians as it symbolised a certain Italian song (melodic, traditionalist, sentimental) that they perceived to be outside modernity. Young musicians, then, had to fight against such hegemony in order to regain their freedom, to attach their music to what was going on in Italy and in the rest of the world and to feel, instead, inside modernity. This chapter aims to investigate the growth of Neapolitan music over the last 50 years in parallel with the influence that new musical trends – particularly those thought of as countercultural – had on Neapolitan musicians, and the relationship this music has had with this 'object', which needed first to be distanced and deconstructed, to be afterwards critically recuperated and used as a model for new compositions. Thus, in the beginning, while young musicians were experimenting with new creative ideas, the Neapolitan song had to be violated, debunked, stripped bare of its stock conventions and bent to unheard of expressive possibilities.

Among the first Neapolitan performers to try working outside the format of the Neapolitan song were the Showmen, a band who, though they were active for only a short period in the late 1960s, left a mark on Neapolitan music; some of the band's members (James Senese and Elio D'Anna) were later to form prominent bands like Napoli Centrale and Osanna. Jazz and rhythm and blues were the main musical influences for the Showmen and the fact that Senese and bass player Mario Musella were the sons of American soldiers and Neapolitan mothers (both were born when American troops occupied Naples in 1945: Senese's father was an African American and Musella's a Native American), seemed to give them a natural affinity for the music of Black America. Although the Showmen wrote their own songs and often sang in Italian, they intentionally confronted the Neapolitan song tradition. A meaningful example is their recording of 'Catarì (marzo)', a classic love song written by Salvatore Di Giacomo and Mario Pasquale Costa in 1893. the Showmen's version of this romantic and melodic composition is stretched and performed dramatically in a 'black mood'. With Senese being a central protagonist of the music scene for some years (Musella died in 1979), his origin helped build the myth of the new Neapolitan music being the music of Italian 'niggers'. Furthermore as Neapolitans were considered the despised race of the 'meridionali' – that is, the people of the South discriminated against by those of the North (Teti 1993) – young musicians of the 1960s, and the growing number of journalists specialising in music, began to associate marginalisation with cultural subordination and creative energy. And just as the renewal of American music was seen to originate in the African American community, so the renewal of Italian music was seen to originate, for the press of the time, among those referred to as 'the niggers of Vesuvius'. 'Why did they take so long to appear?' asked journalist and rock producer Renato Marengo. 'Because the obscurantism of the Neapolitan song – unpopular, not folk, not genuine, a flirtatious and touristic knock-off, giving a decadent, false, uncultured vision of Neapolitan music – meant nobody gave the Neapolitan credit. Consequently young Neapolitans felt frustrated and lacked the courage to "come out"' (Marengo 1974 my translation).

Black music was not the only foreign trend in which young musicians were interested, as both progressive and psychedelic rock were highly influential at the time. Bands like Osanna and Il Balletto di Bronzo looked towards the English progressive scene, the first to Genesis and Jethro Tull (Osanna's live acts were highly theatrical, incorporating face paint and dramatic light shows), the second, with piano virtuoso Gianni Leone, towards 'keyboard heroes' like Keith Emerson and Rick Wakeman. Both groups recorded concept albums, like Osanna's *L'Uomo* (1971) and *Palepoli* (1973), and Il Balletto di Bronzo's *Ys* (1972). Other artists included Alan and Jenny Sorrenti (both from a Welsh mother), who were considered the most unusual singers of the time. Jenny founded Saint Just in 1973, a band combining English folk influences with classical sounds, and later became one of the few Italian 'cantautrici' (female singer-songwriters), recording a number of popular albums as a solo artist. According to producer Lilli Greco, Jenny has been one of the most outstanding musicians to record on the RCA label, 'an exceptional singer ... far above her possible competitors' (Becker 2007; my translation). Jenny's brother Alan recorded his first album, *Aria*, in 1972 and his second, *Come un vecchio incensiere all'alba di un villaggio deserto*, in 1973 and both, like the Saint Just albums, were published by Harvest, the English label created by EMI to promote progressive rock. Alan's music was highly experimental, ethereal and rarefied, comprising long psychedelic compositions accompanied by cryptic lyrics; in 1974, though, he recorded 'Dicitencello vuje', a Neapolitan song written in 1930: his vocalised version, delivered in falsetto style (thus challenging established purists), was both original and astonishing and showed how young interpreters could perceive and work with classic songs. Two years later he wrote 'Sienteme', still a popular song that could be classified as an attempt to write a 'modern' passionate Neapolitan song. In his song 'Vorrei incontrarti' (1972), Sorrenti also wrote one of the most concise couplets to encapsulate the 'spirit of the time': '*Vorrei incontrarti fuori i cancelli di una fabbrica/vorrei incontrarti lungo le strade che portano in India ...*' ['I'd like to meet you outside the gates of a factory/I'd like to meet you on the roads that lead to India']. The factory and India represented the two major poles of the counterculture in Italy: the factory (that is, the 'Fordist' factory, with a conveyor belt production line, which had developed quickly in Italy) was at the centre of the theoretical Marxist speculations of the radical left wing active outside the Communist Party. According to the 'operaisti' (Wright 2002, Tronti 2009), the most influential radical group, a young, unskilled working class, mainly of Southern origin, was reacting to the pressure of factory life with a new subjectivity and an alternative, 'autonomous' community lifestyle that would eventually end up refusing to work and instead take up illegal means to acquire goods that were impossible to buy on ordinary salaries. India, on the other hand, represented the myth of an alternative civilisation, custodian of an ancestral wisdom lost in the industrial world; many Italian hippies in those years, just like the Beatles, travelled to India looking for gurus.

It is interesting to observe the different connections the Neapolitan scene had with the British and American one: for example, Senese and his 'genetic' predisposition to be drawn to jazz; Jenny and Alan Sorrenti recording for the Harvest label; the presence of American musicians Shawn Phillips and Patrizia (née Patricia) Lopez – Phillips a long-haired American singer embodying the spirit of the American counterculture who, before he moved in 1967 to Positano, on the Sorrento coast, not far from Naples, had worked with Donovan and the Beatles (and even performed at the Isle of Wight Festival); and Lopez a singer-songwriter born in Los Angeles who had also moved to Naples, bringing with her the songs of Jefferson Airplane, the Grateful Dead, Joni Mitchell and David Crosby, mixing them with Raffaele Viviani's songs and the Neapolitan 'Villanelle'.[2] It is thus suggested that American and English connections meant for Neapolitan musicians not only faster access to international trends in rock music, but also a closer link to what the English-speaking world was producing in terms of countercultures. Bob Dylan, and all that he was able to absorb and give back in his songs, for example, inspired Edoardo Bennato, one of the most successful Italian 'cantautori' of the 1970s: curly-haired, with small dark glasses and a degree in architecture, Bennato originally performed as a one-man-band, playing 12-string guitar, harmonica and kazoo, while hitting a tambourine with a device attached to his right foot. With his croaky voice, Bennato appeared a cross between Dylan and 'Pulcinella', a folk mask typical of the Naples area that, like all masks, mocked power and symbolised the real voice of the everyman – and Bennato certainly mocked the power and official values of the Italian state: corrupt politicians, the Communist Party, the president of the Republic, even the pope ended up in the barbs of his harsh and anarchic criticism. Bennato immediately targeted a national audience and only occasionally sang in the Neapolitan dialect; nonetheless, he remained closely linked to Naples (the cover of his album *Io che non sono l'imperatore*, 1975, carried the layout of his project for a new Naples underground system that he, provokingly, opposed to the official one). Bennato reached the height of his notoriety in the late 1970s, when he produced three albums (*Burattino senza fili*, 1977, *Uffà Uffà* and *Sono solo canzonette*, both 1980: the first and the last being enormously successful) and, as the first Italian 'cantautore' to achieve such success, managed to sell out stadiums. His 'Cantautore' (1976), which ironically underlines the excessive expectations people had of singer-songwriters in Italy and the unnatural role they had assumed, still stands as a most intelligent song.

---

[2] Raffaele Viviani (1888–1950) was one of the most popular Neapolitan playwrights and the author of many songs for his theatre works. The 'Villanella' is a Neapolitan polyphonic genre of compositions of the sixteenth century. Patrizia Lopez recorded her first Italian album in 1976.

Eugenio Bennato, Edoardo's brother, was one of the founders of the Nuova Compagnia di Canto Popolare (NCCP), a folk revival group to which Neapolitan music owes the unearthing of a huge corpus of folk songs that became the backbone of the Neapolitan folk music revival. The revival of traditional music had been, since the 1960s, a key feature of Italian left-wing culture: rejected by immigrants because they reminded them of the misery of their origins, folk songs were re-evaluated as a repertoire of songs free of commercialism and thus a possible component of a progressive culture. It was folklore itself (investigated by both Antonio Gramsci and the ethnologist Ernesto de Martino) that was seen, with its country festivals, its rituals, its traditional medicine, as a possible repository of anti-capitalist values (and, as such, a counterculture in itself). Folk music was also regarded as the only original and 'authentic' music Italy had, and the only one capable of competing with rock music and its craze – an attitude also found in other folk revivals. For the NCCP, the Neapolitan song, with its lack of originality, was responsible for the elimination of folk music from people's consciousness (and with it the social conditions of the poorest sections of society that expressed it, especially the peasants of the countryside around Naples). To address this and to suggest a possible new direction for Neapolitan music the NCCP took the classic 'Tammurriata nera', written in 1944, and treated it with a folk arrangement.

In 1977 Eugenio Bennato took a further step by leaving the NCCP to launch Musicanova, a folk group that proposed writing new songs based on traditional modes with lyrics criticising the official history of the unification of the country. Here, Bennato's research on the southern peasant resistance of the 1860 Piedmontese conquest of the South that aimed to unify the country was also an attempt to rediscover an alternative culture: that of the bandits – and the communities of small villages that supported them – that opposed the modern lifestyle introduced by the new rulers. In contrast to the NCCP, a group of workers at Alfa Sud, a car factory located in Pomigliano D'Arco, in the Neapolitan hinterland, gave birth to the Gruppo Operaio di Pomigliano D'Arco 'E Zezi ('E Zezi Workers Group), who adopted a polemical stance, singing political lyrics and rejecting the 'philological' research of the NCCP (Vacca 1999).

In the 1970s Naples continued to produce jazz-rock. James Senese, together with performers inspired by black music, formed Napoli Centrale, a more mature project than the Showmen, that was influenced by artists like Weather Report and Miles Davis in his rock period. Between 1975 and 1977 Napoli Centrale recorded three albums. In 1976 the band recruited a young bass player who was destined to become the most popular and probably the most innovative Neapolitan musician of the last 50 years, although the really meaningful part of his career lasted little more than 10 years: Pino Daniele. Guitarist, singer and composer, from a poor family from the centre of Naples, Daniele is a key-figure in Neapolitan music. As a poet, the lyrics of his first songs combined the local dialect with American English to create delicate paintings in the tradition of the classic Neapolitan song as well as passages describing the chaotic life of contemporary Naples; as a musician, he managed to integrate foreign musical influences (rock, jazz, blues, funk) with the melodic profile and the harmonic structures of the classic Neapolitan song; as a singer, he had an expressive nasal voice with blues inflections; and as a guitarist, he played both acoustic and electric guitar with equal proficiency. Last but not least, he was symbolic in embodying Neapolitan music at its most ripe, namely in tradition, in the creative assimilation of new trends, with a strong link to the city, and with the ability to attract a national audience without necessarily singing in Italian. Daniele seemed to represent, at that time, the critical consciousness of a new generation of young people who had completely assimilated modernity and who wanted to rescue Naples and the whole of the South from their old conditionings. In contrast to the work of Edoardo Bennato, who was more vague and generic in his protest, Daniele's first songs seemed to mirror more faithfully the massive changes the city and its youth had been through since 1968. In the mid-1970s, for example, Daniele's song 'O mare' echoed the aims of the workers' movement Disoccupati Organizzati [Organised Unemployed], which had broken with the traditional policy of patronage with the political power that the Neapolitan subproletariat had been obliged to accept. His first album, *Terra mia*, was recorded in 1977,[3] while his first big hit, 'Je so' pazzo', appeared a year later. Daniele had clearly felt the creative spirit of 1977, a year which marked another turning point for Italian contemporary society; he also demonstrated his commitment to the more widespread concern regarding pollution (another trend of the time), which he invoked in many of his compositions. In tune with his times, Daniele's work also seemed ingrained in the city's deepest folk culture and in the performing style of the 'posteggiatori'. With Pino Daniele, the classic Neapolitan song ceased to be a problem for Neapolitan musicians: the gap had finally been filled and nobody would ever feel uneasy with it in the future.

The Italian 1980s were the reverse of the 1970s: following the neo-conservative wave started by Ronald Reagan in the US and by Margaret Thatcher in the UK, Italy underwent a long period of '*restoration*'. The defeat of workers at the Fiat automobile factory in Turin, following a month-long struggle against the announced dismissal of almost 15,000 employees, signalled an imploding political situation: the march of a number of white-collar workers (the so-called 'march of the 40,000') in favour of breaking the picket line to re-open the factory meant the acceptance of a change in the relationship between the trade unions and industrialists. In reality change had already taken place inside the factory: automation had reduced the need for large numbers of workers and the conveyor belt production line was progressively being substituted by a new form of

---

[3] In 1977, together with political radicalism, the vindication of private needs emerged from a new generation that refused to distinguish between the public and private sphere in life. This marked an explosion of ideas and practices in which, through countercultures, the languages of the visual avant-gardes of the beginning of the twentieth century penetrated into popular arts: originally utilised in alternative forms of political communication, comics, magazines, cinema and theatre, they are now the common languages of advertising and mass culture.

production where cars would be produced on demand and not on a mass scale for a market that was close to saturation.

At the same time, outside the factory, society was invested with a new ideological trend, that of disengagement: the so called 'anni di piombo' (the 'years of lead', the 1970s, with their deep class conflict and terrorism) were replaced by the 'anni del riflusso' (the 'years of reflux' – the years of individualism – a metaphorical wave rolling back to leave only scattered remnants on the shore). These years, with the development of large commercial television networks, the dismantling of the Welfare State, and an emphasis on personal success, prepared the ground for the most recent Italy – an Italy characterised by the cultural hegemony of an aggressive right wing, which found its undisputed champion in the tycoon-politician Silvio Berlusconi. In this new context countercultures became much less fashionable and were driven back into the distant corners of society (in terms of music, mainly in the post-punk and hardcore circuits). In the 1980s, Naples also saw the explosion of the 'camorra', the Neapolitan mafia, with its transformation from an old illegal asset connected to the smuggling of cigarettes into a modern and perfectly organised criminal holding associated with the trafficking of drugs and the control of public works through collusion with political power (Marrazzo 1984). The climate again became highly conservative, with local politicians supporting the central government and the city pushed into social desertification. Music mirrored the situation: while the rest of Italy turned to disco music, the folk music revival disappeared and the political song became unfashionable. Moreover, little of note emerged from Naples in those years: Bennato abandoned his original acoustic satirical folk rock for a trite early rock and roll with watery lyrics (for example 'Viva la mamma', 1989). In 1992, though, together with the blues band Blue Stuff, he recorded a brilliant and original album under the guise of a bluesman named Joe Sarnataro; the NCCP turned to a simplified world music; Teresa De Sio (former singer with Musicanova) hit success with 'well-made' pop songs; and Daniele concluded his golden years to become what he is now, an 'ecumenical' mainstream pop singer for families and television. The suicide in 1983 of Luciano Cilio, a Neapolitan avant-garde composer, appeared to epitomise the decade, and although some artists of note emerged during the period (Enzo Gragnaniello, Enzo Avitabile, Avion Travel), only the Bisca, an underground rhythm and blues band that began working in the 1980s (and who would later play a notable role in the 1990s), can be said to have been part of an underground scene. In the 1990s, in Naples and across Italy as a whole, the alternative popular music scene became once again stimulating and inspired.

The beginning of globalisation is conventionally located in the period between the fall of the Berlin Wall (1989) and the end of the First Gulf War (1991): both events mark a time when the old division between East and West could be said to have come to a close and the planet was unified under the rule of the International Monetary Fund and the World Bank, the two institutions in charge of universally expanding the laws of capitalism. In Italy, furthermore, the collapse of the Soviet Union caused the dissolution of the Communist Party and its transformation into the PDS (Left Wing Democratic Party), later the DS (Democrats of the Left). The old Christian Democrat politicians, and their allies, the Socialists, were both swept away by enquiries into political corruption made by a pool of judges in Milan. Fearing a possible victory at the elections by the PDS, Berlusconi decided to enter politics, organised his party (Forza Italia) and, with the support of his media empire and his wealth, won election in 1994 (Ginsborg 2003).

Meanwhile, the fragmentation of big factories and the re-allocation of industrial production to faraway countries, where labour costs are less, resulted in growing unemployment and the transformation of what were once working-class areas into wastelands. Abandoned schools, disused cinemas, forsaken buildings, old and derelict slaughterhouses and similar spaces became occupied by people expelled from the processes of production and by immigrants and off-site students to become Centri Sociali Occupati Autogestiti (CSOA), that is, 'Occupied Self-Managed Social Centres' (see Adinolfi et al. 1994; Moroni, Farina and Triopodi 1995; Consorzio Aaster et al. 1996). CSOA activists quickly understood the danger of a right-wing turn with Berlusconi in power, and the places they took possession of were soon transformed into spaces of alternative cultural activity and centres of political antagonism. Thus while occupants of CSOAs were not exactly squatters, it was in such places that aspects of the political radicalism of the 1970s – defeated on the surface of society – managed to survive, and that subcultures and countercultures found new ground to develop. In CSOAs people could drink beer at a reduced price, obtain free legal assistance from militant lawyers, socialise and use digital technology, attend concerts at low prices (roughly 20 per cent of the usual rate or less) and so on. CSOAs were also against copyright and refused to pay the Performing Rights Society for music performed inside their premises (frequently musicians also allowed CSOAs to record their concerts and make records or audio cassettes to sell for support). CSOAs further claimed to boycott multinationals and to fight heavy drugs, which the Italian radical left wing has long argued are an instrument of the establishment aimed at defeating social protest. Originally shunned by the authorities, some CSOAs have managed, with the passing of time, to gain recognition from and be aided by municipalities. Yet, they weren't short of a few contradictions: while Coca-Cola was vehemently banned as a symbol of imperialist capitalism, American cigarettes were welcome.

While the Leoncavallo in Milan is probably the oldest CSOA, dating back to the 1970s, in the 1990s they spread like mushrooms in many of the big cities and in some of the smaller ones too. And it was in such places that the new Italian music of the 1990s was born, and Naples soon turned out to be one of the most important cities for the trend: rejecting the isolated figure of the 'cantautore', young performers active in CSOAs started to join groups they themselves often named 'posse', after the name used by black rappers in America. Rap, ragamuffin and reggae were references for musicians based in CSOAs, many of whom worked with samples and montage.

The most singular peculiarity, though, was a new rediscovery of Italian folk music. With globalisation and the digital revolution, there was also a growth in the circulation of the sounds and traditions of world music: as a genre, however problematic its definition may be, its expansion into the Western world, where most of it (especially music originating in the East) constituted previously unheard music, now made it easier to obtain and drew attention once again to traditional musical idioms. It is probably due to this collateral effect of globalisation that Italian musicians rediscovered local dialects and traditional Italian music: all of a sudden, from North to South, bands, even those inspired by the black American posses, started to develop reggae and ragamuffin sung in local dialects with folk music forms. This new folk music revival was very different from the earlier ones, as now folk music was not the object of philological or critical research but was incorporated into new songs in a manner similar to 'bricolage': sampled, treated electronically or by asking folk musicians to join in. As a consequence, old, long forgotten folk musicians, like the 80-year-old Antonio Sacco or the 70-year-old Uccio Aloisi, both from the Puglia region, became the idols of a new generation of teenagers (with Aloisi singing in CSOAs): in short they became 'stars', just like the old bluesmen like Mississippi John Hurt or Son House had become stars in America in the 1960s.

In Naples, where in the 1990s a new left-wing administration worked to do away with the old politics and start up something different (a process that became known as the 'Neapolitan Renaissance'), two bands were destined to find fame: 99 Posse and Almamegretta. Both made their first appearance in Officina 99, a CSOA established at a deserted works on the periphery of Naples. Officina 99 took its name from the number of the building and 99 Posse was basically the house band. Here, subcultures and counterculture coincided even more than in the 1970s. 99 Posse were involved in political action but also exhibited strong symbolic elements of subcultural styles (Mohawk haircuts, heavy-duty boots, chains and nose rings), while Almamegretta's singer Raiz (bald, muscular, aggressive) adopted full identification with Afro-American culture, quoting Malcolm X and sometimes appearing like a gangsta rapper.[4] In Naples there was no 'rediscovery' of the dialect: for local performers it was absolutely natural to sing in Neapolitan, and it was considered exceptional, or defying and innovative, on the contrary, to sing in Italian (as Edoardo Bennato did); thus it was obvious for 99 Posse and Almamegretta to sing in Neapolitan. 99 Posse aligned themselves with 'operaismo', the political stance of the Italian radical left wing of the 1960s and 1970s: their epoch-making hit 'Curre curre guagliò' (1993) was about a love of CSOAs and the struggle to defend them, while their 'Rigurgito antifascista', from the same album, was a violent call against resurgent fascism.[5] 99 Posse was essentially a rap/ragamuffin band, except when they collaborated with the powerful rhythm and blues band Bisca, who joined them on the successful 'Incredibile Opposizione Tour', a long tour of CSOAs around Italy that resulted in the release of a double album in 1994.

---

[4] Raiz came to encapsulate the culmination of a long history of interest in black music and culture shown by Neapolitan musicians.

[5] Many 99 Posse songs were extremely aggressive and caused reactions (once, even a Parliamentary question). The CSOA movement, in general, has often been accused of being connected to political violence.

The collaboration between Bisca and 99 Posse constituted probably one of the most significant moments of Italian music in the 1990s, although the double disc doesn't quite do justice to the exciting atmosphere of the live shows.

Almamegretta's musical inspiration was more elaborate, taking in references to British trip-hop and the dub scene (Massive Attack, Asian Dub Foundation, Adrian Sherwood). Their ant-racist song 'Figli di Annibale' (1992) imagined Hannibal as a black general coming from Africa, ruling Italy for 20 years with his soldiers and generating the 'bastard' Italian race: although probably far from historical truth, the song was forceful, accompanied as it was by a bass riff that sounded like elephant steps. When 99 Posse and Almamegretta began their careers, the controversial relationship Neapolitan musicians had to the classic Neapolitan song had, as mentioned, already been settled.[6] Yet both groups still found it necessary to address the issue: Almamegretta wrote a couple of new songs in the format of the classic song ('Nun te scurdà', 1995, sung with Giulietta Sacco, a famous singer of Neapolitan song, and 'Pe' dint' 'e viche addò nun trase 'o mare', from the same album, with lyrics written by Salvatore Palomba, a local poet who wrote songs for Sergio Bruni, one of the most prestigious interpreters of the classic song); 99 Posse, on the other hand, furiously anti-American, covered 'Tu vuò fà l'americano', a song written in the 1950s to poke fun at Neapolitan teenagers who followed American fashion at the time. Both 99 Posse and Almamegretta, after an initial period in which they recorded for small and independent labels, decided to sign for majors; both collaborated with Pino Daniele and, accordingly, both achieved lasting enormous notoriety.

'Where have all the flowers gone?' What has happened to almost three generations of Neapolitan musicians? Most of them are still around, often transformed in proportion to the success they achieved. Pino Daniele is still the biggest star, filling theatres wherever he goes but with nothing of his original countercultural strength: his songs have for 20 years been the most hackneyed one can possibly imagine. In 2007, the last time I saw him in concert, on a beach near Rome, the audience was composed mainly of families with prams and children, the set list consisted almost entirely of new songs and the three songs he performed from the old repertoire resembled spaceships landing from another planet. Edoardo Bennato is no longer a rock star: though still active, he is unable to reignite the inspiration that made him so important in the 1970s. Alan Sorrenti, after turning to disco music and hitting the charts in 1977 with 'Figli delle stelle' and in 1979 with 'Tu sei l'unica donna per me' (also translated into English), soon disappeared, following stormy personal events, to reappear from time to time without much success. His sister Jenny, instead, continues to work on projects combining her two roots, English folk and Mediterranean traditions. Osanna have been re-formed with a new line up by the singer-guitarist Lino Vairetti and the support of David Cross (ex-King Crimson). James Senese still plays his angry jazz-rock but his

---

[6] In the early 1990s, even Roberto Murolo, an 80-year-old, long-forgotten singer-guitarist of classic Neapolitan song, was rediscovered and celebrated.

music is not as surprising as it once was. Eugenio Bennato rides the wave of the most recent folk revival, popularising a folk music he himself composes but without much substance. Raiz left Almamegretta but has had little success as a solo artist so far. 99 Posse disbanded in 2005 and reformed in 2011 after the singer underwent drug rehabilitation, but they don't make headlines anymore. Bisca are also alive, still exploring their rhythm and blues and still performing in CSOAs, but they never attract the same size audiences that they had in the 1990s when they toured with 99 Posse.

Countercultures and subcultures are dynamic: they help the stagnant and moribund to get going again, and they have often been the ground on which the market has experienced new trends and obtained new possibilities of expansion (Buxton 1975). In Naples, they had a liberating effect, it having taken three decades for Neapolitan musicians to find their own way into modern song and popular music and, at the same time, to recover Naples' glorious tradition. Countercultures were a powerful aid in the task, acting as a means of emancipation from what had become an ossified repertoire that brought with it a vision of the world that risked causing the city to be cut off from what was happening in Italy and the rest of the world. As such, Neapolitan music has grown in the last 40 years, detaching itself from its parents' hands and starting to walk alone. Today the legacy of the Neapolitan song is no longer an obstacle and a new generation of performers has chosen it as a favourite genre and has even extended its interest to the repertoire from before the 'classic' period (1880–1945): Brunella Selo, for example, or Gianni La Magna, the latter originally a folk musician who has recorded an album (*I Cottrau a Napoli*, 2005) on which he sings the old songs contained in *I Passatempi musicali*. These were a number of music albums containing songs published between 1824 and 1845 by Guillame Cottrau, a musician of French origin who worked in Naples and collected, re-wrote and composed songs mainly for an international market of foreign visitors and aristocrats who came to Naples and wanted to bring back with them mementos of the city.[7]

While musicians rediscover classic songs, the considerable number of scholars attracted to the Neapolitan song means that attitudes towards it have definitely changed and this is certainly very positive, as only through its history can Naples look to its past and better understand its heritage, consciously integrating Neapolitan song with the new sounds of a global music.

---

[7] The work of Guillame Cottrau was continued after his death by his son Teodoro (1827–79). Many of the songs of the 'Passatempi' derived from folk songs or from songs written by artisans of the old city, a repertoire which often circulated on broadsides and which is now largely forgotten, owing to the success of the 'classic' song.

Bibliography

Adams, B., Jardine, L., Maloney, M., Rosenthal, N., Shone, R. and Shand Kydd, J. 1997. *Sensation: Young British Artists from the Saatchi Collection*. Royal Academy of Arts, exhibition catalogue, 18 September–28 December 1997. London: Thames and Hudson.

Adinolfi, F. et al. 1994. *Comunità virtuali I centri sociali in Italia*. Rome: Manifestolibri.

Adorno, T.W. 1984. 'La situation du narrateur dans le roman contemporain', in *Notes sur la littérature*. Paris: Flammarion, 37–43.

———. 1991. 'Culture and Administration', in *The Culture Industry: Selected Essays on Mass Culture*. London: Routledge, 107–31.

———. 1994. 'On Popular Music', in *Cultural Theory and Popular Culture: A Reader*, edited by J. Storey. Hemel Hempstead: Harvester Wheatsheaf, 202–14.

Agnew, J.-C. 1986. *Worlds Apart: The Market and the Theater in Anglo-American Thought, 1550–1750*. Cambridge: Cambridge University Press.

Albiez, S. 2003. 'Know History!: John Lydon, Cultural Capital and the Prog/Punk Dialectic', *Popular Music*, 22(3), 357–74.

Alloway, L. 1974. 'The Development of British Pop', in *Pop Art*, edited by L.R. Lippard. London: Thames and Hudson, 27–66.

Allum, P. 1973. *Politics and Society in Post-War Naples*. Cambridge: Cambridge University Press.

Althusser, L. 1975 [1970]. *Ideologia e apparati ideologici di Stato*. Rome: Editori Riuniti, 65–123.

Anderson, I. 2007. *This Is Our Music: Free Jazz, the Sixties, and American Culture*. Philadelphia, PA: University of Pennsylvania Press.

Anon. 1960. 'Music: Beyond the Cool', *Time*. [Online] Available at: http://www.time.com/time/magazine/article/0,9171,827683-1,00.html [accessed: 14 September 2011].

Anon. 1968a. 'Dim View of Beatles Newest Disc', *Berkeley Barb*, 7(8), 30 August–5 September, 6.

Anon. 1968b. 'Paul, a Raccoon, "Top Hats and Noise!"', *New Musical Express*, 30 November, 3. Reprinted in *The Beatles 1960–1970: NME Originals*, edited by S. Sutherland, 1(1) (2002), 126.

Anon. 1969. 'Rock: The Revolutionary Hype', *Time*, 3 January. [Online] Available at:http://www.time.com/time/magazine/article/0,9171,900514,00.html[accessed: 26 March 2013].

Anon. 1976. 'Billboard's Recommended LPs', *Billboard*, 27 November, 78.

Anon. 2001. *Hair Metal*. Milwaukee, WI: Hal Leonard.

Appadurai, A. 1990. 'Disjuncture and Difference in the Global Cultural Economy', in *Global Culture: Nationalism, Globalisation and Modernity*, edited by M. Featherstone. London: Sage, 295–310.
——. 2000. 'Global Flows: Disjuncture and Difference in the Global Cultural Economy', in *Modernity at Large: Cultural Dimensions of Globalization*. Minneapolis, MN: University of Minnesota Press, 27–47.
Aptheker, B. 2002. 'Gender Politics and the FSM: A Meditation on Women and Freedom of Speech', in *The Free Speech Movement: Reflections on Berkeley in the 1960s*, edited by R. Cohen and R.E. Zelnik. Berkeley, CA: University of California Press, 129–39.
Aquin, S. 2003. 'The 1960's: World Wide Waves', in *Global Village: The 1960's*, edited by S. Aquin. Montreal: Snoeck Publishers, 13–18.
Arnold, G. 1993. *Route 666: On the Road to Nirvana*. New York: St. Martin's Press.
Artieri, G. 1961. *I posteggiatori*. Milano: Longanesi.
Attali, J. 1977. *Bruits: Essai sur l'économie politique de la musique*. Paris: Presses Universitaires de France.
——. 1985. *Noise: The Political Economy of Music*, translated by Brian Massumi. Minneapolis, MN: University of Minnesota Press.
Baddeley, G. 1999. *Lucifer Rising*. London: Plexus.
Baldvig, F. 1982. 'Crime and Criminal Policy in a Pragmatic Society: The Case of Denmark and Christiania, 1960–1975', *International Journal of the Sociology of Law*, 10, 9–25.
Balestrini, N. and Moroni, P. 1997. *L'orda d'oro*. Milano: Felltrinelli.
Balmer, R. 2006. *Thy Kingdom Come: An Evangelical's Lament: How the Religious Right Distorts the Faith and Threatens America*. New York: Basic Books.
Banes, S. 1993. *Greenwich Village 1963: Avant-Garde Performance and the Effervescent Body*. Durham, NC: Duke University Press.
Bangs, L. 1987. *Psychotic Reactions and Carburetor Dung*, edited by Greil Marcus. New York: Vintage Books.
Bannister, M. 2006. *White Boys, White Noise: Masculinities and 1980s Indie Guitar Rock*. Aldershot: Ashgate.
Barber, D. 2008. *A Hard Rain Fell: The SDS and Why It Failed*. Jackson, MI: University Press of Mississippi.
Barrett, E. 2011. *Kristeva Reframed: Interpreting Key Thinkers for the Arts*. London: I.B. Tauris.
Barsam, R.M. 1973. *Nonfiction Film: A Critical History*. New York: Dutton.
Barthes, R. 1964. *Mythen des Alltags*. Frankfurt am Main: Suhrkamp.
——. 2000. *Mythologies*. London: Vintage.
Baudrillard, J. 1981. *For a Critique of the Political Economy of the Sign*. St. Louis, MO: Telos.
——. 2002. *Screened Out*, translated by C. Turner. London and New York: Verso.
Bebbington, D.W. 2005. *The Dominance of Evangelicalism: The Age of Spurgeon and Moody*. Downers Grove, IL: InterVarsity Press.
Becker, H.S. 1982. *Art Worlds*. Berkeley, CA: University of California Press.

Becker, M. 2007. *C'era una volta la RCA. Conversazioni con Lilli Greco*. Rome: Coniglio Editore, 218–26.
Bell, D. (ed.). 1999. *Woodstock: An Inside Look at the Movie That Shook Up the World and Defined a Generation*. New York: Barnes and Noble.
Benjamin, W. 1968. *Illuminations*. New York: Shocken.
———. 1986. *Reflections*: New York: Shocken.
Bennato, E. 2010. *Brigante se more*. Rome: Coniglio Editore.
Bennett, A. 1999. 'Subcultures or Neo-tribes? Rethinking the Relationship between Youth, Style and Musical Taste', *Sociology*, 33(3), 599–617.
———. 2000. *Popular Music and Youth Culture: Music, Identity and Place*. Basingstoke: Palgrave Macmillan.
———. 2001. *Cultures of Popular Music*. Buckingham: Open University Press.
——— (ed.). 2004. *Remembering Woodstock*. Aldershot: Ashgate.
———. 2005. *Culture and Everyday Life*. London: Sage.
———. 2010. 'Popular Music, Cultural Memory and Everyday Aesthetics', in *Philosophical and Cultural Theories of Music*, edited by E. de la Fuente and P. Murphy. Leiden: Brill, 243–62.
———. 2011. 'The Post-Subcultural Turn: Some Reflections Ten Years On', *Journal of Youth Studies*, 14(5), 493–506.
Bennett, G. 2005. *Soft Machine: Out-Bloody-Rageous*. London: SAF Publishing.
Benson, B. 2003. *The Improvisation of Musical Dialogue: A Phenomenology of Music*. Cambridge: Cambridge University Press.
Berardi, F. 2009. *Precarious Rhapsody: Semiocapitalism and the Pathologies of the Post-Alpha Generation*. London: Minor Compositions.
Berman, M. 1982. *All That Is Solid Melts Into Air: The Experience of Modernity*. New York: Simon and Schuster.
Bhabha, H. 1994. *The Location of Culture*. London: Routledge.
Bielefeldt, C., Dahmen U. and Großmann, R. 2007. *PopMusicology: Perspektiven der Popmusikwissenschaft*. Bielefeld: transcript.
Birgy, P. 2012. '"Si cette histoire vous amuse, on peut la recommencer." Le yéyé et l'importation de la contre-culture américaine', *Volume! La revue des musiques populaires*, 9(1), 'Contres-Cultures 1: Théorie et Scènes', edited by S. Whiteley. Nantes: Éditions Mélanie Seteun, 151–67.
Bivens, J. 2008. *Religion of Fear: The Politics of Horror in Conservative Evangelicalism*. New York: Oxford University Press.
Bjelajac, D. 2000. *American Art: A Cultural History*, London: Laurence King.
Blake, A. 1997. *The Land without Music: Music, Culture and Society in Twentieth-century Britain*. Manchester: Manchester University Press.
Bloch, E. 1976. *The Principle of Hope, Vol. 1*. Cambridge, MA, The MIT Press.
Bloomfield, T. 1993. 'Resisting Songs: Negative Dialectics in Pop', *Popular Music*, 12(1), 13–31.
Bockris, V. and Malanga, G. 2003. *Up-Tight: The Velvet Underground Story*. London: Omnibus.

Bolham, P.V. 2002. *World Music: A Very Short Introduction*. New York: Oxford University Press.

Boltanski, L. and Chiapello, E. 1999. *Le nouvel esprit du capitalisme*. Paris: Gallimard.

Bonz, J. 2001. *Sound Signatures: Pop-Splitter*. Frankfurt am Main: Suhrkamp.

Boone, G. 1997. 'Tonal and Expressive Ambiguity in "Dark Star"', in *Understanding Rock: Essays in Musical Analysis*, edited by J. Covach and G.M. Boone. New York: Oxford University Press, 171–210.

Borthwick, S. and Moy, R. 2004. *Popular Music Genres: An Introduction*. New York: Routledge.

Bourdieu, P. 1992. *Les règles de l'art: genèse et structuration du champ littéraire*. Paris: Seuil.

——. 1993. *The Field of Cultural Production*. Oxford: Polity Press-Blackwell.

——. 1994. *Raisons pratiques: sur la théorie de l'action*. Paris: Seuil.

Bourriaud, N. 2005. 'Yoko Ono and Gentle Energy', in *Yoko Ono: Horizontal Memories*, edited by G. Arbu. Oslo: Astrup Museum of Modern Art, 39–46.

Boyd, J. 2007. *White Bicycles: Making Music in the 1960s*. London: Serpents Tail.

Bradbury, M. and Macfarlane, J. 1976. *Modernism: 1890–1930*. Harmondsworth: Penguin Books.

Braudel, F. and Reynolds, S. 1982. *The Wheels of Commerce, Volume II: Civilization and Capitalism, 15th–18th Century*. Vol. 1. New York: Harper & Row.

Braunstein, P. and Doyle, M.W. 2002. *Imagine Nation: The American Counterculture of the 1960s and '70s*. New York: Routledge.

Brautigan, R. 1968. 'All Watched Over', from *The Pill vs. The Springhill Mine Disaster*. New York: Dell.

Breines, W. 2004. 'The Emergence of the New Left', in *The Counterculture Movement of the 1960s*, edited by W. McConnell. San Diego, CA: Greenhaven Press, 32–44.

Buckley, D. 2005. *Strange Fascination: David Bowie – The Definitive Story*. London: Virgin.

Bugliosi, V. with Gentry, C. 1994. *Helter Skelter: The True Story of the Manson Murders*. Second edition. New York: Norton.

Bull, M. 2004. 'Smooth Politics', in *Empire's New Clothes: Reading Hardt and Negri*, edited by P.A. Passavant and J. Dean. New York and London: Routledge, 217–30.

Bürger, P. 1984. *Theory of the Avant-Garde*. Minneapolis, MN: University of Minnesota.

Burke, D. 2011. 'Five Facts about Dominionism', *The Christian Century*. [Online] Available at: http://www.christiancentury.org/article/2011-09/five-facts-about-Dominionism [accessed: 26 March 2013].

Burner, D. 1996. *Making Peace with the 60s*. Princeton, NJ: Princeton University Press.

Buxton, D. 1975. *Le rock: Star-système et société de consommation*. Grenoble: La Pensée Sauvage.

C, Jay. 2007. 'Pauline Kael vs. Gimme Shelter', *Thedocumentaryblog. com*, 10 July. [Online] Available at: http://www.thedocumentaryblog.com/index.php/2007/09/10/pauline-kael-vs-gimme-shelter/ [accessed: 6 July 2008].

Cagle, V.M. 1995. *Reconstructing Pop/Subculture: Art, Rock, and Andy Warhol*. London: Sage.

Cairncross, A. and Cairncross, F. (eds). 1992. *The Legacy of the Golden Age: The 1960s and Their Economic Consequences*. London: Routledge.

Calinescu, M. 1987. *Five Faces of Modernity: Modernism, Avant-garde, Decadence, Kitsch, Postmodernism*. Durham, NC: Duke University.

Campbell, M. and Brody, J. 2008. *Rock and Roll: An Introduction*. Second edition. Belmont: CA, Thomson Schirmer.

Carey, J. 2005. *What Good Are the Arts?* London: Faber.

Cartmel, D., Hunter, I.Q., Kaye, H. and Whelehan, I. (eds). 1997. *Trash Aesthetics: Popular Culture and Its Audience*. London: Pluto Press.

Chambers English Dictionary. 1988. Edinburgh and Cambridge: Chambers.

Chambers, I. 1985. *Urban Rhythms: Pop Music and Popular Culture*. London: Macmillan.

Chaney, D. 1996. *Lifestyles*. London: Routledge.

———. 2002. *Cultural Change and Everyday Life*. Basingstoke: Palgrave.

———. 2004. 'Fragmented Culture and Subcultures', in *After Subculture: Critical Studies in Contemporary Youth Culture*, edited by A. Bennett and K. Kahn-Harris. Basingstoke: Palgrave, 36–48.

Charone, B. 1976. 'Aerosmith: Hammersmith Odeon, London', *Sounds*, 23 October. [Online] Available at: http://www.rocksbackpages.com/article.html?ArticleID=10002 [accessed: 26 March 2013].

Christianias Baggrundsgruppe. 2006. *Oplæg til Christianias egen Udviklingsplan*. Copenhagen: Christiania.

Christianias lokalhistoriske arkiv. [n.d.]. [Online] Available at: http://www.christianiaarkiv.dk [accessed: 29 September 2012].

Clarke, D. (ed.). 1990. *The Penguin Encyclopedia of Popular Music*. London: Penguin.

Clarke, J., Hall, S., Jefferson, T. and Roberts, B. 1976. 'Subcultures, Cultures and Class: A Theoretical Overview', in *Resistance through Rituals: Youth Subcultures in Post-War Britain*, edited by S. Hall and T. Jefferson. London: Hutchinson, 9–74.

———. 1997. 'Subcultures, Cultures and Class', in *The Subcultures Reader*, edited by K. Gelder and S. Thornton. London and New York: Routledge, 100–111.

Clecak, P. 1983. *America's Quest for the Ideal Self: Dissent and Fulfilment in the 60s and 70s*. Oxford: Oxford University Press.

Clover, J. 2009. *1989: Bob Dylan Didn't Have This to Sing About*. Berkeley and Los Angeles, CA, and London: University of California Press.

Cohen, R. 2002. 'The Many Meanings of the FSM', in *The Free Speech Movement: Reflections on Berkeley in the 1960s*, edited by R. Cohen and R. Zelnik. Berkeley, CA: University of California Press, 1–53.

Cohen, S. 2007. *Decline, Renewal and the City in Popular Music Culture: Beyond the Beatles*. Aldershot: Ashgate.

Cohn, N. 1968. 'A Briton Blasts the Beatles', *The New York Times*, 15 December, 7–8.

Conrad, P. 1998. *Modern Times Modern Places: Life and Art in the 20th Century*. London: Thames and Hudson.

Consorzio Aaster/Centro sociale Cox 18, Centro sociale Leoncavallo and P. Moroni. 1996. *Centri sociali: geografie del desiderio*. Milano: Shake.

Cope, A.L. 2010. *Black Sabbath and the Rise of Heavy Metal Music*. Farnham: Ashgate.

Corbin, A. 1994. Les *cloches de la terre*. Paysage sonore et *culture* sensible dans les *campagnes au* XIXe siècle. Paris: Albin Michel.

Croft, J. 1997. 'Youth, Culture, and Age', in *British Cultural Identities*, edited by M. Storry and P. Childs. New York and London: Routledge, 163–98.

Daniele, P. 1994. *Storie e poesie di un mascalzone latino*. Napoli: Pironti.

Danto, A.C. 2005. *Unnatural Wonders: Essays from the Gap between Art and Life*. New York: Farrar, Straus and Giroux.

Davis, M. 2007. 'Notes and Documents: Riot Nights on Sunset Strip', *Labor/Le Travail*. [Online] Available at: http://www.historycooperative.org/journals/llt/59/davis.html [accessed: 16 September 2011].

Davis, R.P. 1979. 'Christiania: Legal and Criminological Issues Arising from Denmark's "Social Experiment"', *The Dalhousie Law Journal*, 5, 791–809.

Debord, G. 2007. 'The Decline and Fall of the Spectacle-Commodity Economy', in *The Situationist International Anthology*, edited by K. Knapp. Berkeley, CA: Bureau of Public Secrets, 194–202.

Debord, G. and Nicholson-Smith, D. 2006. *The Society of the Spectacle*. New York: Zone.

Debray, R. 1979. 'A Modest Contribution to the Rites and Ceremonies of the Tenth Anniversary', *New Left Review*, 1(115) (May–June), 45–65.

DeGroot, G.J. 2008. *The Sixties Unplugged: A Kaleidoscopic History of a Disorderly Decade*. London: Harvard University Press.

DeKoven, M. 2004. *Utopia Limited: The Sixties and the Emergence of the Postmodern*. Durham, NC and London: Duke University Press.

Den Tandt, C. 2004. 'From Craft to Corporate Interfacing: Rock Musicianship in the Era of MTV and Computerized Instruments', *Popular Music and Society*, 27(2), 139–60.

Denning, M. 1987. *Cover Stories: Narrative and Ideology in the British Spy Thriller*. London: Routledge and Kegan Paul.

Des Barres, P. 1987. *I'm with the Band: Confessions of a Groupie*. Chicago, IL: Chicago Review Press.

DeVeaux, S. 1997. *The Birth of Bebop: A Social and Musical History*. Berkeley, CA: University of California.

Dickens, C. 2003. *A Tale of Two Cities*. New York: Toby LLC.

Didion, J. 1979. *The White Album*. New York: Simon and Schuster.

Doyle, M.W. 2002. 'Staging the Revolution: Guerrilla Theatre as a Countercultural Practice. 1965–68', in *Imagine Nation: The American Counterculture of the 1960s and '70s*, edited by P. Braunstein and M.W. Doyle. New York and London: Routledge, 71–98.

Drakeford, J.W. 1972. *Children of Doom: A Sobering Look at the Commune Movement*. Nashville, TN: Broadman Press.

Drenching, T.H.F. 2005. '"Watermelon in Easter Hay": The Function of the Reverb Unit and the Poverty of the Individual Spirit', in *Academy Zappa: Proceedings of the First International Conference of Esemplastic Zappology (ICE-Z)*, edited by B. Watson and E. Leslie. London: SAF Publishing, 89–98.

Dunn, K.C. 2004. '"Know Your Rights!": Punk Rock, Globalization, and Human Rights', in *Popular Music and Human Rights. Volume 1: British and American Music*, edited by I. Peddie. Aldershot: Ashgate, 27–38.

Dunn, T.L. 2004. 'Sovereignty, Multitudes, Absolute Democracy: A Discussion between Thomas L. Dunn and Michael Hardt about Hardt and Negri's *Empire*', in *Empire's New Clothes: Reading Hardt and Negri*, edited by P.A. Passavant and J. Dean. New York and London: Routledge, 163–73.

Durkheim, E. 1915. *The Elementary Forms of Religious Life*. New York: Free Press.

Eagleton, T. 1976. *Marxism and Literary Criticism*. Berkeley, CA: University of California Press.

Easton, P. 1989. 'The Rock Music Community', in *Soviet Youth Culture*, edited by J. Riordan. Bloomington, IN: Indiana University Press, 45–82.

Echaurren, P. and Salaris, C. 1999. *Controcultura in Italia 1967–1977*. Torino: Bollati Boringhieri.

Echols, A., 1999. *Scars of Sweet Paradise: The Life and Times of Janis Joplin*. New York: Henry Holt.

Ehrenreich, B. 2007. *Dancing in the Streets: A History of Collective Joy*. New York: Metropolitan Books.

Ehrlich, P.R. 1975 [1968]. *The Population Bomb*. Rivercity, MA: Rivercity Press.

Elliott, M.C. 1990. *Freedom, Justice, and Christian Counter-Culture*. London: SCM Press.

Erikson, E.H. 1968. *Identity, Youth, and Crisis*. New York: W.W. Norton.

Eshun, K. 1999. *Heller als die Sonne: Abenteuer in der Sonic Fiction*. Berlin: ID-Verlag.

Eskridge, L. 1998. 'One Way: Billy Graham, the Jesus Generation, and the Idea of an Evangelical Youth Culture', *Church History*, 67(1), 83–106.

——. 2005. 'God's Forever Family: The Jesus People Movement in America 1966–1977'. Unpublished dissertation, University of Stirling.

Eyerman, R. and Jamison, A. 1998. *Music and Social Movements: Mobilizing Traditions in the Twentieth Century*. Cambridge: Cambridge University Press.

Featherstone, M. 1991. *Consumer Culture and Postmodernism*. London: Sage.

Fenemore, M. 2007. *Sex, Thugs and Rock'n'Roll: Teenage Rebels in Cold-War East Germany*. New York: Berghahn.

Field, P. 1978. 'Rock Albums', *Gramophone*, March, 114.

Fineberg, J. 2000. *Art Since 1940: Strategies of Being*. London: Laurence King.
Fiske, J. 1994. 'The Popular Economy', in *Cultural Theory and Popular Culture: A Reader*, edited by J. Storey. New York: Harvester Wheatsheaf, 495–512.
Ford, S. 1999. *Wreckers of Civilisation: The Story of COUM Transmissions and Throbbing Gristle*. London: Black Dog.
Foster, H. 1993a. 'Postmodernism: A Preface', in *Postmodern Culture*, edited by H. Foster. London: Pluto Press, vii–xiv.
——. (ed.). 1993b. *Postmodern Culture*. London: Pluto Press.
Frank, R. 2008 [1959]. *The Americans*. Göttingen: Stiedl.
Frith, S. 1981. '"The Magic That Can Set You Free": The Ideology of Folk and the Myth of Rock', *Popular Music*, 1, 159–68.
——. 1983. *Sound Effects: Youth, Leisure and the Politics of Rock*. London: Constable.
——. 1988. *Music for Pleasure: Essays in the Sociology of Pop*. Oxford: Polity Press.
——. 1996. *Performing Rites*. Oxford: Oxford University Press.
Frith, S. and Horne, H. 1987. *Art into Pop*. London: Methuen.
Gaar, G.G. 1992. 'Punk Revolution', in *She's a Rebel: The History of Women in Rock & Roll*. Seattle, WA: Seal Press, 189–225.
Gair, C. 2007. *The American Counterculture*. Edinburgh: Edinburgh University Press.
Galasso, G. 1978. *Intervista sulla storia di Napoli (a cura di Percy Allum)*. Bari: Laterza.
Gans, D. 2002. *Conversations with the Dead: The Grateful Dead Interview Book*. Second edition. New York: Da Capo.
Garcia, J., Reich, C. and Wenner, J. 1972. *Garcia: A Signpost to New Space*. San Francisco, CA: Straight Arrow.
Gendron, B. 2002. *Between Montmartre and the Mudd Club: Popular Music and the Avant Garde*. Chicago, IL: University of Chicago Press.
George-Warren, H. 1995. *Garcia*. Boston, MA: Little, Brown and Company.
Gibson, W. 2010. *Zero History*. London: Penguin Group.
Giddens, A. 1991. *Modernity and Self-identity: Self and Society in the Late Modern Age*. Cambridge: Polity Press.
Giesecke, M. 2006. *Die Entdeckung der kommunikativen Welt – Studien zur kulturvergleichenden Mediengeschichte*. Frankfurt: Suhrkamp.
Gillett, C. 1983. *The Sound of the City: The Rise of Rock and Roll*. New York: Pantheon Books.
Ginsberg, A. 1956. *Howl*. San Francisco, CA: City Lights Books.
Ginsborg, P. 1990. *A History of Contemporary Italy: Society and Politics 1943–1988*. London: Penguin.
——. 2003. *Italy and Its Discontents*. New York: Palgrave Macmillan.
Gitlin, T. 1987. *The Sixties: Years of Hope, Days of Rage*. New York: Bantam Books.
——. 1993. *The Sixties: Years of Hope, Days of Rage*. Revised edition. New York: Bantam Books.
Glanzer, P.L. 2003. 'Christ and the Heavy Metal Subculture: Applying Qualitative Analysis to the Contemporary Debate about H. Richard Niebuhr's *Christ and Culture*', *Journal of Religion and Society* 5, 1–16.

Glass, G. 1992. 'Why Don't We Do It in the Classroom?', in *Present Tense: Rock 'n' Roll and Culture*, edited by A. DeCurtis. Durham, NC: Duke University Press, 93–100.

Gleason, R.J. 1972 [1969]. 'A Cultural Revolution', in *The Sounds of Social Change*, edited by R.S. Denisoff and R.A. Peterson. Chicago, IL: Rand McNally, 137–46.

Goff, P. and Heimert, A. 1998. 'Revivals and Revolution: Historiographic Turns since Alan Heimert's *Religion and the American Mind*', *Church History*, 67(4), 695–721.

Goldstein, S. 1998. 'The Wild One and Gimme Shelter', *National Film Board Registry*. Library of Congress, 10 November. [Online] Available at: http://www.loc.gov/film/goldstein.html [accessed: 10 October 2008].

Goodwin, A. 1993. *Dancing in the Distraction Factory: Music Television and Popular Culture*. London: Routledge.

Gracyk, T. 1996. *Rhythm and Noise: An Aesthetics of Rock*. Durham, NC: Duke University Press.

Gramsci, A. 2007 [1975]. *Quaderni dal carcere*, Vol. III. Torino: Einaudi.

Granata, C.L. 2003. *Wouldn't It Be Nice: Brian Wilson and the Making of the Beach Boys' Pet Sounds*. Chicago, IL: A Cappella Books.

Gray, M. 1994. *Mother: The Frank Zappa Story*. London: Plexus.

Greenfield, R. 1996. *Dark Star: An Oral Biography of Jerry Garcia*. New York: William Morrow and Company.

Grossberg, L. 1983–84. 'The Politics of Youth Culture: Some Observations on Rock and Roll in American Culture', *Social Text*, 8, 104–26.

——. 1984. 'Another Boring Day in Paradise: Rock 'n' Roll and the Empowerment of Everyday Life', *Popular Music*, 4, 225–58.

——. 1992. *We Gotta Get Out of This Place: Popular Conservatism and Postmodern Culture*. New York: Routledge.

Gruber, K. 1997. *L'avanguardia inaudita*. Genova: Costa & Nolan.

Guentcheva, R. 2004. 'Sound and Noise in Socialist Bulgaria', in *Ideologies and National Identities: The Case of 20th Century Southeastern Europe*, edited by J.R. Lampe and M. Mazower. Budapest and New York: CEU Press, 211–34.

Hajdu, D. 2001. *Positively 4th Street: The Life and Times of Joan Baez, Bob Dylan, Mimi Baez Fariña, and Richard Fariña*. New York: Picador.

Hale, J.A. 2002. 'The White Panthers: "Total Assault on the Culture"', in *Imagine Nation: The American Counterculture of the 1960s and '70s*, edited by P. Braunstein and M.W. Doyle. New York and London: Routledge, 125–56.

Hall, S. 1968. *The Hippies: An American 'Moment'*. Birmingham: Centre for Contemporary Cultural Studies, University of Birmingham.

Hall, S. and Jefferson, T. (eds). 1976. *Resistance through Rituals: Youth Subcultures in Post-War Britain*. London: Hutchinson.

Hamelman, S.L. 2004. *But Is It Garbage? On Rock and Trash*. Athens, GA: University of Georgia Press.

Hansen, L. and Gonzalez, N. 2004. *Provos, Drugs and Illusions*. Copenhagen: People's Press.

Hannerz, U. 1996. *Transnational Connections: Culture, People, Places*. London: Routledge.

Hardt, M. and Negri, A. 2001. *Empire*. London and Cambridge, MA: Harvard University Press.

——. 2004. *Multitude: War and Democracy in the Age of Empire*. New York: Penguin.

Harrison, D. 1997. 'After Sundown: The Beach Boys' Experimental Music', in *Understanding Rock: Essays in Musical Analysis*, edited by J. Covach and G.M. Boone. New York: Oxford, 33–57.

Harrison, S. 2001. *Pop Art and the Origins of Post-Modernism*. Cambridge: Cambridge University Press.

Harron, M. 1988. 'McRock: Pop as a Commodity', in *Facing the Music: Essays on Pop, Rock and Culture*, edited by S. Frith. New York: Pantheon, 173–220.

Hart, M., Stevens, J. and Lieberman, F. 1990. *Drumming at the Edge of Magic: A Journey into the Spirit of Percussion*. San Francisco, CA: HarperCollins.

Harvey, D. 2007. *A Brief History of Neoliberalism*. New York: Oxford University Press.

Haslett, M. 2000. *Marxist Literary and Cultural Theories*. New York: St. Martin's Press.

Hassan, I. 1987. *The Postmodern Turn: Essays in Postmodern Theory and Culture*. Columbus, OH: Ohio University Press.

Hatch, N.O. 1989. *The Democratization of American Christianity*. New Haven, CT: Yale University Press.

Hayden, T. 2009. *The Long Sixties: From 1960 to Barack Obama*. Boulder, CO: Paradigm.

Heale, M.J. 2001. *The Sixties in America: History, Politics and Protest*. Chicago, IL and London: Fitzroy Dearborn Publishers.

Hebdige, D. 1979. *Subculture: The Meaning of Style*. London: Methuen-New Accents.

——. 1988. *On Images and Things*. London: Routledge.

Hedvard, Z. [n.d.]. *Christiania mit hjerte*. [Online] Available at: http://www.zofiart.dk/ [accessed: 29 September 2012].

Hegarty, P.M. 2007. *Noise/Music: A History*. New York: Continuum.

Hein, F. 2012. 'Le DIY comme dynamique contre-culturelle? L'exemple de la scène punk rock', *Volume! La revue des musiques populaires*, 9(1), 'Contres-Cultures 1: Théorie et Scènes', edited by S. Whiteley. Nantes: Éditions Mélanie Seteun, 105–26.

Heinrich, Max. 1968. *The Beginning: Berkeley 1964*. New York and London: Columbia University Press.

Hendricks, J. (ed.). 1990. *Yoko Ono: To See the Skies*. Milan: Mazzotta.

Heylin, C. 1991. *Dylan: Behind the Shades*. London: Penguin Books.

Holl, E. 1996. *Die Konstellation Pop: Theorie eines kulturellen Phänomens der 60er Jahre*. Hildesheim: Universität Hildesheim.

Hoskyns, B. 1996. *Waiting for the Sun: Strange Days, Weird Scenes, and the Sound of Los Angeles*. New York: St. Martin's Press.
——. 1997. *Beneath the Diamond Sky: Haight-Ashbury 1965–1970*. London: Bloomsbury.
Howard, J.R. and Streck, J.M. 1999. *Apostles of Rock: The Splintered World of Contemporary Christian Music*. Lexington, KY: University Press of Kentucky.
Hughes, R. 1980. *The Shock of the New*. London: BBC.
Hunter, I.Q. and Kaye, H. 1997. 'Introduction', in *Trash Aesthetics: Popular Culture and Its Audience*, edited by D. Cartmel, I.Q. Hunter, H. Kaye and I. Whelehan. London: Pluto Press, 1–13.
Hunter, R. 1990. *A Box of Rain*. New York: Viking.
Hunter, R., Peters, S., Wills, C., Jackson, B. and Mcnally, D. 2003. *Grateful Dead: The Illustrated Trip*. London: Dorling Kindersley.
Huxley, A. 1954. *The Doors of Perception*. London: Chatto and Windus.
Jacke, C. 2004. *Medien(sub)kultur: Geschichten – Diskurse – Entwürfe*. Bielefeld: transcript.
Jackson, B. 1983. *Grateful Dead: The Music Never Stopped*. New York: Delilah.
Jackson, K.T. 1985. *Crabgrass Frontier: The Suburbanization of the United States*. New York: Oxford University Press.
Jacobs, J. 1961. *The Life and Death of Great American Cities*. New York: Random House.
Jameson, F. 1971. *Marxism and Form: Twentieth-Century Dialectical Theories of Literature*. Princeton, NJ: Princeton University Press.
——. 1990 and 1992. *Signatures of the Visible*. New York: Routledge.
——. 1993. 'Postmodernism and Consumer Society', in *Postmodern Culture*, edited by H. Foster. London: Pluto Press, 111–25.
Janov, A. 1970. *Primal Scream: Primal Therapy: The Cure for Neurosis*. New York: Dell.
——. 1991. *The New Primal Scream: Primal Therapy 20 Years On*. Wilmington, DE: Enterprise Publishing.
Joseph, B.W. 2005. 'My Mind Split Open: Andy Warhol's *Exploding Plastic Inevitable*', in *Summer of Love: Psychedelic Art, Social Crisis and Counterculture in the 1960s*, edited by C. Grunenberg and J. Harris. Liverpool: Liverpool University Press, 239–68.
Junker, D. and Gassert, P. 2004. *The United States and Germany in the Era of the Cold War, 1945–1990*. Cambridge: Cambridge University Press.
Kael, P. 1970. 'Gimme Shelter'. *The New Yorker*, 19 December.
Kaiser, C. 1988. *1968 in America: Music, Politics, Chaos, Counterculture and the Shaping of a Generation*. New York: Grove Press.
Kaiser, M. 1997. *Machtwechsel von Ulbricht zu Honecker: Funktionsmechanismen der SED-Diktatur in Konfliktsituationen 1962 bis 1972*. Berlin: Akademie Verlag.
Kaler, M. 2011. 'How the Grateful Dead Learned to Jam', *Dead Studies*, 1, 93–112.

Keightley, K. 2001. 'Reconsidering Rock', in *The Cambridge Companion to Pop and Rock*, edited by S. Frith, W. Straw and J. Street. Cambridge: Cambridge University Press, 109–42.

Keister, J. and Smith, J.L. 2008. 'Musical Ambition, Cultural Accreditation and the Nasty Side of Progressive Rock', *Popular Music*, 27(3), 433–55.

Keltner, S.K. 2011. *Kristeva: Thresholds*. Cambridge: Polity Press.

Keniston, K. 1968. *Young Radicals: Notes on Committed Youth*. New York: Harcourt, Brace & World.

Kent, N. 1973. Review of the New York Dolls' self-titled debut LP, *New Musical Express*, 25 August. [Online] Available at: http://www.rocksbackpages.com/article.html?ArticleID=10876 [accessed: 6 September 2009].

Kesey, K. 1962. *One Flew over the Cuckoo's Nest*. New York: Viking Press/Signet Books.

Kirk, A.G. 2007. *Counterculture Green: The Whole Earth Catalog and American Environmentalism*. Lawrence, KS: University of Kansas.

Klein, G. 2004. 'Image, Body and Performativity: The Constitution of Subcultural Practice in the Globalized World of Pop', in *The Post-Subcultures Reader*, edited by D. Muggleton and R. Weinzierl. Oxford and New York: Berg, 41–9.

Klitsch, H.-J. 2001. *Shakin' All Over: Die Beatmusik in der Bundesrepublik Deutschland 1963–1967*. Erkrath: High Castle.

Koch, A. and Harris, S. 2009. 'The Sound of Yourself Listening: Faust and the Politics of the Unpolitical', *Popular Music and Society*, 32(5), 579–94.

Koestenbaum, W. 2001. *Andy Warhol*. London: Weidenfeld & Nicholson.

Koons, J. 2009. *Popeye Series*, Serpentine Gallery, London, 2 July–13 September. [Online] Available at: http://www.serpentinegallery.org/2008/06/jeff_koons_popeye_series2_july.html [accessed: 23 March 2012].

Korzilius, S. 2005. *'Asoziale' und 'Parasiten' im Recht der SBZ/ DDR: Arbeiten zur Geschichte des Rechts der DDR*. Cologne: Böhlau.

Kracauer, S. 1981. *Le roman policier: un traité philosophique*. Paris: Petite Bibliothèque Payot.

Krims, A. 2007. *Music and Urban Geography*. New York and London: Routledge.

Kristeva, J. 1974. *Revolution in Poetic Language*, translated by M. Waller. New York: Columbia University Press.

——. 1982 [1980]. *Powers of Horror: An Essay on Abjection*, translated by L.S. Roudiez. New York: Columbia University Press.

Kuspit, D. 2000. *Psychostrategies of Avant-Garde Art*. Cambridge: Cambridge University Press.

Kvaran, G.B. 2005. 'Yoko Ono: Horizontal Memories', in *Yoko Ono: Horizontal Memories*, edited by G. Arbu. Oslo: Astrup Museum of Modern Art, 7–12.

Kvorning, J. 2004. 'Christiania og grænserne i byen', in *Christianias lære*, edited by K. Dirckinck-Holmfeld. Copenhagen: Arkitektens Forlag, 85–91.

La Capria, R. 1986. *L'armonia perduta*. Milano: Mondadori.

Lachman, G. 2001. *Turn Off Your Mind: The Mystic Sixties and the Dark Side of the Age of Aquarius*. London: Sidgwick & Jackson.

Laclau, E. 2004. 'Can Immanence Explain Social Struggle?', in *Empire's New Clothes: Reading Hardt and Negri*, edited by P.A. Passavant and J. Dean. New York and London: Routledge, 21–30.

Laing, D. 1985. *One Chord Wonders: Power and Meaning in Punk Rock*. Philadelphia, PA: Open University Press.

Landau, J. 1972 [1969]. 'Beggars' Banquet', in *Rolling Stones*, edited by D. Dalton. New York: Amsco Music Publishing, 328–31.

Landy, E.E. 1971. *The Underground Dictionary*. London: MacGibbon & Kee.

Lash, S. and Urry, J. 1994. *Economies of Signs and Space*. London: Sage.

Lauritsen, P. 2002. *A Short Guide to Christiania*. Copenhagen: Aschehoug Dansk Forlag A/S.

Le Bon, G. 1897. *The Crowd: A Study of the Popular Mind*. Second edition. New York. Macmillan.

Lee, M. and Simms, H. 2008. 'American Millenarianism and Violence: Origins and Expression', *Journal for the Study of Radicalism* 1(2), 107–27.

Lee, M.A. and Shlain, B. 1985. *Acid Dreams: The Complete Social History of LSD: The CIA, the Sixties, and Beyond*. New York: Grove Press.

Lefebvre, H. 1995. *Introduction to Modernity: Twelve Preludes, September 1959–May 1961*. New York: Verso.

——. 1996. *Writings on Cities*, edited by Elonore Korfman and Elizabeth Lebas. Malden, MA: Blackwell.

Leigh, M. 1963. *The Velvet Underground*. New York: Macfadden Books.

Lescop, G. 2012. 'Skinheads: du Reggae au Rock Against Communism', *Volume! La revue des musiques populaires*, 9(1), 'Contres-Cultures 1: Théorie et Scènes', edited by S. Whiteley. Nantes: Éditions Mélanie Seteun, 129–49.

Lesh, P. 2005. *Searching for the Sound: My Life with the Grateful Dead*. New York: Little, Brown.

Levitz, T. 2005. 'The Unfinished Music of John and Yoko', in *Impossible to Hold: Women and Culture in the 1960's*, edited by A.H. Bloch and L. Umansky. New York and London: New York University Press, 217–39.

Levy, A. 2006. *Female Chauvinist Pigs: Women and the Rise of Raunch Culture*. London: Pocket Books, Simon & Schuster.

Liebing, Y. 2005 *All You Need Is Beat: Jugendsubkultur in Leipzig 1957–1968*. Leipzig: Forum Verlag.

Lindenberger, T. 1995. *Straßenpolitik: Zur Sozialgeschichte der öffentlichen Ordnung in Berlin 1900 bis 1914*. Bonn: Dietz.

——. 2003. *Volkspolizei: Herrschaftspraxis und öffentliche Ordnung im SED-Staat 1952–1968*. Cologne: Böhlau.

Lippard, L.R. (ed.). 1974. *Pop Art*. London: Thames and Hudson.

Livingstone, M. (ed.). 1991a. *Pop Art*, Royal Academy of Arts, exhibition catalogue, 13 September–15 December 1991. London: Weidenfeld & Nicholson.

——. 1991b. 'In Glorious Techniculture', *Pop Art*, Royal Academy of Arts, exhibition catalogue, 13 September–15 December 1991. London: Weidenfeld & Nicholson, 12–19.

Lochhead, J. 2001. 'Hearing Chaos', *American Music*, 19(2), 210–46.
Loppen Christiania. [n.d.]. *Loppen*. [Online] Available at: http://www.loppen.dk/ [accessed: 13 October 2011].
Lowe, K.F. 2006. *The Words and Music of Frank Zappa*. Westport, CT and London: Praeger.
Ludvigsen, J. 1971. 'Emigrer med linie 8', *Hovedbladet*, 39(1), 10–11.
———. 2003. *Christiania: Fristad i fare*. Copenhagen: Ekstar Bladets Forlag.
Luhr, E. 2009. *Witnessing Suburbia: Conservative and Christian Youth Culture*. Berkeley, CA: University of California Press.
Lukács, G. 1971. *History and Class Consciousness: Studies in Marxist Dialectics*. London: Merlin Press.
Lynskey, D. 2011. 'The Monkees' Head: "Our Fans Couldn't Even See It"', *The Guardian*, 28 April.
McCone Report. 1995. 'The Watts Riots', in *Takin' It to the Streets: A Sixties Reader*, edited by A. Bloom and W. Breines. New York: Oxford University Press, 42–51.
MacDonald, I. 1995. *Revolution in the Head: The Beatles' Records and the Sixties*. London: Pimlico.
McDonough, F. 1997. 'Class and Politics', in *British Cultural Identities*, edited by M. Storry and P. Childs. New York and London: Routledge, 201–23.
McGuigan, J. 1992. *Cultural Populism*. London: Routledge.
McKay, G. 1996. *Senseless Acts of Beauty: Cultures of Resistance Since the Sixties*. London: Verso.
Macke, A. 2012. 'Les Taqwacores: émergence d'une contre-subculture américano-musulmane', *Volume! La revue des musiques populaires*, 9(1), 'Contres-Cultures 1: Théorie et Scènes', edited by S. Whiteley. Nantes: Éditions Mélanie Seteun, 85–102.
McNally, D. 2002. *A Long Strange Trip: The Inside History of the Grateful Dead*. New York: Broadway Books.
McNeil, L. and McCain, G. 1997 and 2003. *Please Kill Me: The Uncensored Oral History of Punk*. London: Abacus.
MacPhee, J. and Reuland, E. 2007. *Realizing the Impossible: Art against Authority*. Oakland, CA: AK Press.
McRobbie, A. 2000. *Feminism and Youth Culture*. London: Routledge.
McRobbie, A. and Garber, J. 1976. 'Girls and Subcultures', in *Resistance through Rituals*, edited by S. Hall and T. Jefferson. London: Routledge, 209–22.
———. 1997. 'Girls and Subcultures', in *The Subcultures Reader*, edited by K. Gelder and S. Thornton. London and New York: Routledge, 112–20.
Madoff, S.H. 1997. 'Wham! Blam! How Pop Art Stormed the High-Art Citadel and What the Critics Said', in *Pop Art: A Critical History*, edited by S.H. Madoff. Berkeley, CA: University of California Press, xiii–xx.
Madsen, J.H. [n.d.]. *Den Rullende Opera*. [Online] Available at: http://denrullendeopera.dk/ [accessed: 13 October 2011].
Maffi, M. 2009 [1972]. *La cultura underground*. Bologna: Odoya.

Maharaj, S. 1991. 'Pop Art's Pharmacies: Kitsch, Consumerist Objects and Signs', in *Pop Art*, edited by M. Livingstone, Royal Academy of Arts, exhibition catalogue. London: Weidenfeld & Nicholson, 20–29.

Malvini, D. 2007. '"Now Is the Time Past Believing": Concealment, Ritual, and Death in the Grateful Dead's Approach to Improvisation', in *All Graceful Instruments: The Contexts of the Grateful Dead Phenomenon*, edited by N. Meriwether. Newcastle. Cambridge Scholars Publishing, 1–18.

Mandel, E. 1986. *Meurtres exquis: histoire sociale du roman policier*. Montreuil: PEC.

Mann, P. 1991. *The Theory-Death of the Avant-Garde*. Bloomington, IN: Indiana University Press.

Mann, W. 1987. 'The New Beatles' Album', in *The Lennon Companion: Twenty-Five Years of Comment*, edited by E. Thompson and D. Gutman. Basingstoke and London: Macmillan, 152–4 [original *The Times*, 22 November 1968].

Marcus, G. 1989. *Lipstick Traces: A Secret History of the Twentieth Century*. Cambridge, MA: Harvard University Press.

——. 1993. *Ranters and Crowd Pleasers: Punk in Pop Music, 1977–92*. New York: Anchor Books.

——. 1997. *Lipstick Traces: A Secret History of the Twentieth Century*. London: Picador.

Marcuse, H. 1973. *An Essay on Liberation*. Harmondsworth: Penguin Press.

Marengo, R.M. 1974. Untitled article published in E. Bennato, *Dirotterotti*. Rome: Edizioni Modulo Uno, 1979. From an article originally included in the magazine *Ciao 2001*. No page numbers given.

Marrazzo, G. 1984. *Il camorrista*. Napoli: Pironti.

Martinussen, N. 2007. *'Jensen på sporet' Christianiaopera 1976*. [Online] Available at: http://home6.inet.tele.dk/niels_ma/acv/ncv008.htm [accessed: 2 March 2009].

Marx, K. and Engels, F. 1998. *The Communist Manifesto: A Modern Edition*. New York: Verso.

Mason, N. 2005. *Inside Out: A Personal History of Pink Floyd*. San Francisco, CA: Chronicle Books.

Matheu, R. 2009. *The Stooges: The Authorized History and Illustrated Story*. New York: Abrams.

Medhurst, A. 1997. 'Negotiating the Gnome Zone: Versions of Suburbia in British Popular Culture', in *Visions of Suburbia*, edited by R. Silverstone. London and New York: Routledge, 240–68.

Meriwether, N. 2007. *All Graceful Instruments: The Contexts of the Grateful Dead Phenomenon*. Newcastle: Cambridge Scholars Publishing.

Middleton, R. 2000. *Reading Pop: Approaches to Textual Analysis in Popular Music*. Oxford: Oxford University Press.

Miles, B. 1968. 'Multi-Purpose Beatle Music'. *IT*, 45 (29 November–12 December), 10.

——. 1997. *Paul McCartney: Many Years from Now*. London: Secker & Warburg.

——. 2004. *Frank Zappa*. London: Atlantic Books.
Miles, S. 2000. *Youth Lifestyles in a Changing World*. Buckingham: Open University Press.
Miller, D.E. 1999. *Reinventing American Protestantism: Christianity in the New Millennium*. Berkeley, CA: University of California Press.
Miller, T. 1999. *The 60s Communes: Hippies and Beyond*. Syracuse, NY: Syracuse University Press.
——. 2002. 'The Sixties-Era Communes', in *Imagine Nation: The American Counterculture of the 1960s and 70s*, edited by P. Braunstein and M.W. Doyle. London: Routledge, 327–52.
Monson, I. 1967. *Saying Something: Jazz Improvisation and Interaction*. Chicago, IL: University of Chicago Press.
Moore, A. 2002. 'Authenticity as Authentication', *Popular Music*, 21(2), 209–23.
Morat, D., Bartlitz, C. and Kirsch, J.-H. 2011. 'Politics and Culture of Sound in the Twentieth Century', *Zeithistorische Forschungen/Studies in Contemporary History*, 8(2). [Online] Available at: http://www.zeithistorische-forschungen.de/16126041-Inhalt-2-2011 [accessed: 21 March 2012].
Moroni, P., Farina, D. and Tripodi, P. (eds). 1995. *Centri sociali: che impresa!* Rome: Castelvecchi.
Mueller, C. 2008. 'The Music of the Goth Subculture: Postmodernism and Aesthetics'. PhD dissertation, Florida State University.
Muggleton, D. 2000. *Inside Subculture: The Postmodern Meaning of Style*. Oxford: Berg.
Muggleton, D. and Weinzierl, R. 2004. *The Post-Subcultures Reader*. Oxford: Berg.
Muldoon, R. 1968. 'Subculture: The Street-Fighting Pop Group', *Black Dwarf*, 13(6) (15 October), 8.
Müller, J. 2011. 'The Sound of Silence: Von der Unhörbarkeit der Vergangenheit zur Geschichte des Hörens', *Historische Zeitschrift*, 292(1), 1–29.
Müller, W. 1961. 'Der Jazz Saloon und seine Folgen', *Deutsche jugend. Zeitschrift für Jugendfragen und Jugendarbeit*, 9(4), 162–7.
Munroe, A. 2000. 'The Spirit of YES: The Art and Life of Yoko Ono', in *Yes: Yoko Ono*, edited by A. Munroe and J. Hendricks. New York: Japan Society and Harry N. Abrams, 10–37.
Negri, A. 2005 [1989]. *The Politics of Subversion: A Manifesto for the Twenty-First Century*. Cambridge: Polity.
Neville, R. 1971. *Play Power*. London: Paladin.
Nielsen, K.P. 1985 (repr. 2004). *Christiania Sange af Tage Morten*. Christiania: Christiania.
Nietzsche, F. 1954a. *Thus Spoke Zarathustra*, in *The Portable Nietzsche*, edited and translated by W. Kaufmann. New York: Viking.
——. 1954b. *Twilight of the Idols*, in *The Portable Nietzsche*, edited and translated by W. Kaufmann. New York: Viking.
——. 1966a. *The Birth of Tragedy*, in *Basic Writings of Nietzsche*, edited and translated by W. Kaufmann. New York: Random House.

——. 1966b. *Ecce Homo*, in *Basic Writings of Nietzsche*, edited and translated by translated by W. Kaufmann. New York: Random House.

——. 1967. *On the Genealogy of Morals*, translated by W. Kaufmann and R.J. Hollingdale. New York: Random House.

Nimmermann, P. 1966. 'Beat und Beatlokale in Berlin', *Deutsche jugend. Zeitschrift für Jugendfragen und Jugendarbeit*, 14(11), 495–504.

Nutall, J. 1970 [1968]. *Bomb Culture*. London: HarperCollins.

Ohse, M.-D. 2003. *Jugend nach dem Mauerbau: Anpassung, Protest und Eigensinn (DDR 1961–1974)*. Berlin: Ch. Links.

Oldfield, D.M. 1996. *The Right and the Righteous: The Christian Right Confronts the Republican Party*. Lanham, MD: Rowman & Littlefield.

——. 1992. 'Preface', in *She's a Rebel: The History of Women in Rock & Roll*, by Gillian G. Gaar. Seattle, WA: Seal Press, xiii–xiv.

——. 2005. 'Horizontal Memories', in *Yoko Ono: Horizontal Memories*, edited by G. Arbu. Oslo: Astrup Museum of Modern Art, 125–32.

Palmer, T. 1968. 'The Beatles' Bulls-eye', sleeve notes to *Yellow Submarine* by the Beatles, Apple Records.

Passavant, P.A. 2004a. 'Postmodern Republicanism', in *Empire's New Clothes: Reading Hardt and Negri*, edited by P.A. Passavant and J. Dean. New York and London: Routledge, 1–20.

——. 2004b. 'From Empire's Law to Multitude's Rights: Law, Representation and Revolution', in *Empire's New Clothes: Reading Hardt and Negri*, edited by P.A. Passavant and J. Dean. New York and London: Routledge, 95–119.

Perry, C. 1984. *The Haight-Ashbury: A History*. New York: Random House.

Peterson, R. and Berger, D. 1990. 'Cycles in Symbol Production: The Case of Popular Music', in *On Record: Rock, Pop and the Written Word*, edited by S. Frith and A. Goodwin. London: Routledge, 140–59.

Picker, J.M. 2003. *Victorian Soundscape*. Oxford and New York: Oxford University Press.

Poiger, U.G. 2000. *Jazz, Rock and Rebels: Cold War Politics and American Culture in a Divided Germany*. Berkeley, CA: University of California Press.

Powell, M.A. 2002. *The Encyclopedia of Contemporary Christian Music*. Peabody, MA: Hendrickson Publishers.

Prato, P. 2010. *La musica italiana*. Rome: Donzelli.

Pratt, R. 1990. *Rhythm and Resistance: The Political Uses of American Popular Music*. Washington, DC: Smithsonian Institution Press.

Pressing, J. 1988. 'Improvisation: Method and Models', in *Generative Processes in Music: The Psychology of Performance, Improvisation, and Composition*, edited by J.A. Sloboda. Oxford: Clarendon Press, 129–78.

Putnam, R.D. 2000. *Bowling Alone: The Collapse and Revival of American Community*. New York: Simon & Schuster.

Rauhut, M. 1993. *Beat in der Grauzone: DDR-Rock 1964 bis 1972 – Politik und Alltag*. Berlin: Basisdruck.

——. 2008. *Rock in der DDR 1964 bis 1989*. Bonn: Bundeszentrale für politische Bildung.
Redhead, S. 1990. *The End-of-the-Century Party: Youth and Pop Towards 2000*. Manchester: Manchester University Press.
Reich, C.A. 1971. *The Greening of America*. Harmondsworth: Allen Lane.
Reid, J. 1987. *Up They Rise: The Incomplete Works of Jamie Reid*. London: Faber and Faber.
Reimer, B. 1995. 'Youth and Modern Lifestyles', in *Youth Cultures in Late Modernity*, edited by J. Fornas and G. Bolin. London: Sage, 76–92.
Reising, R. 2009. 'Melting Clocks and the Hallways of Always: Time in Psychedelic Music', *Popular Music and Society*, 32(4), 523–47.
Reynolds, S. 2005. *Rip It Up and Start Again: Postpunk 1978–1984*. New York: Penguin.
Reynolds, S. and Press, J. 1995. *The Sex Revolts: Gender, Rebellion, and Rock 'n' Roll*. Cambridge, MA: Harvard University Press.
Riesman, D. 1950. *The Lonely Crowd: A Study of the Changing American Character*. New Haven, CT: Yale University Press.
Rifkin, A. 1993. Street Noises: Parisian Pleasures 1900–40. Manchester: Manchester University Press.
Roberts, R.E. 1971. *The New Communes: Coming Together in America*. Englewood Cliffs, NJ: Prentice-Hall.
Robinson, M.F. 1972. *Naples and Neapolitan Opera*: Oxford: Oxford University Press.
Rockwell, J. 1982. 'Rock and Avant-Garde: John and Yoko's Record Collaborations', in *The Ballad of John and Yoko*, edited by J. Cott and C. Doudna. New York: Rolling Stone/Doubleday/Dolphin, 272–7.
Rogers, N. 1998. *Crowds, Culture, and Politics in Georgian Britain*. Oxford: Clarendon.
Rosenberg, H. 1972. *The De-definition of Art: Action Art to Pop to Earthworks*. New York: Horizon Press.
Rossinow, D. 1998. *The Politics of Authenticity: Liberalism, Christianity, and the New Left in America*. New York: Columbia University Press.
——. 2002. 'The Revolution Is about Our Lives', in *Imagine Nation: The American Counterculture of the 1960s and '70s*, edited by P. Braunstein and M.W. Doyle. New York and London: Routledge, 99–124.
Roszak, T. 1970 [1969]. *The Making of a Counter Culture: Reflections on the Technocratic Society and Its Youthful Opposition*. London: Faber and Faber.
Rotundo, A. 1993. *American Manhood: Transformations of Masculinity from the Revolution to the Modern Era*. New York: HarperCollins.
Rowe, D. 1995. *Popular Cultures: Rock Music, Sport and the Politics of Pleasure*. London: Sage.
Russell, E.A. with Van der Leun, G. 2009. *Let It Bleed: The Rolling Stones, Altamont, and the End of the Sixties*. New York: Springboard Press.
Salaris, C. 1997. *Il movimento del settantasette*. Bertiolo: AAA Edizioni.

Sandbrook, D. 2006. *White Heat: A History of Britain in the Swinging Sixties*. London: Little Brown.
Sassen, S. 2004. 'The Repositioning of Citizenship: Emergent Subjects and Spaces for Politics', in *Empire's New Clothes: Reading Hardt and Negri*, edited by P.A. Passavant and J. Dean. New York and London: Routledge, 177–201.
Saunders, D. 2007. *Direct Cinema: Observational Documentary and the Politics of the Sixties*. London: Wallflower Press.
Savage, J. 1991. *England's Dreaming: Sex Pistols and Punk Rock*. London: Faber and Faber.
Scaduto, A. 1975. *Mick Jagger*. Frogmore, St Albans: Mayflower Books.
Schaeffer, F. 2009. 'The Only Thing Evangelicals Will Never Forgive Is Not Hating the "Other"', *Religion Dispatches*. [Online] Available at: http://www.religiondispatches.org/archive/rdbook/2097/the_only_thing_evangelicals_will_never_forgive_is_not_hating_the_%E2%80%9Cother%E2%80%9D/?page=2 [accessed: 29 March 2013].
Schafer, R.M. 1973. 'The Music of the Environment', *Cultures*, 1(1), 15–52.
——. 1977. The Tuning of the World. New York: Knopf.
Schaffner, N. 1978. *The Beatles Forever*. New York: McGraw-Hill.
Schreck, N. (ed.). 1988. *The Manson File*. New York: Amok Press.
Schuster, U. 1994. 'Die SED-Jugendkommuniqués von 1961 und 1963, Anmerkungen zur ostdeutschen Jugendpolitik vor und nach dem Mauerbau', in *Jahrbuch für zeitgeschichtliche Jugendforschung 1994/1995*. Berlin: Metropol, 58–75.
Schweighauser, P. 2006. The Noises of American Literature 1890–1985: Towards a History of Literary Acoustics. Miami, FL: University of Florida Press.
Scott, J.W., Dolgushkin, M. and Nixon, S. 1999. *Deadbase XI: The Complete Guide to Grateful Dead Song Lists*. Cornish, NH: Deadbase.
Sculatti, G. 2005. 'The Acid Test', booklet notes to *The Acid Test*, CD, Acadia/Evangeline Records, ACAX 500.
Shapiro, P. 2005. *Turn the Beat Around: The Secret History of Disco*. London: Faber and Faber.
Shires, P. 2007. *Hippies of the Religious Right*. Waco, TX: Baylor University Press.
Showalter, D.F. 2000. 'Remembering the Dangers of Rock and Roll: Toward a Historical Narrative of the Rock Festival', *Critical Studies in Media Communication* 17(1), 86–102.
Shumway, D. 1990. Rock & Roll as a Cultural Practice, in *Present Tense: Rock 'n' Roll and Culture*, edited by A. DeCurtis. Durham, NC: Duke University Press, 116–33.
Silverstone, R. (ed.). 1997. *Visions of Suburbia*. London and New York: Routledge.
Simon, R.K. 1999. *Trash Culture: Popular Culture and the Great Tradition*. Berkeley and Los Angeles, CA: University of California Press.
Sinclair, J. 1995. 'Rock and Roll Is a Weapon of Cultural Revolution', in *Takin' It to the Streets: A Sixties Reader*, edited by A. Bloom and W. Breines. New York: Oxford University Press, 301–3.

Sjöholm, C. 2005. *Kristeva and the Political*. New York: Routledge.
Sklower, J. 2006. *Free Jazz, la catastrophe féconde. Une histoire du monde éclaté du jazz en France (1960–1982)*. Paris: L'Harmattan.
——. 2008. 'Rebel with the Wrong Cause: Albert Ayler et la Signification du Free Jazz en France', *Volume! La revue des musiques populaires*, 6(1–2). Nantes: Éditions Mélanie Seteun, 193–219.
Slater, P.E. 1970. *The Pursuit of Loneliness: American Culture at the Breaking Point*. Boston, MA: Beacon Press.
Smith, A. 1968. 'God Bless You Beatles', *New Musical Express*, 9 November, 3 and 5. Reprinted in *The Beatles 1960–1970: NME Originals*, edited by S. Sutherland, 1(1) (2002), 124–5.
Smith, M.M. 2001. Listening to Nineteenth-Century America. Chapel Hill, NC: University of North Carolina Press.
——. 2008. Sensing the Past: Seeing, Hearing, Smelling, Tasting, and Touching in History. Berkeley, CA: University of California Press.
Smith, P. 2010. *Just Kids*. London: Bloomsbury.
Sontag, S. 1964. 'Notes on "Camp"', *Partisan Review*, 31, 515–30. [Online] Available at: http://www9.georgetown.edu/faculty/irvinem/theory/sontag-notesoncamp-1964.html [accessed: 29 July 2011].
——. 2005 [1966]. 'One Culture and the New Sensibility', in *Against Interpretation and Other Essays*. Ueland: Hanne Beate, 293–304.
Spalding, J. 2012. 'Damien Hirsts are the Sub-prime of the Art World', *The Independent*. [Online] Available at: http://www.independent.co.uk/opinion/commentators/julian-spalding-damien-hirsts-are-the-subprime-of-the-art-world-7586386.html [accessed: 27 March 2012].
Spector, S. 2009. 'How the Music Played the Band: Grateful Dead Improvisation and Merleau-Ponty', in *Dead Letters Volume 4*, edited by N. Meriwether. Columbia, SC: Dead Letters Press, 195–205.
——. 2010. 'When "Reason Tatters": Nietzsche and the Grateful Dead on Living a Healthy Life', in *The Grateful Dead in Concert: Essays on Live Improvisation*, edited by J. Tuedio and S. Spector. Jefferson, NC: McFarland and Company, 180–90.
Spitz, B. 2005. *The Beatles: The Biography*. New York: Little, Brown and Company.
Sragow, M. 2000. 'Gimme Shelter: The True Story', *Salon.com*, 10 August. [Online] Available at: http://www.salon.com/2000/08/10/gimme_shelter_2/ [accessed: 26 March 2013].
Stahl, H. 2009. 'Musikpolitik im geteilten Berlin – Die Aushandlungen des Hörfunksound und die Einarbeitungen von Popmusik 1962 bis 1973', in *Heißer Sommer – Coole Beats: Zur Popmusik in der DDR und ihren medialen Repräsentationen*, edited by S. Trültzsch and T. Wilke. Frankfurt am Main: Peter-Lang, 159–78.
——. 2010. Jugendradio im Kalten Ätherkrieg. Berlin als eine Klanglandschaft des Pop (1962–1973). Berlin: Landbeck.

Stannard, N. 1983. *The Long and Winding Road: A History of the Beatles on Record*. London: Virgin Books.
Stansell, C. 2000. *American Moderns: Bohemian New York and the Creation of a New Century*. New York: Metropolitan Books.
Stapleton, S. 2001. 'A Little History', booklet notes to *Chance Meeting on a Dissecting Table of a Sewing Machine and an Umbrella* by Nurse with Wound, CD, World Serpent/United Dairies NWW 1.
Stazio, M.L. 1991. *Osolemio*. Rome: Bulzoni.
Storey, J. 1998. 'Postmodernism and Popular Culture', in *The Icon Critical Dictionary of Postmodern Thought*, edited by S. Sim. Cambridge: Icon, 147–57.
Stowe, D. 1994. *Swing Changes: Big-Band Jazz in New Deal America*. Cambridge, MA: Harvard University Press.
———. 2011. *No Sympathy for the Devil: Christian Pop Music and the Transformation of American Evangelicalism*. Chapel Hill, NC: University of North Carolina Press.
Sundberg, J. 1991. *The Science of Musical Sounds*. San Diego, CA: Academic Press.
Svede, M.A. 2000. 'All You Need Is Lovebeads: Latvia's Hippies Undress for Success', in *Style and Socialism: Modernity and Material Culture in Post-War Eastern Europe*, edited by S.E. Reid and D. Crowley. Oxford: Berg, 189–208.
Swiss, T., Sloop, J. and Herman, A. 1998. *Mapping the Beat: Popular Music and Contemporary Theory*. Malden, MA: Blackwell.
Taylor, N. 2010. *Documents and Eyewitnesses: An Intimate History of Rough Trade*. London: Orion Books.
Teti, V. 1993. *La razza maledetta*. Rome: Manifestolibri.
'The Alternative Jesus: Psychedelic Christ', *Time*, 21 June 1971. [Online] Available at:http://www.time.com/time/magazine/article/0,9171,905202,00.html[accessed: 26 March 2013].
Théberge, P. 1991. 'Musicians' Magazines in the 1980s: The Creation of a Community and a Consumer Market', *Cultural Studies*, 5(3), 270–93.
Thompson, D. 2009. *Your Pretty Face Is Going to Hell: The Dangerous Glitter of David Bowie, Iggy Pop and Lou Reed*. Milwaukee, WI: Backbeat Books.
Thompson, E. 2002. The Soundscape of Modernity: Architectural Acoustics and the Culture of Listening in America, 1900–1933. Cambridge, MA: The MIT Press.
Thompson, H.S. 1993 [1971]. *Fear and Loathing in Las Vegas*. London: Flamingo.
Thorgerson, S. and Powell, A. 1999. *100 Best Album Covers*. London: Dorling Kindersley.
Thornton, S. 1996. *Club Cultures: Music, Media, and Subcultural Capital*. Hanover: University Press of New England.
Thrills, A. 1978. 'Complete Control: Siouxsie in Wonderland', *New Musical Express*, 24 June.
Tiber, E. and Monte, T. 2007. *Taking Woodstock*. Garden City Park, NY: Square One.
Tonooka, T. 2011 [1981]. 'Black Flag: Interview' in *Ripper*, in *White Riot: Punk Rock and the Politics of Race*, edited by S. Duncombe and M. Tremblay. London: Verso, 75–7 [original *Ripper*, 6, 1981].

Tronti, M. 2009. *Noi operaisti*. Rome: Derive Approdi.
Tuedio, J. and Spector, S. 2010. *The Grateful Dead in Concert: Essays on Live Improvisation*. Jefferson, NC: McFarland and Company.
Turner, F. 2006. *From Counterculture to Cyberculture: Stewart Brand, the Whole Earth Network, and the Rise of Digital Utopianism*. Chicago, IL: University of Chicago Press.
Udo, T. 2002. *Charles Manson: Music, Mayhem, Murder*. London: Sanctuary.
Vacca, G. 1999. *Il Vesuvio nel motore*. Rome: Manifestolibri.
———. 2008. 'Canzone e mutazione urbanistica', in *Studi sulla canzone napoletana classica*, edited by E. Careri and P. Scialò. Lucca: Lim 431–47. [Online] Available at: www.giovannivacca.com [accessed: 10 March 2013].
van Dijck, J. 2007. *Mediated Memories in the Digital Age*. Stanford, CA: Stanford University Press.
van Donselaar, J. 1993. 'The Cult of Violence: The Swedish Racist Counterculture', in Racist Violence in Europe, edited by T. Bjorgo and R. Witte. New York: St Martin's Press, 62–79.
Vesterberg, H. 2007. 'Sangene Kan de Ikke Slå i Hjel', *Politiken*, 13(7), 14–15.
Waksman, S. 1998. 'Kick Out the Jams!: The MC5 and the Politics of Noise', in *Mapping the Beat: Popular Music and Contemporary Theory*, edited by T. Swiss, J. Sloop and A. Herman. Malden, MA: Blackwell, 47–75.
Walley, D. 1972. *No Commercial Potential: The Saga of Frank Zappa and the Mothers of Invention*. New York: Dutton-Sunrise.
Walser, R. 1993. *Running with the Devil: Power, Gender and Madness in Heavy Metal Music*. Hanover, NH: Wesleyan University Press.
Watson, B. 1993. *Frank Zappa: The Negative Dialectics of Poodle Play*. London: Quartet Books.
———. 1997. 'Frank Zappa as Dadaist: Recording Technology and the Power to Repeat', in *The Frank Zappa Companion*, edited by R. Kostelanetz. New York: Schirmer Books, 151–90.
Watson, B. and Leslie, E. (eds). 2005. *Academy Zappa: Proceedings of the First International Conference of Esemplastic Zappology*. London: SAF Publishing.
Watson, S. 1995. *The Birth of the Beat Generation: Visionaries, Rebels, and Hipsters 1944–1960*. New York: Pantheon.
———. 2003. *Factory Made: Warhol and the Sixties*. New York: Pantheon.
Watts, A. 1962. *The Joyous Cosmology*. New York: Pantheon.
Webster, C. 1976. 'Communes: A Thematic Typology', in *Resistance through Rituals: Youth Subcultures in Post-War Britain*, edited by S. Hall and T. Jefferson. London: Hutchinson, 127–34.
Weinstein, D. 1991. *Heavy Metal: A Cultural Sociology*. New York: Lexington Books.
———. 1998. 'The History of Rock's Pasts through Rock Covers', in *Mapping the Beat: Popular Music and Contemporary Theory*, edited by T. Swiss, J. Sloop and A. Herman. Oxford: Blackwell, 137–51.

——. 2000. *Heavy Metal: The Music and Its Culture*. Revised edition. Cambridge: MA: Da Capo Press.
Wenner, J. 1968. 'Beatles', *Rolling Stone*, 24 (21 December), 10–13.
——. 2000. *Lennon Remembers*. London and New York: Verso.
White, E. 1986 [1980]. *States of Desire: Travels in Gay America*. Picador: London.
Whiteley, S. 1992. *The Space between the Notes: Rock and the Counterculture*. London: Routledge.
——. 1997a. 'Introduction', in *Sexing the Groove: Popular Music and Gender*, edited by S. Whiteley. London: Routledge, xiii–xxxv.
——. 1997b. *Sexing the Groove: Popular Music and Gender*. London: Routledge.
——. 2000. *Women and Popular Music: Sexuality, Identity and Subjectivity*. London: Routledge.
——. (ed.). 2012a. *Volume! La revue des musiques populaires*, 9(2), 'Contres-Cultures 2: Théorie et Scènes'. Nantes: Éditions Mélanie Seteun.
——. (ed.). 2012b. *Volume! La revue des musiques populaires*, 9(2), 'Contres-Cultures 2: Utopies, Dystopies, Anarchie'. Nantes: Éditions Mélanie Seteun.
——. 2012c. '*Electric Ladyland*: And the Gods Made Love'. *Volume! La revue des musiques populaires*, 9(2). Nantes: Éditions Mélanie Seteun, 163–75.
——. 2013. 'Kick Out the Jams: Creative Anarchy and Noise in 1960s Rock', in *Resonances: Noise and Contemporary Music*, edited by N. Spelman. New York: Continuum, 13–23.
Wiener, J. 1995. *Come Together: John Lennon in His Time*. London: Faber and Faber.
——. 1998. 'Pop and Avant-Garde: The Case of John and Yoko', *Popular Music and Society*, 22(1), 1–16.
Wierling, D. 2008. 'Youth as Internal Enemy: Conflicts in the Education Dictatorship of the 1960s', in *Socialist Modern: East German Everyday Culture and Politics*, edited by K. Pence and P. Betts. Ann Arbor, MI: University of Michigan Press, 157–82.
Williams, R. 1983. *Keywords: A Vocabulary of Culture and Society*. Revised edition. New York: Oxford University Press.
Williams, R. 2009. *The Blue Moment: Miles Davis's* Kind of Blue *and the Remaking of Modern Music*. London: Faber.
Willis, E. 1996. 'Velvet Underground', in *Stranded: Rock and Roll for a Desert Island*, edited by G. Marcus. New York: Da Capo Press, 71–83.
Willis, P. 1978. *Profane Culture*. London: Routledge and Kegan Paul.
Winner, L. 2007. 'Trout Mask Replica', in *Stranded: Rock and Roll for a Deserted Island*, edited by G. Marcus. New York: Da Capo, 58–70.
Wolfe, T. 1968. *The Electric Kool-Aid Acid Test*. New York: Bantam Books.
Woo, J.A. 2006. 'The Post-War Art of On Kawara and Yoko Ono: As If Nothing Happened. Doctoral dissertation, University of California Los Angeles.
Wright, S. 2002. *Storming Heaven: Class Composition and Struggle in Italian Autonomist Marxism*. London: Pluto Press.

Wright, W. 1975. *Sixguns and Society: A Structural Study of the Western*. Berkeley, CA: University of California Press.

Yoshimoto, M. 2005. *Into Performance: Japanese Women Artists in New York*. New Brunswick, NJ and London: Rutgers University Press.

Young, S. 2011. 'Jesus People U.S.A., the Christian Woodstock, and Conflicting Worlds: Political, Theological, and Musical Evolution, 1972–2010'. Unpublished PhD dissertation. Michigan State University.

Zappa, F. 1966. Liner notes to *Freak Out!* by The Mothers of Invention, MGM Records.

Zappa, F. and Occhiogrosso, P. 1989. *The Real Frank Zappa Book*. London: Picador.

Žižek, S. 2004. 'The Ideology of Empire and Its Traps', in *Empire's New Clothes: Reading Hardt and Negri*, edited by P.A. Passavant and J. Dean. New York and London: Routledge, 253–64.

Discography

Aerosmith. 1991. *Pandora's Box*. Columbia.
Alice Cooper. 1972. 'School's Out'. Warner Bros.
Alice Donut. 1994. *Dry Humping the Cash Cow (Live at CBGB)*. Alternative Tentacles.
Almamegretta. 1993. *Animamigrante*. Anagrumba.
Armchair Radicals. 1997. *Here Comes the King*. Self-released.
Ash Ra Tempel and Leary, T. 1998 [1972]. *Seven Up*. Purple Pyramid.
B-Machina. 2009. 'Conspiracy', on *In Memory of Miguel Serrano* by Various Artists. Valgriind.
Balletto di Bronzo. 1972. *Ys*. Polydor.
Beach Boys, The. 1965. 'California Girls', on *Summer Days (and Summer Nights!!)*. Capitol.
——. 1966. *Pet Sounds*. Capitol.
——. 1990 [1967]. *Smiley Smile*. Capitol.
Beatles, The. 1965. *Rubber Soul*. Parlophone.
——. 1966. 'Eleanor Rigby', on *Revolver*. Parlophone.
——. 1967a. *Sgt. Pepper's Lonely Hearts Club Band*. Parlophone.
——. 1967b. 'All You Need Is Love'. Parlophone.
——. 1968a. *The Beatles* ['White Album']. Apple.
——. 1968b. 'Hey Jude/Revolution'. Apple.
——. 1976 'Got to Get You into My Life'/'Helter Skelter'. Capitol.
Benatar, P. 1981. *Precious Time*. Chrysalis.
——. 1996a. *Heartbreaker: Sixteen Classic Performances*. Capitol.
——. 1996b. *The Very Best Of: Vol. 2*. Chrysalis.
——. 1998. *Premium Gold Collection*. Emi Electrola.
——. 1999. *Best*. Vereinigte Motor-Verlage.
——. 2002a. *The Divine*. EMI Plus.
——. 2002b. *In the Heat of the Night*. Disky.
——. 2003. *Greatest Hits Live*. King Biscuit Flower Hour Records.
Bennato, E. 1974. *I buoni e i cattivi*. Ricordi.
——. 1978. *Burattino senza fili*. Ricordi.
Berry, C. 1955. 'Maybellene'. Chess Records.
——. 1957. 'School Day (Ring! Ring! Goes the Bell)'. Chess Records.
——. 1964. 'Promised Land', on *Saint Louis to Liverpool*. Chess Records.
Black Sabbath. 1970. 'Electric Funeral', on *Paranoid*. Vertigo.
Bloodgood. 1987. *Detonation*. Frontline.
——. 1989. *Out of the Darkness*. Intense Records.
Bon Jovi. 1996. *These Days*. Mercury.
Bonemachine. 2008. *Erste Rotation (eine Retrospektive von Krieg und Zeit)*. Sabbathid Records.

Buffalo Springfield. 1967. 'For What It's Worth'. Atco.
Byrds, The. 1969. 'Jesus Is Just Alright', on *Ballad of Easy Rider*. Columbia.
Cabaret Voltaire. 1985. *The Covenant, the Sword and the Arm of the Lord*. Virgin.
Caliban. 2011. *Coverfield*. Century Media Records.
Can. 1970. *Soul Desert*. Spoon Records.
Captain Beefheart. 1969. *Trout Mask Replica*. Straight/Reprise.
Celtic Frost. 2002. *Prototype*. Self-released.
Chic. 1978. 'Le Freak', on *C'est Chic*. Atlantic.
Clash, The. 1980. 'Stop the World', on *Black Market Clash*. Epic.
Cochran, E. 1959. 'Teenage Heaven'. Liberty Records.
Coleman, O. 1959. *The Shape of Jazz to Come*. Atlantic.
Country Joe and the Fish. 2009. 'Fixin' to Die Rag', on *Woodstock: Music from the Original Soundtrack and More*. Rhino.
Cream. 1969. *The Best of Cream*. Atco/RSO.
Cure, The. 1979. *Three Imaginary Boys*. Fiction Records.
——. 1980. *Seventeen Seconds*. Polydor.
——. 1981. *Faith*. Fiction Records.
——. 1982. *Pornography*. Fiction Records.
Daniele, P. 1979. *Pino Daniele*. EMI.
——. 1980. *Nero a metà*. EMI.
——. 1981. *Vai mò*. EMI.
Dark One Lite. 2005. *A Guitar Tribute to Mötley Crüe*. Tribute Sounds.
Diamond Reo. 1976. *Dirty Diamonds*. Kama Sutra.
Dimension Zero. 2003. *Penetrations from the Lost World*. Regain Records.
Dylan, B. 1965. *Highway 61 Revisited*. CBS.
——. 2005. 'Visions of Johanna', on *No Direction Home, the Soundtrack*. Columbia/Legacy.
Electric Hellfire Club. 1993. 'Black Bus', on *Burn Baby Burn!*. Cleopatra.
——. 1995a. 'Creepy Crawler', on *Kiss the Goat*. Cleopatra.
——. 1995b. 'Night of the Buck Knives' (Coming Down Fast Mix), on *Kiss the Goat*. Cleopatra.
Eno, B. 2009. *Discreet Music*. E.G. Records.
Fogerty, J. 1969. 'Bad Moon Rising', on *Green River*. Fantasy.
Fripp, R. 1979. *Exposure*. Polydor.
Gamalon. 1991. *High Contrast*. Virgin.
Gillan. 1988 [1982]. *Magic*. Virgin.
Gloomys, The. 1967. 'Calling Mayfair'. Capitol.
Grateful Dead. 1968. *Anthem of the Sun*. Warner Bros.
——. 1969a. 'Dark Star', on *Live/Dead*. Warner Bros.
——. 1969b. 'The Eleven', on *Live/Dead*. Warner Bros.
——. 1971. 'Playing in the Band', on *Grateful Dead*. Warner Bros.
——. 1975. 'Help on the Way > Slipknot', on *Blues for Allah*. Grateful Dead Records.

——. 2009 [1968]. 'Viola Lee Blues', on *Carousel 2-14-68. Road Trips*, vol. 2, no. 2. Grateful Dead Productions.
Greenbaum, N. 1969. 'Spirit in the Sky', on *Spirit in the Sky*. Reprise.
Grimm, MF (featuring Ill Bill and Block McCloud). 2006. 'Karma', on *American Hunger*. Day by Day.
Gruppo Operaio di Pomigliano D'Arco. 1974. *'E Zezi, Tammurriata dell'Alfasud*. I dischi del sole.
Guardian. 1989. *First Watch*, Enigma.
——. 1997. *Bottle Rocket*. Warner/Word.
Haley, B. and His Comets. 1954. 'Rock around the Clock'. Decca.
Harrison, D. 1977. *Not Far from Free*. Mercury.
Heatherington, D. 1980. 'Helter Skelter'/'Mr. Nice Guy'. Epic.
Heavy Tuba and Jon Sass. 1998. *Sagenhaft*. ATS.
Hendrix, J. 1967. 'Purple Haze'. Track Records.
——. 1968. *Electric Ladyland*. Reprise.
——. 2009. 'The Star Spangled Banner', on *Woodstock: Music from the Original Soundtrack and More*. Rhino.
Holy Soldier. 1990. *Holy Soldier*. Myrrh Records/A&M.
Honk, Wail and Moan. 1999. *Saturn Swings!*. Uffda.
Hoo Doo Soul Band. 1997. *Live at Oldfield's*. Self-released.
Hüsker Dü. 1986. 'Don't Want to Know If You Are Lonely/All Work and No Play/ Helter Skelter'. Warner Bros.
Idora. 1991. 'Helter Skelter', on *Best Run Fast Vol. 2*. MCR.
Jackson, J . 1982. *Night and Day*. A&M.
Jars of Clay. 1995. *Jars of Clay*. Essential/Silvertone.
——. 1997. *Much Afraid*. Essential/Silvertone.
Joplin, J. 1971. 'Mercedes Benz', on *Pearl*. Columbia.
KC and the Sunshine Band. 1976. '(Shake, Shake, Shake) Shake Your Booty', on *Part III*. TK Records.
Kesey, K. and the Merry Pranksters. 2005 [1966]. *The Acid Test*. Acadia/ Evangeline Records.
La Magna, G. 2005. *I Cottrau a Napoli*. Frame.
Lamé Gold. 1998. *Limit*. Studio 54.
LeFevre, M. and Broken Heart. 1978. 'Crack the Sky', on *Crack the Sky*. Myrrh.
Led Zeppelin. 1971. *Led Zeppelin*. Atlantic.
Lennon, J. and Ono, Y. 1968. *Unfinished Music No. 1. Two Virgins*. Apple.
Lopez, P. 1976. *Patrizia Lopez*. RCA.
Lords, The. 1967. 'John Brown's Body'. Columbia.
McCartney, P. 2009. *Good Evening New York City*. Hear Music.
McGuire, B. 1965. 'Eve of Destruction', on *Eve of Destruction*. Dunhill.
Mad Mongols. 1994. *Cripple Satan Scream*. Teichiku Records.
Mamá Ladilla. 2004 [1994]. *Directamente de la Basura: Diez Años Macerando*. Boa.
Manson, C. 1970. *Lie: The Love and Terror Cult*. Awareness Records.
MC Einar. 1989. '28 grader i skyggen', on *Arh Dér!*. CBS.

Mighty Sphincter. 1986. *The New Manson Family*. Placebo Records.
Mitchell, J. 1970. 'Woodstock', on *Ladies of the Canyon*. Reprise.
——. 2009. 'Woodstock', on *Woodstock: Music from the Original Soundtrack and More*. Rhino.
Morrissey. 1995. *Southpaw Grammar*. RCA/Reprise.
——. 1997. *Maladjusted*. Island.
Mothers of Invention, The. 1966. *Freak Out!*. Verve.
——. 1968. *We're Only in It for the Money*. Verve.
Mötley Crüe. 1983a. 'Helter Skelter'/'Helter Skelter'. Elektra.
——. 1983b. *Shout at the Devil*. Elektra.
——. 1999. *Live: Entertainment or Death*. Mötley Records.
——. 2005. *Red, White and Crüe*. Mötley Records.
——. 2006. *Carnival of Sins: Live*. Mötley Records.
Mungo Jerry. 1970. 'In the Summer Time'. Pye Records.
Musicanova. 1978. *Musicanova*. Philips.
My Life with the Thrill Kill Kult. 1994. 'After the Flesh', on *The Crow* by Various Artists [original soundtrack]. Atlantic.
Napoli Centrale. 1975. *Napoli Centrale*. Ricordi.
Necro Tonz, The. 1987. *Are You Dead, Yet?*. Last Beat.
Negativland. 1989. *Helter Stupid*. SST Records.
Nine Inch Nails. 1994. *The Downward Spiral*. Interscope Records.
Norman, L. 1972. 'I Wish We'd All Been Ready', on *Only Visiting This Planet*. Verve.
Nuova Compagnia di Canto Popolare. 1973. *NCCP*. RCA.
Nurse With Wound. 1979. *Chance Meeting on a Dissecting Table of a Sewing Machine and an Umbrella*. United Jnana.
Ocean. 1970. 'Put Your Hand in the Hand', on *Put Your Hand in the Hand*. Kama Sutra.
Ono, Yoko. 1970. *Yoko Ono/Plastic Ono Band*. Apple.
——. 1971. *Fly*. Apple.
Ono, Yoko and John Lennon. 1972. *Sometime in New York City*. Apple/EMI.
Osanna. 1973. *Palepoli*. Fonit Cetra.
Osbourne, O. 'Revelation (Mother Earth)', on *Blizzard of Oz*. 1980.
Peel, D. and the Lower East Side. 1993. 'Hemp Hop Smoker', on *Comin' Down Fast! A Gathering of Garbage, Lies and Reflections on Charles Manson* by Various Artists. Helter Skelter Records.
Petards, The. 1966. 'Pretty Miss'. CCA Records.
Petra. 1983a. 'Not of This World', on *Not of This World*. StarSong/A&M.
——. 1983b. 'Grave Robber', on *Not of This World*. StarSong/A&M.
——. 1987a. 'This Means War!', on *This Means War!*. StarSong.
——. 1987b. 'He Came, He Saw, He Conquered', on *This Means War!*. StarSong.
——. 1990. 'Armed and Dangerous', on *Beyond Belief*. DaySpring Records/Word/A&M/Epic.
Phillips, S. 1970. *Second Contribution*. A&M.

Pink Floyd. 1967. *A Nice Pair – The Piper at the Gates of Dawn*. Harvest.
——. 1968. *A Saucerful of Secrets*. Harvest.
——. 1969. *Ummagumma*. Harvest.
——. 1973. *The Dark Side of the Moon*. Harvest.
——. 1975. *Wish You Were Here*. Harvest.
Ramones, The. 1984. 'Planet Earth 1988', on *Too Tough to Die*. Sire.
Ramrods, The. 2004. *Gimme Some Action*. Young Soul Rebels.
Reed, L. 1975. *Metal Machine Music*. RCA.
Rolling Stones, The. 1968a. *Their Satanic Majesties Request*. Decca.
——. 1968b. *Beggars Banquet*. Decca.
——. 1968c. 'Street Fighting Man'/'No Expectations'. London.
——. 1969a. 'Midnight Rambler', on *Let It Bleed*. Decca.
——. 1969b. 'Gimme Shelter', on *Let It Bleed*. Decca.
——. 1970. *Get Yer Ya-Ya's Out! The Rolling Stones in Concert*. Decca.
——. 1971. *Sticky Fingers*. Decca.
Rosetta Stone. 1994. *Nothing*. Minority/One Records.
Sacred Warrior. 1988. *Rebellion*. Intense Records.
Saint Just. 1973. *Saint Just*. Harvest.
Santana. 1969. 'Soul Sacrifice', on *Santana*. Prime Cuts.
Secession. 1986. *Michael/Helter Skelter*. Siren Records.
SexA. 1990. *No Sleep 'Till Pussy/Fuck Piction*. FV Založba.
Showmen, The. 1969. *The Showmen*. RCA.
Simon, P. and Garfunkel, A. 1970. 'El Condor Pasa'. CBS.
Siouxsie and the Banshees. 1978. *The Scream*. Polydor.
——. 1984. 'Blow the House Down', on *Hyæna*. Polydor.
Sisters of Mercy, The. 1985. 'Black Planet', on *First and Last and Always*. Merciful Release/WEA.
Sixpence None the Richer. 1994. *The Fatherless and the Widow*. R.E.X.
——. 1995. *This Beautiful Mess*. R.E.X.
——. 1997. *Sixpence None the Richer*. Squint Entertainment/Elektra.
Skinny Puppy. 1989. *Rabies*. Nettwerk.
Skrew. 1997. *Angel Seed XXIII*. Metal Blade.
Sonic Youth. 1985. *Bad Moon Rising*. Homestead.
Sorrenti, A. 1972. *Aria*. Harvest.
Soundgarden. 2011 [1996]. *Live on I-5*. A&M.
Spite Extreme Wing. 2008. *Vitra*. Avantgarde Music.
Stooges, The. 1970. *Fun House*. Elektra.
Stryken. 1987. *First Strike*. Chrystal Records.
Stryper. 1985. *Soldiers Under Command*. Enigma.
Sunday Fury. 2009. *Men from the Grey Town*. Nail Records.
That Petrol Emotion. 2009 [1994]. *Final Flame (Fire, Detonation and Sublime Chaos)*. Self-released.
Trouble. *Live Dallas Texas 03/12/90* [official bootleg]. Trouble Inc.
Turner, J.L. 1999. *Under Cover, Vol. 2*. Shrapnel.

U2. 1988. *Rattle and Hum*. Island.
Ubangis, The. 1992. *Lovesick/Grandma Dynamite/Helter Skelter*. DeCeased Records.
Urban Dance Squad. 1996. *Beograd Live*. SKC.
Various Artists. 1976. *Christiania*. Christiania/CBS.
Various Artists. 2003. *Nye Christiania Sange*. Helicopter Records.
Various Artists. 2004. *Bevar Christiania*. Karma Music.
Various Artists. 2008. *Christiania Forever*. Phantom Sound & Vision.
Velvet Underground, The. 1967. *The Velvet Underground and Nico*. Verve.
Vow Wow. 1989. *Helter Skelter*. Arista.
Watts, A. 1962. *This Is IT!*. MEA.
White Zombie. 1993. *Resurrection Day* [bootleg]. KTS.
Yoshida, M. 1998. *Mitsue*. Kojima.
Zappa, F. 1976. *Zoot Allures*. Warner Bros.
——. 1978. *Live in New York*. DiscReet.
——. 1979a [1978]. *Sheik Yerbouti*. Zappa Records.
——. 1979b. *Joe's Garage*. Zappa Records.
——. 1981a. *You Are What You Is*. Barking Pumpkin.
——. 1981b. *Tinseltown Rebellion*. Barking Pumpkin.
——. 1982. *Ship Arriving too Late to Save a Drowning Witch*. Barking Pumpkin.
——. 1985. *Zappa Meets the Mothers of Prevention*. Barking Pumpkin.
——. 1986. *Jazz from Hell*. Barking Pumpkin.
——. 1994 [1967, 1991, 1992]. 'N-Lite', on *Civilization Phase III*. Barking Pumpkin.
——. 2004 [1970–78]. *QuAUDIOPHILIAc*. Barking Pumpkin.
99 Posse. 1993. *Curre curre guagliò*. Esodo Autoproduzioni.

Filmography

Fiction

Badham, J. 1977. *Saturday Night Fever*. Paramount Pictures.
Brooks, R. 1955. *The Blackboard Jungle*. Metro-Goldwyn-Mayer.
Dreifuss, A. 1967. *Riot on Sunset Strip*. American International Pictures.
Dunning, G. 1968. *Yellow Submarine*. United Artists.
Gries, T. 1976. *Helter Skelter*. Lorimar Productions.
Klane, R. 1978. *Thank God It's Friday*. Columbia Pictures.
Lee, A. 2009. *Taking Woodstock*. Focus Features.
Rafelson, B. 1968. *Head*. Columbia Pictures.
Scott, R. 1991. *Thelma and Louise*. Metro-Goldwyn-Mayer.
Zappa, F. 1979. *Baby Snakes*. Intercontinental Absurdities.

Video Art / Experimental Films

Nameth, R. 1966. *The Exploding Plastic Inevitable*. [Online] Available at: http://www.jonbehrensfilms.com/experimental005.html [accessed: 13 July 2011].
Warhol, A. 1963. *Sleep*.
——. 1964a. *Empire*.
——. 1964c. *Couch*.
——. 1965. *Vinyl*.
——. 1966. *The Chelsea Girls*.
——. 1968. *Flesh*.
——. 1970. *Trash*.

Documentary Films

Bate, P. 1994. *Witness: Manson – The Man Who Killed the Sixties*. A Box Production for Channel 4.
Cohen, R.C. 1967. *Mondo Hollywood*. Hollywood International Pictures.
Kowalski, L. 1980. *D.O.A.: A Rite of Passage*. High Times Films.
Lerner, M. 1996. *Message to Love*. Castle Music Pictures.
Maysles, D. and Maysles, A. 1970. *Gimme Shelter*. Maysles Films/Cinema 5.
Moore, M. 2004. *Fahrenheit 9/11*. Dog Eat Dog Films.
Pennebaker, D.A. 1967. *Monterey Pop*. Leacock Pennebaker.
Riefenstahl, L. 1936. *Triumph of the Will*. Universum Film AG.

———. 1938. *Olympia*. Tobis/Müller.
Roeg, N. and Neal, P. 1972. *Glastonbury Fayre*.
Scorsese, M. 2011. *George Harrison: Living in the Material World*. Grove Street Pictures.
Wadleigh, M. 1994 [1970]. *Woodstock: 3 Days of Peace and Music*. Warner Bros.

Television Series

Various Directors. 1952–70. *Death Valley Days*. Syndicated.
Various Directors. 1987–91. *thirtysomething*. MGM Television.
Various Directors. 1997–present. *Girls Gone Wild*. Girls Gone Wild.

Video Clips

Kahn, J. 2009. Eminem: 'We Made You'. Shady/Aftermath/Interscope. [Online] Available at: http://www.youtube.com/watch?v=V90a88q2qEg [accessed: 14 March 2012].
Lawrence, F. 2009. Lady Gaga: 'Bad Romance'. Streamline/Kon Live/Cherrytree/Interscope. [Online] Available at: http://www.youtube.com/watch?v=qrO4YZeyl0I&ob=av2e [accessed: 14 March 2012].

Various

Warhol, A. 1964b. 'Andy Warhol on Pop Art', interview. [Online] Available at: http://www.youtube.com/watch?feature=endscreen&NR=1&v=deRMRh8Zjgg [accessed: 10 March 2012].

Index

99 Posse, 247–8, 249
    'Curre curre guagliò', 247
    'Rigurgito antifascista', 247
    'Tu vuò fà l'americano', 248

Ache
    'De Skæve Drømme', 219
acid, *see* LSD
acid rock, *see* psychedelic rock
Adler, Lou, 39
Aerosmith
    'Helter Skelter', 99–100
Almamegretta, 247–8, 249
    'Figli di Annibale', 248
    'Nun te scurdà', 248
    'Pe' dint' 'e viche addò nun trase 'o mare', 248
Aloisi, Uccio, 247
Alpert, Richard, 35
Altamont, xviii, 5, 9, 43, 98, 99, 124, 125, 126, 127, 133–7
alternative, xvii, 189
    aesthetic, 46
    community, 18, 20, 83, 150, 241, 242
    culture, 18, 243, 246
    lifestyle, 4, 17, 18, 25, 82, 205, 206, 241
    music, 45, 90, 92, 104, 245
    scene, 89
    value system, 17
American Forces Network, 225
Amon Düül, 152
Amon Düül II, 152
Anissette, 218
apocalypse, xviii–xx, 7, 9, 84, 98, 104, 154
    and Christianity, 112, 114, 115–20
Apple, 90
Aptheker, Bettina, 183–4, 185
Arkadia-Combo, 225
art rock, 141

Ash Ra Tempel, 152–3
    Seven Up, 153
Ashcan School, 51
Asian Dub Foundation, 248
Atlantics, 225
authenticity, xix, 42, 43, 62, 70, 71, 145
    and music, 7, 30, 120, 152, 154, 155, 156, 198, 199, 207, 210, 216, 218, 220–21, 243
avant-garde, 10, 11, 49, 50, 61, 62, 86, 87, 92, 96, 101, 141–5, 149, 152–6, 172–3, 181–2, 244n3
Avion Travel, 245
Avitabile, Enzo, 245

Bachman-Turner Overdrive, 100
Baez, Joan, 31
Balin, Marty, 37
Barrett, Syd, 60, 63n20, 151, 197
Beach Boys, 39–41, 43, 60, 231
    Beach Boys Party, 150
    'California Girls', 39
    Pet Sounds, 40–41
    Smiley Smile, 150
Beat movement/music, xvii, 3–4, 7, 18, 36, 50–51, 61, 62, 84, 86, 112, 115, 205, 237
    in Berlin, 227, 228, 230, 231
    'New Vision', 52n8
Beatlers, 225
Beatles, xvii, 18, 36, 54, 60, 61, 66, 86, 89, 91, 99, 143, 144, 150, 156, 172, 218, 220, 242
    break up, xviii, 98
    'All You Need Is Love', 18
    'Eleanor Rigby', 7, 88
    'Helter Skelter', xix, 8, 96–8, 99–107
    'Hey Jude', 95
    'Long, Long, Long', 96
    'Revolution', 95, 96

'Revolution 1', 96
'Revolution 9', 96, 98, 105, 143
Rubber Soul, 40
'Sexy Sadie', 96
Sgt. Pepper's Lonely Hearts Club Band, 60, 54n11, 87, 143, 231
The Beatles ('White Album'), 54n11, 92, 96, 98, 99, 105, 143
Yellow Submarine, 83–4
'Yellow Submarine', 150
Beaulieu Jazz festivals, 125
Beefheart, Captain, 4, 189
Trout Mask Replica, 42–3
'Veteran's Day Poppy', 43
Benatar, Pat
'Helter Skelter', 102
Bennato, Edoardo, 242, 244, 248
Burattino senza fili, 242
'Cantautore', 242
Io che non sono l'imperatore, 242
Sono solo canzonette, 242
Uffà Uffà, 242
'Viva la mamma', 245
Bennato, Eugenio, 243, 249
Berkeley student riots, 183–4
Berlin
East, 13–14, 223, 225–8, 233–4
West, 13–14, 223, 225, 228–9, 230–34
Berlin Radio, 13, 227
Berlusconi, Silvio, 245, 246
Berry, Chuck, 83, 89, 97
'Cadillac Coupe', 7, 88
'School Days', 81
Bevar Christiania, 218
Bifrost, 217, 218
Big Beats, 225
Big Brother and the Holding Company, 37
Bisca, 245, 247–8, 249
Black Flag, 102
Black Panthers, 112
Black Sabbath, 103
'Electric Funeral', 75
Blackboard Jungle, 81
Blake, Peter, 53
Sgt. Pepper's Lonely Hearts Club Band, 54n11
Blake, William, 145
Bloodgood, 118, 120

Blue Stuff, 245
blues, 89, 97, 100, 103, 245
Bon Jovi
'Helter Skelter', 103, 106
Bonemachine
'Helter Skelter', 106
Bonnaroo, 126
Bottles, 225
Bowie, David, 6, 10
Boyd, Joe, 129
Bozzio, Dale, 198
Brakhage, Stan, 51
Breton, André, xvi
Brightles, 225
Brill Building, 38, 39, 62
British Forces Network, 225
British subcultures, 70, 71, 72–7
Brittles, 225
Bruni, Sergio, 248
Buddhism, 51, 61, 146, 173
Zen, 181
Buffalo Springfield, 41
'For What It's Worth', 41
Burroughs, William, 52, 84
Burton, Tim, 200
Bus Stop Four, 233
Butlers, 228
Byrds, 41
'Jesus Is Just Alright', 8, 115

Cabaret Voltaire, 48–9
Cabaret Voltaire (band)
The Covenant, the Sword and the Arm of the Lord, 105
Cage, John, 7, 51, 84, 146, 181
Cale, John, 59, 62, 64
Caliban
'Helter Skelter', 103
camp, xvii, xix, 6, 8, 10, 73, 104
Camp, Steve, 120
Can, 153, 232
cannabis, 209, 210, 219, 220
Cants, 225
capitalism, xvii, xix, 6–7, 18, 20–21, 31, 34, 38–9, 47, 50, 52, 65, 66–78 *passim*, 82, 91, 136, 137, 209, 227
Capitol Records, 39

Carnivore
   'Helter Skelter', 103
Cash, Johnny, 8, 115
Cassady, Neal, 157
Castañeda, Carlos, 84
CBS, 151
CCM (contemporary Christian music), 117–22
Celtic Frost
   'Helter Skelter', 103
Centri Sociali Occupati Autogestiti (CSOA), 246–7, 249
Chess, 89
Chic
   'Le Freak', 194
Children of God, 8, 115
Christian metal, 117–20, 121
Christian punk, 118, 119–20, 121
Christian rock, 113, 115, 116, 117–22
Christiania, 4, 12–13, 206–9, 210, 212–15, 215, 219–22
   Den Grå Hal, 210
   Det Gule Værtshus, 210
   Genbrugsstationen, 212
   Jazzhus Loppen, 210
   Månefiskeren, 210
   Månekabareten, 210
   Maskinhallen, 212
   music in, 209–12, 216–22
   Musik Loppen, 210, 213, 214
   Nemoland, 211, 211, 213
   Operaen, 210
   Støttefest (support festivals) for, 210, 214
   Woodstock, 211–12
Christiania Forever, 218–19
Christianity, xviii, 8–9, 109–11
   and apocalypse, 112, 114, 115–22
   and environmentalism, 113–14, 122
   and politics, 111–15, 117–18
   see also Jesus Movement
Cilio, Luciano, 245
Cizik, Richard, 113–14
Claiborne, Shane, 115
Clapton, Eric, 8, 115
Clash, 43
   'Stop the World', 75
classic rock, 83, 91–2

Claus, Tømrer
   'Christiania Sangen', 219
Cochran, Eddie, 83, 88, 91
Coil, 153
   'How to Destroy Angels', 154
Cold War, 13–14, 19, 32, 35, 118, 223–35
Coleman, Ornette, 5, 29–30, 62
   The Shape of Jazz to Come, 29
Coltrane, John, 158, 167
Columbia, 90
Compassion International, 121
Constanten, Tom, 160, 161
Cooper, Alice
   'School's Out', 81
Copenhagen, 12–13, 206, 207, 212–15, 217, 221
Copenhagen Jazz Festival, 211
Cornell, Chris, 123
Cornerstone Music Festival, 121–2
Costa, Mario Pasquale
   'Catarì (marzo)', 240
Costello, Elvis, 89
Cottrau, Guillame, 249
Cottrau, Teodoro, 249n7
counterculture, 3–5, 63, 65, 66, 82–3, 98–9, 103–4, 106, 124–5, 133, 141–2, 148, 149, 150, 151, 152, 155–6, 167, 171, 174, 180, 182, 189, 197, 201, 205–6, 237, 238, 241, 242, 243, 244n3, 245, 246, 247, 249
   and apocalypse, xviii–xx, 7, 9, 84, 104, 112, 122, 154
   and Christianity, 109–12, 114–15, 121–2
   and collective identity, 12, 38, 238
   and community, 12–14, 18, 20, 36–8, 206, 212–15, 219–22
   in a contemporary context, 25–6
   defined, xvi, 17
   and digital communication technologies, 24
   and dystopia, xvii, xviii, 5, 7, 9, 62
   and lifestyle sites and strategies, 23–5
   and modernism/modernity, xvi–xviii, 5, 33–5, 42–3, 180
   and noise, 4, 43
   origins of, 18–20

problematising, 20–22
re-theorising, 22–3
as set of antagonistic fields, xv–xviii
and space, 12, 13, 205, 206–7, 212–15, 219–22, 224
and utopia, xviii–xx, 5, 7, 9, 34, 83–8, 93, 95, 145, 155, 180
and vocalisation, 182–5
cover versions, 159, 161; *see also* 'Helter Skelter'
Crazy World of Arthur Brown, 63n20
Cream, 54, 96
Best of Cream, 54n11
Creedence Clearwater Revival, 100
'Bad Moon Rising', 8, 115
Crosby, David, 242
Crosby, Stills and Nash, 125n2
'Woodstock', 132
Cross, David, 248
Crystals, 39
Cubism, 48
Cure, 89, 92
Current 93, 153, 154

D'Anna, Elio, 240
Dachluke, 230, 232
Dadaism, xvi, 43, 48–9, 142, 144, 145, 147, 151, 152, 153, 156
Dale, Dick, 39
Damned, 89
Daniele, Pino, 243–4, 245, 248
'Je so' pazzo', 244
'O mare', 244
Terra mia, 244
Davis, Miles, 50, 86, 243
De Sio, Teresa, 245
Democratic National Convention, Chicago, xviii
Depeche Mode, 89
Des Barres, Pamela, 41, 42
Det Internationale Sigøjnerkompagni, 218
Devo, 43
Di Giacomo, Salvatore
'Catarì (marzo)', 240
Diamond Reo
'Helter Skelter', 100
Diana Show-Band, 225
Diddley, Bo, 89

Diggers, 38, 112
Dimension Zero
'Helter Skelter', 103
Dine, Jim, 51
Best of Cream, 54n11
Dio, 119
disco, 193–4, 196, 199, 245, 248
Disoccupati Organizzati, 244
Dissing, Povl, 218
Dobson, James, 113–14
documentary film, 9, 51–2, 59; *see also* *Gimme Shelter*; *Woodstock: Three Days of Peace and Music*
Dolenz, Micky, 152
Donovan, 242
Doors, 84, 150, 158
Dorfkrug, 230
drag, 6, 10, 56, 57
drugs, 4n1, 18, 20, 24, 25, 30, 33, 35, 41, 48, 54, 56, 57, 58, 60, 61, 84, 119, 135, 137, 148, 149, 150, 151, 154, 205, 209, 213, 246; *see also* cannabis; heroin; LSD; psychedelics; speed
dub, 248
Duchamp, Marcel, 49
Fountain, 49, 144, 155
Dylan, Bob, xvii, xviii, 5, 7, 8, 18, 30–31, 36, 62, 86, 90, 115, 196, 231, 242
'All Along the Watchtower', 104
Highway 61 Revisited, 91
'Rainy Day Women #12 and 35', 150
'Subterranean Homesick Blues', 193
'Visions of Johanna', 134
dystopia, xvii, xviii, 5, 7, 9, 62, 194

East Berlin, 13–14, 223, 225–8, 233–4
echo-team, 225
Edge, 104
Ehrlich, Paul
The Population Bomb, 133
Electric Hellfire Club, 105
Emerson, Keith, 241
Emerson, Lake and Palmer, 88
EMI, 90
Empire (and Multitude), 6, 66–9
and subcultures, 69–71, 72–9
Eno, Brian, 89, 92

Ernst Knaack, 226
ethnicity, 21, 22, 24, 52, 74, 76, 88, 89, 93
experimentation, 33, 34
  commercial, 8, 90
  musical, 30, 31, 36, 37, 85, 86, 96, 141, 143–4, 152, 153, 155, 156, 157, 161, 171, 172–3, 176–7, 180, 182, 185, 238, 241
  see also avant-garde; freak culture/freak out

Factory (Warhol's), 45, 56–7, 59, 60, 62–3
Factory Records, 89, 92
Fast Product, 89
Faust, 153, 154
femininity, 11–12, 48, 51n4, 91, 131, 136, 178, 192; *see also* gender; masculinity; sex; sexuality
feminism, 11, 81, 171, 173, 177, 185, 199
Festival di Sanremo, 237
festivals, 9–10, 38, 123–9, 136–7, 210, 214, 237
Festsäle, 230
Fiction, 89
Fisher, Wild Man, 189
Five Stones, 225
Fleetwood Mac, 8, 115
Fluxus, 51, 156, 181
Flying Burrito Brothers, 125n2
Fællessange, 216–17
Fogerty, John, 158
folk music, xvii, 36, 37, 38
  Italian, 14, 237, 243, 245, 246–7, 249
  in New York, 5, 30–31, 33
folk rock, 91
Foulk, Ron, 129
Frampton, Peter
  'I'm in You', 196
Frank, Robert, 51
  Cocksucker Blues, 51n5
  Pull My Daisy, 51n5
  The Americans, 51
Franke-Echo-Quintett, 225
freak culture/freak out, 10–12, 141–2, 145–9, 150–56, 194, 199
Free Berlin Station, 229, 230, 232, 233, 234
Free Speech Movement (FSM), 182–5
Freundschaft, 226

Fri Galaxe, 220
Fripp, Robert, 92
Fromme, Lynette 'Squeaky', 105
Futurism, xvi, 48

Gang of Four, 89
Garcia, Jerry, 36, 159, 160, 162, 164, 165, 167, 169
Gardian, 118
gender, xv, xix, 3, 4, 6, 8, 10, 11, 21, 22, 23, 48, 65, 73–4n3, 74, 77, 81–2, 91, 93, 131, 136, 171–2n2, 187, 191, 196, 199
  and voice, 171, 173, 174, 178–9, 180–82, 183–4
  see also femininity; masculinity; sex; sexuality
Genesis, 241
George, Boy, 6, 10
Gibson, William
  Zero History, 92
Gillan, Ian
  'Helter Skelter', 103
Gimme Shelter, 9, 124, 126, 127, 133–7
Ginsberg, Allen, 4n1, 50, 84, 155, 157
  Howl, 145
Giorno, John, 57
glam, 64
Glastonbury Fayre, 126, 129
Glastonbury Fayre, 129n5
glitter, 64
Gloomys, 232
Gnags, 218
Godspell, 9, 116
goth, 20, 64, 70, 73, 74, 75, 76, 77, 101, 104, 115
Gragnaniello, Enzo, 245
Graham, Bill (concert promoter), 38, 157
Graham, Billy (evangelical minister), 109
Grateful Dead, xvii, 4, 10, 35, 36–7, 63n20, 125n2, 146–7, 157–69, 205, 242
  'Alligator', 161
  Anthem of the Sun, 10, 147
  'Caution (Do Not Stop on Tracks)', 147, 161, 163
  'Cold Rain and Snow', 161
  'Cryptical', 161, 163
  'Dark Star', 160, 161–3, 167

'Good Morning Little Schoolgirl', 161
'Help on the Way', 163
'Playing in the Band', 163
'Slipknot', 163
'That's It for the Other One', 147
'The Eleven', 163
'The Other One', 161, 163
'Viola Lee Blues', 161, 163
Greenbaum, Norman
   'Spirit in the Sky', 8, 115
Greenhorns, 225
Greenwich Village, 30–31
Groening, Matt, 200
grunge, 64
Gruppo Operaio di Pomigliano D'Arco
   'E Zezi, 243
Guardian, 118
Guess Who, 100
Guetta, David, 92
Guthrie, Woody, 31

Hager, Kurt, 228
Haight-Ashbury, xviii, 25, 36–7
Haley, Bill, and the Comets
   'Rock around the Clock', 81
Hamilton, Richard, 52n9, 53
   The Beatles, 54n11
happenings, 25, 51, 84
hardcore, 89, 104, 245
Hardt, Michael, 6, 65–71, 72–9
Harrison, Don
   'Helter Skelter', 100
Harrison, George, xviii, 91, 96
Hart, Mickey, 160, 161, 162
Harvest, 241, 242
Harvest Crusade, 117
Haus Metzler, 230
Havel, Václav, 187
Havens, Richie, 132, 136
Heartfield, John, 49
Heatherington, Dianne
   'Helter Skelter', 100
heavy metal, 9, 72, 74, 75, 89, 96, 102–3, 104, 106, 219
   Christian, 117–20, 121
Hedvard, Zofia
   'Christiania Mit Hjerte', 218
Helms, Chet, 37, 38

'Helter Skelter', xix, 8, 96–8
   cover versions, 99–107
Hendrix, Jimi, 4, 5, 60, 63n20, 87, 96, 104, 132, 136, 205
   'All Along the Watchtower', 104
   Electric Ladyland, 87
   'Purple Haze', 84
   'Star Spangled Banner', 136
Hermsdorf Star-Club, 230, 232
heroin, xvii, 6, 62
Hinduism, xviii, 4n2
hip-hop, 196, 210, 212
hippies/hippy movement, xvii, xviii, 7, 14, 18, 21, 25, 34, 36, 41, 43, 63, 82, 88, 89, 132, 142, 205, 208, 210, 219, 220, 221, 242
   and Christianity, 109–12, 115
Hockney, David, 53
Holy Soldier, 118, 120
Honecker, Erich, 13, 227
Hot Five, 225
Hunter, Robert, 167
Hüsker Dü
   'Helter Skelter', 104
Huxley, Aldous, 84
   Doors of Perception, 25

I Passatempi musicali, 249
Il Balletto di Bronzo, 14, 240
   Ys, 241
improvisation, 36, 37–8, 100, 201
   freak out and, 141, 143
   Grateful Dead and, 10, 36–8, 157–68
   jazz and, xvii, 29–30, 33, 36
Incredible String Band, 129
indie, 70, 106, 219
industrial, 10, 64, 104, 105, 153
Island, 89
Isle of Wight Festival, 21, 125, 129, 242
Italy, 237–8, 241, 244–6

Jackson, Joe
   Night and Day, 92
Jagger, Mick, 9, 91, 134
Jan and Dean, 39
Janov, Arthur, 184–5
Jarry, Alfred, 151
Jars of Clay, 120

jazz, xvii, xviii, 4n1, 5, 14, 29–30, 33, 36, 37, 42, 50, 62, 81, 82, 86, 143, 153, 157, 158, 160, 164–5, 211, 230, 232, 237, 240, 242, 243, 248
Jazz Saloon, 230
Jefferson Airplane, 37, 60, 63n20, 125n2, 205, 242
Jenkins, Jerry B.
  Left Behind, 120
Jensen på Sporet, 210
Jesus Christ Superstar, 9, 116
Jesus Movement, xviii, 8–9, 109–11
  and apocalypse, 112, 114, 115–22
  and environmentalism, 113–14, 122
  and politics, 111–15, 117–18
Jesus People Army, 114–15
Jesus People USA, 115, 121
Jethro Tull, 238, 241
Johns, Jasper, 53
Jokers, 225
Jones, Brian, 5, 9, 125
Jones, Davy, 152
Joplin, Janis, 5, 37
  'Mercedes Benz', 7, 88
Jørgensen, C.V., 218
Joy Division, 89
Jugendstudio DT 64, 13, 14, 227, 233, 234

Kansas, 115
Kaprow, Allan
  18 Happenings in 6 Parts, 51
Kay, Ella, 229, 230
Kennedy, Bobby, xviii
Kent State shootings, xviii
Kerouac, Jack, 4n1, 50, 51n5
  Pull My Daisy, 51n5
Kesey, Ken, 146, 155, 157–8
  Acid Tests, xvii, xviii, 18, 35, 37, 146–7, 149, 151, 157, 161, 162
  One Flew Over the Cuckoo's Nest, 35
  The Acid Test, 146–7
King, Martin Luther, xviii
King Crimson, 248
Kinks, 99
kitsch, 45
Kosmos, 226
krautrock, 152–3, 154, 155
Kreutzman, Bill, 160, 162

Kristeva, Julia, 11, 171n1, 175, 176, 177–8, 185
Kuba-Klub, 226
La Magna, Gianni
  I Cottrau a Napoli, 249
LaHaye, Tim
  Left Behind, 120
Lamb of God, 119
lang, k.d., 6, 10
Lang, Michael, 130
Larsen, Kim, 218
Le Fevre, Mylon
  'Crack the Sky', 118
Leary, Timothy, 35, 84, 153, 188
Led Zeppelin, 100, 238
  'Kashmir', 100
  Led Zeppelin IV, 92
Leipzig, 228
Lennon, John, 60, 91, 152, 154, 156, 172, 176, 180, 182, 184
  Unfinished Music No. 1: Two Virgins, 10, 11, 142–5, 146, 149, 155, 156, 180n6
Leoncavallo, 246
Leone, Gianni, 241
Lesh, Phil, 36, 159–60, 161, 163, 165, 169
Levene, Keith, 154
Lewis, Jerry Lee, 89
Lichtenstein, Roy, 53
lifestyle, 4, 17, 18, 22–6, 31, 78, 82, 125, 233, 241
Lindsey, Hal, 114, 120
  The Late Great Planet Earth, 112, 117
Liverpool, 207, 216, 218, 220–21
Livgren, Kerry, 115
Lollapalooza, 123
London, 6, 60, 63n20, 220
  suburbs, 191–2
Lopez, Patrizia, 242
Lords, 232
Los Angeles, 5, 33, 38–41, 43, 147, 148, 191
Love, 41
LSD, xvii, xviii, 5, 10, 11, 18, 35–6, 37, 40, 64, 146, 153, 158, 163–4, 180n6
Lunden, Tom
  'I Kan Ikke Slå os Ihjel', 217–18

Lydon, John, 153–4
Lynch, David, 200

Magic Band, 199
Malanga, Gerard, 59
Mamas and the Papas, 39, 60, 231
Manson, Charles, xvii, 5, 8, 98–9, 104
   'Helter Skelter', xix, 8, 98–9, 102, 104, 105–7
   'I'll Never Say Never to Always', 104
   Lie, 104
Manson, Marilyn, 105
Manson Family, xviii, 8, 43, 98–9, 102, 104
Manzarek, Ray, 91
Martha and the Vandellas, 231
masculinity, xvii, 8, 11–12, 48, 51n4, 81–2, 91, 131, 136; *see also* femininity; gender; sex; sexuality
Massive Attack, 248
Matta-Clark, Gordon, 200
Maysles Brothers, 134, 135
MC Einar
   '28 Grader i Skyggen', 219n7
MC5, 4
McCartney, Paul, 60, 61, 91, 97, 101
   Good Evening New York City, 8, 107
   'Helter Skelter', 107
McGuire, Barry, 8
   'Eve of Destruction', 115, 116
McKernan, Ron 'Pigpen', 36, 160
McLaren, Brian, 115
Mekas, Jonas, 51–52
Melanie, 129
Melcher, Terry, 43
Message to Love, 129
MF Grimm
   'Karma', 107
Mighty Sphincter
   'Helter Skelter', 104
Mingus, Charles, 50
Mitchell, Joni, 242
   'Woodstock', 84, 132
Moby Grape, 63n20
mod, 69, 74, 76, 77, 230
modernism/modernity, xvi–xviii, 5, 29–30, 31, 31–5, 41, 42–3, 55, 84–5, 180, 240
Modugno, Domenico
   'Nel blu dipinto di blu' ('Volare'), 237

Mondo Hollywood, 195n9
Monkees, 151–2, 155
   Head, 152, 195n9
Monterey Pop, 130
Monterey Pop Festival, 5, 39, 60, 125
Moody, D.L., 113
Mooney, Malcolm, 153
Mor, Røde, 218
Morrissey, 191–2
   Maladjusted, 192
   'Maladjusted', 192
   Southpaw Grammar, 192
Morrissey, Paul, 54n12, 57, 59
Morrison, Jim, 5, 91
Morrison, Sterling, 59
Morrison, Van, 104
Morten, Tage, 216–17
   'Christianshavn's Saneringshymne', 217
   'Varme vibrationer', 217
   'Vore Drømme', 216–17, 218
Motherfuckers, 112
Mothers of Invention, 150, 199, 231
   Freak Out!, 10, 141, 147–9, 194, 199
   'Return of the Son of Monster Magnet', 148–9, 150
   We're Only in It for the Money, 149, 193
   'Who Are the Brain Police?', 194
Mothersbaugh, Mark, 43
Mötley Crüe
   'Helter Skelter', 102–3, 104, 106
Multitude (and Empire), 6, 66–9
   and subcultures, 69–71, 72–9
Mungo Jerry, 231
Murolo, Roberto, 248n6
Murphy Blend, 233
Musella, Mario, 240
Musicanova, 243, 245
Mute, 89
My Life with the Thrill Kill Kult
   'After the Flesh', 105

Napalm Death, 119
Naples, 238–44, 245, 246, 247–9
Napoli Centrale, 240, 243
Neapolitan song, 14, 239–40, 241, 243, 244, 248, 249

Negativland
   'Helter Stupid', 105
Negri, Antonio, 6, 65–71, 72–9
Neil, Vince, 103
Nettlebeck, Uwe, 153
Neue Welt, 232
New American Cinema Group, 51
New Left, xvii, 3–4, 34, 42, 111, 112, 183, 205, 208
New Manson Family, 104
new wave, 64
New York, 5, 29–31, 33, 38, 51, 53, 60, 141, 147, 172, 181, 205
Newport Folk Festival, 125
Nicholson, Jack, 152
Nico, xix, 57, 59, 64, 147
Nietzsche, Friedrich, 157, 166–9
Nine Inch Nails
   'Gave Up', 105
   The Downward Spiral, 105
noise, 4, 43, 155, 172, 224
Norman, Larry, 116, 120
   'I Wish We'd All Been Ready', 117
Nova, Helga, 220
Nuova Compagnia di Canto Popolare (NCCP), 243
Nurse With Wound, 153, 154
   Chance Meeting on a Dissecting Table of a Sewing Machine and an Umbrella, 154
Nye Christiania Sange, 218

Obama, Barack, 154
Obscure, 89
Ocean
   'Put Your Hand in the Hand', 8, 115
Officina 99, 247
Oldenburg, Claes, 51, 53
Ono, Yoko, 152, 156, 171–4, 180–82
   abject vocalisations, xix, 10–11, 171, 173–7, 179, 184–6
   Cut Piece, 171–2n2
   'Don't Worry Kyoko (Mommy's Only Looking for Her Hand in the Snow)', 11, 173, 177, 179
   Fly, 174, 177
   'Sisters, O Sisters', 171, 173
   Unfinished Music No. 1: Two Virgins, 10, 11, 142–5, 146, 149, 155, 156, 180n6
   'Why?', 173, 175–6
   Yoko Ono/Plastic Ono Band, 174, 175
Osanna, 14, 240, 241, 248
   L'Uomo, 241
   Palepoli, 241
Osbourne, Ozzy, 103
   'Revelation (Mother Earth)', 75
Outs, 232

P-Orridge, Genesis, 6, 10, 154
Paloomba, Salvatore, 248
Paolozzi, Eduardo, 52n9
Parker, Charlie, 86
parody, 73, 96, 148, 196
pastiche, 96, 104, 199
patriarchy, 171, 178–9, 189, 195n7
Peretti, Frank E., 120
Petards, 232
Petra
   'Armed and Dangerous', 118
   'Grave Robber', 118
   'He Came, He Saw, He Conquered', 118
   'Not of This World', 118
   'This Means War', 118
Phillips, John, 39, 60
Phillips, Sam, 89
Phillips, Shawn, 242
PiL, *see* Public Image Limited
Pink Floyd, 60, 63n20, 92, 151
   A Saucerful of Secrets, 231
   Dark Side of the Moon, 88
   'Interstellar Overdrive', 151
   The Piper at the Gates of Dawn, 151, 231
   Ummagumma, 92
place, 11–12, 24, 206, 225–6, 230, 233; *see also* space
Play It Again Sam, 89
politics, xviii, xix–xx, 3, 4, 9, 11–12, 13–14, 17, 20–21, 24, 25, 52, 63, 67–8, 81, 82, 87, 95, 96, 128, 136, 137, 173, 174, 182–4, 185, 187, 188, 194
   and Christiania, 201, 205, 217, 219, 221

and Christianity, 111–15, 117–18
in Cold War Berlin, 223, 225–30, 234
demonstrations, 12n6, 183–4, 206, 207, 228, 238
in Italy, 237–8, 239, 241, 244–6, 247
see also New Left
Pollock, Jackson, 50, 53, 60
Polydor, 90
Pop, Iggy, 6, 10, 128n4, 172
Pop Art, 7, 45, 50–55, 58, 63, 84
Pop-Inn, 232
post-industrial, 10, 153
postmodernism/postmodernity, xvi, 42, 43, 46, 50, 55, 56, 57, 65, 67, 70, 73–4, 76, 84–5, 92, 180
post-psychedelic rock, 83, 88, 89, 91, 92
post-punk, 10, 83, 84, 89, 92, 105, 141, 142, 153–4, 245
Pound, Ezra, xvi, 84
Presley, Elvis, 89, 91
Primal/Scream Therapy, 184–5
progressive rock, 87, 151, 233
Italian, 14, 237, 241
protest songs, 18, 217–19, 238, 243, 244, 247
psychedelic rock, xvi, xvii, 6, 7, 10, 29, 34, 35–8, 60, 63, 83, 87, 91, 150–51, 154, 157, 158, 161, 163, 205, 231
Italian, 14, 241
psychedelics, xvi, xvii, 6, 7, 10, 29, 34, 35–8, 154, 161, 163–4; *see also* LSD
Psychic TV, 153, 154
pub rock, 89
Public Image Limited (PiL), 153–4
punk, 7, 20, 43, 64, 66, 69, 70, 71, 73, 74, 75, 76, 77, 83, 84, 88, 89, 100–102, 115, 118, 119–20, 121, 153–4, 155, 196, 201, 219

Quasimodo, 232
Quicksilver Messenger Service, 63n20

race, xv, 8, 11, 17, 21, 22, 23, 39–40, 51, 65, 73–4n3, 74, 76–7n8, 77, 78, 81, 82, 89, 91, 107, 128, 129, 136, 173, 180–82, 183, 187, 240, 248
Radio Luxemburg, 225, 233
Raelettes, 231

ragamuffin, 14, 246, 247
Rage of Angels, 118
Raiz, 247, 249
Rakha, Alla, 161
Ramones
'Planet Earth 1988', 75
Ramrods
'Helter Skelter', 100
rap, 14, 104, 107, 196, 212, 219, 246, 247
Rauschenberg, Robert, 53
RCA, 153, 241
Reagan, Ronald/Reaganism, 11, 12, 111, 117, 187, 188, 190, 194n6, 195–6, 201, 202, 244
recording studio/techniques, xvi, 10, 36, 39, 60, 61, 91, 92–3, 102, 103, 147, 197
Reed, Lou, 6, 10, 59, 60, 62, 64, 238
Metal Machine Music, 153, 155
reggae, 14, 210, 211, 212, 246, 247
Reich, Charles A., xv, 19–20
Reichel, Ilse, 230
religion, 17, 24, 52, 84, 197; *see also* Buddhism; Christianity; Hinduism; Jesus Movement; spirituality
Religious Right, 111, 112, 114, 117
Resurrection Band, 115
Rez, 115
Reznor, Trent, 105
rhythm and blues, 14, 88, 89, 91, 92, 240, 245, 247, 249
RIAS-Treffpunkt, 233
Rice, Boyd, 102
Richard, Cliff, 89
Richards, Keith, 91–2
Riefenstahl, Leni, 9, 136
Olympia, 130
Righteous Brothers, 39
rock and roll, 7, 14, 36, 45, 83, 88, 89, 91–2, 97, 103
Rock in Rio, 126
Rolling Stones, xvii, 18, 54, 89, 99, 104, 150, 151
at Altamont, 9–10, 133–6
at Hyde Park (London), 9, 125
at Madison Square Gardens (New York), 9, 134
at Waldbühne (Berlin), 13, 228–9

Beggars Banquet, 96
Cocksucker Blues, 51n5
Get Yer Ya-Ya's Out, 134
'Midnight Rambler', 134
'Sing This All Together (and See What Happens)', 151
Sticky Fingers, 54n11
'Street Fighting Man', 95
'Sympathy for the Devil', 134
Their Satanic Majesties Request, 150
Rolling Stones Records, 90
Ronettes, 39
Roskilde, 126
Roszak, Theodore, xv, 3–4, 19, 33–4, 145, 205
Rough Trade, 89
Rubin, Jerry, 4n2
RuPaul, 6, 10

S-f-beat, 13, 230–33
Sacco, Antonio, 247
Sacco, Giulietta, 248
Sacred Warrior, 118
Safebreakers, 232
Saint Just, 241
San Francisco, 5, 6, 25, 33, 36–8, 41, 60, 63n20, 151
Sanctuary, 119
Santana, 125n2, 132
Sarnataro, Joe, 245
Saturday Night Fever, 193
Savio, Mario, 183, 185
scenes, 11–12, 25, 33, 37, 62, 89
Scheff, Robert, 172
Schwitters, Kurt, 49
SDS (Students for a Democratic Society/Party), 111, 112
Sebastian, 218
Secession
'Helter Skelter', 104
Sedgwick, Edie, 60
Selo, Brunella, 249
Senese, James, 240, 243, 248
sex, xvii, 4n2, 6, 11–12, 48, 49, 54, 58, 59, 61, 88, 119, 137, 148, 205
Frank Zappa and, 187–202 *passim*
see also femininity; gender; masculinity; sexuality

Sex Pistols, 90, 141, 153, 154
D.O.A., 195
sexuality, 6, 8, 10, 11–12, 21, 23, 24, 54, 74, 78, 85–6, 91, 117, 137, 205
Frank Zappa and, 187, 189–90, 192–3, 196–7
see also femininity; gender; masculinity; sex
Sherman, Cindy, 6, 10
Sherwood, Adrian, 248
Shouters, 225
Showmen, 14, 240, 243
'Catarì (marzo)', 240
Simon and Garfunkel, 231
Siouxsie and the Banshees, 90
'Blow the House Down', 75
'Helter Skelter', 101–2
Sisters of Mercy
'Black Planet', 75
Situationism/ists, 141
Sixpence None the Richer, 120
Skinny Puppy
'Worlock', 105
Skrew
'Helter Skelter', 106
slagsange, 217–19
Slumstormere, 12, 207
Sly and the Family Stone, 231
Soft Machine, 238
'We Did It Again', 151
Sojourners, 115
Solveig, Martin, 92
Solvognen, 208
Sonic Youth
'Death Valley 69', 104
Sorrenti, Alan, 241, 242, 248
Aria, 241
Come un vecchio incensiere all'alba di un villaggio deserto, 241
'Dicitencello vuje', 241
'Figli delle stelle', 248
'Sienteme', 241
'Tu sei l'unica donna per me', 248
'Vorrei incontrati', 14, 241
Sorrenti, Jenny, 241, 242, 248
soul, 89
sound production, xvi, 10, 36, 39, 60, 61, 91, 92–3, 102, 103, 128, 197

Soundgarden, 123
  'Helter Skelter', 103
soundscape, 185, 224, 231, 233–4
space
  and counterculture, 12, 13, 205, 206–7, 212–15, 219–22, 224
  and subculture, 223–5, 233–5
  see also place
Spector, Phil, 39
speed, xvii, 6, 62
Spencer, Jeremy, 8, 115
spirituality, xviii, 4n1, 4n2, 9, 35, 116, 145, 205; *see also* religion
Spite Extreme Wing
  'Helter Skelter', 103
Sport-Kasino Spandau, 230
Sputniks, 225
Stapleton, Steve, 154, 156
Starr, Ringo, 144, 176
Status Quo, 99
Stax, 89
Stiff, 89
Stockhausen, Karlheinz, 172
Stone, Sly, 136, 231
Stooges, 152
  Fun House, 152
  'L.A. Blues', 152
Stookey, Paul, 115
Støttefest (support festivals), 210, 214
Strummer, Joe, 43
Stryken, 118
Stryper
  Soldiers Under Command, 118
Studio 54, 194
subculture, 3, 5, 6, 14, 17, 20, 22, 23, 25, 65–6, 82–3, 238, 246, 247, 249
  and Multitude (and Empire), 69–71, 72–9
  and space, 223–5, 233–5
suburbia, 188–91
  Frank Zappa and, 187, 188, 190–91, 192–200
Sun, 89
Sunday, Billy, 113
Sunday Fury
  'Helter Skelter', 103
Sunset Strip, 41
surf music, 39–41

Surrealism/ists, 49, 142, 145
Suzuki, Damo, 153
Swan Song, 90

Tamla Motown, 89, 90
Tate, Sharon, 98, 105
Team 4, 225
Telstars, 225
Thank God It's Friday, 195
Thatcher, Margaret, 244
Thelma and Louise, 85–6
Them, 104
thirtysomething, 195
Thompson, Hunter S.
  Fear and Loathing in Las Vegas, 19
Throbbing Gristle, 101, 153
  'Six Six Sixties', 154
Tibet, David, 154
Tin Pan Alley, 38
trash culture/aesthetic, 45–8, 49, 54, 55, 56–7, 58, 59, 61–2
trip-hop, 248
Trouble
  'Helter Skelter', 103, 106
Tucker, Maureen, 59, 62
Tuesday Club, 232
Turba, Kurt, 227
Turner, Joe Lynn
  'Helter Skelter', 103
Twistkeller, 226

U2, 154
  'All Along the Watchtower', 104–5
  'Helter Skelter', 104–5, 106
  Rattle and Hum, 104–5
Ulbricht, Walter, 227
underground, 6, 25, 45, 56, 61, 63, 95, 96, 99, 107, 146, 147, 151, 152, 154, 180, 192, 196, 226, 231, 245
utopia, xviii–xx, 5, 7, 9, 34, 83–8, 90–93, 95, 145, 155, 180

Vairetti, Lino, 248
Velvet Underground, xvii, xix, 6, 45, 47, 48, 51n6, 54, 56, 58–64, 84, 147, 150
  'All Tomorrow's Parties', 60
  'European Son', 10, 147
  'Femme Fatale', 60

'Heroin', 60
'I'll Be Your Mirror', 60n15
'Sunday Morning', 60n15
The Velvet Underground and Nico, 60–62, 147
'Venus in Furs', 60
'Waiting for the Man', 60
White Light/White Heat, 64
Ventures, 39
Vietnam War, 19, 25, 81, 84, 88, 98, 116, 133, 136, 180, 182, 183, 205
violence, xvii, xviii, 6, 7, 10, 85, 88, 98–9, 103, 107, 113, 134, 135
Virgin, 89, 90
Viviani, Raffaele, 242
Vliet, Don Van, 42–3
voice, 164, 182–4
and Yoko Ono, xix, 10–11, 171, 173–7, 179, 184–6
Voorman, Klaus, 176
Vow Wow
'Helter Skelter', 103

Wagner, C. Peter, 114
Wakeman, Rick, 241
Wallis, Jim, 115
Warhol, Andy, 6, 45–8, 52–5, 56–64
Couch, 59
Empire, 57
Exploding Plastic Inevitable, xvii, xviii, 10, 45, 58–60, 61, 62, 147
Flesh, 58
Sleep, 57
Sticky Fingers, 54n11
The Chelsea Girls, 57
Trash, 58
Vinyl, 59
Waters, John, 200
Watts, Alan, 146
This Is It!, 146
Watts, Charlie, 134
Watts riots, 39–40, 41
Weather Report, 243
Weathermen, 99, 112
Weinberg, Jack, 183
Weir, Bob, 160, 162
West Berlin, 13–14, 223, 225, 228–9, 230–34

White Zombie, 105–6
'Helter Skelter', 106
Who, 89, 132
'I Can See for Miles', 97
Wilson, Brian, 40–41, 60, 150
Wilson, Tom, 61, 64
Wir-um zwanzig, 13, 230
Wolfe, Tom, 39
The Electric Kool-Aid Acid Test, 18, 146
Woodstock Music and Arts Fair, 5, 9, 18, 21, 43, 104, 124, 125, 126, 127, 128, 129–33, 136–7, 189
Woodstock: Three Days of Peace and Music, 9, 124, 126, 127, 129–33, 136, 136–7
world music, 245, 246–7
World Vision, 121
Woronov, Mary, 59

Yardbirds, 99
Yellow Submarine, 83–4
yippies, 3, 4n2, 112

Zappa, Frank, 11–12, 144, 149, 152, 154, 155, 187–8, 231
and suburbia, 187, 188, 190–91, 192–200
Baby Snakes, 193n5, 195
Civilization Phaze III, 188
Frank Zappa Meets the Mothers of Prevention, 187
Freak Out!, 10, 141, 147–9, 150, 189, 194, 199
Jazz from Hell, 187
Joe's Garage, 196, 197–9
Sheik Yerbouti, 12, 189, 193n5, 195, 196–7, 200
Ship Arriving Too Late to Save a Drowning Witch, 199
Tinsel Town Rebellion, 198
We're Only in It for the Money, 149, 193
You Are What You Is, 12, 196, 200–202
Zappa in New York, 199
Zoot Allures, 193–4
Zappa, Moon Unit, 199
Zombie, Rob, 105

CPSIA information can be obtained
at www.ICGtesting.com
Printed in the USA
BVHW03s2013070618
518541BV00003B/34/P